VOLUME TWO

the Wilton Way of Cake Decorating

THIS BOOK is dedicated to my mother, Zeda Olive Wilton, and to my father, McKinley Wilton. My sisters, Martha Wilton Ellison and Mary Jane Wilton Turner, and my brother, Wesley Wilton, join me in this expression of love and respect. From our parents we learned the satisfaction of doing a job well, even in difficult circumstances, and of mastering a craft completely.

IN THIS BOOK we explore the roots of the Wilton-American method of cake decorating. In their purest and most characteristic forms, we explain the English method and its descendants, the Australian and South African methods. We display the dramatic Mexican method, the flowery Philippine and Continental methods of decorating.

From these foreign methods, the American decorator has learned, and then expanded, the art form.

THE WILTON-AMERICAN WAY of decorating has added to the traditional body of knowledge and skill that is the treasury of any art. A noticeable innovation is the free, joyous use of color that makes even the simplest cake a work of art.

Another Wilton-American addition to the art of cake decorating is the creation of realistic flowers. To the American decorator, the color and fragile form of a flower is a challenge to re-create it and to add its beauty to a beautiful cake.

As its most important contribution to cake decorating, the Wilton way has brought the American ability of achieving perfection through efficient means. Through study and practice we have discovered quicker, easier ways to attractive effects.

THE WILTON-AMERICAN WAY of decorating is a constantly evolving method, based on old skills used in new ways. Its object is pleasure—the delight of those for whom you practice this art, and your own satisfaction in mastering it. Every decorator, whether novice or master, adds to the art.

SO, TO YOU, THE ADVENTUROUS DECORATOR, I would also like to dedicate this book. To decorate well is not an easy task. It requires a thorough knowledge of the techniques of the past. It needs constant practice to attain the necessary skills. It takes an observant eye and an active imagination to translate skill into beauty. These efforts are more than repaid by the joy and satisfaction of creating not just beautiful cakes—but little works of art.

NORMAN WILTON

CHAPTER ONE

The Flowers of the Fifty States

THE SPLENDID, FIVE-TIERED CAKE shown on the gate-fold frontispiece and again on page 29 is an example of the wonderful possibilities of icing in the skilled hand of the decorator. The cake presents a colorful history of the United States, with the flower of every state arranged on its tiers. Below each flower, a Color Flow shield gives the name of the state and the date of its entry into the union.

Some of the flowers are well-loved favorites of the decorator—Apple Blossom, Violet, Carnation, and of course, the Rose. But most of them are very unusual blossoms, some never before attempted in icing, such as the Lady's Slipper, Sage Brush, Blue Bonnet and Indian Paint Brush.

All together, they form a dictionary of flower-making for the decorator, and one you will turn to again and again. You may not have the occasion to decorate a cake of such noble proportions as this Fifty States Cake, but the flowers will inspire you to decorate many very distinctive smaller cakes. Examples of a few start on page 30.

Use royal icing for all the flowers for precise details and lasting quality. Recipe, and directions for mounting flowers and leaves on wire stems are in **Chapter Twenty.**

ABOVE: THE GREAT SEAL of the United States is executed in Color Flow and mounted on each of the four sides of the 24″ base tier. Directions are on page 28. Patterns for the seal, and the shield shapes that identify each state flower are in The Wilton Way Pattern Book. The next page tells how to pipe the brilliant American Beauty roses that surround the Great Seal.

This view of the top 8" tier shows Camellia and Forget-me-not.

AMERICAN BEAUTY ROSE. To make the flower of the District of Columbia, hold tube 104 with wide end touching number 9 nail and narrow end turned up and inward. Pipe a ribbon of icing into a cone by turning nail. Pipe a coil around cone about ⅓ of the way up from nail to form bud. Pipe a row of three standing, overlapping petals, keeping narrow end of tube straight up and turning nail counterclockwise as you move tube up and back down in an arch. Pipe two rows of five overlapping petals, turning narrow end out slightly more each time so petals open out. Pipe the last row of six petals, turning narrow end of tube far out, so petals are lying almost flat for look of full-blown rose.

CAMELLIA, Alabama's state flower, is easily piped with tube 104 on number 2 nail. Loosely coil a ribbon of icing on nail, turning nail twice. Then pipe another, tighter coil of ribbon over the first, starting about ⅓ of the way up the first coil. Again turn the nail twice while piping to make a rounded bud. Make three flared, overlapping petals by holding narrow end of tube at a slight outward angle. Pipe a row of five fully-opened, overlapping petals to finish the flower. Dry.

Another view of the 8″ tier adorned with Saguaro (cactus flower) and Apple Blossoms.

FORGET-ME-NOT, Alaska's state flower. Use a large number 7 nail, so you can make several of the petite blossoms at one time. Begin by piping a tiny, ¼″ tear-shaped petal, slightly cupped, with tube 101s. Pipe four more petals. Complete flower with a tube 1 yellow dot in center.

APPLE BLOSSOM. The state flower of Arkansas and Michigan is a delicate spring blossom that is simple to duplicate in icing. Fit a decorating bag with tube 101. Spatula-stripe bag above narrow end of tube with a thin stripe of pale pink icing. Fill bag with white icing. Using a flat flower nail, pipe five tiny, identically-shaped, rounded petals, each about ½″ long. Make each petal separate from the others—do not overlap. Pipe a tube 6 dot in center of flower. While icing is wet, push in a cluster of artificial stamens, cut short and tinted pink at tips with food color and small brush. Dry.

As you turn the pages, views of the tiers, adorned with flowers, will be printed before the directions for making the flowers. You will be able to see the way the flowers are arranged on the tier, and identify each flower with the state it represents. Directions for making the Saguaro, Arizona's state flower are on the next page.

SAGUARO, Arizona's state flower, is a large and beautiful cactus flower. To make it in icing, start by lining a small two-piece lily nail with foil. Fit a decorating bag with tube 103, stripe bag with yellow icing above the narrower end of tube, then fill bag with white icing. Begin flower by piping a stand-up ribbon of icing within well-shaped center of nail. Pipe another ribbon of icing on top of first, turning hand almost palm up, so ribbon lies almost flat. Pipe cupped, square-tipped petals directly on top of icing ribbon, keeping them separate and equal-sized until you have a ring of seven petals in all. Then, with tube 4, pipe a spiral string of yellow icing into an inverted cone shape that stands about ⅛″ above center of flower. Brush center smooth with damp brush and insert four white stamens, about ¼″ long. Dip a moistened finger into yellow-tinted sugar and pat cone lightly on top. Dry. Turn blossom over (removing foil) and pipe a large cone of green icing with tube 1A. Immediately push in a 3″ length of florists' wire. Brush icing down onto base of flower with a damp brush. Pipe a thick, shell-shaped pad with tube 1A and green icing, and while still wet, push a 4½″ length of florists' wire into narrow tip. Brush smooth. Add tiny cactus spines with tube 1.

CALIFORNIA POPPY. California's brilliant state flower grows wild on the hillsides of the state. Reproduce this hardy poppy in icing. Press foil halfway into 1¼″ lily nail. Using tube 103, touch center of nail with wide end of tube, pull icing over edge, then straight across and back to center for square, cupped petal. Smooth center of petal with damp brush. Repeat for four completely separate petals. Add a tube 3 dot in center of flower. While icing is wet, push in ½″ long artificial stamens.

One side of the 10″ tier, showing California Poppy, Columbine and Mountain Laurel.

COLUMBINE, Colorado's flower. Pipe petals on a cone, covered with wax paper. Using tube 103 and a downward motion, pipe five white, tapered petals about ½″ long, leaving a tiny hole at center so tip of cone shows. With tube 104 held at a right angle, pull out five blue petals from base of white ones.

Pinch tips into points. Dry, remove from cone. Make loop in end of piece of florists' wire and insert through hole so loop is in flower. Pipe tube 13 mound over loop and insert artificial stamens. Holding flower by wire, pipe five tube 3 nectar tubes at back of petals. Insert into styrofoam to dry.

MOUNTAIN LAUREL, state flower of Connecticut and Pennsylvania. Line the 1¼″ two-piece lily nail with foil. Pipe five tube 67 petals from center to a point just above inner edge, overlapping them. Smooth inside of blossom with damp brush. Dry. Add a ring of tiny red dots to center with paste color. Pipe a tube 13 green star in center, then push ten ¼″ long artificial stamens into star so they lie against petals.

With tube 1, pull out a tiny yellow stalk from one side of green star. Dry, remove foil and pipe tube 1 lines on backs of petals. To form bud, squeeze out icing with tube 20, pulling out to point. Dry and mount on wires. Pipe slender 1¼″ tube 352 leaves on wires. Mount buds and flowers on wires, tape with leaves into spray.

These close-ups show the remaining views of the 10″ tier graced with Peach Blossom, Orange Blossom, Cherokee Rose, Hibiscus and Syringa.

PEACH BLOSSOM. Delaware's state flower blooms profusely in the spring. It is a simple flower to create in icing. With tube 102 on number 7 nail, pipe five small, rounded petals, each about ⅝″ long. Overlap them very slightly at the base of the petals, keeping tips separate. Pinch tips of petals to a point with damp fingers. Pipe dot in center of flower with tube 6. While icing is wet, push in artificial stamens that have been cut short and tinted pink at tips with food color and a small brush.

ORANGE BLOSSOM is Florida's sweetly fragrant state flower. To duplicate it in icing, cover a 1¼″ lily nail with foil, pushing it only about halfway into nail. Pipe a long, slim tube 76 petal. Lightly tap with damp fingertip to round off tip of petal. Pipe four more petals. Brush petals with a small damp brush to deepen groove. Dry. Make center separately with tube 101s, piping icing into a cupped shape. Top with tube 1s zigzag. Make small vertical lines on the outside of the cup with a small brush. Dry. Attach cup to center of flower with a small dot of icing. Pipe a tube 6 oval mound of icing for bud.

CHEROKEE ROSE, the state flower of Georgia is a shrub rose that makes a very dainty cake decoration. Attach wax paper to a number 2 flower nail and pipe the first thin, ruffled, heart-shaped petal with tube 104. Repeat for a circle of five overlapping petals. Pipe a tube 13 green star in center of flower, then add tube 1 yellow dots around it to define a larger star shape. While center is still wet, push in six artificial stamens, cut short. To use the flower flat, on a cake top, pipe tube 4 green stem and buds and add tube 352 leaves. Attach roses at center of leaf clusters with icing.

HIBISCUS, the state flower of Hawaii is a lush, brilliant tropical flower. Line 2¼″ two-piece lily nail with foil. Starting deep in nail, pipe a tube 104 petal, narrow at base, then wider as you move out to edge. Jiggle hand for a 1″ wide ruffle, then decrease pressure as you move back to base. Pipe five petals. Use tube 3 to pipe a line of icing out from base, down center of petal. Pipe a dot of icing in flower center and insert a 1¾″ curved piece of florists' wire. Coat wire with icing by pushing tube over wire and squeezing while pulling away. Top with tube 3 yellow dots, tube 1 green dots.

SYRINGA, state flower of Idaho, is a lovely, fragrant summer flower, quick and easy to make. Cover nail number 6 with foil. Using tube 102, start in center of nail and move out and over high edge, then back to center for a fan-shaped petal. Pipe identical second and third petals, overlapping slightly at base. Complete a circle of six petals, all separated at the tips. Pipe a large tube 8 yellow dot at center of blossom. While icing is still wet, dip a damp finger into yellow tinted sugar and pat lightly on dot.

These close-up photographs of portions of the 12″ tier display Violet, Peony, Wild Rose, Sunflower, Goldenrod and Magnolia. Detailed directions for making these flowers in icing start below.

VIOLET. The state flower of Illinois, New Jersey, Rhode Island and Wisconsin is a cheerful sign of spring. To create it in icing, hold tube 101 at 45° angle with wide end touching center of flower nail, narrow end turned out slightly. Squeeze out three ½″ long high-cupped petals side-by-side, but separate. Finish with two smaller, ¼″ long petals facing the first three petals. Brush thinned white icing in center of flower, then add tube 1 dots. Pipe broad leaves with tube 112.

FLOWER CENTER

COMPLETED FLOWER

PEONY, Indiana's state flower, is unexcelled as a cut flower and has an unforgettable fragrance. To re-create this beautiful, full-blossomed flower, start in the following manner. On number 13 nail, pipe a circle of tube 104 ruffled petals. Hold tube at a 45° angle and, jiggling hand slightly for ruffled effect, pipe each petal about ½″ long. The first row will have about nine petals. Add a second row with same number of petals as first, moving slightly inward. Then add a third row with slightly fewer ruffled petals, again moving inward. Make center of flower separately. Holding tube 60 at almost a 90° angle, pipe a small cupped petal. Surround it with two rows of tube 60 petals. Then pipe two more rows of petals, opening them out slightly. Dry. Attach dried center into middle of flower with a dot of icing. Fill in between center and the outer petals with more tube 60 petals for a full effect.

14

WILD ROSE. This fresh and lovely flower of Iowa is easy to create in icing. Line nail number 4 with foil and beginning at center, pipe a round, cupped petal with tube 103. Pipe four more petals. Pipe a tube 6 dot of icing in center of flower and push in a thick cluster of ½″ long artificial stamens. Slant stamens out so they seem to "explode" from flower center. To pipe bud, begin with a small tube 6 cone, then coil a tube 103 ribbon of icing around it.

SUNFLOWER, floral symbol of Kansas, is piped with tube 352 on number 2 nail. Pipe a short base, lift tube straight up, then stop pressure to produce a ½″ long uptilted, pointed petal. Make a circle of petals around nail's edge, leaving a ¼″ space in middle. Pipe tube 12 mound of icing in center and flatten to diameter of ⅞″ with finger dipped in brown-tinted sugar. When dry, turn flower over and pipe tube 12 dot, then overlapping rows of tube 352 green points around it, lifting tips like petals. To make an opening bud, pipe small green cone with tube 12. Pull tiny yellow petals straight up with tube 65, then pull more petals and sepals outward. Leaves are piped with tube 70.

GOLDENROD, sunny flower of Kentucky and Nebraska. To make on cake top, pipe tube 1 stems and finish with tube 3 dots. Now pipe tube 17 stars at ends of stems and pipe many tube 13 stars over them. Finish with a scattering of tube 1 dots and slender tube 65 leaves. To make standing spray, tape five pieces of florists' wire together at base, and insert ends of wire into decorating cone fitted with tube 17. Pull out elongated shell. Cover shell with tube 13 stars, piling one on another for puffy effect. Add tube 1 dots.

This section of the 12″ tier displays Goldenrod, Magnolia and Pine Cone.

MAGNOLIA, Louisiana's and Mississippi's flower, blooms in the spring on a flowering tree. To make an opening Magnolia bud, shown in top row at left, pipe a round, cupped petal with tube 402. Pipe three overlapping upright petals with tube 402 around edge of cupped petal. Continue piping rows of three overlapping upright petals, making the petals progressively larger, until there are four rows. Dry. Make the center of the bud by piping a tube 6 mound of icing. Smooth into cone shape with a damp brush. Pipe tube 3 green dots down upper sides of cone, then tube 2 yellow dots around lower third of cone. Dry. Attach in middle of bud with dot of icing.

Pipe a fully-opened flower with tube 402. Make a long petal, pinching tip into a point with damp fingers. Make a circle of five petals, overlapping slightly at base. Smooth petals together at center with damp brush. Pipe another circle of five petals on top of first circle, making them stand more upright. Brush smooth. Pipe a final circle of three petals, making them stand almost straight up. Brush smooth. Make center the same as for bud and attach within flower with dot of icing. Mount flower on wire stem.

Pipe slender tube 112 leaves about 2″ long on florists' wire. Dry on curved surface. Tape stems of six leaves around flower stem with floral tape. Bend leaves out into a flat six-pointed star shape behind Magnolia flower.

MAGNOLIA BUD

FINISHED MAGNOLIA FLOWER

PINE CONE, state flower of Maine. To make a Pine Cone, cover a cone shape with wax paper. Using tube 97, drop some icing on tip of cone and smooth with finger to coat tip. Pipe a standing petal at tip, moving hand up and down as for a rose petal. Then pipe second and third petals the same as the first for "bud". Pipe a row of five, then a row of six petals below bud, turning tube so they stand out. Finish Pine Cone by piping a row of six, then a row of seven petals, turning tube so last row of petals is perpendicular to cone. Dry, then remove wax paper with Pine Cone from shape. Peel off wax paper. Tube 1 needles are piped after cones are placed on cake tier.

BLACK-EYED SUSAN, Maryland's beloved state flower, grows in the fields and brightens the roadside. Make this golden wildflower by first piping a cone-shaped mound of dark brown icing with tube 6 on a square of wax paper. Sprinkle it with brown-tinted sugar and dry. Attach a second square of wax paper to a number 7 flower nail with a dot of icing. Using tube 103, pull out thirteen or fourteen long slim petals from center of nail to edge. Complete the circle of petals, then while icing is wet, draw two narrow grooves in each petal with a damp artist's brush. Immediately press dried brown cone into center of flower. Dry flowers on and within curved surfaces for natural effect.

This close-up of the 12″ tier shows Pine Cone and Black-eyed Susan.

These areas of the 12″ tier show Mayflower, Apple Blossom, Lady's Slipper and Magnolia.

MAYFLOWER, The state flower of Massachusetts, grows in clusters against a background of glossy pointed leaves. Using tube 101s, hold tube flat to surface of number 7 nail and press out five small round petals, each about ⅜″ long. Pipe a tube 1 dot in center of blossom. Dry some of the flowers flat and others within a curved surface.

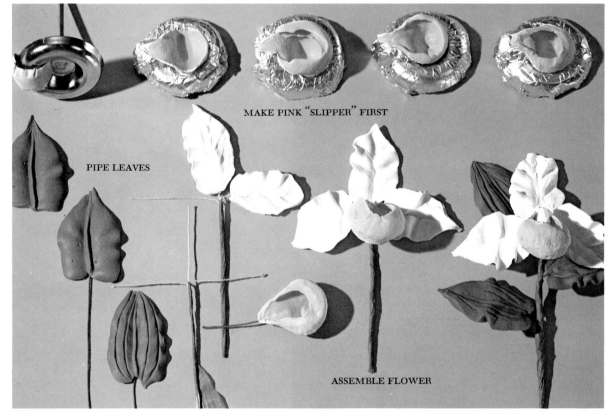

MAKE PINK "SLIPPER" FIRST

PIPE LEAVES

ASSEMBLE FLOWER

LADY'S SLIPPER, Minnesota's native wild orchid. First make the pink "slipper". Fashion a 1¼″ pad of ¾″ width masking tape by folding until it is ⅛″ thick. Tape to raised edge of number 8 nail. Cover nail with foil. Starting in indentation of nail, pipe a wide tube 402 petal, drawing to a point over pad. Pipe stand-up curve around edge of petal to create cup shape. Smooth with damp brush. Now pipe a tube 101 ribbon around edge of cup, brush smooth, dry. Pipe 2″ tube 113 leaves on florists' wire. Mark grooves with toothpick. Dry. Tape lower parts of three 4½″ fine florists' wires together, leaving 1½″ at top. Bend two wires to sides and pipe a tube 103 ruffled petal on each, moving from base to tip, then back. Remove slipper from foil, pipe a tube 3 mound of icing on back, and push a 1½″ length of wire into mound. Brush smooth and dry. Center slipper between petals, taping wire to petal stem. Finally, pipe tube 80 bulb-shaped sepal from center petal into slipper. Tape on leaves.

18

Moving to the 16" tier, just above the arched pillars, we continue our parade of state flowers. In this view we see the Hawthorn, representing Missouri, and the Bitterroot, Montana.

HAWTHORN, Missouri's flower, is a snowy white spring blossom. Make flowers with tube 103 on number 2 nail. Have wide end of tube touching surface of nail, narrow end lying almost flat. Pipe a round petal, slightly cupped at edge. Continue around for a total of five overlapping petals. Pipe a tube 2 green dot in center of flower and surround it with tube 1 yellow dots. Dry some of the flowers flat and others within a curved surface.

STEP ONE   STEP TWO   ASSEMBLE FLOWER

BITTERROOT is Montana's rosy-hued state flower. Create it in two steps, using tube 103. Beginning at the edge of nail number 7, pipe a long, thin petal to the center. Complete a circle of about twelve petals, keeping petals separate but close together and equal in size. Dry in a curved form so petals will tilt upward. Pipe a second ring of petals, this time piping only seven and keeping widely separated on nail. While second ring of petals is still wet, place dried first ring of petals on top of them. Pipe tube 14 star in center of blossom. Cut off tops of a cluster of artificial stamens and push into star while it is still wet. Remove blossom from nail and dry on a flat surface. To make a bud, twirl a tube 103 ribbon of icing around top of a length of florists' wire. Brush smooth with a damp brush. Twirl a tube 103 green ribbon around base of bud and smooth onto wire with damp brush.

Three views of the 16″ tier show Sagebrush, Lilac, Violet, Yucca, Rose and Dogwood.

SAGEBRUSH, Nevada's flower. Create it by piping a cluster of three leaves with tube 102. Pipe with a curving motion in fleur-de-lis shape. While icing is wet, push a 3″ length of florists' wire into base. Smooth leaves together with a damp brush to form single leaf effect and brush icing over wire. Dry. To make flower, push tip of a wire into bag fitted with tube 4 to coat with icing. Starting at top, pipe little tube 2 dots over coated tip until cone shaped. Tape leaves and flowers into a single stalk.

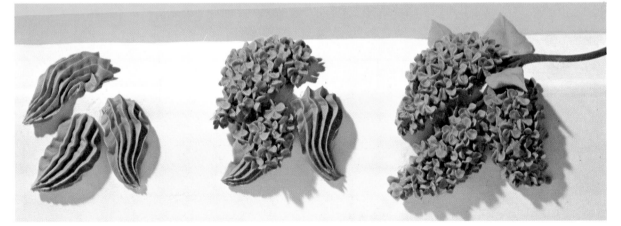

LILAC, New Hampshire's fragrant flower. Make many four-petalled blossoms with tube 101s, each petal less than ¼″ long. Dry. Pipe elongated shells on cake with tube 21. Attach blossoms to shells with dots of icing, covering completely. Add tube 1 buds and tube 4 branch. Pipe tube 352 leaves and short tube 2 stems. To make upright flower on wire stem, pipe shell over end of florists' wire on wax paper. Dry, then attach blossoms and buds. Pipe leaves on wire and tape to flower stem.

20

YUCCA, spectacular flower of New Mexico. Line ½″ two-piece lily nail with foil. Pull out six tube 66 petals from center almost to top of nail, then sharply inward. Dry, remove foil and mount on wires. Make open blossom the same, but do not turn tips of petals in as much. To make green buds and white buds, pipe calyx on wire with tube 3. Dry. Pipe tube 2 lines of icing to a point, then smooth onto calyx with damp brush. Tape buds and blossoms into a single stalk. Pipe about a dozen leaves (not shown) by inserting different lengths of wire into bag of green icing fitted with tube 352, squeezing as you pull out to a point. Tape buds and flowers together, then leaves at bottom of stalk.

ROSE, New York's state flower. Use tube 104 and number 7 nail. Pipe a spiral of icing. Starting about ⅓ of the way up the spiral, pipe a coil of icing. Pipe a stand-up petal, then a second and a third, overlapping each. Pipe a row of five petals, making them open out farther by turning out narrow end of tube. Pipe a final row of five petals, turning out narrow end even farther. To pipe a bud, pipe a coil of icing and then three petals that overlap tightly. Add tube 67 sepals. Mount on wire.

DOGWOOD. North Carolina's and Virginia's flower. To make, use tube 103 at a 45° angle, wide end in center of number 7 nail, narrow end pointed out. Press lightly, then increase pressure for a half petal that fans out slightly. Move straight back to center of nail, then to edge again for second half to complete a heart-shaped petal. Pipe four petals. Brush indents in petals with green, then brown food color. Pipe tube 2 dots in center and dry in curved surface. Mount on wire.

WILD PRAIRIE ROSE is North Dakota's lovely state flower. Create these summer blossoms easily in icing. Pipe a total of five round, high-cupped petals with tube 103. As you pipe, overlap each petal. Dry.

Pipe a tube 13 white star in center of rose, and immediately push in six tiny artificial stamens cut ¼" long. Dry. Pipe tube 67 leaves on wires. Mount roses on wire stems.

CARNATION. The state flower of Ohio is piped with stiffened icing to create the characteristic broken petal effect. Touch tube 104 to the center of number 7 nail and pipe the first petal. Move out about 1⅛", jiggling gently as you go and lifting slightly as you reach petal tips. Curve around, return to center of

nail and stop pressure. Repeat for a complete circle of deeply ruffled petals. Pipe another circle of petals on top of the first, lifting them a bit more upright. Add a third circle of petals, shorter and still more upright. Fill center with vertical petals. Mount several flowers on wires.

MISTLETOE. Oklahoma's state flower has long been a symbol of peace and friendship. Using tube 102, pipe a ¾" petal-shaped leaf on wax paper. Push a 3" length of florists' wire into base of leaf and cover with dot of icing. Brush smooth with a small, damp brush. Dry. Tape two leaves together with floral

tape, keeping one higher than the other. Add more leaves, alternating sides of stem and letting top leaf be the "center" one. Bend wired leaves outward in a natural manner. Pipe tube 3 berries between leaves. Pipe a tiny dot on each berry with copper food color.

These three views of the 16″ tier show Wild Prairie Rose, Carnation, Mistletoe, Oregon Grape, Mountain Laurel, Violet and Yellow Jessamine.

OREGON GRAPE is a fitting symbol for Oregon, a most bountiful state! Pipe a 1″ long tube 70 leaf on wax paper. While icing is wet, pull out points around edge of leaf with a damp brush. Dry some leaves in, others on a curved surface. Peel off wax paper. Attach florists' wire to back of leaf with icing. Dry. Lay a 4″ florists' wire on wax paper and pipe a 1″ long cluster of bulb-shaped grapes with tube 6 over one end, starting at top. Overlap grapes to hold securely. When dry, peel off paper and pipe a line of icing down back of cluster for strength. Tape leaves and grapes together with floral tape.

YELLOW JESSAMINE is South Carolina's fragrant state flower. To pipe it, begin at the center of number 1 nail and pipe a ½″ long tube 101 petal with a slightly turned up tip. Continue around for four more petals. Dip end of a small brush into cornstarch and press into center of blossom to make a hole. Let dry and turn over. Pull out a long, thin cone shape on back with tube 4. Then add a green dot on tip of base with tube 4. Push a length of florists' wire into wet icing and pipe two tiny sepals with tube 1 on either side of dot. To make Jessamine bud, twirl tube 101 ribbon of icing around top of a length of wire. Brush smooth with damp brush. Twirl a tube 101 green ribbon around bud base and brush up into three points on bud. Pipe thin 1″ leaves on wire on wax paper with tube 352, curving tips slightly.

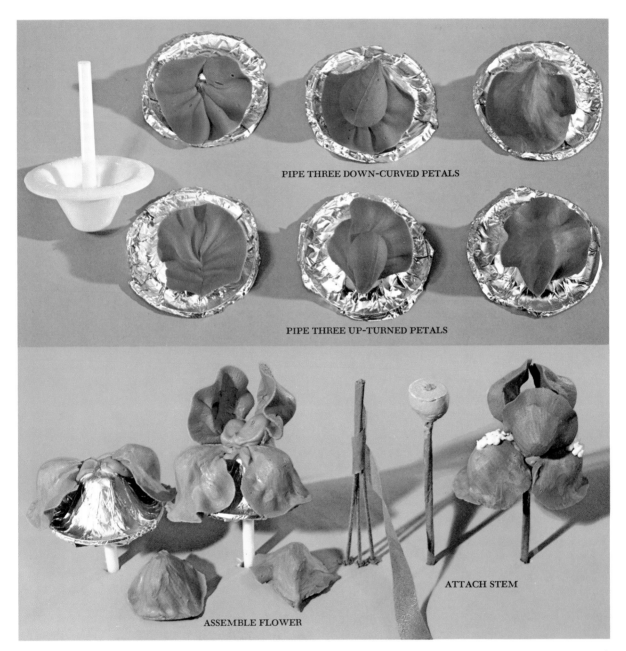

PIPE THREE DOWN-CURVED PETALS

PIPE THREE UP-TURNED PETALS

ASSEMBLE FLOWER

ATTACH STEM

IRIS. Tennessee's lovely state flower takes several steps, but the results are truly worthwhile.

MAKE THREE DOWN-CURVED PETALS FIRST. Turn over half of 1¼″ two-piece lily nail to use as dome-shaped flower nail. Cover smoothly with foil. Beginning at top, pipe a large tube 102 ruffled petal, moving to edge of nail and back to top. Petal should be 1″ wide and ¾″ long. With tube 4, pipe shell-motion bulb in center of petal, tapering to point at base of petal. Brush bulb and petal together. Remove foil with petal carefully to hold shape. Dry.

PIPE THREE UP-TURNED PETALS. Begin top petal at edge of nail, curving up to dome and back to edge. Make same size as down-curved petal. Pipe bulb with tube 4, tapering to edge of nail. Brush bulb and petal together. Remove to dry.

ASSEMBLE FLOWER. Pipe tube 4 dot of icing on tip of each down-curved petal. Arrange in circle on nail. Dry. Pipe a tube 4 dot on tip of each up-curved petal and gently press on top of lower petals as shown. Dry.

ATTACH STEM. Tape three 20-gauge wires together for stem. Pipe tube 6 mound on wax paper, push in stem, brush icing onto wire. Dry. Very carefully attach blossom to stem with dot of icing. Let icing set a few minutes, then pipe iris beards on each down-curved petal with tube 1 dots.

24

Within the arched pillars are pictured Iris, Bluebonnet and Sego Lily.

How to put flowers on bases. *Punch holes in plastic heart bases with a hot nail or icepick. Insert wired flowers through hole. Pipe a little green icing around hole to hide it and to steady flowers.*

BLUEBONNET. To create the Texas state flower in icing, pipe two ½″ long, high-cupped petals with tube 102 over a 4″ length of florists' wire. Overlap petals slightly at base. Pipe bottom petal by pointing tube straight at base of first two petals and squeezing as you turn your hand over. Pull a tube 1 pistil from center of blossom. Tape four or five Bluebonnets into a stalk with floral tape, alternating blossoms. To make leaves (not shown), place a 5″ length of florists' wire on wax paper and with tube 67, pipe a narrow, pointed, 1¼″ long leaf over one end. Dry and peel off paper. Tape five leaves together and bend wires to form a flat circle of leaves.

SEGO LILY. Utah's flower is snow white with inside "painted". Line a 1¼″ two-piece lily nail with foil. Divide nail into quarters with four tube 2 green lines. Dry. Pipe three round, stand-up petals with tube 104. While icing is wet, fold tips of petals into points with damp finger. Smooth flower with damp brush. Dry a few minutes. Using paste colors, paint centers yellow and red inverted "v's". Push a ⅜″ length of wire into center of flower. Pull out four tube 2 points in star fashion at tip. Mount on wires.

25

Within the arched pillars in this close-up are Red Clover, Dogwood and Pasqueflower.

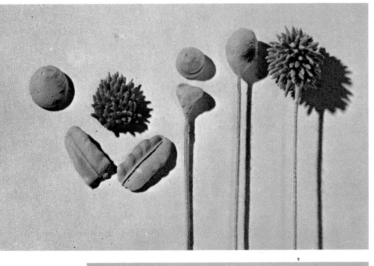

RED CLOVER, Vermont's state flower, makes a most unusual cake decoration. Begin with a clover blossom that will lie flat on cake surface. Pipe a ¾" oval mound of icing with tube 12. With tube 1, pull out tiny points all over mound for blossom, starting at top. Leaves, 1" long, are piped with tube 67 and dried on a curved surface. To make a stemmed clover blossom, begin with a tube 12 cone of icing piped on a square of wax paper. While icing is wet, push in a 5" piece of florists' wire. Brush icing onto wire. Push into styrofoam block to dry. Peel off wax paper and pipe a second tube 12 cone of icing onto flat side of first one. Brush into an oval bulb. Dry, then pull out tiny tube 1 points all over bulb. Push into styrofoam block to dry.

PASQUEFLOWER. The state flower of South Dakota, so named because its European cousin blooms just before Easter. Its richly-hued blossoms were once used to dye Easter eggs. Line a number 8 nail smoothly with foil. Beginning in the indentation of the nail, pipe a petal with tube 352, pulling it to a point over the high edge of nail. Pipe two petals next to it, overlapping them at base. Then pipe three more petals directly across from the first ones. Lightly smooth center of blossom with damp brush. Pipe a thick cluster of yellow dots in center of blossom with tube 2.

The vases on the bottom tier contain Rhododendron (two vases), Violet and Indian Paint Brush.

RHODODENDRON. Washington's and West Virginia's flower starts with five ruffled petals piped with tube 103 in a foil-lined, 1¼″ two-piece lily nail. Pipe from center of nail, increasing pressure as you reach outer edges and then back. Brush center of flower smooth with damp brush. Pipe dot of icing into center and insert cluster of short artificial stamens. Add pistil made by pushing clipped end of artificial stamen into bag of red icing fitted with tube 2 and squeezing gently while pulling out. Dry flowers. Mount on wires. Tape five or six thin florists' wires together, leaving top third free. Bend tops of wires to form a flat circle. Push large wax paper square onto stem, then push stem into styrofoam until paper and wires rest on surface. Pipe a long tube 67 leaf over each wire. Dry, then peel off paper. Spread leaves apart and insert flowers between them. Tape stems together.

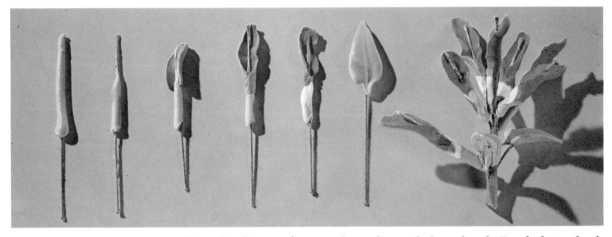

INDIAN PAINT BRUSH. Begin making the flower of Wyoming by coating half the length of a 4″ piece of florists' wire with icing by inserting it through tube 5 into a bag of icing and squeezing gently while pulling wire out. While icing is wet, pinch top half flat with damp fingers to make pistil. Pipe standing petal by placing tube 80 lightly behind narrow part of pistil so curved tip touches thicker part and pull straight up. While icing is wet, brush bottom of

petal together with damp brush. Brush thinned yellow icing on upper half of green base. With tube 65, pipe a spear-shaped leaf ¾″ over one end of a 4″ piece of wire. Tape leaves and blossoms together into a cluster with floral tape, placing leaves slightly below blossoms.

HOW TO ASSEMBLE THE CAKE

Although you may never have occasion to create such a large cake for a civic event, the structure of this one can also be used for a towering wedding cake.

Before beginning, gather the materials you need. These are a 28″ x ½″ square piece of plywood covered with foil, dowel rods, Arched Pillar Tier set, two each of 14″, 12″ and 10″ round separator plates, eight 5″ Grecian pillars, four 3″ Grecian pillars and plastic Wingspread Eagle. You also need six Heart Bases, five Heart Bowls and 13 small American flags. The flowers of all 50 states should be piped in advance (see pages 8 through 28 for directions).

Prepare 50 state name plaques and four Great Seals in advance using Color Flow technique. Using patterns from The Wilton Way Pattern Book, tape them to flat surface and cover smoothly with wax paper. Outline plaques with tube 1 and flow in icing. When plaques are dry, pipe names and dates with tube 2. Chapter Twenty gives a listing of the states, their flowers and the dates they entered the union. Prepare Great Seal in three sections—large circle, eagle and clouds. Outline with tube 1 and flow in color. When pieces are thoroughly dry, pipe 13 stars in cloud section with tube 13 and flatten each with damp finger. Pipe tube 3 beading around edge of large circle. Dry. Join pieces with dots of icing.

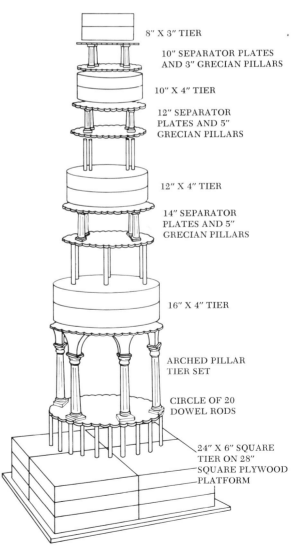

8″ X 3″ TIER

10″ SEPARATOR PLATES AND 3″ GRECIAN PILLARS

10″ X 4″ TIER

12″ SEPARATOR PLATES AND 5″ GRECIAN PILLARS

12″ X 4″ TIER

14″ SEPARATOR PLATES AND 5″ GRECIAN PILLARS

16″ X 4″ TIER

ARCHED PILLAR TIER SET

CIRCLE OF 20 DOWEL RODS

24″ X 6″ SQUARE TIER ON 28″ SQUARE PLYWOOD PLATFORM

Bake and ice tiers. Base tier measures 24″ x 24″ x 6″ and requires twelve cakes, 12″ x 12″ x 2″, stacked in four sections of three layers each. Also bake 16″ x 4″, 12″ x 4″, 10″ x 4″ and 8″ x 3″ round tiers.

When assembling cake, always use dowel rods, clipped off level with top of tier, under the separator plates to prevent cake from collapsing. Use plastic pegs that come with separator plates for additional stability.

STEP ONE. Assemble tiers as shown in diagram. Pipe tube 508 shells around the bottom, top and sides of base tier. Pipe shells on 16″ tier with tube 508 around bottom of tier and tube 506 around top. On 12″ tier pipe shells with tube 506 around bottom and tube 504 around top. Pipe shell borders on top and bottom of 10″ tier using tube 504. Circle 8″ tier with tube 504 shells on top and bottom. Ice a 4″ round piece of styrofoam, 2″ thick, and place it on top of 8″ tier, trimming it with tube 504 shells.

STEP TWO. Ice half-ball of styrofoam and secure into Heart Bowl. Insert 13 American flags and attach bowl between Arched Pillars with icing. Following list of states and flowers in Chapter Twenty , attach the appropriate flowers to Heart Bases as described on page 25. Ice half-balls of styrofoam and secure with icing into Heart Bowls. Insert appropriate flowers.

Tops of 12″ and 10″ tiers will be completely covered by separator plates. To secure flowers to these tiers, holes must be punched through the plates near edges with a heated ice pick or nail. For best results, use gas flame to heat tool.

STEP THREE. Trim the cake with flowers. When attaching flowers, begin at top of cake and work down to bottom to avoid breakage. Using list in Chapter Twenty , attach the appropriate flowers around edge of 8″ tier by pushing wired stems down into cake. Push stems of flowers through holes in separator plates on 10″ and 12″ tiers. On 16″ tier, push stems into cake to secure. Attach a Great Seal and American Beauty Roses on each side of base tier with icing.

Carefully secure Color Flow state plaques to sides of tiers with icing, matching them to their corresponding flowers. On base tier, lean state plaques against Heart Bases and Heart Bowls, securing with dots of icing. Attach Wingspread Eagle to iced styrofoam piece at top of cake with icing. Serves 550.

Just glancing through pages 8 through 28 will inspire you to create many distinctive flower-trimmed cakes. Choose the flower, or group of flowers, most appropriate to the occasion and use them to adorn a masterpiece. We show just three examples here.

CAKE OF NEW YORK (shown on page 32)

STEP ONE. Make Color Flow icing as described on page 76. Tape wax paper over state seal and letter patterns (The Wilton Way Pattern Book) and outline with tube 1. Flow in icing. Dry. Pipe lettering on seal and triangular sun's rays with tube 1s. Use tube 000 to highlight rays and pipe face on sun. Paint in boats and shading on mountain. Pipe beading on inner circle with tube 1 and on outer circle with tube 2.

STEP TWO. Pipe roses and buds with tube 104 and mount on wires. (See page 21.) Pipe tube 67 leaves on wires. Tape into three sprays.

STEP THREE. Bake 12″ x 4″ and 6″ x 3″ round tiers. Fill and ice with buttercream and assemble on tray. Place the 6″ tier toward rear of 12″ tier. Pipe tube 1 script on top of 12″ tier.

STEP FOUR. Attach letters to front of 12″ tier. Pipe

vertical rows of tube 19 stars to resemble city skyline. Pipe tube 21 star border around base of 12″ tier and tube 17 stars around top. On 6″ tier, pipe tube 17 star border around base and tube 16 stars around top. Position flags on 6″ tier. Arrange sprays on top of cake and at each side. Prop seal in position, attaching with dots of icing. Serves 28.

GOLDENROD CAKE (below)

Glowing goldenrod enhances a sheet cake ideal for any fall party. Simple borders set off the flowers.

STEP ONE. Bake a two-layer 9″ x 13″ cake. Fill and ice smoothly with buttercream. Set cake on a foil-covered board.

STEP TWO. Make clusters of goldenrod right on the corners of the cake. Pipe a natural-looking curved sprig with tube 1. After the stems are made, pipe tube 3 dots along the stems and on the ends. Top dots with tube 17 stars, then fill in the flowers with tube 13 stars. Pipe tube 1 dots at random around cluster. Pipe tube 65 leaves. (See page 15.)

STEP THREE. Pipe bottom border of tube 9 balls with tube 5 balls above and between them. Serves 24.

CAKE OF CALIFORNIA

STEP ONE. Prepare Color Flow icing as directed on page 76. Tape wax paper over patterns for sun and letters and outline with tube 2. Flow in thinned icing and let dry.

STEP TWO. Make many California poppies in brilliant yellow, orange and white as directed on page 10. Pipe calyx on back of each flower and mount flowers on wires. Pipe tube 2 leaves on wire, pulling out small spikes.

STEP THREE. Bake 12″ x 4″ and 8″ x 3″ square tiers. Fill and ice with buttercream. Assemble on foil-covered board.

STEP FOUR. For flower effect on bottom borders, use tube 14. Divide side of bottom tier into sixths. Pipe horizontal elongated shells, one from left and one from right to meet at the mark. Pipe a vertical elongated shell above mark starting at top and pulling down toward base. Pipe two additional shells on either side of this, and a star in the center. Repeat around cake to make the flower border around base of tier. Pipe flower border around base of top tier by dividing side of cake into fourths. Pipe tube 14 shell borders around top of both tiers.

STEP FIVE. Place an icing-covered wedge of cake on top of cake to support Color Flow sun. Arrange wired flowers and leaves to frame sun and cascade down sides of cake. Attach letters. Serves 42.

CHAPTER TWO

The Romantic Rose

THE ROSE, throughout history, has been the favorite flower of poets and lovers, commoners and kings. According to legend, it grew in the Garden of Eden and the Hanging Gardens of Babylon. At one time most of the Mediterranean islands must have been covered with wild roses, as the rose is depicted in many early coins, sculptures and even in a Cretan wall painting that dates back 3,600 years. Cleopatra is said to have welcomed Mark Antony in a room carpeted knee deep with rose petals. The Romans draped guests with garlands of roses, washed with perfumed rose water, served rose puddings and rose wines.

With the growth of Christianity the white rose became the Virgin Mary's symbol, and the briar rose was believed to have sprung from drops of Christ's blood, shed as He wore the crown of thorns. In medieval times, Gothic cathedrals were built with glorious rose windows of stained glass.

In France, Napoleon's wife, Josephine, developed some of the greatest rose gardens of all time at her chateau near Paris. She made the rose fashionable, and her skilled gardeners contributed much to the developing science of rose growing. Josephine also commissioned a magnificent series of rose paintings by botanical artist Pierre-Joseph Redouté which remain unequalled for detail and authenticity. Two of these paintings are reproduced above.

The rose appeared on English coins as early as 1344, and about the same time King Edward III established the Order of the Garter, with the rose on its emblem. The Wars of the Roses in the 15th century got their name from the insignia of the two rival families, the red rose of Lancaster and the white rose of York, eventually the winner. Henry VII of Lancaster married a princess of York and began the Tudor dynasty with a rose as its symbol. Henry VIII and Elizabeth I always displayed the Tudor rose in their many portraits, coins and medals. The Victorians used an elaborate language of roses in courtship, and we continue to cherish the rose as a symbol of love and beauty.

THE ROSE is the best-loved flower by cake decorators. In this chapter we show variations on the basic piped rose. You will enjoy duplicating the Peace Rose, Hybrid Teas, wild roses, and fascinating varieties of "old" roses. Pipe them all in royal icing.

THE PEACE ROSE

THE GREATEST ROSE ever bred, according to many rose lovers, is the golden yellow Peace, edged with blushing pink. Developed in France by Francis Meilland, it was introduced to America in 1945.

To create the Peace Rose in icing, use the method described on page 8 for the American Beauty Rose with slight modifications. Immediately after piping, dust fingers with cornstarch and curl edges of petals under. To give the yellow rose a touch of pink, dilute pink food color with water and lightly brush on edges of petals with a small brush.

THE PEACE ROSE
BRIDAL CAKE

Create this spectacular wedding cake featuring the beloved Peace Rose and peace symbol.

STEP ONE. Pipe a quantity of Peace Roses and buds, about 55 of each. Mount on wire stems. Pipe sepals at base of flowers with tube 65. Pipe tube 67 leaves on wires. Dry, then tape into clusters of three. Tape about five roses and five buds with leaves into a spray. You will need seven sprays for sides of cake and one to set between pillars. Make two sprays for the arch for the top of the cake with about 20 roses and buds.

STEP TWO. To prepare top ornament, cut or break the pointed tips off two plastic flower spikes to form hollow tubes. Glue to plate from the Heart Base near back edge with airplane glue. Glue petite bridal couple in front of flower spikes. Dry.

STEP THREE. Bake 16″ round, 12″ hexagon and 6″ round two-layer tiers. Fill and ice with buttercream. Place 16″ tier on foil-covered cake board. Insert dowel rods, clipped off level with cake. Place hexagon tier on a corrugated board cut to size and center on 16″ tier. Insert six 12″ long dowel rods into hexagon tier down to the cardboard, where pillars will be positioned. Place 6″ tier on a foil-covered 7″ cake circle. Do not finish assembling cake until all tiers are decorated.

STEP FOUR. Make patterns for 2″ diameter circles and 3½″ and 4½″ long ovals. Trace larger ovals on 16″ tier, smaller ovals on hexagon tier and circles on 6″ tier.

To decorate 16″ tier, fill ovals with tube 1 cornelli lace and edge with tube 2 beading. Figure pipe tube 9 hearts between ovals and top with tube 5 dots. Pipe tube 9 bottom ball border and trim with tube 6 balls. Pipe tube 9 ball border around top of tier.

STEP FIVE. Cover hexagon tier with tube 1 cornelli lace, leaving ovals on sides empty. Edge ovals with tube 2 beading. Pipe tube 8 ball border around base and top of tier. Position 5″ Corinthian pillars over dowel rods. Attach spray of flowers between pillars with icing. Punch holes half-way through bottom of cake circle below 6″ tier to secure dowel rods. Clip off dowel rods ⅛″ above top of pillars and position 6″ tier atop pillars.

STEP SIX. On 6″ tier, figure pipe tube 7 hearts between circles, and top with tube 5 dots. Pipe tube 7 bottom ball border and trim with tube 5 balls. Fill all but front circle with tube 1 cornelli and edge all circles with tube 2 beading. Pipe peace symbol in front circle with tube 2 beading. Pipe tube 7 top ball border.

STEP SEVEN. Position ornament on top of cake and insert wires of sprays into flower spikes on back of ornament. Place cupids from Musical Trio around pillars. Attach sprays of flowers to sides of hexagon tier with icing. Wrap cake board with ribbon and tie a bow around last spray. Serves 180 guests.

TIFFANY AMERICAN HERITAGE CHRISTIAN DIOR KORDES PERFECTA SIMONE ROYAL HIGHNESS BEWITCHED DAINTY BESS

THE BEAUTIFUL HYBRID TEA ROSES

Most popular of the roses grown today are the beautiful Hybrid Teas. Their large elegant blooms and strong stems, wide range of colors and ability to bloom from early summer until frost in most climates account for their popularity.

The Hybrid Teas are created with tube 104, just as the rose on page 21. The variations are described below.

TIFFANY. Pipe with pink icing, then dust fingers with cornstarch and curl petals under. Brush with yellow powdered tempera color (not edible).

AMERICAN HERITAGE. Stripe bag with tube 4 red string, above narrow end of tube, then fill with yellow icing. Curl petals.

CHRISTIAN DIOR. Pipe large full petals of deep crimson red. Curl petals under.

KORDES PERFECTA. Pipe same as American Heritage using deep and pale pink icing.

SIMONE. To make lavender color, blend pink and orchid. Curl petals under.

ROYAL HIGHNESS. Pipe high-centered double blossoms of pale pink. Curl petals under.

BEWITCHED. Pipe large deep pink petals.

DAINTY BESS. Fill decorating bag with half pale and half darker pink icing, lighter color on top. Pipe five petals, moving hand to ruffle edges. Add tube 1 dots and artificial stamens.

TEA ROSE WEDDING CAKE

STEP ONE. Pipe four of each rose and each bud described above. Mount on wires. Pipe tube 67 leaves on wires. Tape leaves to roses and buds. Arrange into large and small bouquet and two sprays.

STEP TWO. Bake 12″ and 6″ round two-layer tiers. Fill and ice with buttercream. Divide 12″ tier into sixteenths and 6″ tier into eighths.

STEP THREE. Assemble on cake board using 8″ round separator plates and 5″ Grecian pillars. On 12″ tier, pipe tube 16 base shell border, then tube 21 upright shells at marks. Edge base of each with tube 16 shells. Drop two tube 2 strings between upright shells and top with tube 16 rosettes. Pipe three rows of stylized flowers around side, composed of tube 3 dots. Edge separator plate with tube 5 balls and pipe a tube 8 top ball border.

STEP FOUR. Pipe similar design on 6″ tier, using tube 16 for shell border and rosettes and tube 19 for upright shells. Pipe tube 2 beading around edge of separator plate. Make scallop pattern for top of tier, mark on cake and outline with tube 2 beading.

STEP FIVE. Ice two half balls of styrofoam. Insert small bouquet in one and secure between pillars. Add wired sprays to cascade down sides of cake. Anchor second half ball in tea cup with royal icing and insert large bouquet. Center on top. Serves 80.

36

THE WILD ROSE IN CREWEL TECHNIQUE

A wild rose need not be growing wild, in fact more than 200 types exist and many bloom in gardens. Most of them bear graceful, five-petaled blossoms that look more like apple or peach blossoms than garden roses. Three of the loveliest wild roses bloom on this cake, done in a style that looks like crewel stitch.

Max Graf is a hybrid rose created by crossing a tall shrub-type rose and a ground-hugging variety. Its pink clusters and trailing branches make it popular with landscape gardeners.

Rosa Rugosa is a rugged, shrub-type Japanese rose that thrives in cool weather.

Rosa Foetida is also called Austrian Copper. Orange-scarlet backed with yellow, it was brought to Europe before the 13th century by Moors invading from Africa.

STEP ONE. Bake a two-layer oval cake. Fill and ice with buttercream. Pipe tube 7 bottom ball border,

adding tube 5 balls for trim. Pipe a tube 6 ball border at top edge of cake.

STEP TWO. Trace wild rose design on top and side of cake using The Wilton Way patterns. Pipe roses directly on cake. Using crewel stitch technique, fill in pattern by piping many lines using tube 1 and working from outside in. Pipe double row of lines to build up buds. For *Max Graf*, pipe pink petals with darker pink undersides curved over at edges. Add pale pink centers and yellow dots for stamens. For *Rosa Rugosa*, pipe dark pink petals with lighter pink edges curved over. Add pale pink centers and yellow dots. For *Rosa Foetida*, pipe orange-scarlet petals with yellow edges curved over and pipe yellow dots at center.

STEP THREE. Pipe leaves in two shades of green, using tube 1 and crewel technique. Vein of leaf is line of tube 1 beading, as are stems. Serves twelve.

A GROUP OF OLD ROSES

As many people collect antique china or cherish fine old furniture, some rose growers specialize in "old roses". These are varieties which, for the most part, reached their peak before the late 1800's, and have been replaced in public favor by new varieties.

MADAME HARDY is a damask rose, introduced in 1842. Using greenish-white icing, pipe many tube 104 petals for full double flower.

ROSA MUNDI is a French or Gallica rose, cultivated before 1581. Pipe pale pink open rose with tube 104. When dry, paint stripes of red and darker pink. Add artificial stamens.

ROSA MOYESII was introduced in 1894. This hardy shrub rose has red single blossoms. Pipe five tube 104 petals, indenting edge. Add tube 1 dots and artificial stamens.

MME. LOUIS LEVEQUE, introduced in 1898, is a moss rose. Pipe about 50 tube 104 petals, furling lower ones for full double flower.

ROSA EGLANTERIA, grown before 1551, is the first of the fragrant-leaved sweetbriars. Stripe bag with white icing, then fill with pink. Pipe five tube 104 petals, indenting edge. Add tube 1 stamens and a few artificial ones.

LORD PENZANCE, another sweetbriar rose, was introduced in 1894. Stripe bag with yellow icing, and fill with peach. Pipe five-petaled rose, indenting edge. Add tube 1 stamens and some artificial ones.

REINE DES VIOLETTES, introduced in 1860, is a soft, mauve color, one of the Hybrid Perpetuals popular in Victorian times. Pipe many tube 104 petals, leaving center open, and add tube 1 center dots of yellow and green for stamens.

MARECHAL NIEL, introduced in 1864, is a Noisette rose, descended from tea roses brought from China. Pipe many yellow tube 104 petals to make a full double blossom.

ROSE DE MEAUX, a small pale pink cabbage rose, was introduced in 1789. Pipe many small tube 102 petals for each blossom.

PAUL NEYRON, another Hybrid Perpetual, was developed in 1869. Pipe a tube 104 multi-petaled pink rose, leaving center open. Fill center with tube 1 yellow dots for stamens.

MADAME HARDY • ROSA MUNDI • ROSA MOYESII • MME. LOUIS LEVEQUE • ROSA EGLANTERIA • LORD PENZANCE • REINE DES VIOLETTES • MARECHAL NIEL • DE MEAUX • PAUL NEYRON

OLD ROSE BRIDAL CAKE

Ten lovely rose varieties from an old-fashioned garden lend their charm to this elegant wedding cake. Trimmed and edged in dainty ecru lace, it is an ideal choice for a bride who will wear a lacy Victorian wedding gown, and who loves antiques.

STEP ONE. Tape wax paper over patterns and outline leaves and roses with tube 1 and royal icing. Starting from center of rose, pipe short zigzag lines to fill in petals. Fill centers of flowers with tube 1 dots. You will need to make four side pieces and four corner pieces for 16″ tier, and four smaller side pieces for 12″ tier. For projecting cornices on 12″ tier make eight half-patterns, four facing left and four right. Make eight panels to cover pillars, four facing left and four right. For top tier make two roses and four leaf clusters separately, half the leaves facing left and half right. Dry all pieces on flat surface. Overpipe backs of pieces for strength. Make extras as lace is very fragile.

STEP TWO. Make roses as described on page 39. You need six flowers and six buds of each variety, plus tube 68 leaves piped on wires. Mount roses and buds on wires. Bind a matching rose and bud to leaves with floral tape. Combine one pair of each variety into a bouquet. With remaining flowers, make smaller bouquet and four sprays.

STEP THREE. Bake 16″ x 4″ and 12″ x 4″ square tiers and 9″ x 3″ oval tier. Fill and ice with buttercream. Insert dowel rods clipped level with top of tier, into two lower tiers for support. Assemble with 5″ Grecian pillars and two 13″ square separator plates, using cardboard cut to fit under oval tier. Brush lower separator plate and underside of upper plate with thinned royal icing to help anchor lace.

STEP FOUR. Pipe tube 9 bulb border around base of 16″ tier and pipe tube 2 dots between bulbs. Pipe tube 9 and tube 2 scallops around edge of lower separator plate. On 12″ tier, pipe tube 7 bulb border around base using separator plate as guide and trim with tube 2 dots between bulbs. On top edge of tier, pipe tube 6 bulbs and tube 2 dots between them. Around base of oval tier, pipe larger tube 6 bulbs and tube 2 dots. Insert large bouquet in half a styrofoam ball and attach between pillars.

STEP FIVE. Attach lace panels to lower separator plate. At one corner of plate, measure ½″ in from edge and pipe two tube 1 lines about 2″ long and parallel to edge. Set one panel, straight edge toward corner, into icing. Pipe two more tube 1 lines at right angle to first set and position panel facing opposite way. Match edges and pipe tube 2 beading down seam to hold panels together. Panels will be ¼″ below 12″ tier. Repeat for other corners.

STEP SIX. On oval tier, pipe short tube 1 line of icing on one side of top edge of tier. Set lace rose in place. Prop with cotton until dry. Remove cotton and attach lace leaf clusters with icing on each side of rose. Repeat on opposite side of tier. On 12″ tier, attach side pieces with dots of icing. Then, beginning at one corner, attach cornices by piping two tube 1 lines of icing at right angle, ⅜″ in on underside of separator plate. Set in cornice pieces, matching seam. Pipe dots of icing on seam in center of rose to hold pieces together. Then pipe a thin line of icing on seam in petal and brush smooth. Repeat for other three corners.

STEP SEVEN. Position small bouquet in mound of icing on top of cake. On 16″ tier, attach side lace pieces with dots of icing. Attach two sprays on 12″ tier and two on 16″ tier with icing. Then, pipe a line of icing at each corner of 16″ tier and attach corner pieces to stand out from cake at right angle. Pipe a line of tube 2 beading on both sides of pieces. Serves 210 wedding guests.

WILD ROSE WEDDING CAKE

The dainty, fresh-faced wild rose is the perfect choice for decorating a spring or early summer wedding cake. Set off these pretty pink blossoms with cool green baroque scrolls for a dramatic bridal table centerpiece.

DECORATING THE CAKE

STEP ONE. Make a quantity of tube 101 wild roses as directed on page 15. Pipe tube 67 leaves on wires. Mount some roses on wires and combine them with leaves to make one large bouquet for top of cake and two sprays for between pillars. Leave remaining roses without wires for sides of cake.

STEP TWO. Paint 5″ Grecian pillars and 2″ plastic bell with light green royal icing. Make base for bell by covering half a styrofoam ball with balls of green royal icing. Pipe balls in circles, starting with tube 5 at base and tapering to tube 3 balls at top. Dry. Secure bell to base with icing. Insert skewer or thin dowel rod through bell and styrofoam base, long enough to go down into cake.

STEP THREE. Use The Wilton Way patterns for scrolls. Tape pattern for 6″ tier to 6″ curved surface and pipe with tube 5. Tape patterns for square tier to flat surface and pipe with tube 5.

STEP FOUR. Bake 10″ square and 6″ round two-layer tiers. Fill and ice with buttercream. Assemble with painted pillars and two 6″ round separator plates on foil-covered board.

STEP FIVE. Pipe tube 12 balls around base of 10″ tier, then finish framing tier with tube 8 balls on side seam and top edge. Pipe tube 5 balls around base and top of 6″ tier.

STEP SIX. Cut wax paper to shape of scroll patterns and place against tiers. Mark with toothpick to indicate scroll area. Remove paper and pipe tube 1 green dots on tiers within area. Secure scrolls on cake with dots of icing.

STEP SEVEN. Pipe tube 2 stems on either side of scroll on sides of 10″ tier, then pipe tube 67 leaves and attach wild roses with dots of icing. Position flower sprays between pillars, securing with mounds of icing and add petite bridal couple. Secure bell on top of cake by inserting skewer into top tier. Push a block of styrofoam into bell and secure with royal icing. Insert bouquet. A lovely petite cake that serves 65.

CHINA ASTER

ANTIQUE ROSE

FRAMED ON A CAKE: ROSE PORTRAIT I

"Pretty as a picture" describes this elegant cake for a bride or a special anniversary. Make flowers first.

CHINA ASTER. To make this fluffy flower, bend florists' wire into a hook at one end, and pipe a tube 9 ball over it. Pull out many tube 1 stamens, then pipe rows of tube 81 petals around this center. Pipe outer petals with tube 104. Dust fingers with cornstarch and touch inner petals to curve inward. Pipe elongated leaves on wire with tube 67. With tube 65s, pipe points on top of leaves. Brush smooth.

ANTIQUE ROSE. Pipe rose as described on page 21, making about a dozen tube 124 petals. When dry, turn over and pipe a tube 12 ball on back. Smooth with damp brush onto petals. Pipe tube 7 calyx on wire and attach rose. For buds, pipe mounds with tube 6 on hooked ends of wire and furl tube 124 petals over them. Add tube 65 sepals. Pipe tube 69 leaves on wire, pulling out points with damp brush. Make tube 104 roses and buds for garland. Mount on wire (see Chapter Twenty) and form four sprays, adding wired leaves. Pipe tube 1 thorns on stems.

THE PORTRAIT CAKE

STEP ONE. Draw two-piece patterns for lattice, creating a scallop design at the center of each side. Tape wax paper over pattern and outline with tube 2 and royal icing. Pipe lattice with tube 2. Dry.

STEP TWO. Bake 9″ x 13″ rectangular and 9″ oval two-layer tiers. Ice and assemble on cake board.

STEP THREE. Pipe tube 2 string around edge of rectangular tier and down each corner to secure lattice. Set lattice carefully in place, one section at a time. Pipe tube 16 scrolls on center design, then pipe tube 16 shell border around all other sides of lattice. Along top of tier, pipe a second row of shells.

STEP FOUR. Pipe tube 5 string around top edge of oval tier. Pipe one row of tube 16 shells along each side of it. Pipe a third row of shells on top of string. Add tube 4 dots between shells on either side of center row. Pipe tube 18 base border.

STEP FIVE. Arrange flowers on cake. Secure garland with icing. Serves 36.

CREATE A FLORAL PORTRAIT in icing. Here and on page 47 are two stunning cakes which reproduce original paintings by the 18th century French botanical illustrator, Pierre-Joseph Redouté. See them on page 33. Redouté's brilliant craftsmanship earned him a reputation as the "Raphael of Flowers". He recorded the superb roses in the Empress Josephine's famous gardens at Malmaison, near Paris. Later he produced a monumental three-volume series, "Les Roses", which is still the largest single reference work on roses. With care, you can create every detail of Redouté's exquisite bouquets in icing.

DEEP-TONED ROSE · MORNING GLORIES · ROSEBUD · ROSE · VIOLA · DAISY · CARNATION

FRAMED ON A CAKE: ROSE PORTRAIT II

A bouquet gathered from a summer garden and arranged with an artist's touch as pictured by French painter Pierre-Joseph Redouté nearly two centuries ago (shown on page 33) is reproduced on this splendid anniversary or wedding cake.

THE FLOWERS

ROSES. With royal icing, pipe a Mme. Louis Lévêque rose and two Paul Neyron roses, one pink and one white, following directions on page 39. Pipe two roses in dark, shaded colors. Fit bag with tube 104, then stripe with violet and fill with deep rose icing. Using flower nail, pipe three rows of wide-open petals. Add tube 1 yellow dots with three white dots in center and insert a few artificial stamens. Mount all on wires. Pipe leaves on wires in four shades of green with tubes 66, 67 and 68. Tape in clusters of three and five. Brush some dry leaves with red color along edges. Make some separate heavy stems by wrapping wire with floral tape. Pull out tube 1 brown thorns.

ROSEBUDS. Bend florists' wire into small hook and pipe a tube 6 ball of icing over it, tapering toward top. Wind a tube 104 ribbon around ball to form bud. When dry, pipe tube 2 calyx and tube 65 sepals. Pull out tube 1 spikes for bristly look. Dry, then tape a rose, a bud and leaves together.

MORNING GLORIES. With tube 104 and white icing, place wide end of tube into lily nail. Squeeze as you turn nail to form hollow cup, then remove excess icing with toothpick. With tube 103 and blue icing, add ruffle around edge of cup and brush smooth. Brush inside of cup with yellow icing and pipe tube 1 pistil. Mount on wires. Pipe tube 65 sepals on base of flower. Smooth down onto calyx with damp brush. To make buds, start with wire bent into hook. Pipe tube 3 mound of icing on it, then several jagged petals with tube 102 to form slim tube. Brush base lightly with white icing. Pipe calyx and sepals on base of bud with tube 65, brushing icing onto wire. Pipe tube 66 leaves on wires. Tape buds, flowers and leaves into spray, beginning with smallest buds at top and continuing down to the open flowers.

VIOLAS. Pipe two tube 102 upper petals. Then pipe three tube 104 petals in front. Pipe four tube 1 black dots in center and pull out tube 1 pistil. Brush on thin black lines with food color. Mount on wires.

CARNATIONS. Pipe as described on page 22, making one pink, one deep violet and several yellow. For buds, make flowers with upstanding petals only. Dry, then paint red stripes on yellow flowers. Mount on wires, then pipe long tube 4 bulb on either side of flower base and brush together to make calyx. Pipe four tube 66 sepals at base of blossom and brush onto calyx.

DAISIES. Fill decorating bag with pink and red icing swirled together. On small nail, pipe five pairs of flat tube 102 petals, holding tube at right angle to nail with wide end turned outward and starting at outer edge of nail. Pipe cluster of black tube 1 dots and circle them with tube 1 yellow dots. Mount on wires. Pipe tube 66 leaves on wires.

THE PORTRAIT CAKE

STEP ONE. Bake 14" x 3" and 10" x 2" round tiers. Ice with buttercream and assemble on 16" round foil-covered cake board.

STEP TWO. Pipe tube 21 shell border around base of 14" tier and tube 16 shell border around top. Divide tier into sixteenths and drop tube 16 strings between divisions. Trim with tube 13 fleur-de-lis and stars. On 10" tier, pipe tube 14 shell borders around top and bottom. Pipe fleur-de-lis in two sizes with tube 14 at intervals around cake and dot with stars.

STEP THREE. On top of cake, pipe mound of icing as base and position wired flowers and leaves as pictured. Insert heavy stems under bouquet at one end. Tape daisies, violas and leaves into several sprays and position on 14" tier, bending wires so they drape gracefully over side of tier. Serves 50 party-style or 140 wedding-style.

CHAPTER THREE

Decorating with Plain Tubes

THE PLAIN ROUND TUBES, ranging in size from tiny tube 000 to large tube 12, are among the most useful series of tubes for a decorator, and are those that demonstrate a decorator's skill more than any others. Indeed, if no other tubes existed, an infinite number of outstanding cakes could be decorated with just these plain round tubes.

The smallest tubes in this series create a huge variety of decorating effects. The very smallest, tubes 000 through 2, are used for Australian curtaining, English, and South African fine line work, and the most delicate lace, lattice and loop trims.

The graceful swinging loop so important to the art of decorating, is usually piped with tubes 1 through 3. Successful loops and all fine line work, are built on three basics:

CORRECT CONSISTENCY OF ICING. For gracefully curving loops, thin the icing so that it flows easily through the tube with light pressure.

CORRECT POSITION OF THE DECORATING CONE. For perfect loops, be sure to have the cake at eye level, and ideally on a revolving decorating stand. Point the tube straight at the point you wish to attach the icing string—touch point, move away, *not down,* and come back to touch again.

A STEADY, EVEN RHYTHM. Some decorators even play a rhythmic march on their record player as they pipe. To surround even a large cake with loops is a quick procedure if your rhythm is fast and sure.

OTHER USES OF PLAIN TUBES

Tubes 1 through 5 are very versatile. They can describe a curving vine, do elaborate or simple script and lettering, make stylized "dot" flowers (see page 37), pipe dainty "picot" or beading and small ball or bead borders. They can also figure pipe small birds and animals.

Larger plain tubes 4 through 12 are useful for ball borders and especially for figure piping. For borders, even controlled pressure is essential for a neat effect. Each ball must be perfectly round and neatly joined to the next, identical in size. For figure piping a varied pressure to create realistic rounded forms is needed.

DECORATE DAINTY PINK BALLERINA

The delicate stringwork on this cake shows how beautiful and effective curving lines can be. Its feminine look is created without the use of a single flower or ruffle.

BAKE ROUND TIERS, 12" x 4" and 8" x 3". Create the top crown by cutting a 4" x ½" circle of styrofoam. Fill tiers and ice. Assemble on serving plate. Pipe strings and dots with tube 1 and royal icing.

ICE CROWN TIER. After the icing has set, turn crown upside down on fruit can to decorate. Divide lower edge into twelfths and drop strings from point to point. Then pipe tiny loops from each point and top each with tube 1 dots. Drop a second row of strings inside the first, but starting at the upper edge. Pipe a dot in the center of each string. Dry.

DECORATE THE 8" TIER. Cut a pattern with twelve scallops for top of cake. Mark with toothpick. Pipe design with strings and follow with a row of dots, about ⅛" in from strings. Begin side design with a row of strings, using scallops as a guide. Pipe a second row of strings inside first and add a row of dots between the two. Pipe loops between the strings.

Drop two rows of strings from the center point of the first strings. Pipe a loop between them. Drop another row of strings between the pairs of strings, below loops. Pipe dots above strings.

DECORATE THE 12" TIER. Make a second pattern with twelve scallops, but remove center to fit over 8" tier. Mark on tier with a toothpick, then pipe design with strings and a row of dots. Using scallops for a guide, drop a row of strings around side. Pipe a second string inside first and add dots between them. Pipe a loop between pairs of strings.

Drop two rows of strings from the center point of the first pair of strings. Drop a loop between them. Pipe a row of dots above each string.

Make third row of double strings, dropping them from center of strings in the second row. Pipe a loop between them. Add a string between the pairs of strings, below loops. Pipe dots above each string.

ADD FINISHING TOUCHES. Pipe tube 8 ball border around base of 12" tier and tube 6 balls around top. Pipe tube 6 balls around base of 8" tier and tube 3 balls around top. Carefully attach crown to top of cake with dots of icing so the loops are pointing up. Circle the base of the crown with tube 3 balls. Secure dancing ballerina to center of crown and pipe tube 2 beading around its base. Serves 32.

CAPTIVE ROSE

Adorned with suspended loops of icing, this petite shower cake challenges the decorator's skill with beautiful results.

PIPE ROSES with tube 102 and buds with tube 101. (See page 21.) Mount on wires. Pipe tube 66 leaves on wires. Dry, then tape flowers and leaves into two large and four small sprays.

BAKE CAKES in round mini-tier pans. Assemble on cake stand with mini-tier separator set, making sure cakes are perfectly aligned.

PIPE BORDERS. Pipe ball borders around tiers, using tube 7 on base of bottom tier and tube 5 on top. Use tube 5 on base of middle and top tiers and tube 3 on top of both. Secure a large spray between sets of pillars.

PIPE STRINGS on sides of tiers with tube 1. Divide bottom tier into twenty-fourths and drop strings from point to point. Leaving four strings open in front, pipe a longer string between the next four pairs on either side. Pipe another string to connect each pair of longer strings. Repeat pattern on other two tiers, dividing middle tier into twenty-fourths and top tier into sixteenths.

PIPE SUSPENDED LOOPS with tube 1. Let each row of loops dry about an hour before piping next row. Pipe loops with the same technique as on a cake side. Using scallops on separator plate as a guide, drop a loop from each one. Leaving two loops open in front, drop a row of six loops on either side, attaching loops to centers of loops above. Drop five loops from that row, then four, three, two and one. Do not let loops touch tier below. Repeat on middle tier.

Position ornament on top of cake, securing two small sprays around base. Add two small sprays on plate. Serves twelve.

LACE TIARA
described on page 52

51

LACE TIARA (*shown on page 51*)

This larger, more complex cake elaborates on the suspended loop technique and is a greater challenge to the decorator.

STEP ONE. Make the lacy tiara ornament for the cake top. Cover a 7″ tall, 3″ diameter lightweight cardboard cylinder with wax paper. Lay it on its side and secure to prevent rolling. With royal icing and tube 1, pipe a line halfway around the bottom edge of the cylinder. This line will be the base and a guide for how wide to make the tiara. Pipe a random pattern of strings, connecting them to the bottom line and to each other. Then pipe a second pattern of strings over the first. Dry for at least twelve hours. Remove tiara from cylinder and *very gently* peel wax paper from back. Over-pipe back of base line and lower strings and dry again.

STEP TWO. Bake 6″ x 3″, 10″ x 4″ and 14″ x 4″ two-layer round tiers. Ice tiers. Make paper scallop patterns for top of 14″ and 10″ tiers using a 12″ and an 8″ square and marking on tier with a toothpick. Assemble tiers with 8″ and 12″ round separator plates and Crystal-Clear pillars.

STEP THREE. Pipe large tube 2 beading around base of pillars and small tube 2 beading to define scallop pattern on top of tiers. Attach small doves between pillars with icing. Pipe tube 5 ball borders around top and bottom of all three tiers, varying the pressure to make both large and small balls. Add tube 3 blue scallops and dots to borders.

STEP FOUR. On 14″ tier drop tube 1 royal icing double strings around top of tier. Drop a second row of double strings from first. Drop three more pairs of strings in four places on tier, opposite pillars.

On top edge of 10″ tier, drop a row of double strings, then drop a second row overlapping the first. Drop a third row of strings from first two, then add additional rows to form a tapered design as pictured and repeat it three more times around tier.

On 6″ tier, drop strings around top of tier. Drop a row of double strings from first row. Add three more double strings in four places on tier.

STEP FIVE. Drop a series of tube 1 suspended loops from each separator plate, making a tapered design opposite each pillar. Let each row of loops dry about one hour before adding the next.

STEP SIX. Attach bridal couple to petite heart base and secure to top of cake. Very carefully secure tiara behind the ornament. Serves 156.

SPARKLING SNOWFLAKE

STEP ONE. Tape wax paper smoothly over filigree patterns. Outline with tube 1 and royal icing and over-pipe main lines twice. You need 30 half-stars, 18 whole stars and 18 quarter stars. Sprinkle with edible glitter before icing dries. You also need four dimensional stars. To make each, you need one whole and two half-stars sprinkled with edible glitter. Prop whole star with pieces of styrofoam, then attach half-stars at right angles on either side of it with a line of royal icing. Lay a length of fish line in the icing along the edge of one half-star before attaching to whole star so the completed design can be suspended. Make the filigree backdrop in three sections, over-piping main lines for strength. Sprinkle with edible glitter. Attach the three sections with lines of icing, propping until dry.

STEP TWO. Bake seven two-layer 9″ x 4″ hexagons for the bottom tier, a 15″ x 4″, a 12″ x 4″ and a 9″ x 3″ hexagon. Seventh 9″ hexagon of the base tier is in the center for support. Fill and ice.

STEP THREE. Cut ½″ thick piece of masonite or four sheets of corrugated cardboard taped together into base for cake 1″ larger than bottom tier. Cover with foil then assemble bottom tier. Insert dowel rods clipped level with top, into base tier to support tiers above. Place 15″ tier in position. Cut cardboard base 1″ larger than 12″ tier. Cover with foil and glue six stud plates on bottom. Press lightly onto 15″ tier to mark position of pillars. Set 7½″ Corinthian pillars in place. Insert 12″ long dowel rods through pillars down to board under 15″ tier. Clip off level with top of pillars.

Attach 12″ tier to board and place on pillars. Elevate 9″ tier with 9″ hexagon separator plates and six 5″ Corinthian pillars.

STEP FOUR. Pipe tube 6 ball borders around bottom and down sides of base tier, tube 5 balls around top. Pipe tube 5 ball borders on all sides of 15″ tier and around bottom of 12″ tier. Pipe tube 4 balls around lower separator plates, top and sides of 12″ tier and top, bottom and sides of 9″ tier.

STEP FIVE. Position backdrop and bridal couple. Attach half-stars around sides of 9″ tier, then pipe tube 4 balls down seams. Suspend a dimensional star by taping fish line to underside of separator plate. Attach quarter-stars around side of 12″ tier and pipe tube 4 balls down seams. Suspend stars from foil-covered board. Attach half-stars and stars to 15″ and base tier. Serves 292.

SPARKLING SNOWFLAKE
described at left

53

ROSE FILIGREE WEDDING CAKE

This daintiest of all wedding cakes is circled with fragile filigree bevels and graced with blushing roses. Creating this beautiful cake will be a source of pride and satisfaction to any adventurous decorator. As with all the cakes in this chapter, only plain tubes are used, except for piping the flowers.

STEP ONE. To pipe the filigree bevel sections, first make cardboard bevel bases to tape the filigree bevel patterns on. Cut the number of pieces for each bevel as indicated on The Wilton Way patterns. Tape these pieces together, *butting seams*. Now trace this complete bevel base on light flexible cardboard, available at art supply stores. Butt and tape seams to form bevel. To give support to cardboard bevel, attach with icing to a 16″ base bevel pan. Or crumple foil into a beveled wreath shape, 16″ at outer diameter, and place under cardboard bevel. Follow the same procedure for supporting the 12″ and 8″ cardboard bevel bases, but using 12″ and 8″ diameter bevel pans or beveled foil wreaths.

Now tape the filigree bevel patterns to cardboard bases and pipe filigree sections with tube 1 and royal icing thinned with lightly beaten egg white. When dry, over-pipe main lines for strength. Pipe tube 1 beading around curved edges at center. Dry again. Carefully remove from wax paper, turn over and over-pipe main lines again. Pipe no more than three filigree sections at a time on cardboard bevel bases to allow plenty of working space.

STEP TWO. Tape small side heart pattern to 8″ curve and large heart to 12″ curve. Pipe with tube 1 and royal icing. Dry, then pipe tube 1 beading around the outer edges of the hearts. Dry again and carefully remove from wax paper.

Pipe tiny roses and rosebuds with tubes 101s and 101. Pipe larger roses with tube 102.

STEP THREE. Bake a 12″ x 4″ round tier, an 8″ x 2″ round layer and an 8″ top bevel. Fill and ice, making a single tier with 8″ round and bevel layers. Ice a 16″ round cake board and assemble tiers on it. Pipe tube 9 balls around base of 12″ tier and tube 5 balls around base of 8″ tier.

STEP FOUR. Position ornament on top of cake and attach roses to it with icing. Pipe tube 65s leaves. Using patterns as a guide, mark position of roses in openings of filigree panels. Attach roses with icing and pipe tube 65 and 65s leaves. Secure lattice hearts to sides between roses.

Begin attaching filigree panels on top bevel using dots of icing. Handle very gently as they are extremely fragile. Then attach filigree panels at base of 8″ tier. Carefully pipe tube 5 balls around top of 12″ tier. These balls will help secure filigree panels. Finally attach filigree panels at base of 12″ tier. Pipe tube 9 balls around edge of cake board to help secure filigree. Your stunning filigree bevel cake will serve 98 wedding guests.

This breathtaking wedding cake, adorned with lace and hung with the most fragile curves of icing, is an outstanding example of the decorator's skill.

STEP ONE. Make lace pieces with royal icing using patterns and tube 1. You will need 25 large and 48 small flat pieces, seven large and seven small pieces made on 8″ curve, and 20 large and 18 small pieces made on 12″ curve. Make extras in case of breakage. Dry thoroughly.

STEP TWO. Pipe many tube 101s forget-me-nots. Mount most on wires. Pipe tube 65 leaves on wires. When dry, tape leaves and flowers together into five small bouquets. Make two clusters, tie with ribbon and attach to card-holder cherub's hands. Make a long, thin spray and attach to cherub fountain. Make two crescent-shaped sprays and attach to second card-holder cherub's hands. Glue cherub to 3″ plastic bell and surround seam with forget-me-nots, adding tube 65 leaves.

STEP THREE. Bake round two-layer tiers 8″, 12″ and 16″ in diameter. Fill and ice smoothly with boiled icing. To assemble you need two 8″ and two 12″ round smooth-edged separator plates, 16 stud plates and eight 5″ Grecian pillars.

Place 16″ tier on cake plate or foil-covered board, then center 12″ separator, smooth side up, on tier. Glue four stud plates to it and attach pillars. Mark position of pillars on smooth side of other 12″ plate and attach stud plates. Attach 12″ tier to plate and place on pillars. Position plates and pillars in same way for 8″ tier. Pipe tube 6 balls around base tier, tube 4 around separator plates.

STEP FOUR. When attaching lace, start at top of cake and work down, piping line of royal icing along two points of the lace piece to secure. First, attach ornament to top of cake, then surround with nine large flat pieces of lace, angled out. Divide side of tier into fourths, attach three flowers at each division and pipe tube 65 leaves. Attach large flat piece of lace vertically to left and right of flowers, angling out.

Position cherub fountain between pillars adding forget-me-nots and tube 65 leaves at base. Attach lace pieces dried on 8″ curve around bottom of tier, alternating large and small.

STEP FIVE. Divide top edge of 12″ tier into eighths, then attach 16 small lace pieces dried on 12″ curve around tier. Attach four large curved pieces at even intervals around side. Secure a flat lace piece on two sides of pattern and *very gently* place cotton ball between them until dry.

Secure one bouquet between pillars. Attach large pieces of lace dried on 12″ curve around base of tier going from center back almost to front, then from back almost to front on other side, a total of 16 pieces. Attach small curved piece on either side of front space.

STEP SIX. Divide top edge of 16″ tier into eighths. Find point exactly between marks and divide bottom of tier into eighths starting at this point. Lightly mark diagonal line from point to point with edge of spatula. Attach three small flat lace pieces along each diagonal.

STEP SEVEN. Drop tube 1 loops of icing between the lace pieces on bottom of 8″ tier, on top edge and below 12″ tier and along top edge of 16″ tier. Also pipe loops along inner side of lace pieces on the side of the 16″ tier.

Attach bouquets at sides and back of 16″ tier and in open space between lace pieces at bottom of 12″ tier. Attach card-holder cherub at front of cake, adding forget-me-nots and tube 65 leaves at base. Serves 216.

CONSTRUCT AN ICING BIPLANE

This icing reproduction of an early '20's plane is sure to please any flying or model airplane enthusiast. Be sure to follow the patterns accurately when piping to assure proper fit and use a light touch when assembling.

STEP ONE. Tape patterns for plane parts to boards and cover smoothly with wax paper. Make all pieces flat except for propeller which is made on a small curved surface. Pipe all pieces with royal icing. Use photo for guide to assembly.

Fuselage. Pipe outer ring with tube 5. Pipe crisscross in center of ring and the triangular pieces with tube 3. When dry, assemble with icing. First attach largest triangular piece across the ring, matching up with crisscross lines. Then add the other two pieces on either side, again matching with crisscross lines.

Tail. Outline pieces with tube 4, pipe inner lines with tube 3. Dry, then assemble with icing using a piece of ¼″ high cardboard to elevate the side pieces of the tail to the proper height. Base of center section rests on table.

Propeller. Pipe with tube 3, dry and attach the two pieces with icing.

Axle and Wheels. Pipe with tube 4, dry and assemble on a small styrofoam block.

Lower Wing. Pipe outline and four cross lines as indicated on pattern to support braces with tube 5. Other lines are tube 3. Pipe three braces for each side with tube 4. Make sure the braces are exactly the length of the pattern or the plane will not fit together properly.

Upper Wing. Pipe outline with tube 5 and other lines with tube 3.

STEP TWO. Make sure all pieces are thoroughly dry, then begin assembling plane. Attach fuselage to top of lower wing with icing. Cut a piece of styrofoam 1¾″ high and about 2″ long. Cut a piece out of the block to allow the brace to be attached to the center of the upper wing. Using the block of styrofoam for support, place right half of upper wing in position. Attach braces with icing. Attach left side of upper wing the same way. Prop tail in position with styrofoam and attach with icing. Dry. Prop plane up with a piece of styrofoam and attach wheels and propeller with icing.

STEP THREE. Bake a 10″ square, two-layer cake. Fill, ice and assemble on foil-covered board. Spread white boiled icing on sides and top of cake with spatula to form cloud patterns. Pipe tube 6 ball border around base of cake.

STEP FOUR. Coat a piece of florists' wire with icing and bend about ¼″ to 90° angle. Position plane on cake using wire pushed into cake to support tail end of fuselage. Serves 20.

A LACY, LATTICE BIRTHDAY CAKE

STEP ONE. Make 28 royal icing lattice pieces, using Australian crescent nail and pattern from The Wilton Way Pattern Book. Brush crescent with egg white and smooth pattern onto it, then brush again and apply piece of wax paper ⅛″ larger than pattern. Insert stem of nail into side of styrofoam block so you can turn nail to pipe lattice. Pipe outline with tube 2, lattice with tube 1. Pipe tube 2 beading around outer curve. Dry. To remove from nail, run a slip of parchment paper under wax paper, then peel from lattice piece.

STEP TWO. Using pattern, pipe 120 lace pieces with royal icing and tube 1. Dry.

STEP THREE. Make 25 tube 103 roses (directions on page 21). Mount on wires. Pipe tube 65 leaves on wires. Dry. Tape leaves to flowers.

STEP FOUR. Bake 10″ square two-layer cake. Fill and ice. Pipe tube 7 bottom ball border. Divide sides into fourths, marking at top and center of side. Drop three tube 2 strings from top points. Pipe tube 5 top ball border. Lightly mark a 4½″ square in center of cake top.

STEP FIVE. Insert candles into cake. Push in flower spikes around candles. Place stems of roses into spikes. Attach lattice pieces to top with line of icing, points of pieces touching pattern line. Attach lace pieces to lattice with icing.

Secure lattice pieces to sides of cake with line of icing so points of the pieces meet at marks halfway up side. Pipe tube 2 beading along inner curve. Attach three lace pieces to the outer curve of each lattice piece. Also attach a lace piece at the points where the lattice pieces meet on the side and where the strings meet at the top edge. Serves 20.

CHAPTER FOUR

The Philippine Method
of Decorating

WATER NYMPH
A dramatic Philippine wedding cake,
described on page 62.

The decorated cake is truly a dramatic centerpiece in the Philippines, and one that displays the decorator's skill. Curving borders are piped with large tubes for a sculptural effect. Flowers are used abundantly in sprays, bouquets and fountains.

The Philippine decorator is most inventive in creating handmade trims of wire, icing, ribbon and styrofoam. Plastic pillars and other cake accessories are very difficult to obtain, so the need to make an artistic substitute becomes a challenge. While plastic pillars are shown on the cakes in this chapter, in the Philippines the pillars would be dowels.

With all this ornamentation, the effect of a Philippine cake is dainty and graceful. This is achieved by the use of harmonizing pastel colors and neat, careful workmanship.

Philippine cakes are usually chiffon or butter cakes, covered and trimmed with boiled icing.

WATER NYMPH *(shown on page 61)*

FIRST PIPE FLOWERS. You will need bell flowers, sampaquitas and calachuchis for the six little bouquets that circle the cake and for the larger bouquet in the center. The pages that follow show the unique Philippine way of making flowers. You will also need about fifteen sampaquita sprays piped on 15″ wires (see page 68) and six lotus blossoms.

PREPARE CENTER ORNAMENT. The stand for the figure consists of four circles of styrofoam in graduated sizes, stacked together. Bottom circle is 4″ x 1″ thick, next 3″ x ½″, then 2½″ x ½″ and finally 2″ x 2″ thick. Ice with royal icing and edge with tube 13 stars. (In the Philippines, this base would be made of light cardboard cylinders, the largest pushed through cake to cake board.)

Paint Classique plastic vase with thinned royal icing, dry, then trim figure and vase with tube 16. Attach vase to stand with royal icing and pipe tube 16 swirls, resembling rosebuds, around base.

Fill the vase with styrofoam, securing with icing. Twist the sampaquita sprays together at base of wire, tape and insert in center of vase. Now insert the other flowers that have been taped into clusters with tulle and set the ornament aside.

BAKE A 14″ TWO-LAYER CAKE. Fill and ice smoothly with boiled icing and set on cake board. Insert a circle of dowel rods, clipped level with top, to support ornament. Center a 10″ cake circle on top of cake, mark lightly and remove. Brush blue-tinted piping gel within marked circle.

DECORATE THE CAKE. Pipe tube 21 shell border around gel "lake". Cut ¼″ ribbon into 3″ pieces. Pipe a tube 21 star on every other shell, and insert ribbon pieces as you pipe, to form an arched fence.

Divide cake into twelfths and mark at top edge. At each mark, pipe a curving shell with tube 1G, starting on top of cake and pulling down to side. Pipe a tube 1G shell on either side of this center one. After twelve triple motifs are piped, pipe a tube 21 fleur-de-lis below each one. Base border is done with tube 21 and consists of alternate shells and swirled shells.

GIVE THE FINISHING TOUCHES. Set ornament in center of cake, securing with royal icing. Arrange sampaquita sprays in graceful curves. Attach lotus to base of ornament. Float several swans, each bearing a lotus bloom, on water. Attach six little bouquets around edge of cake. This dramatic expression of Philippine decorating serves 92 guests.

1   2   3   4   HOOK WIRES AND   PIPE PISTILS
                        TWIST TOGETHER

DRY UPSIDE DOWN

THE PHILIPPINE WAY OF PIPING FLOWERS
This method produces dainty blossoms in a fast assembly-line technique.

ROYAL ICING IS USED for all flowers. For larger ones, stiffen icing so petals will hold their shape.

START WITH A PISTIL, as shown on page 62. Cut about 18 6″ pieces of wire, twist into a cluster and make a tiny hook on each wire. Most flowers are piped on 28-gauge fine wire. Spread the wires apart in a fan shape, then insert hooked ends into decorating cone fitted with an appropriate tube. Insert the wire to the depth of the pistil desired. Squeeze very lightly and pull cone away. Repeat until all pistils are piped, then insert cluster into styrofoam block to dry.

The tube used depends on the flower being made. Pistil 1 (page 62) will be the center of a daisy and is piped with tube 7. Pistil 2, tube 5, is for buds and small flowers. Pistil 3, tube 5, is for a calla lily. Pistil 4 is for a large flower and is piped on a heavier, 22-gauge wire with tube 10.

Using a large tube and light pressure, these flower centers are very quick and easy to pipe.

PIPE MOST PETALS UPSIDE DOWN. Holding the wire, twirl it like a flower nail as you pipe. We show the flowers right-side up to give you a better view.

DRY FINISHED BLOOMS UPSIDE DOWN. Weight a cake rack at one end, and let most of it extend beyond table. As each flower is finished, bend end of wire stem, hook it onto the rack and allow it to dry.

PIPE A DAINTY DAISY
Pipe pistils with tube 7 and dry. Starting at center,

pull out many tube 1 strands. Leave at least one-fourth of the pistil uncovered. Dry upside down. Now, holding flower upside down, pull out a circle of tube 81 petals, attaching each firmly to un-covered area of pistil. Dry again, upside down. Now try these daisy variations.

DAISY ONE. Pipe pistil with tube 7. Leave tip of pistil exposed and pull out two rows of tube 1 stamens. Dry upside down about one hour, just to stiffen. Add single row of tube 81 petals and dry.

DAISY TWO. Pipe pistils with tube 10 and sprinkle with granulated sugar, then dry. Pipe three rows of tube 81 petals, leaving tip of pistil exposed. *Dry thoroughly after piping each row.*

DAISY THREE. Pull out points with tube 1 on tube 10 pistil. Dry. Add row of tube 81 petals, dry again.

DAISY FOUR. Surround tip of tube 7 pistil with three rows of tube 1 stamens. Pipe three rows of pointed petals without drying each row. Touch tube 55 to pistil, squeeze, stop squeezing and pull away. Dry thoroughly.

DAISY

DAISY VARIATIONS

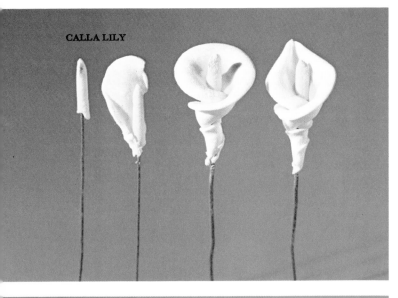

CALLA LILY

Start with a pistil piped with tube 5. Holding wire upside down, touch tube 97 to bottom of pistil, turn wire like a flower nail as you move up. Continue turning to wrap icing around wire. Dip fingers in cornstarch and pinch petal to form point. Dry flower upside down.

For larger flowers, use tube 116, 118 or 119, with a heavier wire and a correspondingly larger pistil for the center.

ROSE

Pipe center, or pistil, with tube 5 on a 22-gauge wire. Pipe flower right side up. Twirl a tube 103 ribbon around pistil, keeping tube parallel to pistil. Add three closed petals, tilting narrow end of tube slightly outward. Surround with five open petals, turning narrow end of tube outward at a 45° angle. Dry upside down.

ROSEBUD

Pipe small pistil with tube 5. Fill decorating cone with orange icing on one side, white on the other. Hold tube 45 parallel to pistil, wide end about halfway from base, narrow end up. Keeping even pressure, twirl wire, slanting tube out as you finish. Note: this flower is made right-side up. Dry upside down on rack.

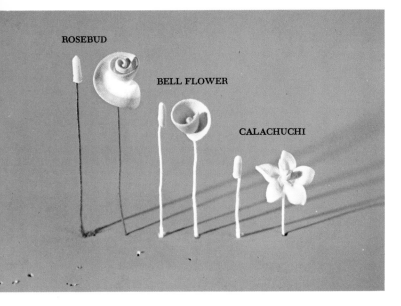

BELL FLOWER

This flower grows in the Philippines on a tree called Yellow Bell. It is piped in a similar fashion to the rosebud. Start lower on the pistil and hold tube 45 on a slant. Twirl wire just once and break off the ribbon of icing.

CALACHUCHI

Use small tube 5 pistil. Working with pistil upside down, touch wide end of tube 97 to center of pistil. Hold tube at 45° angle. Using light pressure, "scrape" tube on pistil, stop pressure, pull away. Dry upside down.

CARNATION

This flower is made right-side up. Pipe tube 9 balls on 22-gauge wire for centers, and dry. Using tube 103, light pressure and stiffened royal icing, pipe petals on top of ball, jiggling hand for ruffled effect. Continue piping petals as you move down side of ball, turning wire as you pipe. Complete by entirely covering ball with petals for full rounded effect. Dry upside down.

SAMPAQUITA, NATIONAL FLOWER OF THE PHILIPPINES

Use tube 59 and pistil piped with tube 7. Holding end of wire with pistil down, touch wide end of tube to pistil and pipe three closed petals, turning wire like a flower nail. Immediately add six outer petals, holding tube at 45° angle to pistil. Dry upside down on rack.

DAMA DE NOCHE

This little flower is piped with tube 55 on a tube 5 pistil. Hold wire upside down, touch tube to pistil at 90° angle and squeeze gently. Pull away for pointed petal. Continue for six-petal flower. Dry upside down on rack.

LOTUS

The lotus, or water lily, is another unusual Philippine flower in that it is piped on a number 7 nail, not on a wire. The royal icing should not be too stiff. Attach wax paper square to flower nail and pipe a tube 6 mound in center of nail. Touching tube to base of mound, pipe a circle of nine pointed petals with tube 81. Squeeze, stop pressure, pull away. Holding tube straight up, pipe three upstanding, interlocking petals in center of mound. Now add more petals between inner and outer rows, holding tube at 45° angle. Dry thoroughly.

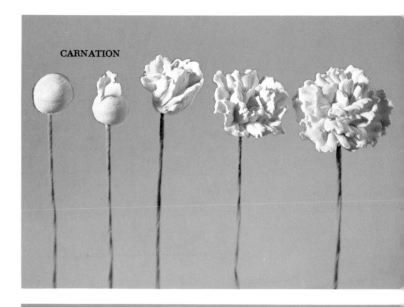

ASSEMBLING FLOWERS INTO BOUQUETS

Philippine decorators have an especially dainty way of grouping their pastel flowers.

Make leaves for the bouquets by inserting a 6″ length of 28-gauge wire into a decorating cone fitted with tube 67. Pull out leaf, increasing pressure slightly for ruffled effect. Dry on rack, upside down.

Loop ribbons, bind with fine 6″ wires. If you would like to add the airy touch of tulle to your bouquets, cut 4″ squares and bunch at center with wires. Now twist the wired flowers, leaves, ribbons and tulle into small bouquets. The twisted stems are inserted into the cake and the bouquets removed at serving time. If you need a larger bouquet, combine several of the small ones and tape the stems together.

DAISY FOUNTAIN

A radiant Philippine wedding cake heaped with dainty pastel daisies.

FIRST MAKE MANY DAISIES, following directions on page 63. Arrange three large bouquets with lavish ribbons to set on cake surface. Group several smaller bouquets into a tapering shape to insert into vase at top of cake. Make four slender sprays to cascade from "fountain".

MAKE FOUNTAIN ORNAMENT. Glue a 5″ Grecian pillar to center of a 10″ round separator plate. Glue the rounded side of a 6″ half-ball of styrofoam to top of pillar. Dry thoroughly. Turn upside down on styrofoam flat surface, heap royal icing on ball and pillar and brush into a smooth vase shape. When dry, turn upright and ice top smoothly. Fill Cupid plastic vase with styrofoam half-ball, securing with icing. Attach Cupid vase to "fountain" and trim with tube 2. Paint top of fountain with blue-tinted piping gel and insert tapered bouquet in Cupid vase.

BAKE A TWO-LAYER, 14″ round cake. Fill and ice with boiled icing. Set on cake board and center with fountain ornament. Do base border with tube 21, piping a circular motion shell for scallop shape. Pipe a tube 16 star on the cake board at the curve of each scallop.

DECORATE FOUNTAIN. Pull up points with tube 2 all around gel "water". Frame top of fountain with tube 21 zigzag and add a row of tube 2 dots at eight places on sides.

Edge separator plate with tube 2 zigzags and add dots on top of cake.

DIVIDE TOP EDGE of cake into twelfths and mark lightly. Drop a double row of tube 21 curves from mark to mark, one row on top and overlapping the second. Trim with tube 2 beading. Clip stems of daisies and secure to side of cake with icing.

FINISH THE CAKE by attaching four sprays to top of fountain, then set three bouquets on cake surface. Serves 92 wedding guests.

"I'M EIGHTEEN!"

In the Philippines, a young girl's 18th birthday is a very important event. It symbolizes the end of girlhood and the beginning of adult responsibilities —much as American "debuts" once did. A large party is held with the cake as centerpiece.

MAKE SAMPAQUITA SPRAYS. This is the national flower of the Philippines. Fill decorating cone with orange icing on one side, white on other. Use tube 59° and pipe the flowers directly on 8″ 28-gauge wires. The method is the same as shown on page 65. Start at the tip of the wire by piping just three petals to form a bud. Pipe two more buds at ½″ intervals on the wire, then add more petals as you progress down wire. You need about 32 sprays.

Make the bouquets and sprays with rosebuds (page 64) and sampaquitas (page 65), adding leaves, tulle, ribbon and sampaquita sprays. You will need five bouquets for the base tier, and four for the two upper tiers. Make a larger bouquet for the top of the arch and two sprays for either side.

CUT ARCH AND NUMBERS from 1″ thick styrofoam, using Wilton Way patterns. Ice "18" with thinned royal icing and sprinkle with edible glitter. Pipe vertical lines with tube 1 on base and top panels. Edge numerals with tube 1 beading.

Cut a 4″ and a 3½″ square from ½″ thick styrofoam for steps for doll to stand on. Ice and stack, then edge with tube 1 beading. Ice arch with thinned icing and edge with tube 1 orange beads. Attach arch to rear of steps with long pins. Cover

all sides of arch with tube 13 swirls.

DECORATE DOLL CAKE. Use small Wonder Mold pan and mini doll pick. Mark off curving line at lower edge of bodice, cover bodice area with thinned icing and sprinkle with edible glitter. Cover skirt area with thinned icing and mark four scallops near hem. Fill with tube 59° ruffles. Pipe puff sleeves with same tube. Now add tube 1 beading, dots and bows as pictured. Tie doll's hands together, pipe a mound of icing in them and push in a "bouquet" of sampaquitas and damas de noche.

PREPARE SEPARATOR PLATES that elevate top tier. Only two pillars are used, with the number "18" substituting for the other two. With a pliers, break off two of the projections that hold the pillars on a 7″ square separator plate. Do the same with a second plate. Now assemble the two plates with two 7½″ Corinthian pillars and the styrofoam numerals. Glue numerals to plates with royal icing. Dry thoroughly.

BAKE, FILL AND ICE with boiled icing two 6″ x 3″ and one 12″ x 4″ square tiers. Assemble on cake board with 7″ square plates and 7½″ Corinthian pillars. Use prepared plates below top tier.

ON 12″ TIER, lightly mark four scallops near the top of each side. Fill area between base of tier and scallop marks with "sotas" or cornelli-like lace work. With tube 1, pipe curls, V's and C's of icing very close together until area is completely covered. Edge base of tier with tube 22 shells. Pipe ribbed zigzag garlands on scallop marks with tube 98. Top garlands with tube 1 ovals. Above garlands pipe graduated tube 1 dots with dots extending on top of tier to separator plate. Accent ovals at points of scallops with a tube 4 orange dot. Edge separator plate with tube 13 zigzag and frame with tube 1 orange dots.

AT BASE OF CENTER TIER, pipe tube 13 swirls, resembling rosebuds. Accent with orange tube 1 dots. Mark scrolled "V" design on sides of tier and pipe with tube 1. Pipe a tube 13 "rosebud" border at base of top tier, adding tube 1 orange dots. Pipe a scalloped border on top of tier similar to one on base tier, but use tube 13 for scalloped garland. Print name on front of tier with a toothpick, then pipe with tube 2 beading.

FINISH DECORATION by securing steps and arch to top tier with icing. Attach sprays to either side of arch, and center arch with bouquet. Arrange bouquets on all tiers. Finally set doll on steps. Cut into 108 wedding-size slices or 60 party servings.

SAMPAQUITA SPRAYS

68

DRAMATIC HOLIDAY CAKES FROM THE PHILIPPINES

Christmas and New Year's Day are major holidays in the Philippines, and gaily decorated cakes are part of the festivities. Often, a colorful cake is given to an employer, teacher or dear friend at Christmas. In the Philippines, it's not Christmas without the scarlet poinsettia! New Year's Day is a family day, climaxed by a lavish dinner and a beautifully trimmed cake.

MERRY CHRISTMAS

PIPE POINSETTIA PETALS. Insert a 5″ length of 28-gauge wire into a decorating cone filled with red royal icing and fitted with tube 69. Using a light, gentle pressure, pull out the wire. Taper petal at base by running your finger down edge to remove excess icing. Bend wire and hang on rack upside down to dry. You will need three poinsettias, each with 14 to 18 petals of varying lengths to decorate cake. When thoroughly dry, twist wires together to form a flower, placing shorter petals in center. Pipe tube 2 stamens. Tape three blossoms together with looped ribbon.

BAKE A TWO-LAYER, 10″ round cake. Fill and ice with boiled icing. Place on ruffle-edged cake board. Criss-cross cake with tube 104 ribbons, starting at top center and continuing down sides to base. Edge base with tube 2 "e" motion border.

Pipe "Merry Christmas" with tube 2, outlining wider parts of letters and filling in with same tube. Add green flourishes with tube 2. Finish border with tube 2 holly leaves and add red dots with same tube. Position poinsettias on cake top and serve to 14.

HAPPY NEW YEAR

DECORATE THE LARGE BELLS on top of cake. Ice two 3¼″ plastic bell molds with thinned royal icing. Mark eight scallops at base of each bell. With tube 1, pipe diagonal lines across bell, from point of one scallop to point of scallop on opposite side. When bell is completely covered, pipe diagonal lines in opposite directions for a lattice effect. Edge scallops with tube 2 beading. Pipe tube 2 scrolls and leaves on side of bells and add tiny poinsettias with tube 55. Center flowers with tube 1 dots. Dry thoroughly, then brush exposed scallops at base of bell with water and sprinkle with edible glitter.

Decorate 2″ plastic bell molds for corners of cake. Cover with thinned royal icing, then pipe diagonal lines with tube 1. Trim with dots and scallops piped with same tube. Dry thoroughly.

PIPE TINY POINSETTIAS on wire in a method similar to that used for Dama de Noche, page 65. Pull out six tube 55 petals, dry upside down, then add tube 1 yellow dots. You'll need about 24 flowers.

Tape 12 flowers and ribbon loops together into a bouquet (see page 66). Pass fine wires through holes in top of two large bells and tape to bouquet stem. Make sure finished stem extends 3″ below bells to insert into cake.

Make smaller clusters with two small bells, ribbon loops and a few poinsettias for corners of cake.

DECORATE THE CAKE. Bake a 9″ x 13″ x 3″ cake, ice with boiled icing and set on cake board. Sketch "Happy New Year" on wax paper and transfer to top of cake. Pipe capital letters with tube 6 and trim with tube 1. Pipe lower case letters with tube 2 and trim with same tube.

Now pipe scrolls and holly leaves on corners and front edge of cake with tube 2. Pull out points on leaves with damp brush. Clip stems of three wired poinsettias and place on front edge of cake.

PIPE A BASE BORDER on cake board with tube 2A. Stripe with tube 101, alternating red and green. Push stems of bell bouquets into cake. Serves 24.

LOVE'S STAIRWAY

This spectacular, soaring wedding cake displays all the dramatic flair that is characteristic of Philippine decorating.

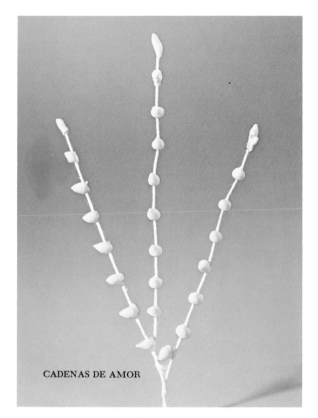

CADENAS DE AMOR

LOVE'S STAIRWAY

PIPE ROYAL ICING FLOWERS. You will need daisies in variety (page 63), calla lilies (page 64), tube 67 leaves (page 66) and sprays of cadenas de amor. Pipe the sprays with tube 2 on 10″ lengths of 28-gauge wire. Starting at tip of wire, touch tube, squeeze lightly, pull away. As you move down, keep the tube almost perpendicular to the wire.

Form the flowers, with ribbons, into bouquets as pictured. Make four bouquets for corners of base tier, plus tiny clusters for within pillars and at base of stairway. Make three bouquets for center tier and a large one for top tier. Page 66 shows how to group flowers.

MAKE STAGE, INITIALS AND STAIRS. The little stage on top tier is formed of 5″ and 4″ circles of styrofoam, ½″ thick. Ice with royal icing and cover with "sotas" (see page 68) piped with tube 1.

Cut the initials of the couple's last names from light cardboard, using your own pattern. Glue a 10″ 22-gauge wire to back of each, leaving most of wire exposed to push through stage and cake tier. Paint with tempera paint, sprinkle with glitter.

Transfer Wilton Way stair patterns to light cardboard. Cut out with X-acto knife. Trim railings and side pieces with royal icing and tube 1. Dry, then assemble with airplane glue.

PREPARE SEPARATOR PLATE for center tier. Glue two 11″ squares of corrugated cardboard together. Paint with thinned royal icing and dry. Measure 1½″ in from edges and glue on plastic stud plates.

BAKE AND ICE THE TIERS. Use a firm pound cake recipe and bake three tiers, 6″ x 3″ round, 10″ x 4″ square and 16″ x 4″ square. Fill and ice with boiled icing. Decorate tiers separately, then assemble.

SET 6″ ROUND TIER on 8″ separator plate from Crystal Clear pillar set. Divide tier into eighths, cut arch pattern and mark on side with toothpick. Outline scalloped edge of arches with tube 1 in "e" motion. Add inner arch shape with tube 1 beading. Use same tube to pipe small center arch shape. Pipe tube 16 shell borders at base and top of tier. Pipe tube 3 dots on plate, outside of base border.

SET CENTER TIER on prepared plate. Divide each side of tier into fourths and mark triangles at base with toothpick. Outline triangles with tube 1 scallops and trim with tube 1 dots and shells. Pipe tube 16 zigzag base border. Edge corners of tier with tube 16 shells. Just below top edge of tier, pipe tube 1 "e" motion scallops and finish with dots. Pipe tube 16 top border. (Note: cardboard separator plate will be edged after assembly.)

SET BASE TIER on 20″ foil-covered cake board. Divide each side into thirds and cut scalloped pattern for top and side. Mark on tier with toothpick. Use tube 1 to edge scallop with "e" motion, then fill area with tube 1 "sotas" (see page 68). Add dots and shells with tube 3. Pipe shell border at base with tube 22 and add tube 16 shells on board.

ASSEMBLE CAKE according to diagram. Mark position of Crystal Clear pillars on base tier by pressing center tier on surface. Insert pillars in base tier, edge each with tube 3. Mound royal icing on top of each pillar and set center tier in position. Cover edge of separator plate with tube 13 shells. Position pillars in center tier by the same method, pressing top tier lightly into surface.

Now add the stairways, attaching at top and bottom with mounds of royal icing.

Set stage on top tier, insert spray of flowers and initials. Steady initials by wiring "stem" to flower stems. Attach petite bridal couple

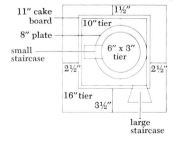

to stage with royal icing. Complete cake by inserting bouquets as pictured. A decorating triumph that serves 194.

A SUNNY DAY IN THE PHILIPPINES

This astonishing example of the Philippine decorator's ingenuity and artistry sums up the complete Philippine Method. Study the pictures well before starting to decorate this showpiece.

PIPE A BANANA TREE

MAKE LEAVES. Fill decorating cone, fitted with tube 112, with green icing. Insert a 5″ 28-gauge wire and pull out while squeezing gently. Taper ends with fingers and hang on rack to dry. You'll need eight or nine 2½″ long leaves for each tree.

MAKE TRUNK. Push an 8″ length of 20-gauge wire into a block of styrofoam covered with wax paper. Wrap wire with floral tape, leaving about 1″ at top uncovered. Curve wire slightly, then pipe many tube 2 lines on part of wire covered with tape, making lines heavier toward base. Brush to smooth. With brown food color paint streaks on trunk. Dry thoroughly. Paint streaks on leaf edges also.

ASSEMBLE TREE by twisting leaf wires to exposed wire on top of trunk. Clip off excess wire. Arrange leaves in natural positions and pipe a bunch of bananas on tree with tube 2.

MAKE THE DOLL IN NATIVE DRESS

The doll starts with a wire armature, much like that a sculptor would use, and uses royal icing and figure piping techniques to finish the figure.

MAKE ARMATURE. Use a 12″ length of 22-gauge florists' wire. On one end pipe head with tube 8, much like the pistil used for flower making. 4″ below chin line, bend wire outward and form circle for base. Attach 4″ lengths of 28-gauge wire to form cone shape for skirt, in five sections, 3″ up from base. Twist a 4″ length of 22-gauge wire for shoulders and arms, one hand up. Wind it just below chin.

PIPE UPPER BODY FIRST. Use tube 4 to build up head. Cover it with lines, tapered toward neck. Pipe a horizontal line for forehead and short vertical lines for nose, chin and cheeks. Dip a small brush in water and stroke face to smooth. Build up upper body and arms the same way, piping a little more icing for bust. Smooth with wet brush.

When head and upper body are formed, pipe fingers with tube 1, then hair with same tube. Brush to smooth. Dry thoroughly, then paint features with food color and small brush.

COVER FRAMEWORK of skirt area with tube 4. Stand figure on wax paper. Cover wires, then pipe strokes connecting wires. Dry. Using tube 4, fill in skirt heavily with white icing and brush to smooth. Brush food color from base of skirt up. Dry.

Pipe tunic with tube 2 and white icing. Build up sleeves in an arch over shoulders. Brush all to smooth and dry. Pipe scalloped hem on tunic with tube 1. Paint trim with food color.

Make broad-brimmed hat. Using a 14″ length of 22-gauge wire, form a circle about 3″ in diameter for edge of brim. Twist to secure, then bring rest of wire into center of circle and form a second smaller circle for head band. Twist wire to secure. Use fine 28-gauge wire to wind back and forth between circles in spoked "spiderweb" formation. Fold a 4″ length of 28-gauge wire in half, and twist each end around inner circle to start crown of hat. Repeat to form peaked crown, with four "spokes". Make a little hook of wire at edge of brim to use to hang from rack for drying.

With tube 2 and brown icing, pipe many lines over brim and crown of hat. Hang by hook on rack to dry. Turn hat over and pipe more tube 2 lines on underside of brim. Conceal hook with icing and dry. Secure hat to head of doll with icing.

PIPE BAMBOO AND MAKE BRIDGE

Insert an 8″ length of 22-gauge wire into decorating cone fitted with tube 9. Pull out wire about 1″ while squeezing, hesitate but continue to squeeze. The pause creates the ridge in the bamboo. When you have four or five ridges, remove wire from cone, stand in styrofoam block and cut off excess wire at tip. Hollow out tip with brush. Dry.

Make bridge by laying two bamboo lengths on wax paper, parallel and about 3½″ apart. Attach bamboo lengths across this base with royal icing.

PUT THE CAKE TOGETHER

Make bouquets of daisies, sampaquitas, rosebuds, and sampaquita sprays (pages 63-65 and 68).

Bake cake. Use a pound cake batter to bake a 9″ x 13″ x 3″ cake. Chill, then carve out a long curve from back of cake to front corner for brook. Ice cake smoothly on sides, roughly on top with green boiled icing. Ice brook area with blue icing. When dry, make brown path with many lines of tube 2, then brush slightly to smooth.

Build fence by inserting bamboo sections along path. Join sections with tube 4 string, *starting at bottom*, then attaching near top of each section.

Add the finishing touches. Pipe a bamboo border on board at base of cake with tube 12. Use technique similar to that used for bamboo sections. Squeeze, hesitate while continuing to squeeze, exerting light pressure. Hollow out ends of bamboo at corners with damp brush.

Streak top of cake by brushing with brown-tinted water. Pipe grass by pulling out with tube 2. Push in banana trees and bouquets and set bridge in position. Set doll on path. Serves 24.

CHAPTER FIVE
The English Method of Decorating

Decorating in England is a highly developed art, perfected through centuries by the work of skilled chefs and bakers. Until rather recently, cake decorating in Great Britain was practiced only by these professionals, but now there is a lively interest in decorating as a hobby, and housewives by the thousands are perfecting their skill.

The English Method has enormously influenced the Wilton-American style. Swinging curves of borders, piped flowers, and insistence on perfection of execution are a few of the characteristics the two methods have in common. Our Color Flow technique was inspired by the English run-in work. And of course, the Australian and South African methods are direct descendents of the English.

The English Method is divided into four distinct styles, each of which slightly overlaps the others. The *Nirvana Style* is distinguished by cakes covered completely, or almost completely by "run-in" work with a fine porcelain finish. The result is highly architectural. The *Over-piped Style* produces impressive cakes characterized by accurate piping and over-piping in graceful curves and scrolls. It is sometimes known as the Lambeth Style after Joseph Lambeth, its best-known practitioner. In addition, English decorators produce many pastries, tortes and gateaux decorated in the *Continental Style*, explained in Chapter Nine. They also produce colorful *Novelty Cakes*, trimmed with flowers and artificial "favors". These cakes are similar to American novelty cakes.

THE NIRVANA STYLE

Cakes in this unmistakable style are so decorated that they resemble imposing miniature buildings or monuments. The architectural effect is achieved by covering a round cake almost completely with pieces of run-in work, outlined, flowed in and carefully dried to a smooth porcelain finish. Patterns and measurements must be exact. Assembly of these pieces is done in a predetermined order to insure final perfection. The run-in pieces are trimmed with fine line and bead work done with a writing tube, and sometimes with daintily piped flowers. Cakes are white, or in very pale tints with stronger colors reserved for accents.

With all of this regimentation, there is still plenty of room for originality in the Nirvana Style. Subtle variations in the curves and shapes of the base collars and top splays and carefully placed openings in the run-in pieces to accentuate the design make each cake a unique work of art. The side panels offer the most opportunity for the creative decorator. Opened by "windows", one looks into garden scenes or groups of flowers. Often, within the opening of the top splay, a beautifully lettered name in run-in work is placed to celebrate a birthday.

Both Nirvana and Over-piped cakes start with a rich, heavy fruitcake covered with marzipan, then iced with two thin smooth coats of royal icing.

MARZIPAN RECIPE
2 cups almond paste (two 8 ounce cans)
4 egg whites, unbeaten
6 cups confectioners' sugar
1 teaspoon vanilla or rum flavor

Knead almond paste by hand in a bowl. Add egg whites and mix well. Knead in sugar, one cup at a time, and flavoring until marzipan has the consistency of heavy pie dough. If stored properly, marzipan dough will keep for months. To store, cover with plastic wrap and place in a tightly sealed container in the refrigerator. After storing, let stand at room temperature until soft enough to work. If still stiff, soften with a drop or two of corn syrup.

COLOR FLOW ICING RECIPE
English decorators use egg white royal icing for their run-in work, thinning as necessary with lemon juice. Since Color Flow is equally strong and dries much faster we used it for the Nirvana cake at right. To soften the icing for flowing in, see page 79.

15 ounces water
6 pounds confectioners' sugar
¾ cup Color Flow mix

Combine three-fourths of the sugar, the Color Flow mix and the water. Mix at slow speed, adding remainder of the sugar, then mix for five more minutes. Use at once for outlining run-in pieces.

THE NIRVANA STYLE of decorating is perfectly illustrated in the cake at right. Mother Goose rides across the top splay and favorite characters are seen within the arches of the side panels. The pages following explain step-by-step how to construct it.

STEP ONE. Start with a fruitcake (recipe Chapter Twenty). Make a recipe of marzipan following the instructions on page 76. Attach a cardboard cake circle the same size as the cake onto the top of the cake with royal icing. Pack the empty space between the cardboard and the cake with pieces of marzipan so the cardboard is level and the side of the cake is perfectly straight. This is now the bottom of the cake. Now fill any fruit holes or cracks in the cake with marzipan, using a small spatula to level surface. Dust work surface and rolling pin with confectioners' sugar and roll out a ball of marzipan into a circle ⅜″ thick and slightly larger than the cake diameter. Brush the top of the cake with warm apricot glaze (heat one cup apricot jam to boiling and strain). Place cake upside-down on marzipan.

STEP TWO. Cut around cake with a sharp knife to remove excess marzipan.

STEP THREE. Lift cake and turn upright. Brush cake sides with warm apricot glaze.

STEP FOUR. Shape remaining marzipan into a long narrow roll and flatten with a rolling pin. Using a ruler as a guide, trim one long side so it is straight. Place cake on its side on strip. Set bottom edge of cake along straight edge of strip and roll, patting marzipan into place. Trim seam so the edges butt.

STEP FIVE. Turn cake upright and carefully trim off excess marzipan around top.

STEP SIX. Press side seam together with fingers and smooth. Pat the cake all over to smooth out any irregularities in the covering. Let harden 48 hours before icing with two very thin smooth coats of royal icing (recipe in Chapter Twenty). Drying time is needed so almond oil will not discolor icing.

In doing run-in work, the icing is a very important factor. Use Color Flow recipe on page 76 and make 1½ recipes to do run-in work for nursery rhyme cake. Use icing right from batch for outlining pieces, then thin icing for running-in. To thin, put a portion of icing into a container and add a few drops of water at a time, stirring by hand. Never beat icing! To test for proper consistency, spoon out a teaspoon of icing and let it drop back into container. When it takes a full count of ten for spoonful to disappear completely into mixture, icing will run-in and set up perfectly. After thinning, let icing sit, covered, 24 hours to allow air bubbles to surface.

Use same technique as for Color Flow work and patterns from The Wilton Way Pattern Book. Outline side panels, splays and collars with tube 2 and unthinned icing. Outline risers with tube 1. Outline Mother Goose and goose with tube 1s. Let dry. Then start run-in work with thinned icing and cone with cut tip. Have two half-filled cones ready when running-in collars and splays.

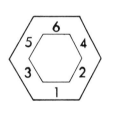

The order of running-in is important. Color Flow icing crusts quickly and crust lines will show on finished design. For collars and splays, work quickly and follow order on diagram. Keep run-in work thin and flat.

When you have completed running-in pieces, dry under a heat lamp placed two feet above them, until

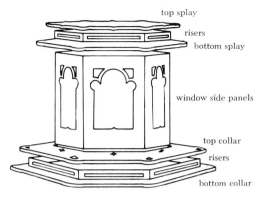

top splay
risers
bottom splay

window side panels

top collar
risers
bottom collar

a crust forms. This gives a glossy finish to pieces. Then complete drying process for at least 72 hours.

When pieces are completely dry, edge collars, windows and splays with tube 1 beading. Pipe cross-stitch design on risers with tube 1. Pipe tube 2 dots and teardrops on top splay. Trim Mother Goose and her goose with tube 1.

PREPARE AND ICE CAKE. Bake 7″ round fruitcake layers, each about 2¼″ high. Stack, spreading buttercream or apricot glaze between them, until they reach a height of about 6¾″. Then prepare cake as described on page 78 and ice with two thin coats of royal icing, drying after each coat. Make very sure that finished height of prepared cake is *exactly* 7⅛″. It must be this height so bottom splay does not rest on side panels. Any weight on them will cause them to break.

OUTLINE FIGURES. Tape patterns to 10″ curved surface, tape wax paper over, then outline with tube 1s. Dry. Run-in thinned icing, then dry. Trim figures with tube 1. Outline sun with tube 1 and run-in icing heavily to create rounded effect. Sun is dried flat. With green icing and a clean sponge, pat icing around bottom of cake for grassy effect.

PREPARE CAKE BOARD. Cover an 18″ round masonite board with gold foil, or tape four 18″ circles of corrugated cardboard together and cover with foil. Attach cake with icing in center, and pipe tube 4 beading around bottom. Using bottom collar pattern as guide, pipe riser lines on board with tube 3. Dry thoroughly.

ASSEMBLE THE CAKE
WITH ROYAL ICING

Start with bottom collar. Pipe dots of royal icing between riser lines on cake board to anchor bottom collar. Very carefully, slip bottom collar over cake, being certain to center it around the cake. Press down gently all around collar to secure to icing. Pipe a tube 2 line of icing, 1″ from inner edge of collar and set one riser against it. Add a line of icing to one side edge of this riser to attach to next riser. Continue piping lines of icing and setting in risers all around cake. Let dry for at least one hour before adding top collar.

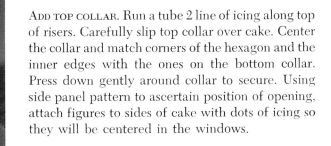

Add top collar. Run a tube 2 line of icing along top of risers. Carefully slip top collar over cake. Center the collar and match corners of the hexagon and the inner edges with the ones on the bottom collar. Press down gently around collar to secure. Using side panel pattern to ascertain position of opening, attach figures to sides of cake with dots of icing so they will be centered in the windows.

Add side panels. Set a side panel between the cake and collars. Run a tube 2 line of icing along one side edge, and place another panel in position. Hold to let icing set for a few minutes and then continue on around the cake, adding one panel at a time. Pipe a line of tube 2 beading along the seam lines between the panels.

THEN ADD BOTTOM SPLAY. Pipe six tube 2 dots of icing on the top of the cake. Set bottom splay in position, matching corners with the bottom collars. Run a tube 2 line of icing along one side of the hexagon shape that marks the division between the blue and yellow areas of the splay. Place riser in position against icing line. Add a line of icing to one side edge of riser to attach to next riser. Continue around the cake. When all the risers are in place, allow to harden for at least one hour before adding the top splay.

FINALLY COMPLETE CAKE by adding the sun and the top splay. The top of the finished cake will have three levels—that of the bottom splay, slightly higher, the sun, and finally the top splay. This gives a characteristic three-dimensional effect. First, using top splay pattern for a guide, attach sun in position on bottom splay with tube 2 dots of icing. Then run a line of icing along top edges of risers. Center top splay, matching corners with bottom splay. Secure to risers by pressing very lightly all around splay.

Your beautiful English Method Nirvana cake is ready to display with pride! Since the fruitcake is so completely covered, it will remain fresh for weeks. To serve the cake, break the run-in work by tapping with a silver knife or a tiny silver hammer, as is done in England, then slice. Cut each layer into 16 wedges. Serves 48 guests.

PANEL ONE

PANEL TWO

PANEL THREE

PANEL FOUR

PANEL FIVE

PANEL SIX

A MASTERPIECE FOR CHILDREN

Mother Goose rhymes have been favorites of children both young and old since the 18th century. Although the identity of Mother Goose remains a mystery, her English origin is clearly discernable through her verses and thus becomes an appropriate subject for this breathtaking Nirvana-style cake.

PANEL ONE

To market, to market, To buy a fat hog;
Home again, home again, Jiggety jog.

PANEL TWO

Bobby Shafto's gone to sea,
Silver buckles on his knee;
He'll come back and marry me,
Bonnie Bobby Shafto!

PANEL THREE

Ride a cock-horse to Banbury Cross,
To see a fine lady upon a white horse;
With rings on her fingers and bells on her toes,
She shall have music wherever she goes.

PANEL FOUR

Jack, be nimble,
And, Jack, be quick;
And, Jack, jump over
The candlestick.

PANEL FIVE

Christmas is coming, the geese are getting fat,
Please to put a penny in an old man's hat;
If you have n't got a penny, a ha' penny will do,
If you have n't got a ha' penny, God bless you.

PANEL SIX

Hot cross Buns!
Old woman runs!
One a penny, two a penny,
Hot cross Buns!

TOP SPLAY

A stunning example of an English Over-piped cake.
Turn the page to learn how to reproduce it.

THE ENGLISH OVER-PIPED STYLE

THIS STYLE IS A JOY and a challenge to the adventurous decorator. It is distinguished by curving scrolls and borders over-piped with complete accuracy and finished with precise and dainty linework. Proportions of the cakes are much different than American eyes are accustomed to and bevels are frequently used. The result is marvelously sculptural with the graceful repeated curves giving a strong rhythmic effect.

English Over-piped cakes are done in white or pale colors, the light and shade of the sculptured piping giving sufficient contrast. They are often trimmed with skillfully piped flowers in bright hues, but these are subordinate to the border designs.

Just as in the Nirvana style, fruitcakes are used, covered with rolled marzipan (page 78), then iced with two thin coats of royal icing. Royal icing is

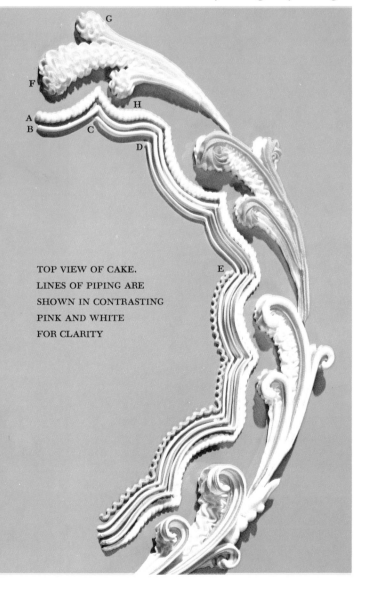

TOP VIEW OF CAKE.
LINES OF PIPING ARE
SHOWN IN CONTRASTING
PINK AND WHITE
FOR CLARITY

used for all trim. (Recipe, **Chapter Twenty**)

AN ENGLISH OVER-PIPED WEDDING CAKE

This is a stately and traditional cake, 10″ round, 5″ high, set on a 14″ base bevel for a final height of 6″. Bake it of fruitcake (recipe Chapter Twenty), filling the 2½″ high layers with buttercream or apricot glaze. Cover with marzipan, explained on page 78, and ice with royal icing. If you want a cake for show use only, build it of styrofoam. Set the cake on a sturdy, foil-covered 18″ cake board.

All patterns are in The Wilton Way Pattern Book.

PIPE THE TOP TRIM

First pipe the violets as shown on page 14. Make the little tassels on wax paper with repeated strokes of tube 1, following pattern. The top trim consists of an inside scalloped border surrounded by scrolls.

DO INSIDE SCALLOPED BORDER. *A very important point to remember:* when over-piping, complete only two lines of piping before allowing work to dry. If more than two lines are piped before drying, the work may shift or collapse from weight. While work is drying, do piping on other areas of cake. Mark the patterns for top designs lightly on the cake. Starting from the outside edge, pipe a tight zigzag line, A, tapering as it nears points of scallops. Now drop tube 2 line, B, within this zigzag. Over-pipe it with a second tube 2 line, and then with tube 1. Pipe line C with tube 2, over-pipe with tube 1. Pipe line D with tube 1. Finish with tiny scallops, E, piped with tube 1s. Add tube 1 dots at points of all scallops.

PIPE SCROLL DESIGNS outside of scalloped border. Pipe first layer of scrolls F, G and H with tube 16 in zigzag shape, wide at ends and tapering to a fine point. Let crust while you go on to work on other areas of cake. Now over-pipe scrolls with tube 15, then tube 5 and allow to dry. On scroll F, over-pipe with a tube 3 line, then a second tube 3 line. Over-pipe scrolls G and H with a tube 3 line, then a tube 1 line. Finish scroll F with a tube 1 line. Add a leaf, piped with a cut bag, at the point where F and G join. Pipe graduated dots with tube 2.

PIPE TOP SIDE BORDER

First divide the top edge of cake into sixteenths. The base structure of this border is built of two zigzag garlands and a ruffle garland, topped with over-piped scallops.

PIPE BASIC STRUCTURE. Within each division, drop a shallow curved guideline with tube 3. Fill in with tube 14 zigzag, increasing pressure at center and tapering off to points at divisions. Below first garland, pipe a tube 102 ruffle in garland shape. Smooth top of ruffle with spatula. Just above ruffle, pipe another tapered garland on side of cake.

Do OVER-PIPED SCALLOPS. To frame first zigzag garland, drop a tube 3 string. Over-pipe with tube 3, then with tube 2 and tube 1.

Just above ruffle garland, drop a tube 3 string and over-pipe with tube 2, then tube 1.

Just below ruffle, drop a tube 3 string, and over-pipe with tube 2, then tube 1.

Below this scallop drop a tube 2 string and over-pipe with tube 1. Add one more scallop with tube 1. Finish with tube 1s dots. Top point of each scallop with tube 1 dot.

PIPE BASE CAKE BORDER

Use same cake division as for top border. Border is made up of four parallel over-piped scallops.

STARTING WITH BOTTOM SCALLOP, mark points on cake division ¾" up from join of bevel and cake. Drop tube 3 scallops from these points. Then over-pipe six times with tubes 3, 3, 2, 2, 1 and 1. *Be sure to allow work to dry after piping twice.*

Just above this scallop drop a tube 3 string. Over-pipe four times with tubes 3, 2, 2 and 1.

Drop third scallop from bottom with tube 2, and over-pipe with tube 2, then with tubes 2, 1 and 1. Fourth scallop is piped with tube 1. Add tiny scallops above with tube 1s, and finish points of all scallops with tube 1s dots.

DECORATE THE BEVEL

Lightly mark scroll pattern on bevel using same division as base cake border above. Following the diagram, pipe and over-pipe the scrolls, making sure the icing dries after each two pipings. Use similar technique as for scrolls on top of cake, starting zigzags wide, and tapering to a point where they meet.

PIPE EACH SECTION with a tube 16 zigzag. Now proceed with over-piping in this order: *Sections 1 and 3*, tubes 5, 3, 3, 2 and 1. *Section 2*, tubes 5, 3, 2 and 1. *Section 4*, tubes 3, 3, 1 and 1. Pipe a leaf with cut bag at point where sections 3 and 4 join. Add graduated dots piped with tube 2. Now edge bevel with tube 18 shells.

ADD THE FINISHING TOUCHES

Attach flowers to top and bevel scrolls with icing. Trim with leaves piped with cut cone. Secure tassels to upper side of cake. Serves 112 guests.

SIDE AND BEVEL OF CAKE

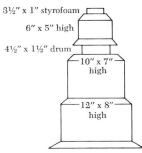

3½″ x 1″ styrofoam
6″ x 5″ high
4½″ x 1½″ drum
10″ x 7″ high
12″ x 8″ high

This magnificent cake is a beautiful statement of the Over-piped style. Lavishly trimmed with cushion lattice, built up borders and flowers, its perfect proportion gives it an appearance of dignity.

Bake the cake from a fruitcake recipe (Chapter Twenty) in the sizes shown in the diagram. Use as many layers as necessary, sandwiching them together with filling, to achieve the proper heights for the tiers. Bake layers for the tops of the 10″ and 12″ tiers in bevel top pans. Trim the top of the 6″ tier to bevel shape, measuring 1″ in on the top of the tier and 1″ down from top edge on side. Base bevels are added later. Cover the tiers with rolled marzipan as explained on page 78. You will need two recipes of marzipan to cover. Dry 48 hours, then ice with two thin coats of royal icing.

Set the 12″ tier on a 16″ cake circle. Measure 1″ up from bottom of tier and mark the side. Now heap royal icing on the cake board and form a smooth bevel with a spatula from edge of cake

board to marked side of tier. Set the 6″ tier on an 8″ circle, mark side at 1″ from base of tier and create bevel in the same way. Dry thoroughly. Assemble the two lower tiers on an 18″ cake board. All patterns are in The Wilton Way Pattern Book.

MAKE TRIMS IN ADVANCE

Prepare for decorating by making these trims ahead of time. Royal icing is used for all.

PIPE APPLE BLOSSOMS with tube 101s and add tube 1 centers. You will need about 2400.

MAKE EIGHT FLOWERED HEARTS. Tape pattern to small curved surface, then tape wax paper over. Pipe the heart shape with tube 5. When dry, attach flowers with dots of icing. Trim with leaves piped with a cut cone.

PIPE EIGHT SMALL PINK HEARTS for bottom tier. Tape pattern on board, tape wax paper over and outline with tube 1. Flow in with thinned icing, building up for rounded shape.

MAKE THE DRUM below top tier from a 1½″ thick circle of styrofoam 4½″ in diameter. Ice the top and bottom with royal icing and cover the side with a strip of rolled gum paste, attaching with egg white (recipe, Chapter Ten). Cover the drum with vertical lines piped with tube 3. Add beading at top and bottom with tube 4. When dry, attach flowers in eight garlands. Pipe leaves with cut cone.

MAKE THE CROWN on top of cake from gum paste (recipe in Chapter Ten) using pattern. Roll out ⅛″ thick and cut eight side pieces and octagon base. Dry the side pieces on a 6″ curved surface, base flat. Cut a 3½″ circle from 1″ thick styrofoam and ice. When all pieces are dry, assemble crown with royal icing. Attach octagon base to styrofoam. Using tube 3, pipe a line of icing on the side of base. Set a curved section on it, pipe icing on one side and on base and add a second section. Continue until all eight sections are attached, propping to hold. Dry eight hours.

Fill in all cracks with royal icing, dry, and lightly sand crown until smooth. On the inside of crown, pipe a tube 2 line over each seam and around oval openings. Add a tube 1 line around ovals. On outside of crown, pipe a tube 3 line over each seam and on top edge. Over-pipe a second tube 3 line on top edge. Finish with tube 1 outlines and dots.

PIPE 48 TASSELS with tube 1. Tape pattern to stiff board, tape wax paper over and pipe with tube 1. Build up tiny knot at top and make fringe with repeated strokes. Add three lines for binding.

MAKE EIGHT OVAL FRAMES for base tier. Tape pattern to 12″ curved surface and tape wax paper over. Outline shape with tube 2. Over-pipe with tube 1, adding a little curl above curve near base. Pipe beading within outline.

On outside of frame, pipe tube 4 oval shape. Dry thoroughly.

PIPE BLUEBIRDS, eight facing right and eight left. Tape patterns to stiff board and tape wax paper over. First do wings. Pipe tube 1 lines from inside to tip, then brush together. Dry.

Pipe tail of bird with lines of tube 1, starting at body and working to tip. Brush to smooth. Figure pipe breast with tube 2, joining smoothly to tail. Pipe a ball for head and continue to form back. Slip rear wing under back and insert front wing into body. Pipe beak with tube 1 and make hole for eye. When bird is thoroughly dry, brush breast with thinned red icing.

DECORATE THE CAKE

This is a challenge to your decorating skill and steadiness of hand, but taken in careful steps will produce a work of art. We show the decorating tier by tier, but you will find it necessary to move from one tier to another as you work, without finishing any tier completely at one time. The over-piped borders and cushion lattice consist of many layers of piping, and *no more than two layers can be piped before the piece is set aside to dry*. If more than two layers are piped at once, the trim may collapse. So proceed from one area to another, allowing time to dry after over-piping only once.

DECORATE TOP TIER

PIPE LATTICE CUSHION RING on top bevel of top tier. This consists of seven layers of crisscrossed lines, piped over a base circle. Each complete crisscross (two lines, piped in opposite directions) is a set.

In center of bevel, pipe a zigzag ring with tube 199 about 1″ wide. Dry about four hours. Now pipe diagonal lines over ring, very close together, with tube 5. Let dry about one hour, then pipe tube 5 lines in the opposite direction to form the first set. Dry about two hours.

Continue to pipe sets of crisscross lines to form cushion. Pipe two more sets with tube 5, then two sets with tube 3 and finally two sets of tube 2, allowing time to dry after piping each set.

As you pipe each diagonal line, *make sure it is directly over the line in the same direction below*. As the lattice builds, it will become more airy, with the lines farther apart, giving a beautiful effect of light and shadow.

PIPE TRIPLE LINES below cushion ring. Pipe a tube 5 line directly below the cushion. Over-pipe with another. Just below this built-up line pipe another tube 5 line. Just below that pipe a tube 3 line.

TRIM LOWER SIDE OF TOP TIER. This consists of four rows of built-up scallops topped by a tiny scallop trim. Divide cake into sixteenths. Starting where bevel joins cake, pipe a tube 2 scallop in each division. Over-pipe with same tube. About ⅛″ above this scallop, pipe a second scallop with tube 2. When these have dried, over-pipe the first scallop twice with tube 1, and the second scallop twice with tube 1. Pipe a third scallop above these two with tube 1 and over-pipe with same tube. Then pipe the fourth scallop with tube 1.

Finish the border with tiny tube 1s scallop edging and add a tube 1 ball at joints of all scallops.

PIPE BASE BEVEL TRIM. First do scallops at edge of bevel. Directly below scallops on side of cake, pipe shallow scallops with tube 2 and over-pipe with same tube. Above these scallops, pipe a second row with tube 2. Edge with tube 2 balls.

Pipe an elaborated "C" scroll on bevel, below each scallop above, with tube 362. Over-pipe first with tube 6, second with tube 4, then with tube 3, and finally with tube 2 for built-up effect, allowing time to dry after first two over-pipings.

DO SIDE FLOWER BORDER. In center of side of tier, pipe a wavy line for vine with tube 3. There will be an "up curve" and a "down curve" above each scallop below. Pipe projecting short stems in each curve. Attach flowers within each curve with dots of icing and add leaves made with cut cone.

DECORATE MIDDLE TIER

Divide tier into sixteenths and then proceed with the over-piped borders.

DECORATE TOP BEVEL. With tube 2, pipe scallops at very top edge of bevel. Below these pipe another tube 2 scallop, and over-pipe once with same tube. Below second scallop pipe another tube 2 scallop and finish with tiny scallop trim with tube 1.

Now pipe borders at lower edge of top bevel. This consists of five parallel scallops, with varying over-piping. Use border piped on top edge of bevel as your guide in placing scallops.

On edge of bevel pipe a row of scallops with tube 1. Second row of scallops, just below is piped with tube 2 and over-piped once. Third and center row of scallops is piped with tube 2 and over-piped four times. Fourth row is piped with tube 2, over-piped twice. Fifth and lowest row is piped with tube 2 and over-piped once. Finish with tiny scallops

piped with tube 1. Pipe a tube 1 ball at point of each scallop.

On side of cake, just below bevel, pipe tube 1 balls, following line of scallops above.

DECORATE LOWER SIDE of tier. Mark curved shapes at base of tier. Each shape occupies the space of two scallops piped on bevel above. Starting at bottom, pipe and over-pipe the borders. First pipe tube 2 curves and over-pipe three times. Just above, pipe tube 2 curves and over-pipe once. Pipe a final tube 2 curve above this. Add scallops with tube 1. Pipe a tube 1 ball at point of each curve.

ADD FLOWER GARLANDS to sides of tier. Drop a tube 1 guideline from top of tier. Mound extra icing at center of curve and attach flowers. Pipe leaves with cut cone.

TRIM TOP BEVEL with flowers. Mound a little icing within scallops on top bevel and press in flowers. Trim with leaves made with cut cone.

DECORATE BASE TIER

TRIM EDGE OF TOP BEVEL. Divide tier into eighths. Using pattern, mark curves and points just below border curves of tier above. All piping is done with tube 2. Border consists of five rows of piping. Starting at edge of bevel, outline shapes and over-pipe six times. Repeat outline just above, over-pipe five times. Pipe third and center row, over-pipe four times. Fourth row is over-piped three times and fifth and last row over-piped once. Add tube 2 balls just below border. Pipe a tube 1 ball at point of each curve.

PIPE BASE BORDER. Mark scallops with pattern at base of tier, lining up with bevel border above as pictured. Border is made up of three rows of scallops, all done with tube 2. Outline scallops at lower edge of border and over-pipe three times. Just above, repeat outline and over-pipe twice. Add a final outline above that. Finish with tiny tube 1 scallops and add tube 1 beads to points of all curves.

DECORATE BASE BEVEL. Mark pattern for over-piped border and scrolls just below border on lower side of cake above.

First do the cushion lattice. With tube 3 pipe diagonal lines in one direction, then opposing direction, starting well within space allowed. Dry and repeat for another set with same tube. Now add two sets with tube 2 for a total of four sets, or eight layers, starting and stopping each set beyond the preceding one. Pipe each line directly above preceding line piped in same direction.

Now pipe the border above lattice, a series of three scallops, with tube 2. Outline curve nearest lattice and over-pipe three times. Just above, outline again and over-pipe twice. Finally add third outline. Pipe a tube 1 ball at point of each curve.

Pipe curved scrolls below lattice following pattern. Outline scrolls with tube 15. Over-pipe with tubes 6, 4, 3 and 2 in that order. Finish bevel with a tube 5 bulb border.

SET DRUM ON CENTER TIER, attaching with royal icing. Attach top tier to drum. Set crown on top tier. Pipe a heavy line of icing around base of crown and press in flowers.

MARK POSITIONS OF OVAL FRAMES on base tier. Drop a double row of tube 2 strings from just below bevel to top of frame area. Pipe double bows and drop strings for ends of bows. Attach frames with icing, then attach pink hearts within frames.

ATTACH ALL TASSELS to cake with dots of icing as picture shows. Set flowered hearts on top bevel of base tier, securing with icing.

ADD FLOWERS to base bevel, securing on mounds of icing. Trim bows and tops of oval frames with flowers. Add leaves piped with cut cone to all flowers.

FINALLY, ATTACH BIRDS to frames with dots of icing. Pipe tube 1 ribbons to hearts, then to beaks of birds with ends resting on cake side.

Your regal, three-tier Over-piped cake is now ready to take the place of honor on the reception table. It will serve 400 guests.

CHAPTER SIX

The Australian Method of Decorating

DAINTY is the adjective best describing the Australian Method. Cakes are small and perfectly proportioned and all trim is meticulously executed.

While Australian decorators do create colorful novelty and children's cakes, using techniques and icings much like our own, this chapter is concerned with the "pure" and unmistakable Australian style.

Colors used for Australian cakes are pale pastels. Flowers, either piped or hand-modeled from gum paste are used in a discreet and airy way, never in masses or heavy clusters.

Two of the most striking characteristics of decorating are *extension* work where fine strands of icing join a curved, built-out "shelf" of icing, and dainty *"free hand"* embroidery. Sometimes this embroidery incorporates "flood work," similar to our Color Flow, where an outline is piped directly on the cake, and then filled in. For both of these techniques, very fine tubes and tiny hand-made paper cones are used. Well-controlled pressure is extremely important to maintain the fine, even line work. Small lace pieces, made off the cake, are frequently used as trim.

Lace designs are sometimes piped on fine tulle. Bows, butterflies, leaf shapes and even entire handkerchiefs done in this way give an airy, softening look to the cake. Narrow ribbons, inserted or banded, add to the dressmaker effect.

Australian cakes start with a rich fruit cake, covered with marzipan, then with rolled fondant, or "plastic icing". Both of these coverings are smoothed over the cake in one piece, giving a soft, feminine appearance.

AUSTRALIAN ROYAL ICING

This is the icing used for all piped work. Make sure that all utensils are perfectly clean and free from grease. Use a small or medium bowl and a wooden spoon kept especially for this purpose.

The pure icing sugar in this recipe is confectioners' sugar, free from any cornstarch. If this is unavailable, ordinary confectioners' sugar, sieved three times through fine nylon or silk is acceptable. This is an important step, as even the tiniest lump makes the fine line work impossible.

  1 egg white, room temperature
  10 ounces (approximately) pure icing sugar,
    sieved
  ½ teaspoon lemon juice

Place egg white in bowl and add the sugar, a tablespoon at a time, beating well by hand after each addition. When mixture has consistency of thin syrup, add the lemon juice, and beat for two minutes. Continue adding sugar, a spoonful at a time, and beating after each addition.

When the icing is firm enough to hold a peak on the back of the spoon it is ready for use, and you have used enough sugar. This usually takes 20 minutes of hand beating. *Never* beat this icing with an electric mixer as it may cause too much aeration. Tint as desired with liquid food color, added sparingly, a drop at a time.

Store well-covered in an air-tight container. When in use, keep covered with a damp cloth to prevent crusting.

AUSTRALIAN ROLLED FONDANT

This fondant remains soft indefinitely and gives a satin-like surface to the cake.

  2 pounds pure icing sugar, sieved (see above)
  ½ ounce gelatin
  ¼ cup water
  ½ cup glucose
  ¾ ounce glycerine
  2 or 3 drops of clear flavoring, as desired
  liquid food color, as desired

Put the gelatin and water in a small pan and heat *very gently* just until dissolved. Put the sieved sugar in a large bowl and make a well in the center. Now add the glucose and glycerine to the dissolved gelatin and mix well. Pour this mixture into the well in the sugar and mix with your hands to a dough-like consistency.

Transfer the dough to a smooth surface lightly dusted with cornstarch and knead until it is smooth and pliable. Add the flavoring and food color during the kneading process. If mixture seems too soft, knead in additional sieved sugar. If it is too stiff, add a very small amount of boiling water, drop by drop.

Use this fondant immediately, or store in an air-tight container at room temperature until needed. Knead again before rolling out. If storing for more than a week, refrigerate, but bring to room temperature before kneading and rolling out. This recipe makes enough fondant to cover a 9″ x 3″ round cake.

HOW TO DECORATE THIS CLASSIC AUSTRALIAN CAKE

STEP ONE. Bake an 8″ square fruitcake 3″ high. Cover cake as directed on page 94 and center it on a 12″ square foil-covered board. Divide each side in fourths to position arches.

STEP TWO. Using patterns from The Wilton Way Pattern Book, pipe separate lace pieces with Australian royal icing. Use tube 1s (or Australian tube 0) and pipe extras, since lace is fragile. Dry thoroughly. Following instructions on pages 95 and 96, model Dainty Bess and Elementary roses and the hyacinths.

STEP THREE. Pipe tube 17 shell border at base of cake. Next do script on top using tube 3 and white icing. Over-pipe with tube 1 and pink icing. Now mark off curves of arches with a toothpick to define position of lace pieces. Add embroidery work above base border with tube 1s and with tube 1 pipe pink beads to support lace pieces on arches. Do only a few beads at a time, secure lace piece, then repeat procedure. Pipe curved stem on top, place Dainty Bess and Elementary roses in position and secure with icing. Place hyacinths along stem near roses and position others in spray at corner of cake. Finally, pipe leaves with "V" cut cone for both sprays and complete arrangements by adding tube 1 pink dots. Serves 32.

STEP ONE. Bake a fruitcake, attach a cardboard cake circle to cake and fill holes and crevices as directed on page 78. Prepare a recipe of marzipan (page 76). Brush cake top and sides with apricot glaze. Dust work surface with confectioners' sugar, then roll out marzipan to a ⅜″ thick circle large enough to cover the entire cake surface. Fold the marzipan over the rolling pin, place on edge of the cake and unroll marzipan onto the cake.

STEP TWO. Gently press marzipan into place around cake and smooth with palms of hands. Marzipan has no stretch and sometimes when covering a cake, cracks will appear. If this happens, pinch the crack together and rub it gently with palm of hand until there is a smooth surface.

STEP THREE. Using a sharp knife, cut off excess marzipan at base. Let harden for at least twelve hours. Now the cake with its seamless covering is ready to be covered with rolled fondant. (Recipe is on page 92.)

STEP FOUR. Brush marzipan covering with apricot glaze. Coat work surface with a thin layer of non-stick pan release and dust with cornstarch. Roll fondant out to a ¼″ thick circle large enough to cover entire cake. Fold the fondant over the rolling pin, place on end of cake and unroll. Smooth fondant into place.

STEP FIVE. Cut off excess fondant around base. Then smooth again with hands and trim excess fondant off so the bottom edge is perfectly even. Transfer cake to cake board or serving plate.

STEP SIX. Now the cake is ready to be decorated. The layers of marzipan and rolled fondant seal in the moisture of the fruitcake and give a perfectly smooth surface on which to decorate.

AUSTRALIAN MODELED FLOWERS

The Australian method of making gum paste flowers differs from the American method in that the petals are hand-modeled, rather than cut out. The size of the petal is determined by the size of the ball of gum paste you start with. Australians use a mixture of gum arabic and water for attaching pieces, but we have used egg white which is just as effective and easier to obtain.

DOUBLE DAINTY BESS

ROLL A BALL of gum paste ½″ in diameter (recipe on page 142). Flatten the ball into a petal about 1½″ in diameter, then thin the edges by pressing between the thumb and forefinger.

SHAPE THE PETAL over the thumb, curling back the edges slightly. Make four more petals using the same procedure. Let the petals dry a short time before assembling. Pipe a mound of royal icing and insert petals into it, overlapping them slightly.

MAKE FIVE SMALLER PETALS using the same procedure, but starting with a ball about ⅜″ in diameter and flattening to about 1″ in diameter. Assemble them in the center of the first circle of petals on a dot of royal icing.

PIPE A DOT of royal icing in the center and insert pearl-tipped artificial stamens at an outward angle. Dry flower thoroughly. To make a Single Dainty Bess, omit the second row of petals.

ELEMENTARY ROSE

MOLD A CONE from a ¾″ diameter ball of gum paste (recipe on page 142). Flatten a ⅜″ ball into a circle for petal, thicker at one edge. Shape around thumb.

ROLL PETAL starting at thin edge. Attach to top of cone with egg white. Make three identical petals and attach thicker edge to cone with egg white.

MAKE FIVE PETALS with a slightly larger ball. Flatten, then thin edges with fingers and cup petal by holding in palm of hand and pressing with thumb. Attach petals to cone, slightly lower than last row. Furl edges.

MAKE SEVEN LARGER PETALS using same technique and a ½″ ball. Attach to cone in same manner. Add another row of petals for a fuller rose. Dry.

TO MAKE A BUD, bend a piece of florists' wire into a hook and dip in egg white. Roll first petal around wire. Secure second row of three petals to rolled petal with egg white. Dry.

CHRISTMAS ROSE

ROLL A ⅜″ BALL of gum paste (recipe is on page 142). Flatten it into a 1⅛″ petal and thin the edges on one side between the thumb and forefinger.

MAKE FOUR MORE PETALS the same way. Place all five petals along the sides of the indentation on the bottom side of a shot glass, overlapping them and leaving a small hole in the center of the flower. Glue each in position with egg white. Dry thoroughly.

MAKE THE CALYX by rolling two short, thin "strings" of gum paste. Flatten them, then lay them in a cross and press together. Brush the calyx with egg white and form it up onto the base of the flower.

MAKE THE CENTER by rolling a ¼″ ball of gum paste. Insert a few artificial stamens and attach the ball in the center of the flower with egg white. Dry thoroughly. The completed flower is shown on the cake on the opposite page.

MOLD LEAVES. Roll a ⅜″ ball of gum paste and model it into a teardrop shape. Flatten it into a leaf shape. Use a knife to press in the veins and the serrated edges. Dry leaf on a curved surface. To add the stem, attach a piece of florists' wire to the back of the leaf with egg white.

HYACINTH

MAKE A ½″ CONE of gum paste (recipe on page 142). With a pointed stick, hollow out the center by working the stick around and around.

CUT THE EDGES of the hollow cone with a sharp knife in six places about halfway up to the point. Press down on the cone lightly to spread out the cut sections.

TRIM EACH SECTION into a point with a sharp knife to create a five-petaled flower. Then insert an artificial stamen through the center of the flower, pinching the base of the flower to hold the stamen in place. This becomes the stem. Indent the center of each petal with a pointed stick and dry the hyacinth upside down on a cotton ball.

THE BLUSHING CHRISTMAS ROSE

The Christmas Rose cake is another example of how elegant even the smallest of the cakes decorated in the understated Australian manner can be! Because of their simplicity, the decoration on these cakes must be executed to perfection.

STEP ONE. Bake an 8″ round fruit or heavy butter cake, 3″ high. Cover cake as directed on page 94, rolling out fondant to between 14″ and 15″. Center cake on 14″ foil-covered board. Use excess fondant to make two ropes, each 32″ long and approximately ¼″ in diameter. Twist these together and encircle base of cake.

STEP TWO. Cut a paper template from a circle 10″ in diameter and from it make a pattern for a six-pointed star. Transfer pattern to cake.

STEP THREE. Use crimper to form outside star pattern. Following pattern, insert crimpers into fon-dant about ¼″ apart. Then squeeze crimpers to-gether to about ⅛″ apart, leaving small mound and tiny "cut in" marks. Pipe scallops on either side of crimped star with tube 1s. Using same tube, add inner star and heart shapes with "snail trail" technique, similar to a shell border. Complete embroidery with dots and vertical lines as pictured.

STEP FOUR. Following procedure on opposite page, model four Christmas Roses and a bud from gum paste. Make 15 to 18 leaves, attaching wire stems to each with egg white. Dry thoroughly.

STEP FIVE. Form gum paste plaque 2″ in diameter by ½″ thick and insert roses and leaves. Arrange single Christmas Rose and bud at base of cake using gum paste stem and wired leaves. Position centerpiece roses on plaque . Serves 30.

AN ELEGANT AUSTRALIAN WEDDING CAKE

Delicate embellishments of icing lace and precision curtaining make this cake unique and artistic.

STEP ONE. Bake two-layer 6″ x 3″ and 9″ x 4″ square fruitcakes. Cover tiers as directed on page 94. Center on 9″ and 13″ square foil-covered cake boards.

STEP TWO. Using excess fondant, make four 5″ high columns in column molds as follows: cut ¼″ dowel rods exactly 5″ higher than the height of the base tier and center these with top of dowel at top of column when molds are made, so that exposed dowel can be pushed through bottom tier and carry weight of top tier. Dry thoroughly.

STEP THREE. Pipe about 90 lace pieces, following Wilton Way patterns, and allow to dry.

STEP FOUR. Model from gum paste four Elementary roses, and four rosebuds (see page 95). Make lilies of the valley by hollowing ¼″ balls of gum paste with rounded stick. Insert stem of artificial stamen through hollowed ball, securing with egg white. Buds are artificial stamens. Wrap stems with floral tape into spray for lower tier. Add 4″ squares of tulle for cluster on top tier.

STEP FIVE. Starting with 12″ and 9″ squares of parchment, cut patterns for cornelli borders and mark on top of each tier. Pipe cornelli with tube 1 and snail trail on inner edges with tube 00. Add tube 14 shell border at base of each tier.

STEP SIX. Make patterns for extension work on each tier. Cut 2″ strips of paper long enough to go around each tier and mark off points for 20 scallops on each. Mark points on tiers with a toothpick.

From mid-points of the two scallops at center base of each tier measure up 1″. At corner of tiers, measure 2″ up from board and mark points with a toothpick. Now connect these points with a diagonal line. This becomes top of curtaining.

STEP SEVEN. Next insert ribbon, which must be done while fondant is soft. About 1″ from top of each tier, mark a line parallel to cake board, up to cornelli. Make slits in fondant, press ribbon in at each end, lining up with mark.

STEP EIGHT. Pipe extension work with tube 3, dropping string from point to point to make an even scallop. Over-pipe string on string to form ledges. Do not add more than two lines before drying or structure will collapse. Build scallops out to eight-string width on base tier, to six on top. When dry, brush thinned royal icing over " ledges" to provide greater strength for curtaining.

STEP NINE. Pipe tube 1 snail trail on diagonal curtaining lines. Do curtaining first on top tier, then on bottom, using tube 00. Position lines as close to one another as possible, so close that in no case could a line be added between any two. Using same tube, add small scallops at base of curtaining. Pipe a line of tube 0 dots above and below ribbons on each tier. Attach ribbon bows with icing.

STEP TEN. Position flower spray and cluster on tiers and assemble with pillars. Attach lace pieces to lower edge of cornelli area. Set each piece on a short line piped with tube 1. Add tube 0 dots below lace. A masterpiece that serves 46.

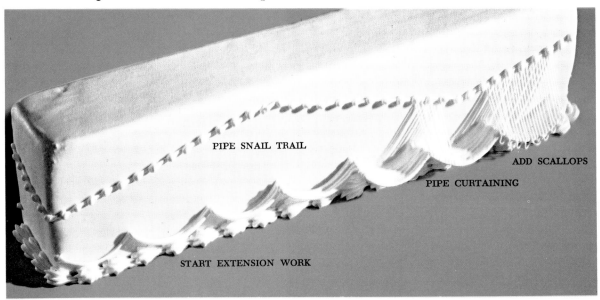

PIPE SNAIL TRAIL

ADD SCALLOPS

PIPE CURTAINING

START EXTENSION WORK

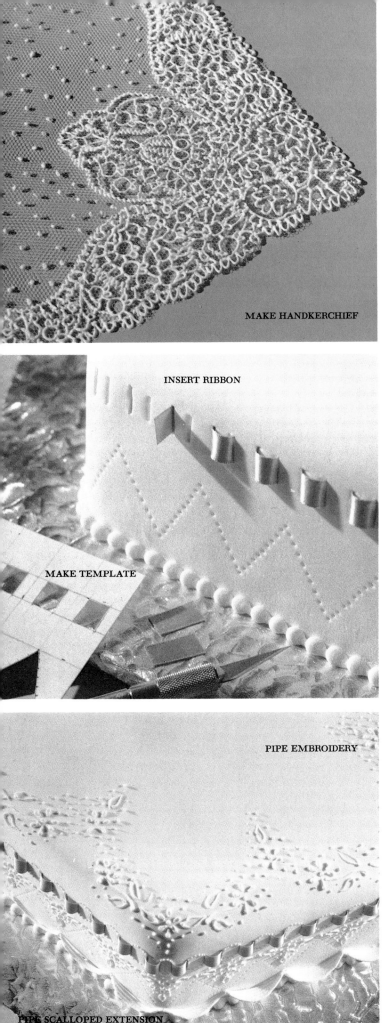

MAKE HANDKERCHIEF

INSERT RIBBON

MAKE TEMPLATE

PIPE EMBROIDERY

PIPE SCALLOPED EXTENSION

PERFECTION: HALLMARK OF THE AUSTRALIAN METHOD

The handkerchief which appears to be made of delicately-woven antique lace is really the creation of a skilled decorator—and is piped with precision in an old world pattern on sheer white tulle! This jewel of a cake shows to advantage many of the decorating techniques that have made the Australian method so unique and artistic.

STEP ONE. Model from gum paste three Elementary Roses and three hyacinths following instructions on pages 95 and 96, mounting roses on wire stems. Next model and attach to wire stems seven gum paste leaves. Set all aside to dry thoroughly.

STEP TWO. Pipe "lace" handkerchief. Place pattern from The Wilton Way Pattern Book on a 10″ square of cardboard, cover this with wax paper and stretch over this a 9″ square of fine tulle. Secure pattern, wax paper and tulle to board with pins on outer edges. Using tube 1 and thinned royal icing, maintain even pressure control and pipe pattern on tulle. Use a slight "hooking" motion with the tube to secure icing to tulle. Dry thoroughly. Trim edges of tulle with X-acto knife.

STEP THREE. Bake a 9″ hexagon-shaped fruitcake 3″ high. Cover cake, following procedure outlined on page 94. Center cake on 14″ foil-covered hexagon board. Add tube 3 bulb border at base.

STEP FOUR. Make light cardboard template for ribbon insertion and for base triangles that define areas of curtaining. (Shown in photo at left.) This will provide for eight equally-spaced loops of ⅜″ ribbon on each side of cake. Top of ribbon is approximately ¾″ below top level of cake. Mark triangles on cake with pin or toothpick. Using an X-acto knife, cut precise slits in still-soft fondant just long enough to accommodate ribbon. Now cut ⅝″ lengths of ribbon and, using point of X-acto knife, insert ends into slits to make eight ribbon loops in each side. Repeat for each of the six sides.

STEP FIVE. Pipe embroidery freehand with tube 000 starting first on top and then working down each side. On top, start embroidery design first in center and then work to either side.

STEP SIX. Pipe scalloped extension to serve as base for curtaining with tube 2. First line is piped full width of base of triangle. Each succeeding line is shorter until you have piped a total of four lines. After piping two lines, allow to dry before proceeding. Pipe a finishing line around each scallop. Brush surface with thinned royal icing. Dry.

100

STEP SEVEN. Pipe curtaining, as shown in photo at right, using tube 000. Using controlled pressure, space lines close enough so that another line of icing can not be piped between any other two lines in the curtain. After curtaining is thoroughly dry, complete trim with tube 000. Pipe scallop border on sides of curtain area. Next add snail trail at bottom of curtaining and, finally, drop tube 000 strings from base.

STEP EIGHT. Pick up handkerchief in center so that folds fall gracefully and position it on cake. Tape flowers and leaves into a small bouquet and tie with ribbon bow. Place on cake. Handkerchief and flower arrangement can be removed and saved when cake is cut. Serves 22 wedding guests.

PIPE CURTAINING   ADD TRIM

CHAPTER SEVEN

The South African
Method of Decorating

The South African method of cake decorating has been established for less than 100 years and is a direct descendant of the English method. Yet it has developed a look and character so distinctly its own, it could not possibly be mistaken for any other.

This is not surprising, as South Africa itself is unique. It lies at the tip of a continent of incredible contrasts, with great jungles, golden deserts, towering mountains, vast meadowlands and thousands of miles of ravishing seacoast. The drama and variety of their surroundings are bound to be reflected in everything South Africans do and cake decorating is certainly no exception.

Within the South African method of decorating, there are two distinct styles. The *Lacework Style* is an elaboration of the English and Australian styles, but the lace pieces are done in a more showy way, frequently in the form of large "wings" which give the cake an airy feeling of flight. The *Run-in Style* is based on the English Nirvana style with cakes almost completely covered with china-like run-in work. The run-in work is done in a three-dimensional fashion for very dramatic effects. Lacework and Run-in cakes begin with rich fruitcakes.

South African decorators also make colorful novelty cakes for birthdays or special occasions. These are made of a light batter, much like our layer cakes, iced and trimmed with buttercream.

Flowers play a large part in South African decorating. These are piped off the cake in royal icing or carefully modeled in gum paste or marzipan by hand. Other flowers are piped directly on a novelty cake in buttercream, using abbreviated but effec-

tive techniques. Modeled and painted marzipan fruit is also used for trim.

The decorating syringe is used in South Africa for most borders and piping. Lace and trellis work is done with a parchment paper cone for best control.

THE LACEWORK STYLE

Fanciful and elaborate lace wings that rise above the tiers are the most dramatic highlights of this style. These fragile wings are piped with a very fine writing tube, then the main lines over-piped. Built-up trellis, or lattice-work, is often used to cover edges of the cake for a soft cushioned effect, reminiscent of the English Over-piped style. A flat trellis often covers the entire top of a South African cake. Other techniques inherited from the English include over-piped scrolls called "hollow line work", lace and lattice work shapes piped on net nails, and over-piped curves and scrolls.

A lacework cake starts with a rich heavy fruitcake covered in marzipan, then double-iced in royal icing in white or a pale tint.

ICING FOR LACE AND LINEWORK

The recipe for Egg White Royal Icing in Chapter Twenty is suitable for covering the cake. For trellis work, lacework and hollow line piping you must be very sure the icing has no tiny lumps or bubbles that might clog the fine tubes used. Therefore, use the recipe for Australian Royal Icing on page 92.

THIS SPLENDID WEDDING CAKE is a perfect example of the South African Lacework Style. The next pages show how to decorate it.

1

2

3

A SOUTH AFRICAN WEDDING CAKE IN THE LACEWORK STYLE

Parts of this impressive cake are piped in careful steps, then assembled for a breath-taking effect. If you are not accustomed to this fine line work, it is advisable to practice until your hand becomes adept in following the curves accurately. All patterns are in The Wilton Way Pattern Book.

PIPE THE LACE WINGS

STEP ONE. Tape patterns to a piece of glass or plastic. Now tack wax paper smoothly over patterns with dots of icing.

Using a paper cone, tube 1s and Australian royal icing (page 92), work from the outside of the wing in to the center. Pipe the outer edges of the circles.

STEP TWO. Add the lace points on the outer edges. Now, working with one circle at a time, add the "spokes" of the circles by moving the tube in a very tight zigzag motion. Pipe the inner circular shape, then add the "S" curves, making sure there is a good join on all curves. You may need to nudge the line of icing gently into place with the tip of a fine artist's brush to make sure it falls directly on the pattern line.

STEP THREE. Continue piping the wings until the entire pattern is completed. Very accurately, pipe the finishing right-angle line which will rest on the top and side of the tiers. Continue to pipe additional wings. You will need fifteen to trim the cake.

Now pipe the top ornament in three sections in the same manner as you piped the wings. Let all pieces dry thoroughly.

Remove pieces from the wax paper by sliding the blade of a small spatula carefully under the wax paper. Turn the pieces over, and over-pipe the main circular lines that define the "wheels" and the straight lines at edges. This will add strength and give a finished effect to the lace when seen from both sides on the cake.

PIPE THE LACE POINTS

You will need about 600 of these trims to edge the trellis work and cake boards, and it is wise to make extras, as they are very fragile. To work more quickly, rule an 8½" x 11" sheet of parchment or other transparent paper into 1" squares. Trace the lace point pattern in the center of each of these squares. Tape this sheet to a piece of glass or plastic, tack wax paper over with dots of icing and you are ready to begin. Use a paper cone, tube 1s, and Australian royal icing.

104

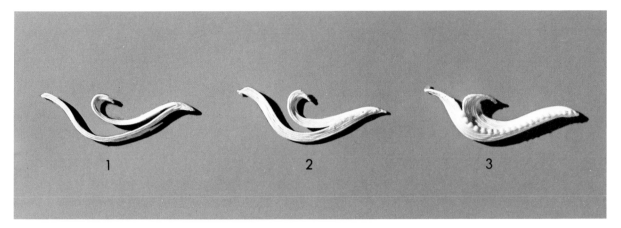

PIPE THE ROSES

Use royal icing and tube 102. Slightly stiffen the icing by adding a little confectioners' sugar, and use the method described on page 21. You will need about one dozen roses. Set aside to dry.

PIPE THE ORNAMENT BASE

The top ornament rests on a run-in plaque. South African decorators use royal icing for this, but Color Flow icing is preferable for it dries more quickly. Recipe is on page 76. Tape pattern to piece of glass or stiff board, tape wax paper smoothly over and outline with tube 2. Thin icing as described on page 79, and flow in the plaque using a paper cone with tip cut. Dry thoroughly, then edge with tube 1 beading.

DO THE HOLLOW LINE WORK

STEP ONE. This technique is similar to the English over-piping. Tape patterns to 16" curved form and tape wax paper smoothly over. Use paper cone, tube 1s and Australian royal icing prepared as described on page 92.

STEP TWO. Starting at outside edges, trace curve of pattern. Over-pipe these lines with second lines piped on top of and very slightly within the first. *After the second lines are piped, allow to dry.* This drying time is necessary so work will not collapse from weight. Continue over-piping each line in the same manner, gradually building up a hollow scroll, and allowing to dry after piping two lines. You will need nine lines to complete the scroll. When scroll is dry, brush lightly with thinned icing. Finish with a row of tube 1 dots.

STEP THREE. Make six left-facing and six right-facing scrolls on 16" form for base tier. Make three pairs of scrolls on 8" form for top tier.

PREPARE THE TIERS

BAKE THREE TIERS, using the fruitcake recipe in Chapter Twenty , or your own favorite. Top tier is 8" round by 3" high. Middle tier is 12" x 4", base tier is 16" x 4".

COVER TIERS with marzipan, exactly as shown on page 78. First fill in any cracks or holes to make cake as smooth as possible. Before covering, set each tier on a cardboard cake circle the same diameter as the tier, using a little royal icing to secure as directed on page 78.

ICE TIERS with royal icing, using recipe in Chapter Twenty . Set tier on turntable, and apply thick coating of icing to sides. Hold a knife perpendicular against side and revolve turntable to spread icing smoothly on side. Cover top of cake as smoothly as possible and trim off any excess build-up of icing on edge. Dry about twelve hours.

Now add a second thin coat of icing to the side of the tier in the same manner as before. With tube 2, pipe a line of icing around top edge of cake, and dry. Thin the icing with a little water and flow in the top surface, allowing the icing to run out to the piped line. Dry to a smooth finish.

SET EACH TIER on a silver foil-covered cake board cut 2" larger in diameter than the tier, and securing with icing. Arrange roses in center of base tier on a small mound of icing. Add leaves piped with tube 66. Heap small mound of icing in center of middle tier and arrange roses. Trim with tube 66 leaves.

ASSEMBLE THE TIERS as pictured on page 103. Use three 5" Grecian pillars between base and middle tiers and three 3" pillars between middle and top tiers. As you place the pillars, push a ¼" dowel rod through pillar to cake board below tier, then clip off level with top of pillar. Set the cake on a large silver tray, or sturdy masonite circle 2" larger in diameter than base cake board. Now you are ready to decorate.

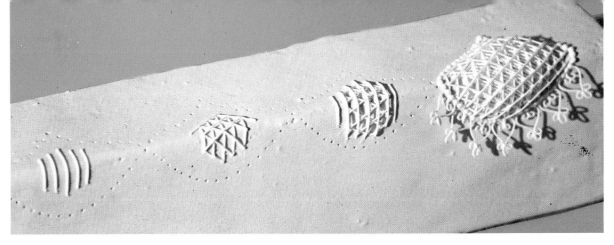

DECORATE THE CAKE

It is best to take the tiers apart and decorate each separately, then assemble again. As you decorate, make sure the work is at eye level. Accurate measuring is essential for the success of this cake.

STEP ONE. Pipe base borders on all tiers. For base tier, pipe a ball border with tube 5 at the point where the cake meets the cake board. On top and slightly above this border add another with same tube. Then add a third tube 5 ball border in front of the first, resting on the cake board. This will create a slight bevel effect. Pipe similar border on middle tier, using tube 4. Do border on top tier with tube 3.

STEP TWO. Prepare to pipe the trellis puffs that cover the top edges of the tiers. Divide lowest tier into sixths. Measure ½" from either side of these divisions. *This inch of space will be left vacant to accommodate the lace wings.* Now prepare a pattern for the puffs. There will be two puffs between each lace wing. Puffs extend about one inch below top edge of tier on side, and about one inch from edge of tier on top surface. Mark pattern on tier with toothpick.

Divide middle tier into sixths and make similar pattern for puffs and mark on tier. *Make sure to leave one inch of space for wings between every two puffs.* Make pattern and mark top tier, first dividing into thirds, and leaving one inch free for three wings.

Now pipe the trellis on each tier with tube 1s. For each puff, pipe a vertical line in center of puff, then two shorter ones on each side. Crisscross these lines with diagonal lines. Continue to pipe vertical lines, then diagonal lines, piping each line directly above the line going in the same direction below it. Gradually extend the length of the lines until the final set touches the edge of the marked pattern.

Edge trellis on cake top with tube 1 beading. Cover edge of trellis on cake side with beading, adding a lace piece after just a few beads are piped. Set lace pieces at a perky angle as you attach them.

STEP THREE. Attach hollow line pieces to sides of top and bottom tier with icing.

STEP FOUR. Run a line with tube 1 from center of Color Flow plaque to one point of plaque. Set one lace piece on line, prop to hold. Then pipe a line on center edge of lace piece, second line on plaque and place second lace piece. Prop to hold and add third lace piece in the same way. Pipe tube 1 beading at base of lace pieces and where they join at center. Dry thoroughly, then place ornament on top tier, securing with icing.

STEP FIVE. Assemble tiers, piping mound of royal icing on top of each pillar to secure.

STEP SIX. Attach lace wings to tiers, starting with top tier. Pipe a line of tube 1 beading on top of tier and down side, in center of open space between puffs. Carefully set wing in position. Prop until dry. Repeat until all wings are in position.

STEP SEVEN. Edge cake boards of all tiers with tube 1 beading and lace pieces. Pipe just a few beads, attach lace piece, and continue until tiers are completely edged. A spectacular wedding cake that serves 216 guests.

THE SOUTH AFRICAN RUN-IN STYLE

This colorful Safari cake is typical of the South African Run-in style—a method similar to American Color Flow, and the direct descendant of the English Nirvana style. Geometrically shaped cakes are enclosed in run-in frames, with more run-in panels adorning the top. Often three-dimensional scenes, created with several layers of run-in work, are placed within the frames. These cakes may commemorate important happenings in a person's career, or events in the history of an organization or community. The colors used are rich and vivid.

As is true of all important South African cakes, the Safari cake is a rich fruit cake, covered with marzipan, then with royal icing. The scenes on the sides show native animals in their natural settings. Decorating directions are on the following pages.

107

Prepare all the components of this handsome South African cake step by step, just as for the English Nirvana cake described on pages 79 through 81. South African decorators use royal icing to outline their run-in pieces, then thin the icing to run-in the areas, but Color Flow icing is equally strong and dries more quickly, so it was used for this cake. Recipe is on page 76.

An unusual feature of the Safari cake is that all the run-in work is done in ivory-tinted icing. Color is applied after the pieces have dried.

PREPARE THE SIDE FRAMES. Tape Wilton Way patterns to rigid surface and tape wax paper over them, making sure pattern is smoothly covered. Using Color Flow icing and tube 2, outline the six frames. While the outline sets, thin the icing with water. Correct consistency is reached when a spoonful of icing dropped into the batch disappears at the count of ten. Let thinned icing stand for 24 hours for air bubbles to rise to the surface.

Use a parchment cone with a cut tip for running-in the thinned icing. Flow in heavily for a rounded, raised effect. Start in the center of one side of frame and fill in on either side, then move to center of adjacent side. Work quickly so no crust lines form. Use a small artist's brush to coax the icing into small areas. Dry the frames under a

heat lamp placed two feet above them for two hours to give a glossy finish. Then complete drying for 24 to 48 hours.

Edge the inside of the dried frames with tube 1 beading. Outline the curved edge with tube 1 and use the same tube for the dot and teardrop trim. Set aside to dry thoroughly.

DO THE SIX FLOWERED TOP PANELS. Tape Wilton Way patterns to smooth surface and tape wax paper over them. Outline with tube 1 and let outlines set. Thin the icing as described for side frames and fill in the areas with ivory-tinted icing. Fill in very heavily so petal and leaf shapes have a rounded raised surface, almost like a low relief. Dry under a heat lamp, two feet above, for two hours, then dry thoroughly for 24 to 48 hours.

When panels are completely dry, thin paste food color with a little water and paint the flowers and leaves in natural hues with an artist's brush. Brush deeper color around centers of flowers. Dry.

BEGIN THE PICTORIAL SCENES. You will enjoy using your originality and artistic ability in creating these realistic pictures. It's a good idea to read page 299 on Classic painting for ideas on techniques before starting. Each panel is composed of four layers, or levels, attached to give a three-dimensional

effect. Patterns for the native South African animals are in The Wilton Way Pattern book, but the background layers are done free hand.

Start with the zebra panel. Draw a 6″ x 4¼″ rectangle on parchment paper. Sketch the outline of the hill in the background against the sky. This will be your background or main pattern. Cover the sketch with another sheet of parchment paper and draw the closer hill and the outline of the pond. This will be the second run-in level or layer. The third layer will be the animals. Cover the sketch again and draw the small hill in the foreground. This will be the fourth and last layer of the three-dimensional picture.

Using these sketches as patterns, tape them to a stiff surface, tape wax paper over, then outline with tube 1 and fill in the areas. Use only ivory-tinted icing. Dry 24 hours.

PIPE THE ANIMALS. Tape Wilton Way patterns to smooth surface, tape wax paper smoothly over, and outline zebras and giraffe with tube 1 and ivory icing. Use a slightly thicker icing for this run-in work. Thin the icing so a spoonful dropped back in batch is still visible at the count of ten. Have a cone fitted with tube 1 and filled with stiff royal icing at hand. Cut tip of a second cone and fill with thinned icing. Flow in outlined shape.

Now use the cone filled with royal icing to create the rounded shape of the animals. Insert tip of tube into icing wherever you want the shape to project—legs, neck and head. Squeeze to the shape you desire, and the flowed-in icing will cover it. Work quickly. A small artist's brush is helpful to "nudge" the icing into the areas. Set aside to dry thoroughly.

PAINT THE SCENES. Use thinned royal icing tinted in natural hues as paint and an artist's brush. Do the background panel first. Paint clouds and sky, then hill. Use paste color to indicate darker areas. Stroke on rushes at foot of hill.

Paint second layer, hill and pond. Then complete the fourth layer, the foreground hill.

The zebras and giraffe figures are painted in paste color, right from the jar. The giraffe is painted a gold color, then spots and details added with paste color. Pipe ears, horns and eyes in royal icing for a dimensional effect.

Attach the layers, or levels, one to another with dots of royal icing, using the first rectangle as a base. After attaching the hill and pond layer, add the animal figures, then the final hill layer. Go back and pipe rocks, grasses and leaves with royal icing. Set panel aside to dry completely.

Do the five other pictorial panels the same way, using your imagination and postcards or pictures to provide scenic backgrounds for the animals.

PREPARE CAKE. Bake a fruit cake in 12″ hexagon pans. A good recipe is on page 323, or use your own favorite. Assemble layers with apricot jam to achieve a cake 4″ high. After assembly, chill cake, and trim to a level top surface. Cover with marzipan as shown on page 78. After drying 48 hours, ice with two coats of royal icing as described on page 105. Use the recipe on page 322. Place cake on foil-covered cake board, 2″ larger all around. Using pattern, pipe tube 1 beading in scalloped design on top. Inside this beading, use tube 1s to pipe a zigzag "lightning" design. Cut the stepped pyramid in center of cake from ½″ slices of cake, or from ½″ thick styrofoam. Assemble and ice with royal icing. Place in center of cake and edge with tube 1. Add lettering with same tube.

ASSEMBLE THE CAKE. Now that all frames, panels and scenes are prepared, put the cake together. Measure ¾″ out from lower edge of cake and mark a line on cake board. Attach assembled pictorial panels to sides of cake with mounds of royal icing and dry. According to pattern, attach flat sugar cubes to cake top to support top panels and pipe a ¼″ high mound of royal icing on each. Dry.

Pipe a tube 4 line of royal icing on cake board as marked, on just one side of hexagon shape. Set a run-in frame against piped line, pipe a line on one side of frame and on cake board adjacent to frame. Set a second frame in position against line on cake board, touching frame that is in position. Hold to steady until set. Starting at top center of first frame, pipe a line of icing to top center of second frame. Pipe a dot of icing on top of dried mound on top of cake and set one flowered top panel in position. Continue piping lines and adding frames and top panels until cake is completely circled. Always add a top panel as soon as two adjacent side frames are in position.

ADD FLAGS. Purchase small cloth flags, 1¼″ x 3½″. Roll out gum paste 1/16″ thick (recipe, page 142), cut to same measurement, brush with egg white, and press to back of flags. Prop flags in wind blown position and dry. Insert in center of pyramid. Edge all seams where frames and panels meet with tube 16 shells. Your South African masterpiece cuts into 50 slices, 1″ x 2″.

Use the same techniques and your artistic abilities to create cakes for other important occasions—an anniversary or a special celebration for a club or organization.

CHAPTER EIGHT

The Mexican Method
of Decorating

THEATRICAL best describes the colorful Mexican method of decorating. Gum paste figures, or "dolls", are meticulously dressed in detailed costumes, usually from a former time. They appear in realistic room settings with furniture and accessories carefully created to scale, or in formal gardens. Most of these tableaux are arranged on drums or platforms that are in turn set on the cakes.

Even when dolls are not used, the cakes still have a dramatic, story-telling mood, as displayed in the Mexican cakes on pages 113 and 114.

HOW TO PREPARE THE CAKE

Mexican cakes are made with a firm pound cake batter. After baking, level the cake and trim off all irregularities. Make crumbs from these trimmings and mix with any clear jelly. Use this jelly-crumb mixture to fill the layers and pack any crevices. Coat the entire cake with jelly.

Center the cake on a ⅜" plywood cake board, 4" larger on all sides than the cake. Strips of 1" x 1" wood of suitable length should be glued on the underside of the board as legs.

Cover the cake with rolled fondant.

MEXICAN ROLLED FONDANT

2 pounds + 4 tablespoons sifted confectioners' sugar
1 tablespoon tragacanth gum
1 tablespoon glucose
5 tablespoons water
Approximately 4 ounces light corn syrup
½ teaspoon almond flavoring

Sprinkle the tragacanth gum over the sifted sugar. Mix glucose and water until the glucose is blended. Slowly add sugar mixture to the glucose mixture, adding small amounts of corn syrup from time to time until it is too stiff to stir, then begin to knead. Add flavoring and the rest of the sugar and knead well. Store fondant in a covered glass container in the refrigerator. Bring to room temperature when ready to use.

Roll out on a surface lightly dusted with cornstarch. Lift occasionally to be sure it is not sticking. Place fondant on cake, rolled side up, and smooth it to completely cover. Trim off excess at base.

Now cover the cake board with puffed foil in the Mexican way. Cut foil in long strips, 7" wide. Form pleats along one long side and glue pleated edge to the board, right next to the cake, with royal icing. Tuck plain, unpleated edge under board and secure with royal icing.

Insert dowel rods, clipped level with surface, into cake to support weight above. Simple borders or other side trim is piped with royal icing, using cut cones or tubes similar to American tubes.

THE THREE PILLARS OF DECORATING

The Mexican method is based on three substances, *royal icing, gum paste* and *pastillage.*

Royal icing is used for piped flowers and borders and to glue pastillage and gum paste pieces.

Gum paste forms dolls' figures and clothing, modeled flowers and small accessories.

Pastillage is a strong hard substance for buildings and structures of all kinds. It is used for drums, or platforms, cylinder-shaped separators, plates, furniture and bases for dolls.

MEXICAN ROYAL ICING

1 egg white (taken from shell the day before)
½ pound confectioners' sugar, sifted
juice of a half lemon, strained

Mix by hand. Beat the egg white until slightly foamy. Add the sugar gradually, a tablespoon at a time, beating after each addition. When mixture becomes very stiff, add lemon juice and beat again.

You may triple the recipe and use an electric mixer *at medium speed* to avoid overbeating.

Practice will teach you the correct consistency, adding lemon juice if too stiff, more sugar if too soft. Strings and fine piping require a *soft* consistency, flowers a *medium* consistency and large flowers, *stiff.* This icing dries quickly—store in a tightly covered jar, and keep covered with a damp cloth while using.

Continued on next page

AT RIGHT: detail from *Autumn,* a Mexican cake that features two ladies dressed in French fashions of 1878. Directions are on page 122.

MEXICAN GUM PASTE

½ pound plus one tablespoon confectioners' sugar
1 tablespoon tragacanth gum
1 teaspoon heavy glucose
3 to 4 tablespoons water (amount depends on humidity)

Sift the sugar and tragacanth gum together into a large bowl. Stir the glucose and two tablespoons of the water together until the glucose is dissolved. Make a well in the sugar mixture and add the glucose-water mixture. Now work with your hands to a *very stiff* dough. If too sticky, add more sugar, if too stiff, add more water, drop by drop. Keep working the paste until pliable and elastic.

To MOLD DOLLS, use the gum paste immediately, or the same day it is made.

To USE FOR FLOWERS, CLOTHING, or anything that requires rolling, use gum paste that has been stored for three or four days. Re-work until pliable, and roll on cornstarch-dusted surface.

STORE GUM PASTE UNCOLORED, wrapped in plastic and in a tightly covered jar. If the weather is warm, keep in refrigerator. It will keep for several months.

COLOR GUM PASTE with paste colors, worked in well until evenly distributed. Pastel colors can be used at once. After adding deep colors, allow gum paste to stand, well-wrapped, until color "ripens"

MEXICAN PASTILLAGE

1 tablespoon powdered gelatin*
½ cup cold water
1 cup granulated sugar
½ cup cold water
2 pounds confectioners' sugar, or more

Dissolve the gelatin in ½ cup cold water. While dissolving, mix granulated sugar and ½ cup cold water in stainless steel or copper pan. (Aluminum will discolor mixture.) Boil to 220° (thread stage). Pour dissolved gelatin into cooked mixture and remove from heat. Stir until well-blended. Add confectioners' sugar by tablespoons, stirring after each addition, until mixture resembles heavy cream. Heap most of remaining confectioners' sugar on table, make a well in center and pour in cooked mixture. Mix with your hands to *very soft dough*, adding more confectioners' sugar if necessary. Store in tightly closed container until ready to use.

*Note: you may substitute sheet gelatin for powdered gelatin. Use six sheets (20 grams or ⅔ ounces). Place in measuring cup and cover with cold water. Soak for 20 to 25 minutes. Strain off water, squeeze out the softened sheets and add to the cooked mixture just as for powdered gelatin. Pastillage made with sheet gelatin can be tinted deep colors. Pastillage made with powdered gelatin can be tinted only in pale colors or used untinted.

HOW TO ROLL PASTILLAGE

When ready to roll out, break off only as much of the soft dough as you plan to use immediately. Knead in more confectioners' sugar until dough is stiff enough to roll. Read the instructions below carefully before starting to roll, as *pastillage dries very quickly*.

PREPARE PATTERN PIECES by tracing them accurately on light cardboard, then cutting out. Check to be sure all pattern pieces needed are at hand. Place all pieces requiring the same thickness in a pile, so they may be cut at one time.

TINT PASTILLAGE by kneading in paste color. Roll pastel tints immediately—allow deep colors, well-wrapped, to set a few minutes. (See note above.)

ROLL PASTILLAGE on smooth formica or marble surface, dusted with cornstarch. Never turn pastillage over, but lift it occasionally to add a little more cornstarch to prevent sticking. Roll to exact thickness needed for piece. Test by cutting off a strip at edge and comparing it with chart on page 113.

LAY LARGEST PATTERN PIECES on rolled pastillage first, holding gently. Use sharp X-acto knife and cut interior openings, such as windows, first, removing cut-out areas. Then cut outer edges. *Cut toward all corners*, not away from them. Cut smaller pieces from leftover areas of rolled pastillage.

WHEN CUTTING THICK PIECES, wet the point of your knife, and move it slowly through the pastillage to preserve a clean edge.

To CUT A SMALL PIECE, first cut out a rough, enlarged shape of the pattern from rolled pastillage, lay on a piece of glass, lay pattern on it and cut around pattern. Remove excess pastillage edges and allow piece to dry on the glass.

DRY ALL CUT PIECES on glass or plexiglass dusted with cornstarch. After drying about 14 hours or more, lay another piece of glass on top of piece, turn over and remove first glass. Dry another twelve or 14 hours on this side.

IF PASTILLAGE BREAKS because of excess working, knead in a few drops of water to soften.

ADD A LITTLE SOFT PASTILLAGE to rolled scraps and knead together before rolling again.

PASTILLAGE THICKNESS CHART

FINE	▬▬▬▬▬▬	1 millimeter
STANDARD	▭▭▭▭▭▭	2 millimeters
SEMI-THICK	▭▭▭▭▭▭	4 millimeters
THICK	▭▭▭▭▭▭	6 millimeters
EXTRA-THICK	▭▭▭▭▭▭	8 millimeters

A CAKE FOR MOTHER

MAKE THE PICTURE FRAME. Use any round or oval frame as a mold—diameter should be 9″ to 13″. Roll out untinted pastillage semi-thick and press gently over cornstarch-dusted frame. Then trim off edges neatly. Dry on frame.

Trace inner edge of frame for pattern for background. Tint pastillage black (allow plenty of time for color to develop after tinting), roll out semi-thick and cut background. Dry. Trace outer edge of frame to use as backing, and cut out of untinted semi-thick pastillage. Dry.

Pipe curves, swirls and beading on frame with soft royal icing and tube 1. Dry, then spray or paint frame gold. Attach background and backing to frame with stiff icing. Roll a cylinder of pastillage, 2″ high, to use as prop for frame.

MAKE GUM PASTE FLOWERS—two roses, four buds and about 25 forget-me-nots in sprays (see page 126). You will also need five sprays of wired gum paste leaves, cut with a leaf cutter. When flowers are dry, attach with stiff royal icing to frame.

MAKE FAN by cutting eleven standard pastillage strips, using Wilton Way patterns. When dry, decorate with soft royal icing. Dry again and paint icing trim gold. Thread cord through holes.

PREPARE CAKE as described on page 110. Trim an 18″ round cake, 3″ high to hexagon shape. Place on 26″ cake board edged with puffed foil. Cover with rolled fondant and edge with tube 18 stars. Set picture on cake, propping with cylinder, drape ribbon and arrange fan. The little gift in front of the picture is a bottle of real perfume. Serves 60.

In Mexico, Christmas is the most important holiday of the year, and no Mexican home is without its festive cake. This cheerful little lighted church is as pretty as a Christmas card and makes a lovely decoration for your home, or to give a friend. Since so much care goes into its making, we suggest you build it on a permanent pastillage "drum" or platform rather than a cake.

The entire church is built of pastillage. Before starting construction, study the recipe and information on pastillage on page 112. Prepare your pattern pieces by transferring them accurately to light cardboard and cutting out. All patterns are in The Wilton Way Pattern Book. Sort the patterns by color—white for all roofs, grey for all towers, green for main church walls and red for chimney and side extension walls. All pieces are rolled to standard thickness except the green door and window frames and the brown main door, which are semi-thick. Refer to thickness chart, page 113.

PREPARE DRUM. Make your own patterns for the drum. You will need two rectangular pieces 3" x 18" and two pieces 3" x 12" for the sides. Also needed are three supports for inside the drum, each 3" x 8". Top of drum is 12" x 18".

Make a recipe of pastillage (page 112), roll semi-thick, and cut the pieces. Cut base for church also. Dry on one side, turn over and dry again.

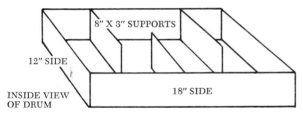

PREPARE CAKE BOARD. This is made of ⅜" plywood, cut to 20" x 26". Glue 1" x 1" strips of wood on underside for legs. On center of top of board draw a 12" x 18" rectangle with a pencil. Draw 8" lines within rectangle where supports will stand. Pipe a line of medium consistency royal icing on one 18" side and adjacent 12" side with tube 5. Set one 18" strip of drum on line, pipe icing on its 3" side and then set a 12" side in position, forming right angle. They will stand by themselves at once. Add other two sides in the same way. Then pipe lines of icing on the board for the supports and set in position. Dry, then pipe a line on top edge of all drum pieces and set top on drum. Fill in cracks or uneven places with icing, smooth with finger and dry. Attach puffed foil to the board (page 110).

CUT PIECES FOR BUILDING. Follow patterns very ac-

curately. Make a second recipe of pastillage using sheet gelatin. Following directions on page 112, roll out to standard thickness and cut all white roof pieces. Divide remaining pastillage in three parts. Tint grey, green and deep red. Roll out and cut the colored pieces, following the order in which the pastillage was tinted. Roll to standard thickness except for semi-thick door and window frames. Cut interior openings first.

Knead red, grey and green scraps together until you arrive at a brown color, roll to semi-thick and cut the two doors. Dry all pieces on two sides.

Hand-model a bell about ½" high. Insert thread through bell while still wet, leaving end hang out of top. When dry, paint with gold paint. Model a grey ball about ¾" in diameter for beneath cross.

ADD DETAILS. With a sharp pencil, draw bricks on grey pieces. Horizontal lines are about ⅛" apart.

The trees are natural twigs. Model two white pastillage cones about 2" wide at base and 2" high. Insert twigs in cones and let dry.

Secure wax paper to back of walls with soft royal icing, covering the window openings. Turn over and pipe window designs with tube 1. When dry, carefully remove wax paper and replace it with colored clear acetate or cellophane, attaching with zigzags to the inside of the walls.

Pipe designs on door with soft icing. Attach window and door frames to front with icing. Trim with tube 2 beading. Attach cross above door.

ASSEMBLE BUILDING with medium royal icing, tinted to match the pastillage pieces. Do this in sections, using the same method you used for the drum. Smooth edges neatly as you assemble. First, erect the walls of the main church on the base and add walls of the side extension. When thoroughly dry, add the roofs, holding in position until set. Dry again. Assemble pointed roofs for the two towers. Now attach the side gable roofs to the main roof and the chimney to the side extension roof. Build the two towers. After arched window section is put on main tower, lay a toothpick across top of walls and hang bell. Attach roofs to towers.

FINISH THE CAKE. Smooth soft icing over all roofs and sprinkle with granulated sugar. Secure ball on top of main tower. Make a cross from stiff florists' wire, cover with icing and attach to ball.

Ice drum smoothly and dry. Set church on drum, slightly to the back, and attach trees. Heap soft icing on top of cake, letting it drape down the sides. Sprinkle with granulated sugar. Pipe "icicles" on trees with tube 3. Your Christmas scene is finished!

FLORIDO, A MEXICAN CHRISTMAS CUSTOM

This charming cake shows two young girls in the costume of their region selling poinsettias in pottery vases, just as girls do in Mexico each year.

MAKING THE DOLLS

Except for the head, all parts of these dolls are modeled by hand, so practice is necessary to achieve an attractive, well-proportioned figure. Diagrams are in The Wilton Way Pattern Book.

Gum glue is used to join two wet pieces of gum paste or pastillage, or one wet and one dry. Add one tablespoon gum arabic to one cup of water in a small jar. Shake well and keep covered. To join two dried pieces, use royal icing.

Make base for figure. Roll pastillage semi-thick (page 113), cut base with Wilton Way pattern and immediately form into cone, leaving a 1″ oval open at top. Dry thoroughly.

Make gum paste head and torso. Use freshly-made gum paste (recipe page 112) and Mexican mold to form the head. Tint gum paste, add a little cornstarch and work well. Form a 1½″ ball and press it into the mold. Remove from mold and smooth back of head. Dip a toothpick in gum glue and insert into neck, leaving about two-thirds of it exposed.

Model upper torso by hand, using the Wilton Way diagram. Start with a ball of gum paste about 1½″ in diameter. After torso is shaped, dip exposed toothpick on head into gum glue and insert in torso for support. Lay on bed of cotton to dry. Attach torso to base with royal icing. Dry.

Using the same gum paste as was used for the torso, model the arms. Diagram is in Wilton Way Pattern Book. Start with a 1″ ball of gum paste. Form into log, then shape elbows and hands. Trim part where arm joins shoulder. Make a "V" cut between thumb and forefinger. Cut between other fingers. Roll each finger to shape and elongate. Place hands in natural position, bend elbow and lay on cotton to dry. Make a left and right arm.

Make up the faces. Blush the cheeks with rouge, then use white, black and colored sharp pencils for the rest of the make-up.

DRESS THE DOLLS

Make skirt. Make your own pattern for the two-piece skirts that meet at side. Experiment on the molded figure with tissue paper. Roll brown-tinted gum paste to standard thickness, cut back of skirt, brush figure with gum glue at waist back and attach skirt back, pleating at sides. Do the same for the skirt front, concealing seam at sides with pleat.

Roll blue gum paste thin as possible for the sleeves. Cut a rectangle about 3½″ long x 3″. Make tiny pleats and attach to top of arm with gum glue. Pleat lower edge and attach to wrist with glue, flattening pleats with your finger. Attach arm to shoulder by melting sealing wax and dropping on flattened end of arm. Hold to shoulder until set. Using pattern, cut the cape-like bodice. Brush upper part of torso with gum glue and put bodice on figure, letting neckline rise on neck. Cut a ⅜″ wide strip of black gum paste, cutting one edge with pinking shears. Attach to edge of bodice with gum glue. Paint two black stripes with paste food color. Pipe hair in front only with tube 1 and dry.

Make turbans. Roll gum paste to standard thickness and cut two streamers, about 3″ long x 1″. Pleat lightly and secure to back of head with gum glue. Now roll gum paste thin as possible and cut

a strip about 1″ x 6″. Wrap around head, letting soft pleats form and finish with a twist at the front. Complete piping of hair.

MAKE LANTERNS from stiff florists' wire about 10″ long. Make a hook at the top and wrap in brown crepe paper. Cut a 1½″ square of thick gum paste, groove with a knife and curve around to form a cylinder. Make a hole on either side with a pin. When dry, decorate with food color, pass a thread through the holes and hang on hook.

MAKE FLOWERS AND BOWLS

CUT POINSETTIA PETALS from thin gum paste using Wilton Way patterns. Each flower is made of about 20 petals in three sizes. Dry petals on cotton to curve. Pipe a mound of red royal icing on wax paper and assemble the petals in three rows, starting at the outside with the longest petals. When dry, add yellow stamens with tube 1. Mount the flowers on wires (page 326).

HAND-MODEL four bowls from freshly made gum paste, 2″, 1½″, 1″ and ¾″ in diameter. When dry, fill three larger bowls with green royal icing and arrange flowers with artificial ferns. Hand-model a tiny bird, 1″ long from freshly made white gum paste. When dry, paint dappled blue feathers with food color. Fill smallest bowl with granulated sugar and attach bird to rim with royal icing.

MAKE THE CAKE

MAKE THE DRUM of semi-thick pastillage tinted a pale green. Make your own pattern. The two long sides are 1¼″ x 15″, two shorter sides 1¼″ x 9½″. You will need 3 supports, 7″ x 1¼″. Top is 9½″ x 15″. Allow all parts to dry, then secure the sides to the top as described on page 115. Add supports as shown in diagram. Let dry thoroughly.

PREPARE CAKE AND BOARD. Bake a 12″ x 18″ cake and cover with rolled fondant as described on page 110. Set on a 20″ x 26″ plywood board, ¾″ thick. Cover with puffed foil (see page 110). Center the cake on the board. Place drum on cake. Pipe tube 5 dots in vertical stripes on sides and edge with tube 7 balls. Pipe tube 9 balls at base of cake and polka-dot the rest with tube 2. Now attach the dolls and flowers on the drum. Cake serves 54.

This cake is an outstanding example of the dramatic quality of Mexican decorating. A bride dressed in 19th century costume dreams of her life to come.

MOLD PASTILLAGE BASE. Roll an oval cylinder of fresh pastillage (page 112). Make it about 1½″ in diameter and 4¾″ high. Increase diameter at base to about 2″ so it will stand firmly. Dip a 6½″ dowel rod, ¼″ thick, in water and insert in cylinder down to the base. Dry 24 to 48 hours.

MOLD TORSO AND HEAD in Mexican mold. Knead color into freshly made gum paste to tint. Add a little cornstarch and work well. Form a long roll and press into front half of mold. Push the gum paste firmly into the top of the mold to define features. Make sure gum paste is level with mold. Trim off excess at waist. Mold back the same way. Remove back by grasping waist and lifting out quickly. Brush with gum glue (page 116) and lay a bamboo stick from head to waist. Remove the front half and press on back half. Smooth seams.

Coat the protruding dowel rod, and the top of the base with gum glue and slide the torso over the dowel rod. Stretch the neck a little and tilt the head. Pinch the waist to thin it. Dry thoroughly. Pad the hips and the bust with a little more gum paste, attaching with gum glue. Dry. Make up the face as described on page 116.

HAND-MODEL THE ARMS from freshly made white gum paste. Only practice will help you to form a natural looking arm. Roll a cylinder of gum paste about 3″ long. Flatten one end into a spoon shape for the hand and trim off the other end to a slant where it will fit against shoulder. Cut a "V" shape to indicate thumb and forefinger, then make three more cuts for other fingers. Shape each finger and the thumb by rolling between your fingers. Since you are making a gloved hand, it will be a little bulky. Curve arm at elbow, position fingers and lay on cotton to dry. Make a left and a right arm.

MAKE PASTILLAGE UNDERSKIRT to support the costume. Roll out freshly made pastillage semi-thick (see page 113), and cut the front, using Wilton Way pattern. Brush the waistline of the figure with gum glue and attach. Cut the back of the underskirt and attach to figure with gum glue, letting it overlap the front. Smooth seam with fingers. The edge will fall in a graceful train. If necessary, place cotton under back of underskirt to support it till dry. This takes 24 to 48 hours.

DRESS THE DOLL

All clothing is made from gum paste aged several days or more, and rolled very thin. Treat the gum paste like fabric, letting it fall in graceful folds. Work very fast. Examine the picture well, then cut your pieces just as you would cut a real dress. Always brush the body with gum glue (page 116) at the point you will attach the gum paste piece. If pieces are too big, trim with sharp scissors.

MAKE BODICE. Cut rough shape for back, about 2½″ long x 2″. Brush back of figure with glue and smooth on, letting top rise for high collar. Trim at neck, armholes and sides. Do the front the same way. Smooth seams, then dry thoroughly.

MAKE SKIRT. Use front underskirt pattern and attach at waist, forming small pleats at side so skirt drapes smoothly. Cut back using back underskirt pattern. Fold in the two sides and attach at waist, slightly overlapping front. Form pleats as you attach so the skirt drapes in folds. Cut long ¼″ streamers and attach on right side of skirt.

Cut a drape about 6½″ long and 4″ wide. Finely pleat one end and attach to lower left side of bodice, letting it fall to the hemline. Flatten pleats on bodice. Make little bows from ¼″ strips and attach to streamers with gum glue. Dry.

MAKE SLEEVES. Cut sleeve about 3½″ long with a very wide armhole. Pleat armhole, brush arm with gum glue, and drape sleeve on arm. Leave area at top of arm uncovered where it will join shoulder. Dry on cotton. Drip sealing wax on uncovered tops of arms and hold to shoulder until set.

ADD FINISHING TOUCHES. Pipe hair with medium royal icing in a cone with cut tip. Using tube 1, cover yoke area on bodice with lines of soft icing and add tiny dots. Pipe embroidery on skirt. Dry.

Gather ⅜″ lace for a ruffled effect and attach around yoke with short lines of soft royal icing. Add lace trim to hem the same way. Cut veil 14″ x 10″ from fine net. Gather on 10″ side and secure to back of head with icing. Model a 1″ x ⅝″ gum paste book, dry, and attach to bride's hand.

MAKE MEN'S ACCESSORIES. Roll black gum paste into a stick about 3″ long. Add a knob and dry. Paint knob with silver paint. Dry. Model two gloves in grey gum paste about 1″ long, using a real glove as a guide. Cover stick with plastic wrap and lay gloves over it to dry. Make top hat from black gum paste. Cut a 1¼″ circle for brim and a ¾″ circle for top. Dry top flat. Dry brim slightly curved on cotton. Form a cylinder from a 1″ x 3″ strip and attach to brim and top with gum glue. Dry thoroughly.

MAKE THE SETTING FOR THE BRIDE

Before building the pastillage furnishings for the scene, review the information on page 112, study the thickness chart on page 113 and prepare and assemble your patterns. All are in The Wilton Way Pattern Book. Be very accurate when cutting the pieces so the furniture will have a professional look when assembled. Roll out pastillage, cut the piece, then remove excess pastillage from edges, leaving the piece undisturbed to dry on both sides.

BUILD THE FIREPLACE

Cut white pieces. The base of the fireplace is cut from thick pastillage, the back semi-thick and the front and exterior sides from standard thickness. Dry all on two sides. Interior side pieces are cut after fireplace is partially assembled. The mirror is a real mirror, cut by a glass cutter to pattern.

Cut "marble" mantel. Lay small pieces of green and black gum paste on white pastillage. Fold over a few times, roll out thick and cut mantel.

Assemble the fireplace with medium royal icing. Lay back flat and pipe a tube 4 line of icing about half way up one long edge. Set exterior side piece in position. Prop to steady. Attach second side piece. Pipe icing on front edges of side pieces and secure front. Attach mantel, then mirror. Dry.

Roll out white pastillage to standard thickness and cut two interior side pieces. Brush gum glue (page 116) on edges of front and on back of fireplace and attach wet pastillage pieces, curving to fit. Dry. Pipe lines of icing on base and set fireplace upright on base.

Edge with beading and decorate with curves and arabesques, using tube 3 and medium icing. Make "logs" from brown gum paste, none larger than a pencil. Cut on a slant to lengths of 1″ to 2½″. When dry, pile in fireplace, securing with icing.

Hand-model the two vases and clock from gum paste, using Wilton Way diagrams. Paint flower design on vases with thinned food color. Edge vases with gilt paint and paint gilt numbers, hands and trim on clock. Roll green pastillage semi-thick and cut an 11½″ circle for rug. Dry.

BUILD THE CHAIR AND TABLE

Cut the pieces. Follow patterns very accurately when cutting all pieces. Make a recipe of pastillage using sheet gelatin (page 112) and tint brown. Following thickness listed on patterns, cut the chair and table pieces. Dry all on two sides.

Assemble the furniture with medium royal icing tinted to match. Pipe a line of icing on two adjacent edges of table top. Set one leg section in position, upside down. Pipe a line of icing on short side of one side piece and set against leg. Add second leg section and side piece the same way. Wipe excess icing from outside of piece as you proceed. Dry.

Assemble the chair seat, leg sections and side pieces and dry upside down. Lay back of chair on table, pipe icing on arm pieces where they will attach to back and set in position. Prop until dry.

Upholster the chair. The upholstery is cut from standard thickness gum paste using patterns, and padded with cotton. Add texture, if you like, with a special steel rolling pin.

Set chair upright and attach a little cotton to seat with gum glue (page 116). Cut seat upholstery and smooth over seat, folding at corners and gluing to legs and side pieces. Press assembled back and arms on seat while upholstery is wet to mark final position on seat. Set aside.

Lay back of chair on table, and pad with cotton. Cut back upholstery, and attach, just as for seat. Cut oval arm upholstery and secure to arms. Also cut the oval table mat. Dry, then secure assembled back and arms to chair seat with icing. Dry.

Add trims. Outline furniture with tube 1 and soft icing, then add beading trim to upholstery with same tube. Secure oval table mat to table.

PREPARE CAKE

Make patterns for drum. Top is 13½″ square. You will need four 13⅜″ strips for sides and two 12″ strips for inner supports, all 1¼″ wide. Cut from standard thickness pastillage, dry and assemble as diagram on page 115.

Decorate cake. Bake a 15″ square cake, 3″ high. Cover with rolled fondant and set on 24″ diameter round cake board. (See page 110.) Set drum on cake. Using soft royal icing, decorate drum with tube 3 beading and scallops.

Edge base of cake with tube 5 balls, then pipe three tube 3 scallops on each side, ending with fleurs-de-lis on top of cake. Make twelve little sprays of gum paste orange blossoms, buds and leaves (page 125) and attach to cake with icing.

Make bride's bouquet. Pipe about 20 baby roses (page 124). Assemble with orange blossom buds and artificial fern. Make a bow and streamers from thinly rolled gum paste and attach to bouquet with gum glue while wet. Lay on table to dry.

Place rug, furniture and bride on the drum. Lay the men's accessories on the chair. This Mexican confection slices into 42 pieces, 1″ x 2″.

This typical example of the advanced Mexican technique is a real challenge for the decorator. The two dolls are dressed in detailed replicas of costumes shown in a French fashion journal of the last century. See a close-up picture on page 111. After some practice, you may want to make three-dimensional replicas of other drawings or paintings.

Since Mexican decorators rely on observation and skill in draping, no patterns are given.

Study the close-up picture well. Experiment with tissue patterns held against the molded doll before rolling and cutting the gum paste clothing. To drape the doll figures in soft folds of thin gum paste and to add the tucks, ruffles and ribbon trims is a real lesson in dressmaking.

Review the directions for the bride doll on page 118, and remember to mold the figures in freshly made gum paste (recipe, page 112), and to use gum paste made several days in advance for the clothing. Gum glue recipe is on page 116.

MAKE THE LADY IN BLUE

MOLD THE FIGURE. The basic figure is done just as described on page 118, gluing the gum paste torso to a pastillage base. Thin the waist, tilt the head and dry. Pad the figure by gluing on more gum paste at bust and hips. Add a pastillage underskirt, keeping the front rather straight, and letting the back drape into a train. The Wilton Way patterns for the bride doll's underskirt may be modified for this. Dry for 24 to 48 hours. Make-up the face.

Do THE SKIRT FIRST. Cut a strip of white gum paste about 1″ wide and texture it with a grooved rolling pin or with thin edge of a ruler. Attach to side of figure from hip to hem. Do the same on the other side. Trim strip narrower at top. Cut the back of the skirt and attach. For the draped front of the skirt you must work very quickly. Roll a strip of gum paste very thin, brush edges of white strips with glue, and attach in folds.

MAKE WHITE BLOUSE by gluing a strip of thin gum paste to front of figure, ending at hipline. Add a strip for a high collar. Cut jacket back and smooth to figure. Cut two-piece front of jacket, allowing enough width to fold back at front into lapels. Glue lapels at waistline and shoulders.

HAND-MODEL THE ARMS and dry. (See Wilton Way diagram.) Cover outside of arm with a narrow strip of white gum paste textured with a rolling pin or ruler. Complete sleeve with blue gum paste. Add ruffle at wrist. Use royal icing to pipe trim on gloves. Attach arms to shoulder with melted sealing wax and smooth armhole.

ADD TRIMS. Cut tiny strips and attach for ribbon trim on sleeves and skirt. You must work very quickly to make the pleated double ruffles. Cut ½″ strips of thin gum paste, paint a thin line of glue in center and pleat. Press with thin edge of ruler for center crease, brush a line of glue on skirt and attach. Pleats will conceal joinings as you add more lengths of ruffle. Add a white single ruffle to back of skirt, then a blue double ruffle.

Pipe the coiffure with a cut cone and medium royal icing. Dry. Cut a gum paste circle 1½″ in diameter, hand-model the little hat and dry on head. Attach to head with icing. Trim with gum paste bows and real feathers. Hand-model a gum paste fan, add a gold cord, dry and attach to hands with royal icing.

THE LADY IN ROSE

MOLD THE TORSO and attach to pastillage base just as for bride doll, page 118. Add pastillage underskirt, keeping smooth and straight in front. A slightly different technique is used for clothing—sections are cut in one piece without a break at waist. Cut a gum paste shape for front of dress and smooth to figure. Trim square neck and arm holes and trim at hem if too long.

Do THE FULL-LENGTH COAT in sections, one for each side front and one or more for back. Brush glue on upper part of figure and attach front sections first. Trim at shoulder, neck and armhole. Add back sections and trim. Smooth seams on upper part of figure and let folds conceal seams in skirt.

Do TRIMS when figure is clothed and dried. Striped pattern on dress is brushed on with food color. Coat is covered with cornelli (punto perdido) done with cut cone and soft icing. Add icing design on front edges of coat. Ruffles are made just as for Lady in Blue and attached to hem. Model arms, attach sleeves and add ruffles at wrist before securing to figure. Cover with cornelli lace. Hand-model hat, dry and put on head. Add gum paste ribbon trim and tiny piped forget-me-nots (page 124). The parasol is hand-modeled over a bamboo stick. Attach to hand with icing.

CREATE THE PARK-LIKE SETTING

THE CAKE IS A RECTANGLE 16″ x 20″ x 3″. Prepare as described on page 110 and set on plywood board 24″ x 28″. Cover with foil and pipe tube 9 ball border at base.

THE TREES ARE TWIGS about 15″ high. Form green

pastillage cones, 2″ wide at base and about 2″ high. Dip twigs in water and insert in cones. Pipe leaves over branches with cone with tip cut in "V" shape.

Tape baby roses and calla lilies (pages 124 and 125) into clusters and curve wire into a circle at base to stand upright.

Figure pipe several icing doves from royal icing and dry. Pipe grey royal icing rocks on wax paper.

Assemble the cake, securing pieces with royal icing. The pond is an oval mirror, about 6″ x 8″, set to side rear of cake. Set trees on the rear corners. Place rocks in front of the trees and around pond.

Sprinkle thickly with green-tinted coconut for "grass", then place the wired clusters of flowers, concealing bases with more coconut. Set the dolls in position. Attach a bird to a tree branch and set others on the "pavement". Attach clusters of calla lilies to the front of the cake and heap coconut around them.

Although this scene was set on a cake, you may prefer to cover a 16″ x 20″ pastillage drum with rolled fondant so you can preserve this showpiece.

This masterpiece of Mexican decorating serves about 80 guests.

MEXICAN PIPED FLOWERS

There are two basic ways of making flowers in the Mexican method of decorating—piped with royal icing and cut from rolled gum paste. Realism is essential to both the piped and gum paste flowers.

Flowers piped using the Mexican method are very small and dainty. They are often used as garlands by attaching them in a series along a piece of florists' wire, attached to wire stems or secured directly to the cake with icing.

CLOUDS. These charming Mexican flowers are commonly used for bouquets and wedding cakes. They are slightly larger than forget-me-nots (see below).

Fit a decorating bag with tube 59° and fill with white icing. Attach a square of wax paper to a flat flower nail with a dot of icing. Press out five tiny heart-shaped petals so the flower, when completed, is about ½″ in diameter. Dry.

For use in garlands, attach flowers with icing to an 8″ long piece of florists' wire. To mount on wire stems, use very fine florists' wire and follow the instructions in Chapter Twenty.

BABY ROSES. Made directly on pieces of florists' wire, these are very dainty blossoms and make beautiful petite bouquets. These flowers are more efficiently done by making 25 or more at once, as each row of petals must dry before adding the next.

Make a small loop in one end of a fine piece of florists' wire. With tube 59° in a vertical position, wrap a ribbon of icing around loop to form a bud. Dry. Add a row of three upstanding petals so they are slightly taller than the bud. Dry.

Change to a lighter tint of icing, then pipe a row of three or four petals, opening them out a bit. Dry. Pipe the final row of petals opening out even farther. Dry. Pipe tube 2 sepals on flower. Dry.

Make leaves on wires (see Chapter Twenty) using a parchment bag with the tip cut in a "V" shape. Jiggle hand while piping to create the ruffled effect of the leaf. Dry.

FORGET-ME-NOTS. These tiny, delicate flowers are used in hundreds of ways on Mexican cakes. They are made without using a tube.

Pipe on wax paper, using a parchment cone with the tip cut. Pipe a yellow dot, then surround it with five blue dots, piping them close together. The flower should be less than ½″ in diameter. Dry.

To make garlands, attach flowers with dots of icing to an 8″ long piece of florists' wire. To mount on wire stems, use very thin florists' wire and follow the instructions given in Chapter Twenty for making calyx and attaching the flower.

LILY OF THE VALLEY. This familiar flower is often used for wedding ornaments and on wedding cakes.

Make centers for flowers by thinning green icing until it is very soft. Make a tiny loop in the end of a piece of very fine florists' wire. Dip loop into the icing, turn it slightly and remove. The icing should form a smooth teardrop shape on the wire. Make a hook in the wire and hang upside down to dry.

Using tube 60 in a vertical position, hold it against the bud and press out a ribbon of icing, turning wire to wrap it around the bud in a bell shape. Let dry about five minutes, then make five or six little cuts in the edge to make the petals. Insert wire into styrofoam to dry.

To create spray, tape three buds together, then attach six pairs of flowers with floral tape.

MEXICAN GUM PASTE FLOWERS

These delicate rolled gum paste flowers are made using special Mexican cutters and a method that is slightly different from the American method. Both piped and gum paste flowers are used together on a Mexican cake, usually on wires.

CALLA LILY. This little flower is used for small bouquets, in tiny baskets and in garden scenes.

Cut thin florists' wire into pieces 4″ long. To make stamen, model a piece of yellow gum paste around wire into a roll ½″ long and about as thick as a toothpick. Dry. Dip into egg white and sprinkle with granulated sugar. Dry.

Roll white gum paste very thin and cut petal with Mexican calla lily cutter. Brush egg white on round part of petal. Lay stamen at center of petal. Fold half of petal over, then overlap other half to form an open cone. Bend point of petal down slightly, lay on a cotton ball and dry.

Cut leaves with Mexican cutter. Mark veins gently with a knife. Attach a fine piece of florists' wire to back of leaf with egg white and a small piece of gum paste. Dry. Tape flowers and leaves into small bouquets with floral tape.

ORANGE BLOSSOM. This is the most frequently used flower for wedding cakes. Make buds and flower centers the same as for the lily of the valley. Dry.

Roll out gum paste very thin and cut a ¼″ wide strip. Make tiny cuts along one long edge to form a fringe. Attach around flower center so fringe extends beyond it. Dry. Paint tips of fringe with yellow food color and dry again.

Cut petals with Mexican cutter. Hold flower center upside down and attach five petals around it with egg white. Bend outward slightly. Insert wires into styrofoam to dry.

LILY OF THE VALLEY

CALLA LILY

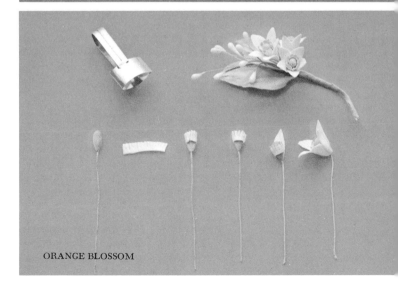

ORANGE BLOSSOM

LARGE ROSE

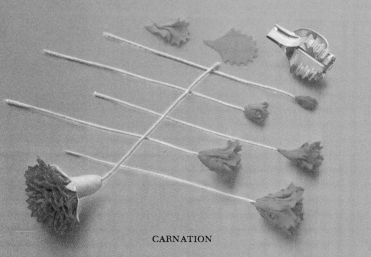

CARNATION

FORGET-ME-NOTS

LARGE ROSE. This flower, one of the most beautiful, is made using five heart-shaped Mexican cutters. Begin by tinting a small ball of gum paste (about the size of a cherry) a very deep color. Then use a piece of this gum paste to tint a larger amount to a very light color.

Roll light colored gum paste very thin and cut nine petals, using the largest cutter. Keep covered to prevent drying. Working with one petal at a time, press all around edge to smooth it, then bend up the two curves of the heart to form small rolls and make two pleats at the point. Place on a cotton ball to preserve the shape and dry.

Darken gum paste and cut eight petals with the next smaller cutter. Curve and pleat the same way and dry. Continue tinting gum paste progressively darker and using smaller cutters and cut seven petals for the third row, six for the fourth and four for the last and darkest row. Let all petals dry.

Assemble by piping a 4″ circle with royal icing and tube 5. Press first row of petals into icing, propping with cotton. Dry. Make a circle of icing on these petals and attach second row. Dry. Add the third and fourth row the same way, then pipe a mound of icing in the center and insert some stamens. Press the final row of petals in place. Dry at least 24 hours.

To make a bud, attach two larger petals together, then attach a second and third size petal on top and in the opposite direction. Dry.

CARNATION. The traditional "gentleman's flower". Tint gum paste a deep red. Cut a piece of medium weight florists' wire 10″ long. Bend the end into a small loop. Roll gum paste very thin and cut petals with Mexican carnation cutter. Cut two petals in half and make two tiny pleats on straight edge of each. Wrap one around loop in wire, attaching with egg white to form bud. Add the other three the same as the first. Dry. Begin to add complete petals until carnation reaches the size of a natural one. Dry flower each time five petals have been added.

For calyx, model a cone and slowly slide it up wire. Attach to base of carnation with egg white. Cut four or five triangular sepals and attach to calyx. Smooth with fingers and dry.

FORGET-ME-NOTS. This flower is frequently used on Mexican cakes because of its charming appearance.

Make flower centers the same as for the lily of the valley (page 125). Dry. Roll blue gum paste very thin and cut flower with Mexican cutter. Push end of wire through flower and attach to flower center with egg white. Lift petals slightly, then push wire into styrofoam to dry.

CHAPTER NINE

Continental Decorating with Chocolate

For centuries, European chefs have evolved this elegant method which combines fine baking with decoration that indicates and enhances the flavor of the delicious confection itself. Only the finest ingredients are used, and the delicate cakes, fillings and icings are frequently perfumed with liqueurs for an excellent flavor.

Working within this framework, and using basic mixtures, every Continental creation is unique.

Of course, chocolate is not an ingredient in every Continental dessert, but its use is so widespread and its decorative possibilities so great, we have made it the subject of this chapter. Almost all the recipes that follow are from *The Wilton Book of Classic Desserts*.

HOW TO TEMPER CHOCOLATE

Before molding chocolate, or using it for cut-out trims, it must be tempered. Heat water in the bottom of a 1½ quart double boiler to 175°F. Remove from heat, place cut-up chocolate, one cup at a time, in the top half of the boiler. Stir occasionally until melted and at a temperature of 110°F. Remove top pan and cool the chocolate until stiff.

To mold, or make cut-out shapes, reheat dark chocolate to 90-92°F. Reheat milk chocolate to 86-88°F before using.

Do not attempt to work with chocolate in hot, humid weather. Summer coating, which has a higher melting point, may be substituted.

CHOCOLATE BOXES present dessert in an elegant manner. Spread chocolate or pastel summer coating on wax paper, cool and cut into 2″ squares. Cut cake into 2″ cubes, fill and cover the top with Continental Buttercream (page 129) or jam. Pipe dots of icing on sides of cake and attach chocolate squares. Garnish with rosettes of Crème Chantilly (page 129), cherries or chocolate cigarettes. Use any of the cake recipes in this chapter. Match the flavors of the jam, Buttercream and Crème Chantilly to the boxes—cherry, strawberry or raspberry for pink, mint or lemon for yellow and chocolate for chocolate. Page 128 tells how to cut the chocolate squares, page 140 how to make the cigarettes.

Making flat chocolate cut-outs and using them to decorate various confections is a frequent practice in Continental decorating.

After tempering and reheating chocolate (see page 127) spread thinly and evenly on a piece of wax paper. Be sure to work quickly before chocolate begins to harden. After it has set, cut shapes with a pizza cutter, an X-acto knife or cookie cutters. To remove shapes from the paper when hardened, invert the wax paper onto another sheet and peel it from the back of the chocolate. The shapes can then be collected and the remainder of the chocolate saved to be used again.

These chocolate cut-outs can be made ahead and stored in a cool (55-60°F) place, away from sunlight or dampness. They should never be attempted in the summer. If it becomes necessary to work with chocolate during the summer months, pastel or chocolate summer coating should be substituted. It does not have to be tempered before using. Just place the cut-up coating in the top of a double boiler and heat to melting point.

Chocolate cut-outs can be used to decorate many types of desserts. Petits fours, ice cream, bombes and mousses are just a few. The cut-outs can be set vertically, at an angle or horizontally as a garnish that can make even a plain dessert elegant.

MAKING A FANCIFUL FAN TORTE

MAKE CUT-OUTS. (Directions above). Spread chocolate on wax paper and let set. Cut 1″ strips into eight 3″ rectangles. Cut these in half diagonally to form triangles. Next cut three 1″ round circles and

cut two in half. Set aside in a cool, dry place.

PREPARE CAKE. Bake cake in 11″ x 17″ jelly roll pan using Chocolate Génoise recipe. Chill, remove crusts then cut into 2″ x 16″ strips. Hold them in place and ice gently with Chocolate Continental Buttercream. This will insure that the icing is the same thickness throughout. Take one strip and roll it jelly roll style. Stand it on end and add a second strip, wrapping it around. Continue adding strips until the cake is about 8″ in diameter.

DECORATE TORTE. Ice sides with Chocolate Continental Buttercream then cover with chopped toasted almonds. Divide top of torte into sixteenths. Using Crème Chantilly (see recipe below), fill each section with tube 21 shells. In center of torte, pipe a tube 18 circle of Crème Chantilly and pipe six rosettes on it. On edge of torte, in the center of each section, pipe a tube 18 rosette. Refrigerate until ready to serve. Immediately before serving, insert chocolate cut-out circles into circle in center of torte, between rosettes. Insert chocolate cut-out triangles between each section of shells on top of torte. Serves 16.

GÉNOISE

This a delicate butter sponge cake.

6 eggs
1 cup sugar
1 teaspoon vanilla
1 cup sifted flour
½ cup clarified butter, melted and cooled

Combine eggs, sugar and vanilla in a large bowl and stir until just combined. Set bowl over saucepan containing 1″ or 2″ hot water. Place over very low heat for five or ten minutes or until eggs are lukewarm. Stir several times to prevent cooking at the bottom. Remove from heat and beat at high speed for 10 or 15 minutes, or until it has tripled in volume and draws out in ribbon form when a spoon is pulled out of it.

Sprinkle the flour, a little at a time, on top of the whipped mixture. Fold in very gently. Then fold in the butter. Do not over mix.

Pour the batter into well-buttered pans, dusted lightly with flour, and bake at 350°F for about 25 minutes, or until cake pulls away from sides of pan. Remove from pans immediately and cool on rack. Makes two 8″ layers or one 11″ x 17″ sheet.

CHOCOLATE GÉNOISE. Follow the recipe above, but substitute ¼ cup dark sifted cocoa for ¼ cup of the flour. Sift flour and cocoa together.

CONTINENTAL BUTTERCREAM

⅔ cup sugar
⅓ cup water
⅛ teaspoon cream of tartar
5 egg yolks
1 cup soft butter

Mix sugar, water and cream of tartar in a sauce-pan. Stir over low heat until sugar is completely dissolved. Raise heat and boil without stirring until syrup tests 238°F.

Beat egg yolks until fluffy. Then pour hot syrup in a thin stream into the yolks, beating constantly. It will become thick and light. Refrigerate until completely cooled. Beat in softened butter, a little at a time until very fluffy. Makes two cups. May be stored in refrigerator a week or two, then rebeaten while chilled to restore texture.

CHOCOLATE BUTTERCREAM. Beat 3 ounces melted, unsweetened chocolate and 3 tablespoons of cognac into two cups Buttercream.

MOCHA BUTTERCREAM. Beat 5 ounces melted, semi-sweet chocolate, 4 tablespoons of extra strong coffee and 3 tablespoons cognac into two cups of Continental Buttercream.

CRÈME CHANTILLY

This is the stabilized whipped cream used for piping from a decorating tube. Add 1 teaspoon gelatin to 2 tablespoons cold water in a metal or pyrex cup. Set in a small pan of boiling water and heat without stirring until gelatin dissolves and looks clear. Beat this mixture into 1 cup heavy cream just as cream begins to thicken. Beat in 2 tablespoons sugar and ½ teaspoon vanilla. Chill.

MOLDING WITH CHOCOLATE

Molding with chocolate is an art in itself. Practice is essential to recognize how much chocolate is needed, how long to let it set and how to remove it from the molds easily. If you don't succeed with your first try, remelt the chocolate and try again. When molding chocolate, a mistake is never wasted.

TYPES AND CARE OF MOLDS

The molds used for chocolate can be either metal or plastic. Metal molds are more durable, but plastic molds are very satisfactory.

The molds are prepared by polishing the inside surface with a soft cloth so it is both clean and highly polished or the chocolate will not leave the mold easily and the finished piece will lack gloss. A sharp instrument should never be used on the molds or they will become scratched which will show on the finished piece.

Molds come in either one or two pieces. The ones with two parts are either totally enclosed or with open ends into which the chocolate can be poured.

CHOCOLATE BARQUETTES AND TARTLETS

These elegant little confections are molded in one-piece molds and are not difficult to make using chocolate and summer coating. Use small tartlet and barquette molds for molding them. Prepare the molds as described on page 130.

Temper chocolate as described on page 127. Reheat and pour into molds, filling to top edge of molds. Let set until chocolate shell is the thickness you desire, then invert mold to drain out excess chocolate. Turn upright and let harden completely. They will leave the molds easily after a slight tap. To make from summer coating, follow the same procedure, but omit the tempering.

Fill the shells with one or more of the fillings given on this page. Pipe a rosette of Crème Chantilly (page 129) on each and garnish with chocolate cut-outs, candied cherries or nuts.

CRÈME PÂTISSIÈRE

This rich, delicate filling is the basis of many variations that are used in Continental decorating. Remember that it is an important part of Continental decorating that the inside of the confection determines the outside decoration—green could be lime or mint-flavored filling, pink could be fruit or peppermint-flavored filling and chocolate could have plain, chocolate or mocha filling.

3 tablespoons flour
⅛ teaspoon salt
⅝ cup sugar
1 cup light cream
4 egg yolks (slightly beaten)
1 teaspoon vanilla

Mix flour, salt and sugar in a heavy saucepan, blend in a little of the cream and place on medium heat, stirring constantly. Add rest of cream and continue stirring until mixture becomes as thick as a medium cream sauce.

Stir a little of the heated sauce into the egg yolks, then pour the egg yolks into the mixture. Return to low heat for a few more minutes until thickened. Do not let boil. Add vanilla after removing from heat and cool.

To prevent a skin from forming over the cream, brush with melted butter. Stir before using. Fills a 9″ tart shell or a dozen or more small tartlets.

CRÈME PLOMBIÈRES

¼ ounce gelatin
¼ cup cold water
1 recipe Crème Pâtissière
1 cup heavy cream, whipped
2 tablespoons cognac

Put water in a metal or pyrex cup, add the gelatin and heat in a small pan of boiling water until clear. Stir into the Crème Pâtissière. Fold the cognac into the whipped cream. Gently fold the two mixtures together. Other liqueurs may be substituted for cognac to vary the flavor.

OTHER VARIATIONS

CRÈME ST. HONORÉ. Make one recipe Crème Pâtissière and cool. Place ¼ cup cold water in a metal or pyrex cup and pour ¼ ounce gelatin over it. Set cup in a small pan of boiling water and heat until contents are clear. It is not necessary to stir. Beat six egg whites with a pinch of salt until stiff. Thoroughly stir gelatin mixture into Crème Pâtissière and carefully fold in egg whites. Chill.

CRÈME AU CHOCOLAT. Make Crème Pâtissière. After removing from heat, add 2 ounces of melted, unsweetened chocolate to mixture along with vanilla. Chill thoroughly.

CRÈME ANGLAISE AU MOKA. Follow the recipe for Crème Pâtissière, but reduce the amount of light cream by 2 tablespoons, substituting 2 tablespoons extra-strong, freshly-brewed coffee.

HOW TO MOLD EASTER EGGS

There are two methods of molding eggs—solid and hollow. When making large eggs, the hollow method is the best.

MOLDING EGGS. After each half of the mold has been prepared (see page 130), pour in tempered chocolate to fill. Let set until the shell is the thickness you desire, then tip mold to empty excess chocolate. Let chocolate shell harden. When shell has cooled completely, it will have pulled away from the sides of the mold. Tap mold to release.

JOINING HALVES. There are two methods of joining the two halves of the eggs. One way is to pipe a little melted chocolate on the edge of one half and set the other on top of it. Or place a baking sheet over a pan of hot water. Pick up the two half-eggs, press their flat edges lightly on the warmed baking sheet, lift and place them carefully together to set. The second method is speedier if you are working with a number of eggs.

After the halves of the eggs are joined and have set, they are ready to be decorated. See the next two pages for the finished eggs and how to decorate them.

Molded chocolate Easter eggs are a delightful and very traditional part of Continental decorating. The eggs can also be molded in pastel or white summer coating. After the eggs are molded and the halves joined they are ready to be decorated. Panorama eggs are made by trimming an opening in one half and creating a scene inside the egg, others are trimmed with marzipan or gum paste plaques.

Decorating these eggs is done in a very traditional way also. Using marzipan (recipe, page 76), gum paste (recipe, page 142) and royal icing (recipe, page 322), the eggs are trimmed with plaques and flowers and the seam between the two halves is cleverly concealed with a decorative trim made of one of the above materials.

When piping royal icing on the chocolate, thin the icing with a little water so it will adhere better. As you pipe, hold the tube so it scratches the surface. The icing will cover the scratches and adhere better to the chocolate. The icing falls off chocolate much more easily than it would from marzipan or gum paste if bumped or jarred.

To make bases for the large eggs, mold a solid half-egg in a 3" egg mold or mold a solid fluted bell in a 2" bell mold. Be sure that chocolate is completely hardened before unmolding. Trim off ½" from top of molded bell base. Attach decorated egg to base with a mound of melted chocolate.

Panorama egg. Mold egg in 5" two-piece egg mold in summer coating as described on page 131. Cut out an oval opening about 3" x 4" in top half of egg with an X-acto knife. Trim very carefully to avoid breaking. Join halves of egg as described on page 131. Mold base in 3" egg mold.

Mold a three-dimensional duck using yellow summer coating, let harden and attach halves using the baking sheet method on page 131. Smooth seam with finger. Paint beak with paste color thinned with kirschwasser and pipe eyes with tube 12 and flatten with a wet finger.

For daisies, roll marzipan 1/16" thick, cut with daisy cutter and dry within a curved surface. Pipe center with royal icing and tube 12 and flatten with a damp finger. Cut leaves with leaf cutter and dry within a curved surface.

Pipe tube 3 scallops with a teardrop between them around seam of egg with thinned royal icing. Pipe the same design around the base with tube 2. Add three tube 4 lines around the edge of the opening and dry.

Fill the lower portion of the egg about halfway with royal icing, let set a few minutes, then fill the rest of the way with blue-tinted piping gel. Position duck inside egg in the piping gel. Secure egg to base with a small mound of melted summer coating. Attach daisies and leaves to egg and base with dots of melted summer coating. Let harden.

Rose trimmed egg. Mold egg in 4½" egg mold with dark chocolate as described on page 131. Mold the base in 2" fluted bell mold. When hardened and unmolded, trim off ½" from top.

Make marzipan roses as described on page 316 and cut leaves with a leaf cutter. Roll marzipan ⅛" thick and cut plaque 1¼" wide and about 4½" long. Attach to egg on a slight angle with a little egg white and trim at seam of egg.

For border covering seam, make a roll of marzipan ⅜" in diameter and about 13" long. Using a crimper, make diagonal design. Brush lightly with egg white so marzipan is sticky and attach around seam of egg. Make letter patterns and transfer to marzipan plaque. Outline letters with tube 1 and brown royal icing. Dry, then fill in with light pink thinned icing. Dry. Paint in shading with paste color thinned with kirschwasser. Pipe tube 1 beading around edges of letters. For trim around plaque, make two 4½" long rolls of marzipan ¼" in diameter and crimp diagonally. Attach over edge of plaque with egg white and trim.

Attach egg to base with a small mound of melted chocolate and let harden. Then attach marzipan roses and leaves in position very carefully with dots of melted chocolate.

Pink heart trimmed egg. Mold egg in 4½" egg mold with white summer coating as described on page 131. Mold base in 2" fluted bell mold with pink summer coating. Trim off ½" from top.

Make gum paste flowers. Roll gum paste as thin as possible and cut flowers with forget-me-not cutter. Curl petals by pressing from edge of petal to base with the round end of modeling stick 5. Pipe tube 1 centers and dry.

Make heart pattern about 2" wide and 1½" high. Cut from gum paste and attach to egg while still wet with a little egg white. Pipe message with tube 1. Cut a ½" strip of thin gum paste and attach around seam of egg with egg white. Make two gum paste bows using ½" wide strips and dry. Add tube 1 beading around ribbon, bows and heart.

Attach egg to base with a small mound of melted summer coating and let harden. Attach gum paste bows to top and bottom of ribbon with royal icing. Secure flowers in position with small dots of melted summer coating and add tube 65 royal icing leaves.

MARY JANE. Mold egg in 4½″ egg mold with milk chocolate as described on page 131. Mold base in 3″ egg mold. When hardened and unmolded, flatten top by pressing against heated cookie sheet used for attaching the egg halves.

Pipe tube 102 five-petaled flowers with royal icing and add tube 1s dots for centers. Dry.

Make oval pattern about 2″ x 2½″. Cut oval from marzipan rolled ⅛″ thick. Attach to egg with a little egg white. Pipe message with tube 1 and royal icing. Make marzipan border to cover seam the same as for Rose Trimmed Egg and attach.

Pipe tube 2 beading around base with thinned royal icing. Pipe tube 2 balls around and slightly over edge of plaque, then circle with tube 1 bulbs.

Secure egg to base with a small mound of melted chocolate and let harden. Attach flowers on egg with dots of melted chocolate and pipe tube 67 royal icing leaves.

FINE LINE PIPING WITH CHOCOLATE

Decorating confections with fine line piping is a specialty in the Continental method. Chocolate, piping gel and royal icing are all used for spectacular, but dainty results. The secret is practice. Although patterns are provided in The Wilton Way Pattern Book, only practice will achieve the steadiness of hand needed to pipe smooth curves.

PREPARING CHOCOLATE FOR PIPING

Before piping with chocolate, it must be specially prepared. For the cake shown above, temper four ounces of chocolate (see page 127). Reheat to the temperature for the type of chocolate you are using, then gradually add ½ teaspoon of kirschwasser. This will cause the chocolate to stiffen up enough to be piped. Use a parchment cone with the tip cut to approximately the size of tube 1s.

HOW TO DECORATE AN ALMOND CAKE

This glowing pink cake is adorned with sweeping curves and arabesques of chocolate. A rim of chocolate marzipan echoes the almond flavor of the cake within. The recipes needed are given below and on the next page.

BAKE AN ALMOND CAKE in an 8″ pan. When it is completely cooled, ice with Continental Butter-cream, almond flavored, (page 128), then cover with poured fondant. Let fondant harden and cool completely.

PIPE FINE LINE WORK in prepared dark chocolate, following the pattern provided in The Wilton Way Pattern Book. It is wise to tape wax paper over the pattern and practice the piping before doing the top of the cake.

ADD MARZIPAN TO SIDES. Roll out chocolate marzipan ¼″ thick. (See next page.) Cut a strip 1¾″ x 24″. Make ribbed design with a grooved rolling pin. Roll strip loosely, ribbed side in and stand it on edge. As you unroll it, wrap it around the cake, securing at the seam with egg white. Serves ten.

ALMOND CAKE

A light, delicate cake with a marvelous texture and flavor. Continental bakers use it for tortes, petits fours and rolled, filled confections.

    ¾ cup sifted flour
    ¼ cup clarified butter, melted and cooled*
    3 eggs
    2 egg yolks
    ½ teaspoon vanilla
    ½ cup sugar

1 teaspoon grated lemon rind
¼ cup almond paste

Combine the three eggs, one egg yolk, vanilla, sugar and lemon rind in a large bowl. Heat over hot water as in Génoise recipe (page 128). When the egg mixture is warm and looks like bright yellow syrup, remove bowl from heat and beat until almost triple in bulk. Cream the almond paste with the remaining egg yolk.

Fold almond paste mixture gently into the beaten egg mixture a little at a time. Sprinkle the flour on top. Fold gently together, pouring in the butter as you fold with a wooden spoon. Do not over mix.

Butter an 8″ round pan, line the bottom with wax paper and butter again. Spread batter in pan and bake at 350°F for 20 to 25 minutes, or until golden and shrunk away from sides of pan.

*To clarify butter, place any quantity in a deep pan and melt over very low heat until foam disappears. Do not allow butter to brown. When clear, remove from heat and pour through a cheesecloth-lined sieve into container, leaving sediment in pan. This pure fat, well-covered, will keep indefinitely in the refrigerator.

WILTON QUICK FONDANT

This fondant is easy to make and dries to a fine gloss. If you prefer to use traditional fondant, complete instructions for making it are in *The Wilton Way of Cake Decorating, Volume One.*

6 cups confectioners' sugar
4½ ounces water
2 tablespoons corn syrup
1 teaspoon almond flavoring

Combine water and corn syrup. Add to sugar in a saucepan and stir over low heat until well mixed and heated just until warm, 100°F. Add flavoring. Place cake on cooling rack with a pan or cookie sheet beneath it. Pour fondant over iced cake, flowing from center and moving out in a circular motion. Yields four cups—enough fondant to cover an 8″ cake or about two dozen petits fours.

CHOCOLATE QUICK FONDANT. Follow the recipe for quick fondant, increasing water to 7 ounces. Just before pouring, stir in 4 ounces unsweetened melted chocolate. You may also stir in 1 teaspoon of almond flavoring. Yields four cups.

CHOCOLATE MARZIPAN

Make marzipan as described on page 76. While marzipan is still somewhat soft (before all the sugar has been added), knead in sifted dark cocoa powder until you achieve the chocolate shade you desire. If too stiff, soften with a little corn syrup or a few drops of brandy or other liqueur.

DAINTY PETITS FOURS TRIMMED WITH LINE PIPING

These petits fours can be made from either Almond Cake or Génoise (page 128). Bake the cake in a sheet pan so it is about 1″ high and cut into 1¾″ square pieces. Split the squares and fill and ice with Continental Buttercream (recipe on page 128). Cover with poured fondant and let harden and cool completely.

FINE LINE PIPING. Patterns for the designs on the petits fours are in The Wilton Way Pattern Book, but as with the cake decorated with fine line piping, practice is the best way to achieve smooth flowing curved lines.

Place prepared piping chocolate into a parchment cone. Cut the tip so the opening is about the size of tube 1s. Pipe the designs on the petits fours and let the chocolate harden.

OUTLINE-FILL IN METHOD. This method is frequently used in Continental decorating to create a raised surface and add color to the design.

Pipe the design with piping chocolate as described above and let it harden. Then fill in areas of the design with tinted warmed fondant placed in a parchment cone with the tip cut. Or fill in with piping gel for a sparkling effect. This method is similar to Color Flow technique, but quicker to do.

These petits fours are a delightful treat to serve at a tea, bridal shower or reception.

A CHOCOLATE TORTE FOR A BIRTHDAY

This lavish torte repeats the chocolate flavor four times—the cake is a chocolate Sachertorte filled with Chocolate Buttercream, the icing is a rich chocolate fondant, the trim is shaped from chocolate marzipan. An apricot glaze under the fondant gives added flavor. A three-dimensional piped ornament and four pink marzipan roses give an especially festive appearance. Elegant ornaments like these are often used in the Continental method on cakes for special occasions.

HOW TO DECORATE THE CAKE

MAKE ROSES. Hand-model four large marzipan roses as described on page 316. Set aside to harden.

PIPE ORNAMENT. Using pattern in The Wilton Way Pattern Book, tape it to a piece of glass or plexiglas and cover smoothly with wax paper. Fill a decorating bag fitted with tube 14 with deep brown royal icing. Pipe four scroll patterns and dry. Turn over, pipe again and dry.

Using chocolate cut-out method (see page 128), cut a 4″ milk chocolate circle. This will be the ornament base.

To assemble ornament, join two of the scroll pieces at right angles with dots of icing. Secure them to the base with a bit more icing. Add the third scroll piece, attaching to the others and to

the base, then attach the fourth piece. Set ornament aside.

PREPARE CAKE. Bake Sachertorte using recipe below. Chill. Trim top so cake is level and about 2″ high. Split into two layers and brush bottom layer with hot apricot glaze (heat one cup of apricot jam to boiling and strain). Spread with Chocolate Buttercream (page 128) and place second layer on top. Brush top and sides with apricot glaze and let harden. Cover with chocolate fondant (page 135) and let harden and cool completely.

MAKE MARZIPAN TRIM. Knead cocoa powder into marzipan until you achieve the color you desire. If marzipan becomes too stiff, soften with a little corn syrup or a few drops of brandy or liqueur of your choice. Roll out the marzipan ⅛″ thick. Make ribbed design by re-rolling with a grooved rolling pin. For side trim, cut twelve triangles 2″ wide at base and 1½″ high. For top trim, cut ten triangles 1½″ wide and 1″ high.

DECORATE CAKE. Place ornament in center of cake, securing in place with a bit of warmed fondant. Attach smaller marzipan triangles around ornament with warmed fondant. Secure marzipan roses on ornament base between the scrolls with warmed fondant. Finally, attach larger marzipan triangles around side of torte with warmed fondant. This lavish birthday cake serves ten.

SACHERTORTE

This is a good, but not necessarily authentic, version of the famous recipe claimed by both the Sacher hotel and Demels, a well-known pastry shop in Vienna. The rich chocolate cake is greatly enhanced by the flavor of apricot glaze.

    ¾ cup butter
    ¾ cup sugar
    6 eggs, separated
    1 teaspoon vanilla
    6 ounces semi-sweet chocolate,
        melted and cooled
    2 cups sifted flour

Cream butter until fluffy, slowly add sugar and beat until well blended. Add egg yolks, one at a time, beating after each addition.

Whip egg whites until stiff and gently fold the chocolate into them. Combine the two mixtures and carefully fold in flour until just blended. Do not over-mix.

Pour batter into a well-buttered 8″ pan and bake at 325°F for 45 minutes or until done. Cool thoroughly. Fill and ice as described above.

A LUXURIOUS CHOCOLATE ROSE TORTE

In this beautiful torte, the chocolate theme is repeated and enhanced by the decoration. The filling and textured icing on the sides are Chocolate Buttercream, the three-dimensional heart ornament is cut from dark chocolate, and the beautiful roses are piped in Chocolate Canache, a totally delicious mixture of chocolate and cream.

The feature of the torte is the heart-shaped ornament beautifully piped with curves and stylized flower shapes in the fine line technique. The half-heart shapes are set on cake wedges to give an interesting three-dimensional effect.

Elegant Continental tortes like this are served at very special occasions—a birthday, anniversary or at a wedding reception on a sweet table.

MAKE HEART ORNAMENT. Melt tempered dark chocolate to 90°-92°F and spread on wax paper to about ⅛″ thickness. Let stiffen and cut out two-piece heart shape with X-acto knife. Pattern is in The Wilton Way Pattern Book. Before piping the fine line design, it is wise to slip the pattern under wax paper and pipe a practice trial before putting design on chocolate. Prepare the royal icing by softening with one or two teaspoons of light corn syrup per cup of icing. Use a parchment cone and clip the smallest possible opening in the tip. Apply more pressure to the cone to pipe the heavier lines, lighten the pressure for the fine lines.

Transfer design to chocolate heart shapes by tracing pattern on parchment paper, laying the paper on the chocolate heart and cutting through to heart with the tip of a very sharp X-acto knife. Pipe the design.

PIPE ROSES. Fit decorating cone with tube 104, fill with Chocolate Canache and pipe six roses. Refrigerate until ready to use. The Canache handles beautifully in the cone and pipes a perfect rose. If you are decorating a cake for a chocolate lover, you will surely want to use this mixture for borders and flower trim, as the flavor is superb.

CHOCOLATE CANACHE

1 cup German sweet chocolate, cut up
⅓ cup whipping cream
1½ tablespoons confectioners' sugar

Temper chocolate, then reheat to 86°-88°F. Mix cream and sugar together, then stir into chocolate until thoroughly mixed. Mixture will be very soft and "soupy". Place in refrigerator for about ten minutes. If it sets too hard, allow it to come to room temperature and stir well before filling cone and piping the roses. Canache may be kept in the refrigerator for weeks if well-covered. When ready to use, bring to room temperature and stir.

Pipe tube 67 leaves on wax paper with the same mixture, but substitute 1 cup of tempered unsweetened dark chocolate for the German sweet chocolate. Reheat to 90°-92°F, then proceed with recipe.

DECORATE THE CAKE. Using Chocolate Génoise recipe on page 128, bake the cake in an 8″ pan. Chill and split into three layers, then fill with Continental Buttercream (page 128). Ice top of torte with Continental Buttercream, then make grooved design with the largest teeth of an icing comb. Ice sides of torte with Chocolate Continental Buttercream and use the largest teeth of an icing comb to make the design.

Ice two small wedges of cake to support the heart. Place them on torte and place the two heart halves in position, securing with a little icing. Place the roses and leaves beneath the up-raised edges of the heart, attaching with dots of icing. Serves ten lavishly.

AN ELEGANT SWAN TORTE

This delightful confection demonstrates the versatility of the Continental method. Here four basic mixtures, Pâté à Chou, Génoise, Crème Chantilly and Crème Pâtissière are combined into a unique and decorative creation. The torte is filled with a delicious Chocolate Mousse. With the basic Continental mixtures mastered, any decorator can compose a masterpiece of form and flavor.

The Swan Torte is completed with chocolate cigarettes, a favorite European trim, tucked jauntily on top.

HOW TO MAKE
CHOCOLATE CIGARETTES

Chocolate cigarettes, also called rolled chocolate, are made by ladling a quantity of tempered chocolate onto a clean, dry marble slab. Spread the chocolate with a spatula until it is a uniform thickness and almost set. Chocolate should still be somewhat warm. With the blade of a knife held at an angle on the surface of the chocolate, pull the knife sideways which gives a cutting action. As this is done, the chocolate will form itself into long thin rolls. Leave the rolls on the slab until completely hardened, then store in a cool dry place until ready to use. If the chocolate begins to harden as you are working, warm the surface with the palm of your hand. If you would like small rolls or cigarettes of a uniform size, score the chocolate on the slab into strips. Score again at right angles to form rectangles. Set knife blade on chocolate and carefully bring the knife forward.

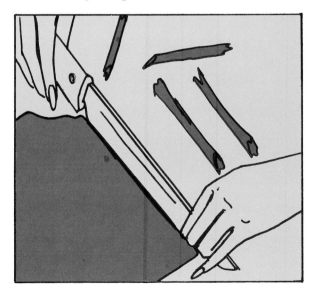

MAKE THE SWANS. Using the recipe and directions below, make the pâté à chou swans. You will need ten to top the cake.

PÂTÉ À CHOU

This is a never-fail recipe and method for perfect cream puffs.

1 cup water
½ cup butter
1 cup sifted flour
¼ teaspoon salt
4 eggs

For best results, have all the ingredients at room temperature and make sure that your oven temperature is accurate.

Put water and butter in a saucepan and bring to a boil. Lower the heat, add the flour and salt all at once and continue to cook, stirring constantly until mixture leaves the sides of the pan and forms a ball. Remove from heat and add eggs, one at a time, making sure each egg is well-blended before adding the next.

This will make 36 swans or small cream puffs, or twelve large cream puffs or eclairs.

Butter a cookie sheet. Fit a pastry bag with tube 8 and press out "S"-shaped swan necks. With tube 2A press out 1½" long, ⅝" diameter mounds for bodies. Allow 2" between bodies and necks for spreading. Preheat oven to 400°F. Bake necks for 20 minutes and bodies for 30 minutes until golden and no beads of moisture show. Turn off heat and leave in closed oven 10 minutes more.

Cut off top of bodies of swans and cut this piece in half to form the wings. Make a recipe of Crème Pâtissière in chocolate or mocha flavor. (See page 131.) Put Crème into a pastry bag fitted with a large plain tube and fill the swans. Insert neck and wings into filling. Before placing swans on cake, sift confectioners' sugar over them.

MAKE AND FILL THE CAKE. Bake a 9" oval cake, 2" high using plain or chocolate Génoise recipe on page 128. Chill and split into three or more layers. Fill with Chocolate Mousse Filling.

CHOCOLATE MOUSSE FILLING

1 cup semisweet chocolate, cut up
4 eggs, separated
1 teaspoon of hot water
4 or 5 drops of vanilla
1 tablespoon brandy
1 cup heavy cream, whipped

Heat the chocolate just until melted in the top half of a double boiler. Remove from heat, cool and beat in egg yolks, one at a time. Add hot water, vanilla and brandy and mix well. Beat the egg whites until stiff and fold gently into the chocolate mixture. Fold in the whipped cream. Refrigerate until ready to use.

COMPLETE THE TORTE. Place torte on serving tray. Cover sides with tube 4B upright columns piped with Chocolate Crème Chantilly. (Fold 2 tablespoons sifted, unsweetened cocoa into one recipe Crème Chantilly after the cream is whipped. Recipe on page 129). Press a chocolate cigarette between every fourth column.

Pipe ten tube 4B shells around top of torte with Crème Chantilly. Pipe tube 4B rosettes in center of torte. Insert chocolate cigarettes into the rosettes. Place swans around top of torte between the shells. Pipe tube 4B stars on either side of swans. Your beautifully elegant torte is ready to serve ten admiring guests.

CHAPTER TEN

The Art of
Making Gum Paste Flowers

The ancient art of gum paste, once practiced only by master chefs, can now be mastered by any adventurous decorator. New cutters, molds and modern techniques allow you to achieve professional effects in a relatively short time.

QUICK METHOD FLOWERS

With practice, working with gum paste is easy and the results are spectacular, especially with the Quick Method of making flowers shown in this chapter. With this method it is not necessary to let each piece dry before assembling. Petals can be cut and put together immediately for most flowers. This saves a great deal of time when making the flowers.

Most of the flower petals are curved on pieces of thin foam toweling rather than on the hand. This procedure greatly simplifies shaping the petals because it leaves both hands free for working.

Another advantage to this method is the set of 26 versatile plastic cutters which is used. Most of the cutters make a whole flower or a combination of several petals, instead of cutting each petal separately. When you become familiar with the process, you will be able to make the flowers with almost assembly-line speed and to create many more varieties than those shown.

GUM PASTE RECIPE

This revised gum paste recipe has been found to be the best one for obtaining true colors.
1 tablespoon Gum-tex™ or tragacanth gum
1 heaping tablespoon glucose
3 tablespoons warm water
1 pound confectioners' sugar (or more)
Mix tragacanth gum and glucose until smooth and dissolved. Add warm water one tablespoon at a time. Add small amounts of confectioners' sugar until you can work mixture with your hands. Continue adding small amounts of sugar as you knead until you have added about ¾ pound of sugar.

Since gum paste handles best when aged, store in plastic bag at least overnight, then break off a piece and work in more sugar until the mixture is pliable, but not sticky.

To store for a length of time, place gum paste in a plastic bag and then in a covered container to prevent drying. It will keep for several months.

To color gum paste, apply a small amount of paste food color with a toothpick. Then knead the gum paste piece until the tint is evenly spread.

To roll gum paste, dust the work surface with cornstarch. Take a small piece of gum paste, keeping the rest well-covered, and work it in your hands. Place it on the cornstarch-dusted area, dust rolling pin with cornstarch and roll out the gum paste to the desired thickness. Remember to roll out only one small piece at a time to avoid drying and to cover every piece you cut with a small glass or plastic container to retain moisture.

To attach gum paste pieces, brush with a small amount of egg white and press gently together.

MATERIALS YOU'LL NEED

Many of the materials you need can be found in your kitchen or in your decorating supplies.

Artificial stamens for the centers of flowers.

Artist's brush to apply color and egg white.

Floral tape and florists' wire to assemble the flowers and make stems. 28, 22 and 20-gauge wire is used.

Foam towels to roll petals on. These come on a roll like paper towels and are available at most large drug stores or groceries.

Gum paste cutters and molds to cut gum paste pieces and imprint them. A set of 26 plastic cutters was used to create all the flowers in this chapter.

Powdered pastels to tint the centers of some flowers. Shave pastel sticks with sharp knife.

Wire cutters and x-acto knife.

Small rolling pin and modeling sticks as numbered here to roll gum paste and shape petals.

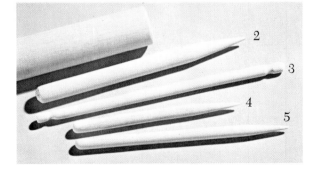

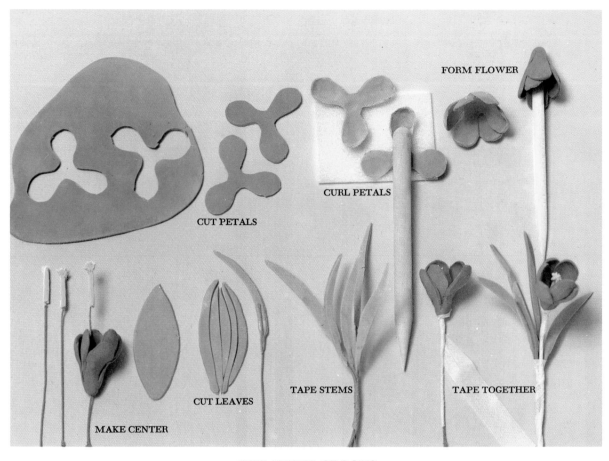

FORM FLOWER

CUT PETALS

CURL PETALS

CUT LEAVES

TAPE STEMS

TAPE TOGETHER

MAKE CENTER

THE PERKY CROCUS
ANNOUNCES SPRING

STEP ONE. Make gum paste as directed on page 142. Tint a piece of it and roll it out 1/16″ thick. For each crocus flower, cut two petal sections with the crocus cutter.

STEP TWO. Lay the petal sections on a piece of soft foam toweling and curl each of the individual petals by pressing from the edge to the center with rounded end of stick number 2.

STEP THREE. Brush the center of one petal section with egg white and attach the second section on top of it. Make sure the petals of the second section are positioned between the petals of the first section for a natural look. Mold the flower over the rounded end of stick number 5 to give it the characteristic crocus shape. Make a hole in the center of the flower with a pointed stick. Make an indentation about ½″ deep in a block of styrofoam with the round end of stick number 2. Place the crocus flower in the indentation to dry.

STEP FOUR. Make the center of the crocus with a length of 28-gauge florists' wire. Insert ¾″ of the wire into a decorating bag fitted with tube 3. Squeeze the bag while pulling out the wire to coat it with icing. Dry, then add tiny tube 1 spikes at the tip. Dry. Brush the center of the flower with egg white, then insert the end of the wire through the flower. Dry.

STEP FIVE. Tint another piece of gum paste and roll out slightly less than 1/16″ thick. Using the lily leaf cutter, cut one leaf for each flower. Then cut it into five pieces with a sharp knife. Attach a piece of 28-gauge florists' wire to each piece with egg white. Dry.

STEP SIX. Tape the wires of the five leaf sections together with green floral tape. Wrap the stem of the flower twice with white floral tape, extending up onto the base of the flower to secure it in position. Then tape the cluster of leaf sections and the flower together with white floral tape.

144

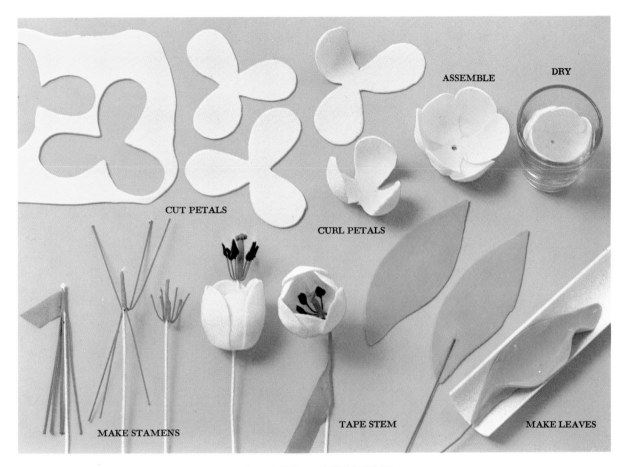

CUT PETALS

CURL PETALS

ASSEMBLE

DRY

MAKE STAMENS

TAPE STEM

MAKE LEAVES

THE BRILLIANT TULIP,
SHOWY AND EASY TO MAKE

A fast flower that's fun to make. When finished, these tulips appear so realistic they could have been cut from your garden. Work quickly so that the gum paste petal sections remain pliable.

STEP ONE. Make gum paste as directed on page 142. Tint a piece and roll about 1/16" thick. Cut one petal section with the small tulip cutter and one with the large tulip cutter.

STEP TWO. Press the edges of each individual petal between the thumb and forefinger to make thinner. Then lay the petal sections on a piece of soft foam toweling and curl with the thumb, pressing from edge of each petal to the center of the piece.

STEP THREE. Brush center of large petal section with egg white and attach small petal section in it. Position petals of the small section so they are between the petals of the large section. Make a hole in the center of the flower with a pointed stick. Place flower over one end of the gum paste rolling pin and cover with a shot glass which has been dusted with cornstarch. Turn the glass up-right and remove the rolling pin. Dry overnight.

STEP FOUR. Make center of tulip by taping one long, heavy wire and six short, 28-gauge thin wires together about ¾" from one end. Bend thin wires up and clip off to about ⅝" length. Insert taped portion into decorating bag fitted with tube 10. Squeeze the bag while pulling out the wire to coat it with icing. Pipe three tube 3 dots on top. Pipe black stamens on each of the thin wires with tube 65. Set in styrofoam block to dry.

STEP FIVE. Insert wire through hole in center of tulip. Wrap stem with green floral tape to hold flower in position.

STEP SIX. Tint another piece of gum paste and roll it out. Cut leaves with the tulip leaf cutter. Attach a piece of florists' wire with egg white and fold end of leaf over wire. Dry within a curved surface, curving edges for a graceful look.

To use in arrangements or bouquets, tape two leaves to each flower, near base of flower stem.

145

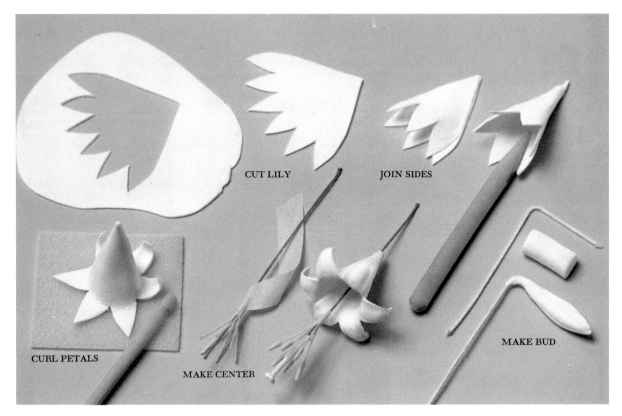

CUT LILY   JOIN SIDES

MAKE BUD

CURL PETALS   MAKE CENTER

A STATELY EASTER LILY

STEP ONE. Make gum paste as directed on page 142. Roll out a piece of it 1/16″ thick. Cut flower with the lily cutter. Attach the two long straight edges with egg white. Smooth seam and shape into cone with stick number 2.

STEP TWO. Bend petals outward and place lily on a piece of foam toweling. Using stick number 3, curl petals by pressing stick from point of petal to base. Insert a small cotton ball into cone, then make a hole in the point of the cone with a pointed stick.

CUT LEAVES

TAPE INTO STALK

Dry upside down, then remove cotton.

STEP THREE. Make center of lily by taping together one 5″ piece of thick 22-gauge florists' wire and six 1½″ pieces of thin 28-gauge florists' wire as pictured. Insert the thick wire into a decorating bag fitted with tube 4. Squeeze bag while removing wire to cover it with icing. Pipe three tube 4 dots on top. Make stamens by covering thin wires with icing, using tube 2 and the above process. Dry. Insert stem through hole in center of flower. Wrap stem with green floral tape, extending up onto base of lily to hold it in place.

STEP FOUR. Make bud with a heavy piece of florists' wire bent to a 90° angle and a 1¼″ long x ⅜″ thick cylinder of gum paste. Model cylinder with hands to form bud shape, then insert wire which has been dipped in egg white. Dry. Wrap stem with green floral tape, extending up onto bud. Make smaller buds with green-tinted gum paste.

STEP FIVE. Tint a piece of gum paste and roll out. Cut leaf shape with the lily leaf cutter. Cut each shape into thirds, then attach a piece of florists' wire to back of each with egg white. Pinch end of leaf around wire and bend leaf. Dry.

STEP SIX. Tape buds, flowers and leaves together into stalks with green floral tape.

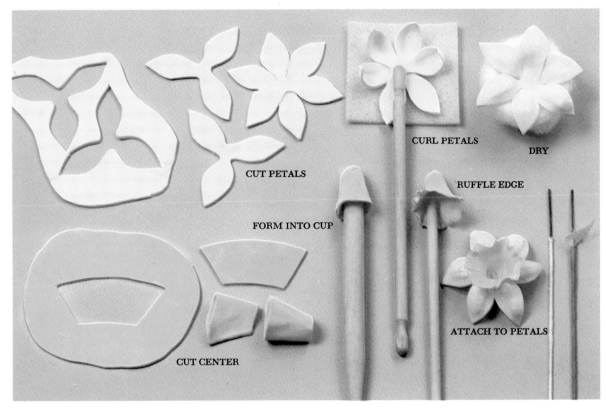

CUT PETALS

CURL PETALS

DRY

FORM INTO CUP

RUFFLE EDGE

CUT CENTER

ATTACH TO PETALS

THE SPRITELY DAFFODIL

STEP ONE. Make gum paste following instructions on page 142. Tint a piece of it yellow and roll out 1/16″ thick. Cut two pieces for each flower with the daffodil petal cutter. Attach with egg white so the petals of one piece fit between the petals of the other. Place petals on a piece of foam toweling and curl by pressing from tip of petal to the base with stick number 3. Make a hole in the center of the piece with a pointed stick. Turn over and dry on cotton ball.

STEP TWO. Tint a piece of gum paste deeper yellow, and roll out 1/16″ thick. Cut one piece for each flower with the daffodil cup cutter. Attach the two short sides together with egg white. Smooth seam and round out with round end of stick number 4. Form into cup shape over round end of stick number 2. Ruffle edge by rubbing and stretching with stick number 5 while holding cup in hand.

STEP THREE. Attach cup in center of petals with egg white. Poke a hole through the center of the cup with a pointed stick to match up with the hole in the petal section. Dry. Insert a heavy piece of florists' wire through hole in flower. Wrap stem with green floral tape to hold flower in position. Coat piece of wire left inside the flower with icing by pushing it into a bag fitted with tube 4 and

then squeezing bag while removing wire. Pipe three tube 4 dots on top to create the pistil of the daffodil. Dry. For finished flower, see page 162.

STEP FOUR. Tint a piece of gum paste and roll out as thin as possible. Cut leaf shapes with tulip leaf cutter and cut each of these in five pieces with X-acto knife. Attach a piece of florists' wire to each one with egg white. Fold ends of leaf over wire, then curve leaf. Dry.

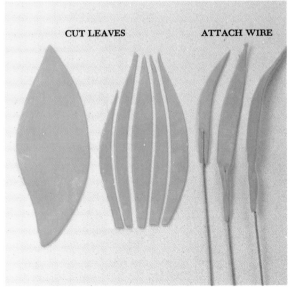

CUT LEAVES

ATTACH WIRE

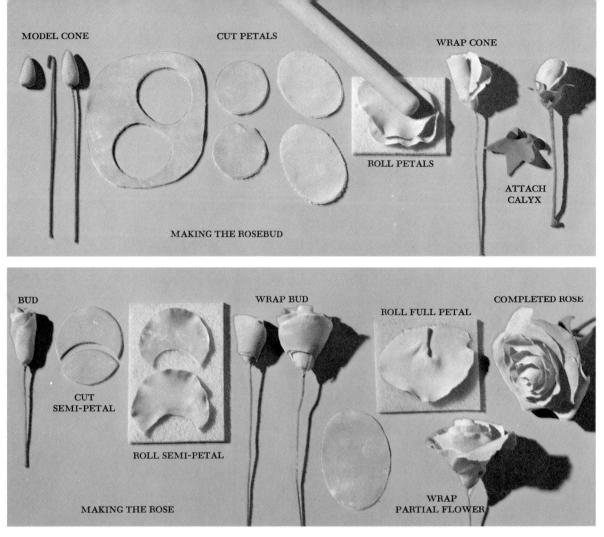

MODEL CONE CUT PETALS WRAP CONE

ROLL PETALS

ATTACH CALYX

MAKING THE ROSEBUD

BUD WRAP BUD ROLL FULL PETAL COMPLETED ROSE

CUT SEMI-PETAL

ROLL SEMI-PETAL

WRAP PARTIAL FLOWER

MAKING THE ROSE

THE DAINTY ROSEBUD

You'll enjoy making these pretty little buds. They go together quickly and easily.

STEP ONE. Make gum paste as directed on page 142 and tint a portion of it. Model a small piece with hands into a ½" tall cone for each bud. Bend the end of a piece of florists' wire into a hook, dip it in egg white and insert it into the base of the cone. Dry thoroughly.

STEP TWO. Roll out a piece of gum paste as thin as possible and cut two petals with the small rose cutter for each bud. Roll each petal with the rolling pin into an oval shape. Place petals on a piece of foam toweling and roll edges of each with stick number 2. When working on one petal, keep the other one covered to prevent drying. Then overlap

the rolled petals leaving about ¼" of the lower petal showing. Wrap them around the cone, attaching with egg white. Bend the outer edges of the petals away from the center of the bud. Dry.

STEP THREE. Tint another piece of gum paste and roll it out less than 1/16" thick. Cut one piece for each bud with the calyx cutter. Place it on a piece of foam toweling and curl the points of the calyx by pressing from the tip to the base with the round end of stick number 5. Make a hole in the center of the calyx. Brush the base of the bud with egg white, insert the wire stem of the bud through the hole in the calyx so the points are curling out and press it to the bud. Wrap the stem of the completed bud with floral tape.

THE LOVELY ROSE, QUEEN OF FLOWERS

This blushing, multi-petaled rose takes a little time and trouble to make, but the beautiful results make it worth the effort.

STEP ONE. Make a bud as described above through Step Two, but do not bend the petals outward. Roll a piece of gum paste as thin as possible, and cut six petals with the medium rose cutter. With

the small rose cutter, remove one-third of each petal. Working with one semi-petal at a time and keeping the others covered, make the outer edge thinner by pressing between the thumb and forefinger. Place a semi-petal on a piece of foam toweling and roll the outer edge with stick number 2. Brush the inner edge with egg white and wrap

148

around bud. Follow the same procedure for the five remaining semi-petals.

STEP TWO. Cut six full petals with the medium rose cutter. Work with one petal at a time, keeping the rest covered. Roll petal into an oval shape with rolling pin. Place it on a piece of foam toweling and roll edges with stick number 2. Make a pleat on one long edge. Brush base of partially assembled rose with egg white, then wrap petal around it with the pleat towards the wire. Bend the upper edge of the petal outward. Continue this same procedure with the remaining five petals, rolling each one progressively larger. Push stem into a piece of styrofoam to dry.

STEP THREE. Tint a piece of gum paste green and roll out thin as possible. Cut one piece with the calyx cutter for each rose. Place calyx on a soft piece of foam and curl points by pressing from the tip to the base with the round end of stick number 5. Make a hole in the center of the calyx and push the wire on the flower through it so the points curl down. Attach it with egg white to the base of the rose. Wrap the stem with floral tape.

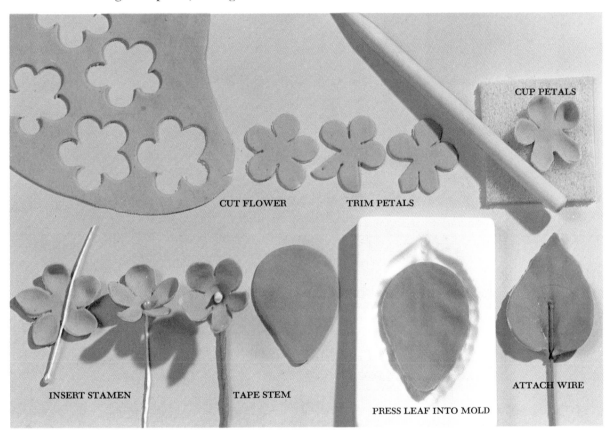

CUP PETALS

CUT FLOWER   TRIM PETALS

INSERT STAMEN   TAPE STEM   PRESS LEAF INTO MOLD   ATTACH WIRE

THE SHY VIOLET, SYMBOL OF SPRING

STEP ONE. Make gum paste following the instructions on page 142. Tint a piece of it and roll it out 1/16″ thick. For each violet, cut one flower with the violet cutter. With an X-acto knife, cut off one-fourth of the petal, lengthwise, on two adjacent petals. Then cut off, at an angle, half of the remaining rounded end on each of the same two petals. This will create the characteristic look of the violet with the two small and three larger petals.

STEP TWO. Place the flower on a piece of foam toweling. Cup the petals with the rounded end of stick number 4 by pressing from the tip to the base of the petal.

STEP THREE. Push an artificial stamen through the center of the violet. Dry violet within a curved surface. Wrap the stem with floral tape and pipe a tube 2 dot of icing over the tip of the artificial stamen. Dry.

STEP FOUR. Tint another piece of gum paste and roll it out 1/16″ thick. Cut a leaf with the large violet leaf cutter. Press it into the leaf mold. Attach a piece of florists' wire to the back of the leaf with egg white and pinch the bottom of the leaf around the wire. Dry.

149

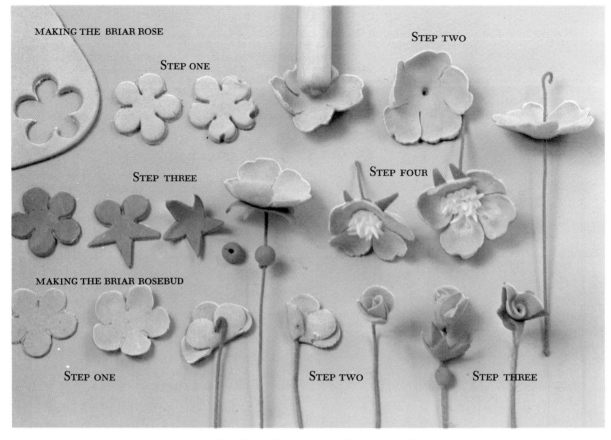

MAKING THE BRIAR ROSE

STEP ONE

STEP TWO

STEP THREE

STEP FOUR

MAKING THE BRIAR ROSEBUD

STEP ONE

STEP TWO

STEP THREE

THE SWEET-FACED BRIAR ROSE

STEP ONE. Make gum paste as directed on page 142. Tint a portion and roll it out to a thickness between ⅛″ and 1/16″. For each flower, cut one piece with the briar rose cutter. Make an indentation in the edge of each petal with the point of stick number 2.

STEP TWO. Using the round end of stick number 2, roll each petal from side to side, concentrating on the petal edge. As you finish each petal, pull the stick from the edge to the center to cup the petal slightly. Make a hole in the center of the briar rose with the point of the stick. Dry it within a curved surface. Make a small hook on one end of a piece of florists' wire and insert it through the hole in the flower, then make calyx.

STEP THREE. Tint a piece of gum paste and roll it out 1/16″ thick. Make the calyx by cutting a piece with the briar rose cutter and trimming the petals

into points with a sharp knife. The calyx can also be made by cutting a piece with the calyx cutter. Using the round end of stick number 5, curl the points of the calyx by pressing from the tip to the base. Insert the flower wire through the calyx so the points curl down. Attach the calyx to the base of the flower with egg white. Roll a tiny ball of gum paste and make a hole through it. Push the wire through the hole in the ball and attach it to the calyx with egg white.

STEP FOUR. Pipe tube 1 spikes of royal icing in the center of the briar rose for stamens. Insert a few artificial stamens in the wet icing. Brush the inner surface of the petals close to the center with powdered white pastel. (Shave pastel stick with X-acto knife.) Dry.

THE BRIAR ROSEBUD

STEP ONE. Roll out a piece of gum paste as thin as possible. Cut a piece for each bud with the briar rose cutter. Curl the petals up slightly by pressing from the tip of the petal to the base with the round end of stick number 5.

STEP TWO. Fold two petals of the flower piece over the other three. Make a small hook in one end of a piece of florists' wire and place it on the folded flower. Brush the left petal with egg white and fold it over to cover the wire. Brush more egg white along the first and second folds and wrap the remaining petals around the wire. Push stem into styrofoam block to dry.

STEP THREE. Tint a piece of gum paste and roll it 1/16″ thick. Make the calyx for the bud by trimming the petals of a briar rose cutter piece into points or by cutting a piece with the calyx cutter. Curl the points of the calyx by pressing from the tip to the base with the round end of stick number 5. Brush the base of the bud with egg white and insert the wire through the calyx so the points are curling up. Press the calyx to the bud. Roll a tiny ball of gum paste and make a hole through it. Push the wire through the hole and attach the ball to the calyx with egg white. Dry.

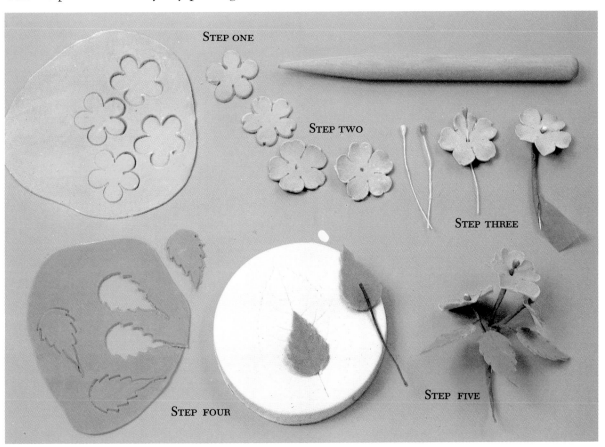

THE SHADE-LOVING IMPATIENS

A charming, flat-faced little flower that is the joy of the city gardener.

STEP ONE. Make gum paste as directed on page 142. Tint a piece of it and roll it out 1/16″ thick. For each impatiens flower, cut one piece with the violet cutter. Make an indentation in the edge of each petal with the pointed end of stick number 2.

STEP TWO. Roll each petal flat with stick number 2, then curl the petals slightly by pulling the round end of the stick from the tip to the base of the petal. Make a hole in the center of the flower with the point of the stick. Dry.

STEP THREE. Dip the head of a pearl yellow artificial stamen into green royal icing. Dry. Insert the stamen through the hole in the flower. Wrap the stem with green floral tape to hold the flower in position. With a small brush, apply a dot of yellow food color on the stamen of the pink impatiens (or apply a dot of red food color on the stamen of the red impatiens).

STEP FOUR. Tint a piece of gum paste and roll it out slightly less than 1/16″ thick. Cut leaves with the small rose leaf cutter. Press each leaf into the leaf vein mold. Attach a piece of florists' wire to the back of each leaf with egg white. Dry.

STEP FIVE. Tape several impatiens blossoms and several leaves together into small clusters with green floral tape.

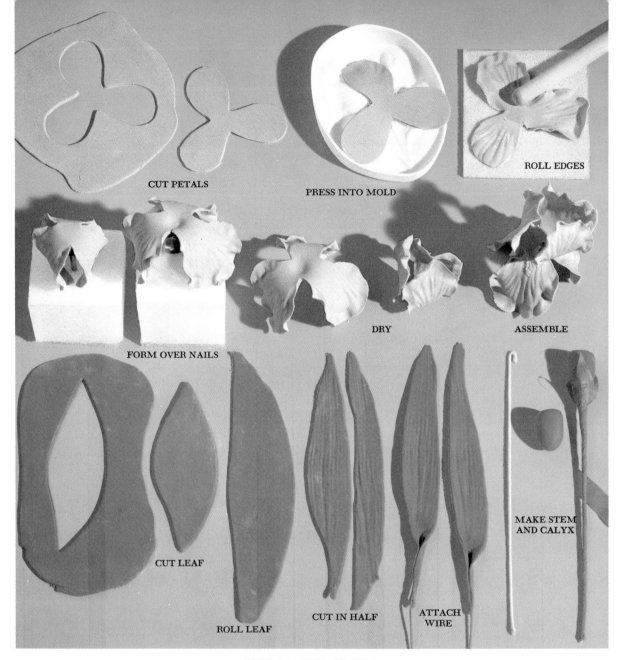

CUT PETALS

PRESS INTO MOLD

ROLL EDGES

FORM OVER NAILS

DRY

ASSEMBLE

CUT LEAF

ROLL LEAF

CUT IN HALF

ATTACH WIRE

MAKE STEM AND CALYX

THE MAJESTIC IRIS

STEP ONE. Make gum paste following the instructions on page 142. Tint a piece of it and roll it 1/16″ thick. For each iris, cut a piece with the small tulip cutter and a piece with the large tulip cutter. Work with one piece at a time, keeping the other one covered. Press the three petals of each piece into the iris petal mold.

STEP TWO. Place the petal sections on a piece of foam toweling and roll the edges with stick number 2. Work around the outside of the petal to ruffle.

STEP THREE. Push a number 1 flower nail into a piece of styrofoam and a number 4 flower nail into another piece. Bend the small petal section over the number 1 nail, tucking the tips of the petals under. This piece becomes the top of the iris. Bend the large petal section over the number 4 nail, pressing the center down into the nail indentation and letting the petals flare out slightly. This piece becomes the bottom of the iris. Dry both petal sections on nails.

STEP FOUR. When thoroughly dry, take a very small piece of gum paste and flatten it with the fingers. Brush both sides of it lightly with egg white. Press it into the indentation in the center of the bottom of the iris and place the top of the iris in position. Press the two pieces lightly together. Pipe tube 1 dots for the "beards" of the iris on the lower petals. Dry thoroughly.

STEP FIVE. Tint a piece of gum paste and roll out to between ⅛″ and 1/16″ thick. Cut a leaf with the tulip leaf cutter. Roll the leaf lengthwise with the gum paste rolling pin until it is almost twice as long as it was. Cut the leaf in half lengthwise to create two thinner leaves.

STEP SIX. *Very lightly,* press with a piece of light cardboard to make lengthwise indentations in the leaves. Do not press too hard, or the cardboard will go all the way through the gum paste. Attach a piece of florists' wire to each leaf with egg white and pinch the bottom of the leaf around the wire.

STEP SEVEN. Make a small hook in one end of a piece of heavy florists' wire. Model a piece of gum paste into a cylinder 1″ long x ½″ wide. Dip the hook in egg white and insert it into the cylinder. Dry. Cut sepals from floral tape and attach them around the base of the cylinder. Wrap the stem with floral tape.

STEP EIGHT. To attach the iris to the stem, flatten a small piece of gum paste with the fingers. Brush both sides of it with a small amount of egg white and press onto the top of the gum paste cylinder. Place the iris on top of the cylinder and lightly press the two together. Insert the stem into a block of styrofoam until the completed flower is dry. See finished flower on stem on page 163.

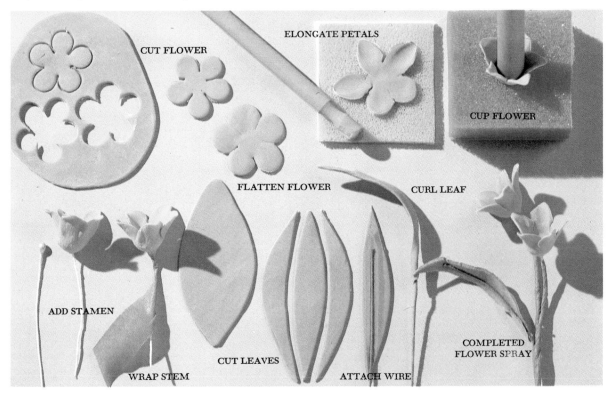

CUT FLOWER
ELONGATE PETALS
CUP FLOWER
FLATTEN FLOWER
CURL LEAF
ADD STAMEN
CUT LEAVES
WRAP STEM
ATTACH WIRE
COMPLETED FLOWER SPRAY

THE DAINTY BLUEBELL

A very pretty little flower that's quick and easy to make. Bluebells make fine "fillers" when used with larger flowers in a bouquet.

STEP ONE. Make gum paste as directed on page 142. Tint a piece of it and roll it out 1/16″ thick. For each bluebell flower, cut one flower shape with the violet cutter. Flatten it slightly by lightly rolling it with the gum paste rolling pin. Be careful when rolling to just flatten the flower and not roll it out of shape.

STEP TWO. Place the flower on a piece of foam toweling and with stick number 3, press along the center of a petal. Pull out slightly while pressing to elongate the petal. Continue around the flower, pressing and elongating each petal.

STEP THREE. Transfer the flower to a foam sponge. Press stick number 2 into the center of the flower to form it into a cup shape. Make a tiny hole in the center of the flower with the point of a stick. Insert a blue pearl artificial stamen through the hole in the flower. Dry the flower upside down on a small ball of cotton. Wrap the stem with floral tape.

STEP FOUR. Tint another piece of gum paste and roll it to a thickness slightly less than 1/16″. Cut a leaf shape with the lily leaf cutter, then cut it into three pieces with an X-acto knife. Attach a piece of florists' wire to each of the leaves with egg white. Pinch the base of the leaf around the wire, then gently bend the leaf into a curved shape. Dry.

STEP FIVE. Tape several completed flowers and leaves together into a spray with floral tape. Keep blossoms above the leaves.

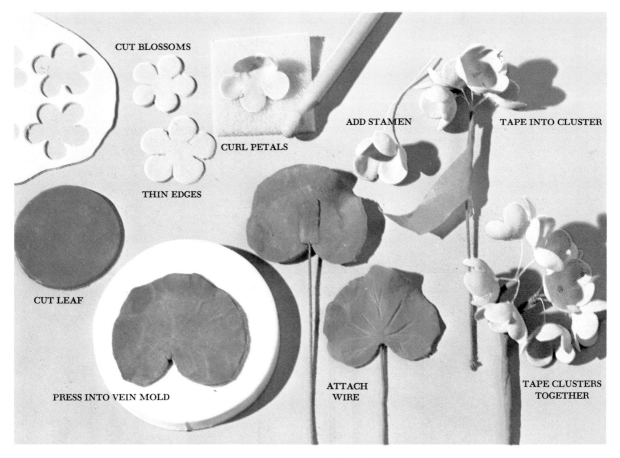

CUT BLOSSOMS

CURL PETALS

THIN EDGES

ADD STAMEN

TAPE INTO CLUSTER

CUT LEAF

PRESS INTO VEIN MOLD

ATTACH
WIRE

TAPE CLUSTERS
TOGETHER

THE MULTI-BLOSSOMED GERANIUM

Multiple flowers like the geranium take a little longer to make, but you'll be delighted with the natural "see-through" effect of the completed flower. See it on page 167.

STEP ONE. Make gum paste following the instructions on page 142. Tint a portion of it and roll out a piece slightly less than 1/16″ thick. Cut the blossoms with the violet cutter. Work with one blossom at a time, keeping the others covered. Press the edges of the petals between the thumb and forefinger to make them thinner.

STEP TWO. Place a blossom on a piece of foam toweling. Curl the petals by pressing from the edge of the petal to the base with stick number 3. Push an artificial stamen through the center of the blossom and secure it in place with egg white. Dry the blossom in an upside down position. You will need 20 to 24 blossoms to create each geranium.

STEP THREE. Tape four blossoms onto a piece of 28-gauge florists' wire with floral tape. Continue taping four blossoms onto pieces of wire until there are six clusters. Tape these six clusters together with floral tape.

STEP FOUR. Tint another piece of gum paste and roll it out 1/16″ thick. Cut a piece with the large rose cutter for each leaf. Press the edges between the thumb and forefinger to make them thinner. Cut out a triangular piece from the edge of the leaf with an X-acto knife to create the characteristic shape of a geranium leaf. Press the leaf into the geranium leaf mold so the cut-out portion is at the bottom of the mold.

STEP FIVE. Attach a piece of florists' wire to the back of the leaf with egg white. Attach a small piece of gum paste with egg white over the wire to help secure it. Ripple the edges of the leaves slightly with the fingers. Dry.

STEP SIX. Make some smaller leaves by cutting pieces of gum paste with the small rose cutter. Follow the same procedure with them as with the larger leaves. When all the leaves are dry, tape several leaves together into a cluster with floral tape. When making an arrangement with the geraniums, be sure the leaves are placed lower than the flowers for a natural look.

CUT PETALS

CUT FLOWER

ROLL PETALS

DRY

ATTACH DISC

CUT LEAVES

PRESS INTO MOLD

ATTACH WIRE

MAKE STEM

COMPLETED DAISY

THE CHEERFUL DAISY

The sunny daisy, so beautiful in a garden or in a cut flower bouquet, needs to be handled gently when made of gum paste to avoid breaking the petals. It is combined with the hardy chrysanthemum into a lovely autumn bouquet on page 168.

STEP ONE. Make gum paste following the instructions on page 142. Tint a piece of it and roll it out 1/16″ thick. For each daisy, cut a piece with the large daisy cutter. Cut each petal in half lengthwise with a sharp knife to double the number of petals.

STEP TWO. Place the daisy on a piece of foam toweling. Roll each petal from side to side with the pointed end of stick number 5. This procedure will make the petals wider and curved. Dry.

STEP THREE. Cut a circle of gum paste with the base of a decorating tube and attach it to the back of the daisy with egg white. This disc will help support and strengthen the petals. Dry.

STEP FOUR. Tint another piece of gum paste and roll it out a little less than 1/16″ thick. Cut a piece for each leaf with the small violet leaf cutter. Press the leaf into the leaf mold. Attach a piece of florists'

wire to the back of each leaf with egg white. Dry the leaf within a curved surface.

STEP FIVE. To make the stem, bend one end of a piece of 22-gauge florists' wire into a small hook. Dip the hook in egg white and push a small ball of gum paste over it. Model the ball into a cone-shaped calyx, the point of the cone extending down onto the wire. Dry. Wrap the wire with floral tape.

STEP SIX. Attach the daisy to the stem by flattening a very small piece of gum paste between the thumb and forefinger. Brush both sides of it with a small amount of egg white. Do not use a lot of egg white or the pieces will not stick together. Press the piece of gum paste to the top of the calyx, then place the daisy on top of it on the calyx. Press very lightly in the center of the daisy to attach it to the calyx. Pipe tube 1 spikes in the center of the daisy with royal icing. Dry. Tape leaves to the stem of the daisy below the flower with floral tape.

To make smaller daisies, use the same procedure as for the large ones, but cut the flowers with the small daisy cutter instead of the large one.

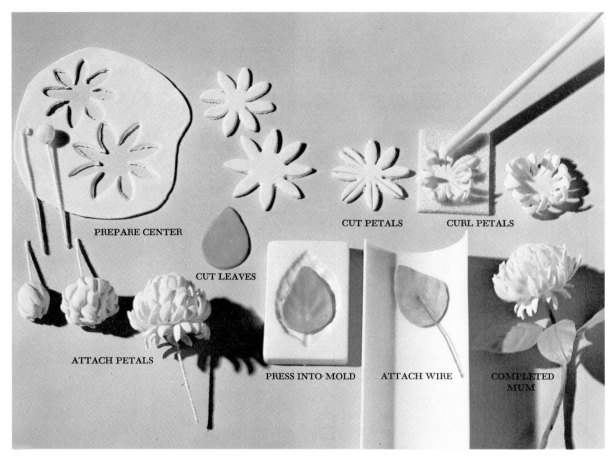

PREPARE CENTER

CUT PETALS

CURL PETALS

CUT LEAVES

ATTACH PETALS

PRESS INTO MOLD

ATTACH WIRE

COMPLETED MUM

THE AUTUMN CHRYSANTHEMUM

STEP ONE. Make gum paste as directed on page 142. Tint a portion of it and set it aside. Bend one end of a piece of florists' wire into a small hook. Dip the hook in egg white and insert it into a ball of tinted gum paste. Dry.

STEP TWO. Roll out a piece of gum paste 1/16″ thick. For each mum, cut three pieces with the small daisy cutter and three pieces with the large daisy cutter. Work with one piece at a time, keeping the rest covered to prevent drying. Cut each petal lengthwise with an X-acto knife to double the number of petals.

STEP THREE. Place a small petal section on a piece of foam toweling. Curl the petals toward the center by pressing from the tip of each petal to the base with the round end of stick number 5.

STEP FOUR. Brush the ball on the wire with egg white, then push the small petal section over the wire. Press it onto the ball so it forms a tight cluster of petals.

STEP FIVE. Curl the petals of the second petal section as described in Step Three. Brush the base of

the first section with egg white and then push the second petal section over the wire, pressing it into position. Follow the same procedure for the third small petal section.

STEP SIX. Working with one piece at a time, curl the petals of two of the large petal sections as described in Step Three and attach to the flower in the same manner as the small petal sections. Curl the petals of the last large petal section in the same way and attach it to the flower with the petals curling down instead of up. Push the wire into a piece of styrofoam for the flower to dry.

STEP SEVEN. Tint another piece of gum paste and roll to a thickness of less than 1/16″. Cut leaves with the small violet leaf cutter. Press them into the leaf mold. Attach a piece of florists' wire to the back of each leaf with egg white and dry them within a curved surface.

STEP EIGHT. Wrap the stem of the mum with floral tape, then tape several leaves to the stem below the flower head.

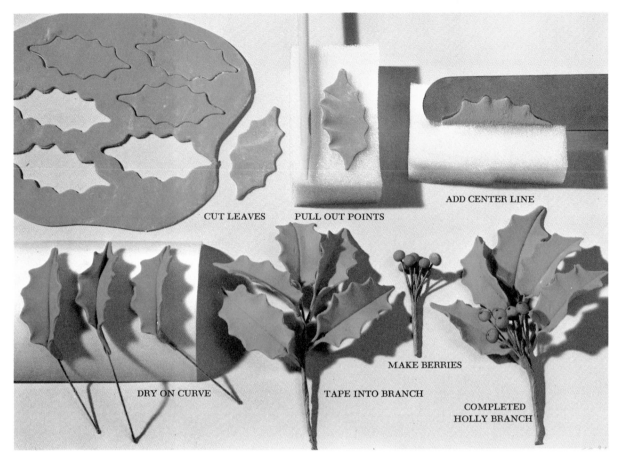

CUT LEAVES   PULL OUT POINTS   ADD CENTER LINE

DRY ON CURVE   TAPE INTO BRANCH   MAKE BERRIES   COMPLETED HOLLY BRANCH

THE CHRISTMAS HOLLY BRANCH

These cheery holly branches are very quick to make. You'll think of lots of ways to use them—forming a lasting Christmas wreath, trimming a candelabra, or garlanding a cake. See a pretty arrangement on page 169.

STEP ONE. Make gum paste following the instructions on page 142. Tint a portion of it and roll out a piece of it into a 5″ circle, 1/16″ thick. Cut leaves from the entire piece with the holly leaf cutter. Keep the leaves well-covered after cutting. You will need about five leaves for each holly branch you plan to make.

STEP TWO. Work with one leaf at a time, keeping the rest covered to prevent drying. Place a leaf on a soft foam sponge. Using stick number 5, pull out the points on the sides of the leaf. Use the pointed end of the stick and press down at each point, then pull the stick out past the edge of the leaf. Press in the center line of the leaf with the edge of a spatula. Do not press too hard or the spatula will cut through the leaf.

STEP THREE. Dip the end of a piece of florists' wire

in egg white and place it at the bottom of the leaf. Pinch the end of the leaf around the wire. Dry the leaf on a curved surface. Repeat Steps Two and Three for each leaf.

STEP FOUR. When dry, tape about five leaves together into a branch with floral tape.

STEP FIVE. Tint a small portion of gum paste and roll small balls for the berries. Dip one end of a 28-gauge piece of florists' wire into egg white and insert it into the berry. Paint a small black dot on the top of each berry with black food color and a small artist's brush. Dry, then tape about six berries into a bunch with floral tape.

STEP SIX. Tape the berries to the leaves with floral tape, positioning them at the same level as the lower leaves.

157

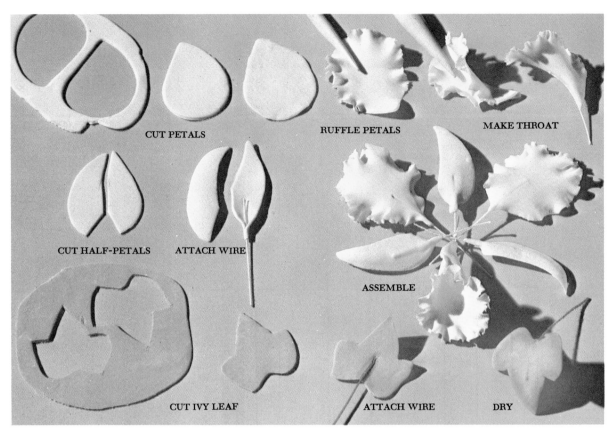

CUT PETALS RUFFLE PETALS MAKE THROAT

CUT HALF-PETALS ATTACH WIRE

ASSEMBLE

CUT IVY LEAF ATTACH WIRE DRY

THE EXOTIC ORCHID

STEP ONE. Follow the instructions on page 142 for making gum paste. Tint a portion of it and roll out a piece 1/16″ thick. For each orchid, cut five petals with the orchid cutter. (You will need to use only four and a half of them.) Keep the pieces you are not working with covered to prevent drying. Thin the edges of one petal by pressing them between the thumb and forefinger. Place the petal on a piece of foam toweling. Ruffle the edges with stick number 5. With the pointed end of the stick, pull the edge of the petal out to stretch and ruffle it.

STEP TWO. Fold the petal over and attach the edges together at the base with egg white. With the pointed end of stick number 2, open the petal up to make the cone-shaped throat. Dip one end of a piece of thin 28-gauge florists' wire in egg white and press it to the back of the cone. Dry on cotton.

STEP THREE. Ruffle two more petals. Working with one petal at a time, thin the edges by pressing them between the thumb and forefinger. Place the petal on a soft piece of foam. With the pointed end of stick number 5, pull the edge of the petal out to stretch and ruffle it. For each petal, dip one end of a thin piece of florists' wire in egg white and press it to the back of the petal. Pinch the base of the petal around the wire. Dry.

STEP FOUR. Cut a wedge from the round end of two orchid petals with a sharp knife, then cut each petal in half lengthwise. Curve three of the half-petals slightly with the fingers, then turn them over and attach a thin piece of florists' wire to the back with egg white. Pinch the end of each half-petal around the wire to help secure it. Dry.

STEP FIVE. When all six petals have been allowed to dry overnight, assemble the orchid. Tape the wires of the two ruffled petals and the throat together with floral tape. Position the three half-petals between them and secure in position by wrapping with floral tape. If you wish to give the orchid a more natural look, brush the inside of the throat with powdered dark yellow pastel. (Carefully shave the pastel stick with an X-acto knife to make the powder.)

STEP SIX. To make the ivy leaves, tint a piece of gum paste and roll it to a thickness of less than 1/16″. Cut some leaves with the small ivy leaf cutter and some with the large ivy leaf cutter. Attach a piece of florists' wire to the back of each leaf with egg white. Curve the leaves slightly with the fingers and then dry them on a curved surface to retain the curve.

CHAPTER ELEVEN

A Gallery of
Gum Paste Flower Arrangements

Flowers made with gum paste are so colorful and realistic they are a pleasure to arrange in corsages, nosegays and bouquets. Their flexible wire stems allow you to turn the blossoms so they may be seen to their best advantage. This chapter shows you thirteen pretty ways to form non-wilt arrangements of gum paste blossoms—you'll think of many more ways to display your artistry. To keep the flowers free of dust, you might cover them with a clear plastic or glass dome.

THREE ORCHIDS, delicate as butterflies, are taped together with ivy leaves to form a dainty corsage. Finish with a ribbon bow.

A DOZEN CHEERFUL CROCUSES in a little Delft sugar bowl bring spring at any season. Fit a block of styrofoam into the bowl, fill crevices with royal icing, then arrange the flowers.

A STATELY MADONNA LILY plant rises from an embossed plastic bowl. Fill the bowl with a half-ball or block of styrofoam, pipe tube 2 royal icing "moss" on top, then insert the lovely lily. A treasure to enjoy for years.

AN EASTER BASKET glowing with tulips and crocuses! You'll need only four tulips and half a dozen crocus flowers to create this spring-time treat. Line a basket with clear plastic wrap, then fill it with styrofoam and pipe the "moss" just as for the lily. You'll have a touch of spring all year long.

BELOW, GOLDEN DAFFODILS spring from a white porcelain tea cup. Prepare the container for them and for the iris at right just as for the lily on page 160.

AT RIGHT, THREE REGAL IRIS blooms are arranged in a brass chocolate pot. Their delicate colors and forms are so beautiful that one can understand why the French chose the iris as their national flower.

Below: arching sprays of fragile bluebells and their grass-like leaves make a charming arrangement. The little urn is made from a plastic bell mold glued to the plate of a wedding ornament base.

Top right: dainty briar roses and buds fill a miniature Paul Revere bowl. Leaves are arranged in lifelike groups of three. Prepare the containers for the roses and bluebells just as for the lily on page 160.

Lower right: one perfect pink rose and its opening bud are framed with fresh violets and edged with a lacy frill. Twist stems together, then pleat a paper doily and insert stems through center. Add a blue ribbon.

BELOW: IMPATIENS in glowing rose and scarlet fill a little brass sugar bowl.

AT RIGHT: PERKY PINK AND RED GERANIUMS are set off by a shiny tin compote you make yourself. Glue a gelatin or bavarian mold to an individual pudding mold, then prepare it, and the container for the impatiens just as for the lily on page 160. You've created a lasting decorative accessory.

A FALL BOUQUET of chrysanthemums and vari-colored daisies is as beautiful as a Dutch still life when arranged in a miniature brass skuttle. Prepare the container just as for the lily, page 160.

A WREATH OF HOLLY LEAVES with bright red berries surrounds four tapers. Cover the reverse side of a 6″ plate from the clear pillar set with green gum paste. The sockets that hold the pillars serve as candle holders. Attach a spray of holly between each candle and set one in the center.

CHAPTER TWELVE

The Wilton Way
of Making Gum Paste Figures

One of the most creative and enjoyable of all the decorating skills is the art of making gum paste figures. These lifelike little people can be posed on award-winning cakes, placed in doll houses, or simply arranged in beautiful tableaux.

No two figures are ever alike—each will take on a personality as you adjust their bodies in expressive poses, bring out their features with color, and drape them in gum paste clothing. Just working with them will bring you the joy and pride of a sculptor.

ADVANTAGES OF THREE-PART MOLDS

All the figures in this chapter were made in three-part plastic molds—one for the head and upper body, one for the legs and lower body and a third for the arms. Thus all parts of the body are in perfect proportion and you are spared the difficulty of hand-modeling legs, arms and hands.

After the figures are molded, you can tilt the heads, turn and bend the torsos, and place the arms and legs in almost any position you desire.

These three-part molds are made in four versions —man, woman, ten year old child and five year old child, each in proportion to one another. The molds for children's figures can serve for boys, girls, angels or fairy tale characters.

Since the molds are made in smooth, strong plastic, the features are finely detailed, and they will not wear or crack as plaster molds do.

MATERIALS YOU'LL NEED

The figures are molded in gum paste, made with the recipe on page 142. Be sure to let gum paste age at least 24 hours before molding figures. Paste food colors are used for tinting, with egg white brushed on to join parts. Limbs are strengthened with toothpicks or cloth-covered wire. Royal icing smooths crevices after drying, and pipes hair and details on clothing. The modeling sticks and rolling pin shown on page 142 shape and ruffle the clothing.

It is important to *dry the molded parts of the figures thoroughly* before assembling—usually 24 hours. Use blocks of styrofoam, cotton balls and popsicle sticks to support figures until dry.

Clothing is made from thinly rolled gum paste, cut out with an X-acto knife to pattern or measurement, and trimmed with a small thread scissors. All patterns needed are in The Wilton Way Pattern Book—but as you master this exciting art you'll make your own to suit the characters you create.

LEARN THE BASICS FIRST

If this method of making gum paste figures is new to you, please study pages 172 to 178 which describe the clown figures. These pages explain the basic procedure of molding, positioning and dressing any figure, and the order in which the work proceeds. Page 178 shows the method for finishing the figures, applying make-up and adjusting hands. But before beginning to make any figure, *read all directions completely.*

HOW TO PRESERVE AND DISPLAY FIGURES

You'll want to preserve these little works of art in permanent displays. When they are finished and completely dry, spray them with two coats of acrylic spray glaze. This will bring out the colors, add sheen, and protect them against moisture which is harmful to gum paste. Then they can be mounted on plastic separator plates, styrofoam or stiff cardboard. Paint these platforms with thinned royal icing. Attach figures with small pieces of gum paste painted on both sides with egg white. This gives a strong, lasting bond.

Two JOLLY CLOWNS frolic on a birthday cake sure to delight any child or circus buff. Make figures as described on pages 172 to 178. Make two hollow sugar balls using 3″ ball mold. Paint with thinned royal icing. Paint a 10″ plastic separator plate with icing. Attach balls to plate with royal icing and figures to ball and plate as described above.

Bake and ice a 14″ two-layer cake. Trim sides with tube 48 diagonal lines, then border with tube 10 balls. Insert dowel rods for support into cake and set clowns (on plate) on top. Edge plate with tube 6 balls and add tapers. Serves 36.

HOW TO MOLD A SEATED CLOWN

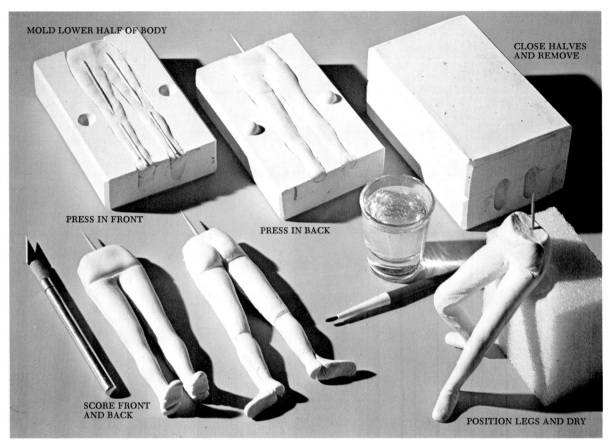

MOLD LOWER HALF OF BODY

CLOSE HALVES AND REMOVE

PRESS IN FRONT

PRESS IN BACK

SCORE FRONT AND BACK

POSITION LEGS AND DRY

For this figure, we are using the man mold. For best results when molding the figures, try to use as close to the correct amount of gum paste to fill the mold as possible. First brush mold with vegetable oil, then wipe out excess with a paper towel. *Be sure to oil every mold you use* in this manner before molding. Rub a little cornstarch onto the gum paste piece before pressing into the mold.

MOLD FRONT OF LEGS. Firmly press a piece of gum paste into the front half of the man's leg mold. First form it into a rectangular shape and make a length-wise cut for the legs with a pair of scissors. Rub with cornstarch, put it into the mold and gently stretch the legs down to the end. To make sure that the gum paste is even with the surface of the mold, press with a small spatula. Trim off excess gum paste flush with mold at feet and waist. With fingers, gently push from edge of gum paste to center to loosen edges slightly. Paint egg white onto the surface of the gum paste, making sure it goes all the way to the edge, but does not seep down into the mold. Press two toothpicks into the surface of each leg, above and below the knee.

MOLD BACK OF LEGS. Using the same procedure as for the front half, firmly press gum paste into the back half of the man's leg mold. Trim excess, then loosen edges. Break a toothpick in half and dip into egg white. Insert it into the waist, pointed end up. Brush surface of gum paste with egg white.

CLOSE THE TWO HALVES of the mold and press together firmly. Push the two halves of the gum paste together at the exposed waist and feet. Loosen the halves of the mold, then remove the back half. Let gum paste "roll out" of the front half of the mold and lift the mold off the tops of the feet. Gently smooth seams with fingers.

MAKE A SHALLOW CUT across the top of the legs on the front and back. Also make a shallow cut across the back of the knees. These score lines allow the legs to bend more easily.

POSITION LEGS. Make an indentation in the edge of a block of styrofoam. Bend lower portion of body at score lines at top of legs and set in the indentation. Bend legs at knees and position as shown. Prop with cotton balls. Dry overnight.

172

MOLD THE TORSO

Always make the back of the torso first. Because of the detail on the face, it is best to unmold the front half of the torso as soon as possible. Oil the halves of torso mold the same as for leg mold.

PRESS IN BACK. Form a piece of gum paste into a rough shape of head, neck and chest. Press it firmly into the back half of the man's torso mold. Flatten gum paste with spatula and trim excess at waist. Gently loosen edges of gum paste from mold. Brush the gum paste with egg white, making sure it goes to the edge but does not seep into the mold. Push a toothpick into the surface of the gum paste to give support to the head and neck.

PRESS IN FRONT. Using the same method as for the back, press a piece of gum paste firmly into the front half of the man's torso mold. Press thumb *very hard* into face to get details. Trim off excess at waist. Loosen edges from mold, then brush gum paste with egg white.

CLOSE THE HALVES of the mold and press firmly together. Push the gum paste together at the exposed waist. Loosen the halves of the mold and remove back half. Let the gum paste "roll out" of the front half. Gently smooth seams.

ATTACH to dried lower half of body. Brush base of torso with egg white and push onto toothpick. Shape and smooth to fit lower half of body. Gently turn head and shoulders to one side and dry.

APPLY CLOWN MAKE-UP after head is completely dry. You need red paste color, a number 1 artist's brush and blue and black lead pencils sharpened to a fine point. Begin on the left side (right side if you are left-handed).

With the black pencil, draw in the eyelid. Add the pupil with the blue pencil. With the artist's brush and red coloring thinned with a *tiny* amount of water, paint in the lines above and below the eye. Do the other eye the same way.

Paint in the line on the forehead and the dot on the nose. Add the make-up on the mouth. Make the top curve first, then the bottom curve and fill in between them. Paint dot on chin. Dry.

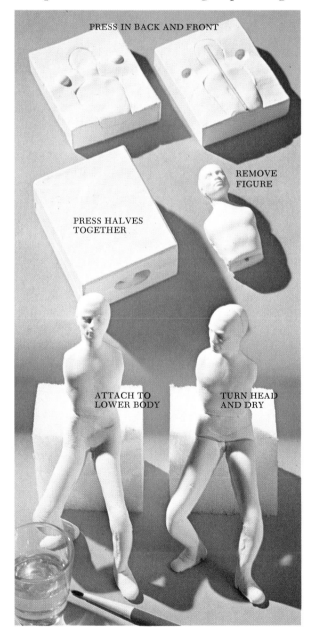

PRESS IN BACK AND FRONT

REMOVE FIGURE

PRESS HALVES TOGETHER

ATTACH TO LOWER BODY

TURN HEAD AND DRY

APPLY MAKE-UP

GUM PASTE IN MOLD

CLOSE HALVES

REMOVE ARM

POSITION AND DRY

CUT RECTANGLE

ROLL CYLINDER

MOLD THE ARMS
FOR THE SEATED CLOWN

For best results, make only one arm at a time. Oil arm mold the same as the leg mold. Be sure to mold both a left and a right arm.

ROLL A PIECE OF GUM PASTE into a cylinder slightly larger than the arm, rub with cornstarch and place it into one half of the man's arm mold. Press it into the mold, being sure to press down in the hand portion of the mold to get the details. Pinch the gum paste back up along the arm so it will fill the other half of the mold.

PRESS THE TWO HALVES of the mold together very tightly. Remove one half of the mold and carefully trim around the arm, while it is still in the mold, with an X-acto knife.

REMOVE THE ARM from the mold and trim the hand with an X-acto knife or a pair of thread scissors. Handle very gently to avoid distorting the shape. Bend the arm into position, prop with cotton balls and dry overnight.

BEGIN TO DRAPE
THE SEATED CLOWN

After the figure has been completely dried, over-night, begin to dress it. When making clothes for gum paste figures, sections of clothing are cut out, draped on the figure and attached with egg white. They must be made and attached very quickly so they will fall into soft folds. If the gum paste begins to dry, it will crack when draped. This takes some practice, but soon you will learn the technique.

MAKE A PANT LEG. Roll a piece of gum paste as thin as possible and cut a 5″ x 4″ rectangle. Fold over to make a cylinder 5″ long and "glue" seam with egg white. Insert the small gum paste rolling pin inside the cylinder and roll, flattening the seam until it is almost invisible. Cut out a large "V" at the seam at one end and a tiny "V" at the other end of the piece with a pair of thread scissors.

SLIP OVER THE LEG with the large "V" at the top and on the inner side of the leg. Attach pant leg at waist and ankle with egg white, pinching together to fit and to give a gathered effect to the pant leg at the ankle. Smooth at waist and ankle with fingers.

MAKE A SECOND PANT LEG the same way and attach to the other leg. Smooth the center seam with fingers in the front and back so the pants appear to be a single piece. Dry thoroughly.

DRAPE BLOUSE

After each piece of clothing is added, make sure it is completely dry (usually overnight) before adding the next. If you rush this process, it is very likely that the clothing will crack or be pushed into an unnatural shape.

After the pants have dried, then add the over-blouse to the figure. This is added before the arms are attached.

ROLL OUT a piece of gum paste as thin as possible. Cut a 6″ x 3″ rectangle for the blouse, then trim the short sides at an angle as shown.

RUFFLE BLOUSE. Lay the rectangular piece of gum paste on a piece of foam toweling. Roll the longest edge with the rounded end of gum paste modeling stick 2, placing the stick about halfway up the piece. This will stretch this edge of the piece and form the flared folds of the blouse.

ATTACH TO FIGURE. Drape the blouse around the figure, attaching it to the upper part of the shoulders with egg white and forming it to fit with the fingers. Arrange the folds on the blouse so they fall gracefully and naturally.

MAKE SHOES
FOR THE CLOWN

The oversize clown shoes are added next, after the blouse has dried thoroughly.

ROLL A 1″ BALL of gum paste for the shoe. Flatten one end with fingers and cut the flattened portion in half from the edge up to the ball.

BRUSH FOOT with egg white. Place the shoe over the foot and wrap the flattened portions around the sides to the back. Trim to fit at the heel. Attach a small ball of gum paste on the toe of the shoe with egg white for a pompon. Repeat process to make the other shoe. Dry.

MAKE THE MITTENS

The arm of the figure will be completely draped before it is attached to the body. The first step is to make the mitten and to form it to the hand.

FOR THE MITTEN, start with a 2″ x 1″ rectangle cut from a piece of gum paste that has been rolled as thin as possible.

BRUSH THE HAND with egg white. Fold the rectangle over the hand. Make a cut for the thumb and trim the remainder of the mitten into a rounded shape.

MOLD THE MITTEN to the wrist and shape it to the hand with the fingers. If the mitten is too large, trim off excess gum paste and reshape. Dry. Repeat for the other mitten.

ATTACH TO FIGURE

CUT AND TRIM RECTANGLE

RUFFLE

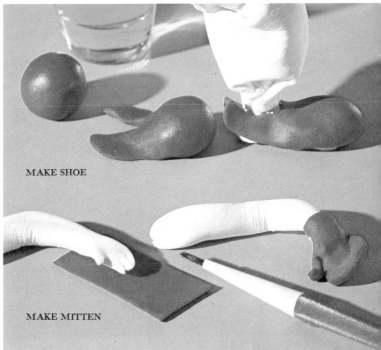

MAKE SHOE

MAKE MITTEN

MAKING COLLAR

MAKING HAT

ATTACH HAT TO HEAD
AND ADD BUTTONS

MAKING SLEEVE

MAKE RUFFLED COLLAR

ROLL OUT a piece of gum paste ⅛" thick. Cut out a 1¾" circle (use end of tube 127D). Remove a circle from center with the end of a standard tube.

RUFFLE COLLAR. Place the gum paste doughnut shape on a piece of foam toweling. With the round end of stick 5, roll outer edge to ruffle it. Cut from the inner circle to the edge.

ATTACH TO FIGURE. Brush egg white around the neck. Place the collar around it, pressing gently in place. Make a second collar the same way and attach, first brushing neck with egg white.

MAKE HAT FOR CLOWN

ROLL OUT a piece of gum paste ⅛" thick and cut a 2" diameter circle. Cut out one-third of the circle in a wedge shape. Roll larger piece into a cone, "gluing" the seam with egg white. Brush egg white inside the bottom edge of the hat. Shape hat to head while the hat and egg white is still wet. Pipe hair with tube 1. Attach a tiny ball of gum paste to the point of the hat with egg white and dry.

ADD BUTTONS to blouse by rolling tiny balls of gum paste and attaching with egg white. Dry.

DRAPE ARM AND ATTACH

ROLL OUT a piece of gum paste as thin as possible and cut a 3" x 2½" rectangle. Fold over to make a cylinder, "gluing" the seam with egg white. Insert a gum paste modeling stick inside the cylinder and roll the seam until it is almost invisible. Cut a "V" shape out at one end on the seam with a pair of thread scissors for under the arm.

BRUSH EGG WHITE on wrist and top of arm. Slip cylinder over the arm. Pinch into gathers to fit at wrist and smooth to the top of the arm. Be sure that the flat part of the arm that attaches to the body is not covered with the sleeve. Roll a string of gum paste for cuff, brush one side with egg white and attach, covering the edge of the sleeve.

ATTACH ARM TO BODY while the sleeve is still wet. Drip a few drops of melted white sealing wax onto the shoulder of the figure where the arm is to be attached. Quickly place the arm in position and hold in place until wax hardens. A second method is to attach a small piece of gum paste to the arm with egg white, brush the piece with more egg white and press to body. Prop until dry. Drape sleeve on the other arm and attach to body. When the figure is thoroughly dry, spray with two coats of clear acrylic spray to protect it from moisture.

176

HOW TO MOLD
A STANDING CLOWN

Now that you have learned to mold a seated clown, you can mold a standing one even more easily. For this figure, we are using the woman mold. It is molded in basically the same way as the seated figure except that the legs are not bent. Be sure to let each piece dry thoroughly as you work.

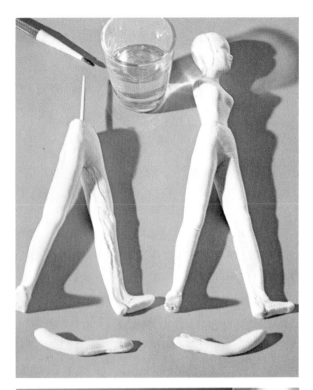

MOLD LEGS. Press pieces of gum paste into the oiled front and back halves of the woman's leg mold as described for the seated figure on page 172. After brushing the pieces with egg white, press a piece of cloth-covered florists' wire into each leg on the front half. Since the legs do not need to bend, the wire gives more support to the legs on a standing figure than the two toothpicks would give. Do not make cuts in the legs.

Position the feet and legs and prop on styrofoam block in an upright position with popsicle sticks until dry. If dried lying down, the piece will flatten and lose its rounded, natural look.

MOLD TORSO. Press pieces of gum paste into the oiled front and back halves of the woman's torso mold in the same way as described on page 173. Attach torso to legs and dry.

After the torso has completely dried, paint on the make-up using the same method as for the seated figure. Let it dry thoroughly to avoid smudging the food coloring.

MOLD THE ARMS in the oiled woman's arm mold using the method on page 174. Bend the arms into position and dry on cotton balls.

TO DRAPE THE FIGURE, follow the steps described on pages 174 through 176. Make and attach the pants, blouse, shoes, mittens, collars and hat in that order. Add the hair and buttons, then drape the sleeves on the arms and attach the arms to the body.

The oversize shoes are very important on this figure because they give it a bigger base and help it to stand without any extra support.

Make the pieces of clothing the same size as for the seated figure. If they are too large, trim them with a pair of thread scissors. Let each piece of clothing dry after it has been draped on the figure before adding the next piece.

When the figure is thoroughly dry, spray it with two coats of clear acrylic spray to protect it from moisture in the air.

YOUR FINISHED GUM PASTE FIGURES will have the look of porcelain figurines. You will find great satisfaction in making these realistic little people.

HOW TO SMOOTH AND FINISH THE FIGURES

Where shoulders, neck or limbs are exposed, you will need to smooth the seam where front and back halves come together. Do this with an X-acto knife, trimming off any excess gum paste gently, after molded parts are thoroughly dry. Then fill seam with royal icing, tinted to match, and smooth with a damp cloth or brush. Occasionally, you will want to paint the entire piece with thinned royal icing after the fill is dry, but this is rarely necessary.

If the clothing is fitted, such as trousers or bodices, smooth seams before putting on clothing.

Spray completed figures with acrylic spray glaze to protect from moisture.

HOW TO MAKE-UP THE FACES

To create the make-up, you will need paste food color, a small artist's brush, pastel sticks, a white pencil sharpened to a point and an X-acto knife. First brush any cornstarch off the face and head with a soft, dry brush. This is the usual make-up for women and children figures. You will vary it for special characters.

BLUSH THE CHEEKS with deep flesh-colored powdered pastel and a soft, dry brush. (To create the powder, shave pastel sticks with the X-acto knife.)

Do EYES. With watered-down copper color, brush in shadow above the eye. Whiten the eye socket with white pencil. With a dot of copper color, designate the pupil. Paint in iris of eye. Darken the pupil, then paint in a thin line for eyelashes. Make the highlight in the eye with the X-acto knife.

PAINT LIPS with thinned food color, starting with the lower one. Define hair area with royal icing before piping hair with a fine writing tube.

VARIATIONS ON BASIC MAKE-UP

FOR A MAN, use slightly darker gum paste to mold than for a woman. Blush cheeks darker and use copper color for lips.

FOR ORIENTAL MAKE-UP, mold head in pale gold color gum paste. Brush white pastel below outside corner of eye to create high cheekbone, then add rose blush on cheeks. Paint copper shadow in eye socket to lower upper lid. Define upper and lower lids with black. Lips are smaller.

FOR AFRO-AMERICAN MAKE-UP, mold head in brown gum paste. Use blended pink, red and brown pastel powder for blush. Eye shadow is thinned brown color. Use black for eyes and lashes. Color lips with white pencil, then apply food color over it.

FOR AMERICAN INDIAN, mold in copper color gum paste. Use blended rust and pink for blush. Apply a lighter color below outer corner of eye to create high cheekbones. Eyes are brown and copper, eyelashes are brown. Paint lips with mixed copper and pink food color.

HOW TO FINISH THE HANDS

Immediately after the arm is taken from the mold, cut between fingers with an X-acto knife. Between second and third fingers, and between third and little fingers, cut out a tiny "v" of gum paste. Gently pinch fingers to point and lengthen. Place them in desired position and dry.

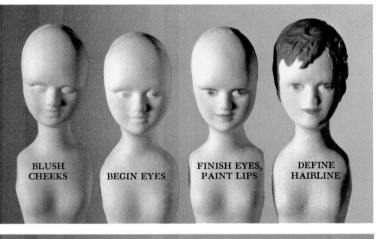

BLUSH CHEEKS   BEGIN EYES   FINISH EYES, PAINT LIPS   DEFINE HAIRLINE

MAKE-UP FOR MAN   ORIENTAL   AFRO-AMERICAN   AMERICAN INDIAN

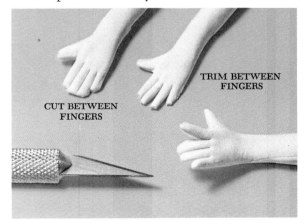

CUT BETWEEN FINGERS   TRIM BETWEEN FINGERS

Two LITTLE FRIENDS, dressed in Victorian style, meet on a flowery cake. The next pages tell how to make the figures. When finished, attach them to a 6″ separator plate, painted with thinned royal icing. Brush small pieces of gum paste on both sides with egg white and attach to soles of shoes, then stand figures on plate. The cake is a 10″ x 3″ square, festooned with garlands, draped with string and brightened with drop flowers.

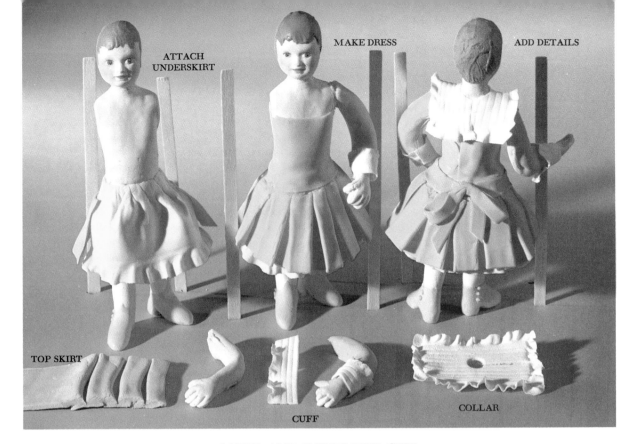

ATTACH UNDERSKIRT

MAKE DRESS

ADD DETAILS

TOP SKIRT

CUFF

COLLAR

MOLD AND DRESS THE GIRL

Mold figure in ten year old child molds as on page 177. While legs are still in mold, cut and attach heel to foot with egg white. Unmold and shape foot. Dry figure 24 hours. Smooth figure and apply make-up as on page 178. Paint boots with royal icing. Dry. Pipe tube 1 buttons.

MAKE UNDERSKIRT. Roll gum paste very thin and cut a 6″ x 2″ rectangle. Ruffle one long edge with stick 5. Brush waist with egg white, then attach unruffled edge, gathering as you attach. Trim excess at back.

MAKE DRESS. Roll gum paste very thin and cut a 7″ x 1½″ rectangle. Fold to form box pleats. Attach at waist with egg white for back of skirt. Trim excess at sides. Make a second piece for the front of the skirt. Attach and trim excess at sides.

Roll gum paste very thin and cut a 4″ x 1½″ rectangle for bodice. Brush body with egg white up to armhole and wrap bodice around, trimming at back. Trim for armhole.

Cut a 6″ x ¼″ belt and attach with egg white, butting it against the skirt. Trim excess at back.

FINISH DRESS. Attach a 2¼″ x 1½″ sleeve to each arm, trimming excess on underside. Cut 2″ x ½″ cuffs. Gently press in lines for tucks with a piece of light cardboard. Ruffle one long edge by rolling with stick and attach with egg white, trimming excess. Attach arms with small pieces of gum paste brushed on both sides with egg white. Prop to dry.

Cut a 1⅞″ x 1⅜″ collar. Cut a hole in center with tube 10, then make a cut from hole in center to edge

so the cut is parallel with the long sides. Gently press in lines for tucks on the collar with a piece of light cardboard, parallel to the cut. Ruffle edges by rolling with stick, then attach with egg white.

MAKE HAT. Start with a 1″ ball of gum paste. Model with fingers so it fits over the end of tube 1A. Then continue modeling to form brim. Dry. Model a dozen tiny Elementary Roses (page 95) on toothpicks. Remove toothpicks and dry. Attach roses to hat with royal icing. Pipe tube 65s leaves. Secure hat on head, then pipe hair with tube 1s.

Make bows for shoulders and hat with ⅛″ wide strips of gum paste. Fold strips to make bows and pinch center. Attach in position with egg white. Make bow at back of dress with a ¼″ wide strip. Attach while still wet with egg white. Pipe beading around collar and cuffs with tube 1s. Roll a gum paste "string" for stick. When dry, attach to hand.

Spray dried figure with two coats of acrylic spray.

MAKING HAT

DRESS LOWER BODY

ATTACH SHIRT

ADD DETAILS

COLLAR

HAT BAND

CROWN OF HAT

MOLD AND DRESS THE BOY

Mold the figure in the ten year old child molds, following the instructions on page 177. Dry, then smooth and apply make-up as on page 178.

BEGIN TO CLOTHE FIGURE. Make and attach boots as for Santa (page 182). Cut ¼″ wide strips of gum paste for socks and attach. Press in grooves with modeling stick 5. Pipe tube 1 buttons on boots.

Cut pant leg using Wilton Way pattern, paint upper leg with egg white, and attach, with seam on inner side. Trim excess. Make a short, lengthwise cut on lower outside edge of pant leg. Flare it to form a flap. Cut tube 2 buttons and attach to flap. Do other pant leg the same. Dry.

ADD SHIRT. Cut a 2¼″ x 2⅛″ piece for front of shirt and attach to figure with egg white. Trim neckline. Cut an identical piece for shirt back and attach. Trim excess at side seams. Trim neckline and armholes. Dry. Cut and attach a triangular neckline insert on the shirt, trimming to fit.

Roll gum paste extra thin and cut the neckerchief from pattern. Lay it on foam toweling and score a line down the middle with stick 5. Turn the piece over and score lines down either side of first line. Pinch the piece to fold it and attach at neckline.

DRAPE AND ATTACH ARMS. Cut a 2½″ x 1½″ rectangle for sleeve. Brush arm with egg white and wrap piece around, trimming to fit. Do other arm the same. Cut cuffs from pattern and attach. Secure arms to body with small pieces of gum paste, brushed with egg white on both sides. Prop to dry.

ATTACH COLLAR. First paint stripes on neckline insert with paste color thinned with kirschwasser or other white liqueur. When dry, cut collar from pattern and attach around neckline with egg white.

Finish neckerchief by attaching two folded ¾″ triangles and a free-form "knot".

MAKE HAT. Cut a strip of gum paste 3″ x ¼″. Form it into a circle and attach to head with egg white. Cut a 1¼″ circle, ¼″ thick for crown. Use stick 5 to form grooves on the underside. Attach to band with egg white. Add a ⅛″ ball to crown and dry.

ADD DETAILS. Paint stripes on collar and cuffs with paste color thinned with kirschwasser. Dry. Pipe ears and hair with tube 1. Make hoop with a long gum paste "string". When dry, attach in hand with egg white. Spray with clear acrylic spray.

BACK VIEW

181

Santa is molded in the ten year old child mold, using the method on page 177. For chubby figure, attach a piece of gum paste to stomach. Dry at least 24 hours.

MAKE THE PANTS FIRST, using Wilton Way pattern. Follow the procedure on page 174, flaring bottoms of legs. Attach at waist and above ankle with egg white, gathering to fit at bottom then trimming straight. Cut a 2¼″ x 1½″ rectangle for each boot. Brush foot with egg white. Wrap long side around foot, extending up to pant leg and smoothing to fit. Cut off excess around sole and in back. Cut a

2¼″ x ⅜″ rectangle for boot cuff. Attach at top of boot, and flare lower edge. Cut a 1⅛″ circle for hat crown. Attach to head with egg white.

MAKE JACKET. Cut a 3″ x 2″ rectangle and roll into a 2″ long open cylinder. Roll seam and flare bottom with stick 5. Slip over head. Attach at shoulders and belt line, gathering at belt line. Pinch shoulder area flat and trim at shoulders and neck. Add a 2⅛″ x ¼″ piece for collar. Score a line down front.

Cut a 3″ x ⅜″ piece for bottom of jacket. Thin one long edge by rolling with stick 5 and attach unrolled edge at belt line. Cut a 3½″ x ¼″ belt and attach. Add belt buckle. Dry three hours.

APPLY MAKE-UP using method on page 178. Paint iris only halfway down eye socket. Paint tiny mouth and blush cheeks, forehead and nose with pink pastel. Add a ¼″ wide cuff around the edge of hat and a small ball at top. Pipe tube 1s "fur" on collar, hat cuff and ball. Pipe tube 1 beard and hair.

HAND-MODEL TINY TOYS. Doll is 1½″ tall, using a ball for head and "strings" of gum paste for arms and legs. Pipe tube 1s hair. Horn is 2″ long. Cut packages, 1″ to 1½″ long and trim with tube 1s. Model a train about 1½″ long and 1″ high. Dry all thoroughly. Model sack from a 1″ ball. Make a short additional strap for the portion extending from Santa's hand. Insert cotton into sack and dry. Attach doll to jacket with egg white. Dry.

MAKE ARMS. Model cylinders 2¼″ long x ⅜″, making one end smaller for shoulder. Press in lines at wider end for "gathers". Bend arms and attach, one holding doll and other bent to hold sack. Attach sack to back. Model mittens from ⅜″ balls and attach to arms. Attach strap portion below mitten. Dry.

ADD FINISHING TOUCHES. Pipe tube 1s "fur" cuffs. Complete hair, beard and eyebrows with tube 1s. Insert packages in sack. Paint a 6″ round separator plate with thinned royal icing and dry. Attach figure to plate by painting small gum paste pieces on both sides with egg white, attaching to soles, then pressing figure to plate. Dry, then spray.

Make two pine trees on iced paper cones. Pull out tube 18 shells from cones, then cover with tube 75 points. Add gum paste star at top. Ice a 10″ round two-layer cake with boiled icing. Pipe a tube 17 shell border. Position Santa and trees on cake. Conceal separator plate with swirled icing. Dust icing and trees with edible glitter. Serves 14.

PAD STOMACH   CLOTHE FIGURE

MODEL SACK   MODEL ARMS   MODEL TOYS

Poised on tiptoe and wearing the daintiest of pink tutus, this ballerina has just stepped out of Tchaikovsky's famous ballet, *The Nutcracker Suite.* Every little girl will be thrilled to see a cake like this, and to keep the pretty figure as a remembrance of a wonderful party. The Sugar Plum Fairy is quite easy to mold with the three-piece woman mold.

MOLD BACK OF LEGS first. Use method for standing figure on page 177. Have at hand 12″ cloth-covered 22-gauge wires. While gum paste is still in mold, lay a wire on one leg, extending 5″ below foot.

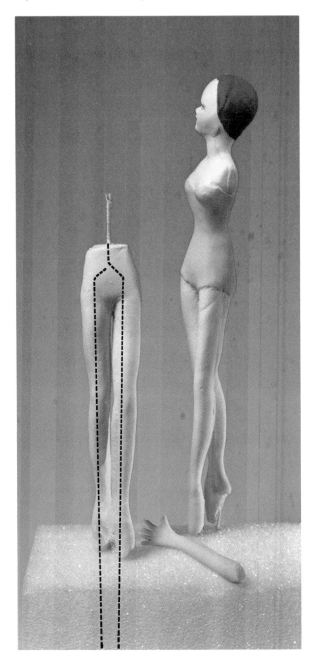

Make an "L" shaped bend in wire at hip and let wire extend above top of mold. Lay second wire on other leg, extending 5″ below foot. Bend at slight angle at hip and clip off.

Mold and join front of legs to back of legs. Immediately bend front of foot down, almost covering wire. Push extended wires into a 4″ thick block of styrofoam. "Turn out" feet to outside. Clip wire extending from top of figure to 1½″ length. Dry at least 24 hours.

MOLD HEAD AND TORSO and place on lower body to dry. Turn head but keep body erect. Mold arms, cut and position fingers. Trim arms diagonally at top of shoulder so they will extend straight out when attached. Dry. Spray arms and figure with acrylic spray glaze.

Roll out gum paste ⅛″ thick and cut a 3½″ circle for base and dry. Paint bodice, tights and shoes with thinned royal icing.

APPLY MAKE-UP as described on page 178 but accentuate painted lines for lashes and add wing-like brows. Paint hair area, then pipe hair with tube 1s. Cut a tiny pointed tiara from gum paste, place on head and dry.

MAKE TUTU. Gather two 60″ x 1¾″ strips of tulle on long edge. Trim edges close to thread as possible. Pull threads to circumference of waistline and knot. Apply line of white glue to figure slightly below waist, wrap one ruffle around and join with a few stitches at back. Attach second ruffle to figure just above first. Adjust top of skirt with point of knife.

ATTACH ARMS to shoulders with small pieces of gum paste brushed on both sides with egg white. Prop with cotton balls on top of tutu until dry. Using Wilton Way pattern, cut tulle arm ruffles. Gather to fit on straight side, trim close to thread, and attach to shoulders with glue. Add design to bodice and tiara with tube 1 dots of piping gel.

BAKE A TWO-LAYER ROUND CAKE from firm pound cake batter. Brush with hot strained apricot preserves, let dry, then cover with rolled fondant. (Method is on page 94, recipe on page 92.) Pipe bulb border at base with tube 6, ruffle with tube 104, beading with tube 2. Make two holes in center of plaque for wires extending from feet and attach plaque to cake. Edge plaque with tube 2. Add scallops and embroidery with tube 1. Place ballerina on cake by pushing wires through plaque and cake to serving tray. An enchanting confection that serves twelve guests.

ATTACH UNDERSKIRT

MAKE DRESS

FINISHED FIGURE

MAKE SLEEVES AND CUFFS

MAKE APRON

BRING A FAIRY TALE TO LIFE

Snow White, a folk tale many centuries old, was set down by the brothers Grimm between 1812 and 1815. Here we show a surprised Snow White and the dwarfs at their first meeting in the forest.

MOLD FIGURE. Using the method on page 177, mold legs from white gum paste, torso and arms from flesh-colored in the woman's molds. Flatten the chest slightly and open the mouth with a pointed stick. To bend the arms at a sharp angle, cut a small "V" from the inner side of the elbow. Position figure in an attitude of surprise. Dry 24 hours.

Finish figure as described on page 178.

BEGIN TO CLOTHE FIGURE. Roll gum paste as thin as possible for all pieces. Cut a 3″ x ¼″ piece for each shoe. Brush it with egg white and wrap around foot, trimming excess at back. Add buckle.

The underskirt is a 5″ circle with a small "X" cut in the center. Ruffle the outer edge by rolling it on a piece of foam toweling with modeling stick 5. Brush hips with egg white, slip underskirt over the head and position it low on the hips. Use cotton balls beneath the underskirt to hold it in position. Dry at least 24 hours before adding dress.

MAKE DRESS. Cut skirt using Wilton Way pattern. Brush waist and slightly below it with egg white and attach skirt slightly above waist, gathering as you attach it. Trim at waist and cut "V" in front.

Cut a 3⅝″ x 2″ rectangle for bodice. Brush piece with egg white and attach to torso, meeting in back and extending down over "V" cut in skirt. Trim

excess in back and at waistline to meet skirt. Cut out neckline and a circle on each side to attach arm. Dry. Cut 1⅞″ x 1½″ sleeves. Brush upper arm with egg white and wrap sleeve around, meeting on underside. Trim excess. Dry.

To paint stripes on dress, thin paste color with kirschwasser and stir in a little cornstarch. Apply with artist's brush. Dry.

Cut apron using Wilton Way pattern. Make a tiny ruffle on the bottom edge, rolling with modeling stick 5 on foam toweling. Pleat apron and attach with egg white. Trim at waist. Dry.

FINISH ARMS AND ATTACH. Cut a 1″ circle for each cuff and cut out center with tube 9. Make a cut from center to outer edge. Ruffle on foam toweling with modeling stick 5. Attach to sleeve with egg white. Dry. Bead edge with tube 1 and dry. Attach arms using a small piece of gum paste brushed on both sides with egg white. Prop to dry. Pipe jewelry with tube 1.

MAKE NECK RUFFLE. Make two pieces the same as for the cuff, except taper the cut ends into curves. Ruffle as for cuff. Attach one on either side of neckline with egg white, meeting in back. Dry.

Trim clothes with tube 1 beading as shown. Make two tiny Elementary Roses on toothpicks instead of cone (page 95). Dry.

Pipe hair with tube 1s. Attach roses with dots of icing and pipe tube 65s leaves. Spray figure with two coats of clear acrylic spray.

CREATE A FANTASTIC CENTERPEICE. Attach an 8″×6½″ × 2″ block of styrofoam to a 14″ styrofoam circle, 1″ thick. Bevel edges of block so top measures 6″ x 5″. Ice with royal icing, giving stucco finish, and place on a 16″ separator plate. Attach figures with small pieces of gum paste, brushed on both sides with egg white. Add wired ferns for forest effect. The children will be thrilled! The next pages tell how to make the dwarfs.

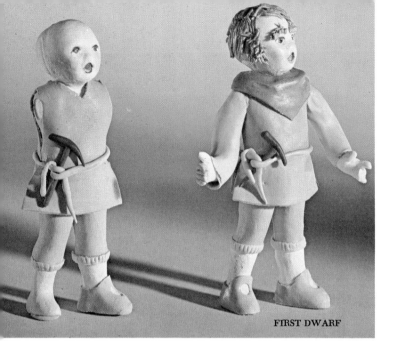

FIRST DWARF

SECOND DWARF

THIRD DWARF

MAKE THE JOLLY COMPANY
OF DWARFS

All these little fellows are molded in the five year o'd child molds, but by varying their postures, hair and clothing, each has a distinct personality. Mold the legs from tinted gum paste, arms and upper body from flesh-colored gum paste. Read pages 172 to 178 for general molding instructions. When dry, the figures are finished and made up as described on page 178.

All pattern pieces for clothing are in The Wilton Way Pattern Book. The arms are attached with a small, flat piece of gum paste brushed on both sides with egg white. Prop arms in position with cotton balls until dry. Hair, beards, eyebrows and trims are piped with royal icing and tube 1s.

To make the tools, roll a small cylinder of gum paste for handle. Insert a piece of florists' wire through it and roll until gum paste covers the wire (shown on page 189). Shovels are cut from a pattern, shaped, attached to handles with egg white and dried. Hammers and picks are hand-molded. When figures are finished, spray with two coats of clear acrylic spray.

FIRST DWARF. After molding torso, open mouth in surprise with a pointed stick. Paint below knee with royal icing and dry. Attach shoes with egg white. Attach pant legs. Secure a thin strip of gum paste to bottom of pant legs, then press in vertical lines on strip. Dry.

Attach shirt, trimming at back and neckline, then cut armholes. Add tunic. Model hammer and attach to figure with egg white. Roll a "string" belt and attach at waist. Dry.

Drape sleeves and trim to fit. Attach arms to body. Dry. Add scarf, then pipe hair and eyebrows.

SECOND DWARF. Prepare figure as described above. Attach shoes with egg white by wrapping from the back to the front. Trim toe of shoe to a point and fold down the top edge. Dry.

Add shirt, making seam in front. Trim neckline and armholes. Attach 1″ circle for crown of hat. Cut brim, make design with a pin and attach to hat. Dry. Make jacket the same as Santa's coat on page 182. Add belt and buckle. Cut hood piece, fold lengthwise and attach around neckline with egg white. Shape the back to form hood. Cut buttons with tube 2 and make holes with a pointed stick. Attach to front of jacket. Dry.

Drape sleeves, gathering at wrist. Attach a ¼″ wide strip for cuff. Attach arms. Pipe shoe laces, hair, beard and eyebrows.

FOURTH DWARF

FIFTH DWARF

SIXTH DWARF

SEVENTH DWARF

MAKE HANDLES FOR TOOLS

THIRD DWARF. Mold and prepare figure as described above. Attach boots the same as the shoes for the Second Dwarf. Dry. Attach shirt, then back of vest. Attach the two front halves of the vest at the shoulder and side seams. Flare out the front edges. Dry thoroughly.

Drape sleeves, gathering at wrist. Add a ⅛″ wide strip for cuff. Add arms to figure. Attach shirt collar around neckline. Pipe trim, hair, beard and eyebrows. Secure pick in hand with egg white. Dry.

FOURTH DWARF. See page 182 for method of dressing in pants and boots. Dry. Now add shirt and tunic the same as for First Dwarf. Attach belt. Drape sleeves, gathering at wrist, then roll a gum paste "string" and attach as cuffs. Secure arms.

After arms dry, attach collar around neck and trim neckline to fit snugly. Secure shovel to hand with egg white. Pipe hair, eyebrows and beard.

FIFTH DWARF. Give surprised expression by opening mouth with pointed stick. Attach shoes as for Second Dwarf. Dry. Attach thin red strip at neckline. Attach back of tunic, then front, cutting away any excess at shoulder. Attach belt, overlapping in front. Drape sleeves, gathering at top and bottom. Add a thin "string" cuff. Secure arms to figure. Dry.

Add a "string" of gum paste where arm meets shoulder. Pipe hair and eyebrows. Secure pick to hand with egg white. Dry.

SIXTH DWARF. Prepare figure as described on opposite page, opening mouth with pointed stick. Make boots the same as for Third Dwarf. Dry. Attach a thin green strip at neckline. Attach back of tunic, then front, trimming excess. Attach belt, then add buckle. Drape sleeve and secure arms to figure. Dry.

Attach cap sleeve for tunic at shoulder seam. Pipe shoe laces, hair and eyebrows. Attach shovel in hand with egg white. Dry.

SEVENTH DWARF. See page 172 for molding the seated figure. Open mouth with pointed stick. Attach tops of shoes, then add soles. Dry.

Attach shirt, trimming at back, neckline and armholes. Add vest, "gluing" at shoulders only. Trim front seam and armholes. Flare bottom. Add kerchief. Drape sleeves on arms, gathering at top and bottom. Add a ¼″ wide cuff. Secure arms to figure. Dry. Add a "string" of gum paste at shoulder seam. Pipe trim, hair, mustache and eyebrows. Dry.

SET FIGURES in their forest scene as shown on page 187. Call the children to admire!

189

SHIRT AND SHOES ON

FRONT OF PANTS ADDED

MAKING TENNIS RACKET

A TRIBUTE TO A CHAMPION

Mold figure in man molds (see pages 172 through 178). Extend wire between halves of legs 1″ beyond feet. Remove cloth covering from exposed portion. When figure is dry, fill seams with royal icing and apply make-up as shown on page 178. All patterns are in The Wilton Way Pattern Book. Roll gum paste for clothing 1/16″ thick.

BEGIN TO CLOTHE FIGURE. Cut shoes and attach to feet. Trim excess. Score a line around edge of shoe to form sole, then add markings on top. Dry.

Cut a 5¼″ x 2¾″ shirt and attach, seam in front. Cut away excess, then trim neckline and armholes. Make folds in shirt with modeling stick 5. Dry. Cut collar and attach at neckline.

Add ½″ x 1¾″ socks. Wrap around ankle, trimming excess at back. Make vertical cuts for ribbing.

ADD TENNIS SHORTS. Cut a 2¼″ x 1″ rectangle as front of shorts. Brush piece with egg white and attach to front of hips. Make a cut between legs and smooth to make pant legs. Press in folds with modeling stick 5. Make back of shorts the same.

Cut a ¼″ wide strip and attach as waistband. Press in marks for closure.

MAKE TENNIS RACKET. Cut a 1/16″ wide strip of gum paste 12″ long. Shape into racket, following the pattern. Dry. Draw lines on a piece of clear acetate with waterproof ink to create webbing. Trim to size and attach to back of racket with egg white. Wrap handles with white, red and blue gum paste and press in diagonal lines. Dry.

ATTACH ARMS. Wrap a 1¾″ x 1½″ strip around the top of the arms for sleeves, pressing with modeling stick 5 to form folds. Dry. Break off fingers and thumb of right hand. Attach racket in right hand with royal icing. Pipe fingers around racket handle with tube 2. Dry. Attach arms with gum paste brushed with egg white. Prop until dry.

Paint stripes on shoes and collar with thinned paste color. Pipe tube 1s hair. Dry, spray figure.

DECORATE CAKE. Paint smallest separator plate from round Mini-tier Set with thinned royal icing and dry. Determine where feet of tennis player will be and poke a hole at each spot with a heated nail. Bake a 10″ x 4″ square cake and ice. Transfer lattice pattern to sides of cake and pipe with tube 2. Edge with tube 17 curves.

Push separator plate into top of cake. Write message with tube 2. Pipe bottom star border with tube 17 and top border with tube 16. Push wires on figure's feet through holes in separator plate and secure with royal icing. Serves 20.

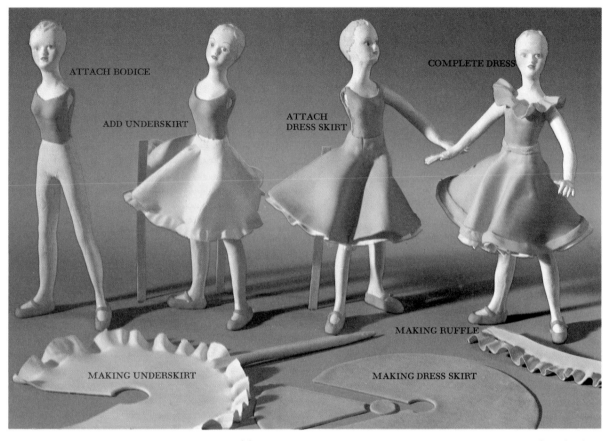

MOLD FEMININE DANCER in woman molds using technique described on pages 172 through 178. Place heavy cloth-covered wire between the two halves of the legs and torso for support. Dry, then fill seams with royal icing. Apply make-up as on page 178, painting in eyebrows with copper color. Designate hairline by painting with royal icing. Roll gum paste 1/16″ thick for clothes.

ATTACH SHOES AND BODICE. Cut ¼″ wide strip and wrap around foot, trimming excess in back. Add a ⅛″ wide strap. Cut bodice from pattern. Attach back first, then front, "gluing" with egg white.

MAKE AND ATTACH SKIRT. For underskirt, cut from pattern, then make a ruffle along edge by rolling with modeling stick 4 on foam toweling. Brush egg white on waist and seam, then attach to figure so it swings out to one side. Use cotton balls to hold it in place. Dry thoroughly.

Cut dress skirt from pattern and attach with egg white the same as for underskirt. Dry.

Cut a strip 3/16″ wide for belt. Wrap around waist, attaching with egg white. Make bow and streamers from 3/16″ wide strips of gum paste. Dry on cotton balls. Cut a ¼″ wide strip and attach around hem of skirt.

ATTACH ARMS with pieces of gum paste brushed on both sides with egg white. Prop until dry.

FINISH FIGURE. Roll a piece of gum paste ⅛″ thick and cut a strip ¾″ wide for collar. Using modeling stick 4, ruffle strip on piece of foam toweling. Cut ruffle away from rest of piece (it should be ½″ wide). Brush neckline with egg white, then attach collar by pressing in place with a pointed stick, keeping folds of ruffles close together. Pipe hair and beads with tube 1. Attach bow to belt with a dot of royal icing. Spray dried figure with two coats of acrylic spray glaze.

DECORATE THE CAKE

Paint a 6″ round separator plate with thinned royal icing and dry. Bake a 10″ x 4″ square two-layer cake. Ice and place on a foil-covered cake board. Position separator plate in center of cake and circle it with tube 13 shells.

Pipe tube 1s flowers over entire cake in a calico pattern. Make scroll bottom border with tube 17. Nestle a star into each curve. Pipe tube 14 top shell border. Attach figures to separator plate with pieces of gum paste brushed on both sides with egg white. Dry thoroughly. Serves 20.

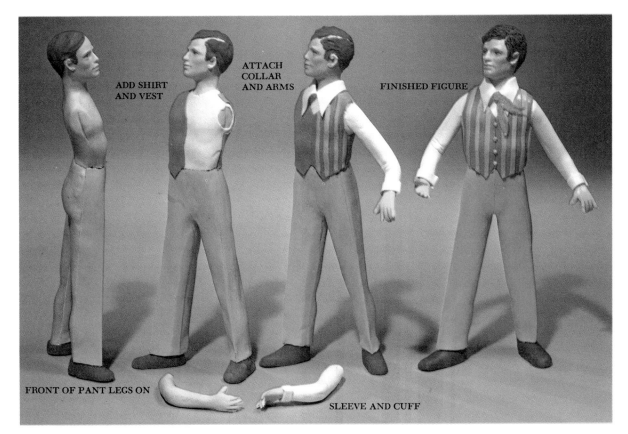

ADD SHIRT AND VEST

ATTACH COLLAR AND ARMS

FINISHED FIGURE

FRONT OF PANT LEGS ON

SLEEVE AND CUFF

MOLD THE PARTNER FOR
THE SQUARE DANCE

Mold figure in the man molds following the procedure on pages 172 through 178. When dry, fill seams on head and neck with royal icing. Apply make-up as described on page 178. Paint on royal icing to define hairline, then pipe ears with tube 1. Roll gum paste 1/16″ thick for clothes. All patterns are in The Wilton Way Pattern Book.

BEGIN TO DRESS FIGURE. Cut shoes using pattern and attach with egg white. Trim excess, smooth seam.

Cut front of pant leg from pattern. Score on dotted line, being careful not to cut completely through gum paste. Attach front of pant leg so score will fall in the middle of the toe of the shoe. Trim to fit, cutting away excess at waist, cuff and along leg seam. Attach other front pant leg the same. Let dry before adding backs of pant legs. Cut backs of pant legs from pattern and score on dotted line. Attach to legs so score falls in middle of heel. Trim excess at waist, cuff and sides. Dry.

ADD SHIRT AND VEST. Cut a 2″ x 4⅝″ rectangle for shirt. Attach to figure with seam in back. Cut away excess in back and at shoulders. Trim neckline and armholes. Dry.

Cut back of vest from pattern and attach. Trim excess. Add the front halves of the vest. Be sure front closing is straight, then trim excess. Add ⅛″ strips on the front of the vest for vertical stripes.

Cut collar from pattern and score on dotted line. Attach around the neckline of the shirt with the two long points in front. Dry.

ADD SLEEVES AND ATTACH ARMS. Cut a rectangle 1½″ x 2½″ for sleeve. Attach smoothly around arm with egg white, trimming excess from seam under arm. Add a ¼″ x 1½″ shirt cuff. Dry. Make other sleeve and cuff the same way.

Attach a piece of gum paste to arm where it will attach to shoulder with egg white. Brush piece with egg white again and press in place on shoulder. Prop until dry with popsicle sticks and cotton balls.

FINISH FIGURE. Make scarf from two triangles, each about ¾″ long. Attach between the points of the collar. Make knot from a tiny ball of gum paste by pressing in marks with a pointed stick and then attaching with egg white. Pipe buttons on vest with tube 1 and hair with tube 1s. Dry, then spray with two coats of acrylic spray glaze. Set both dancers on separator plate in center of cake. Attach with small pieces of gum paste brushed on both sides with egg white.

TWO FRIENDS ON A SUMMER DAY

Make the gum paste figures as described on pages 196 and 197. Bake a two-layer 9″ oval cake. Fill, ice and place on a foil-covered board. Mark off a curved section on top, pat with damp sponge for stucco effect. Ice two small pieces of cardboard to hold figures. When dry, press into icing where figures will stand. Conceal with icing.

Cut 75 gum paste flowers using forget-me-not cutter. Curl petals by pressing from edge to center with stick 5. Dry, then pipe tube 2 centers. Attach 30 flowers to wire stems (see Chapter Twenty). Insert along edge of stucco area. Add tube 65s leaves. Pipe tube 2 stems around side of cake. Add flowers and tube 65s leaves. Pipe bulb borders with tube 5 on top and tube 7 on bottom. Attach figures to cardboard with gum paste brushed on both sides with egg white. Serves twelve.

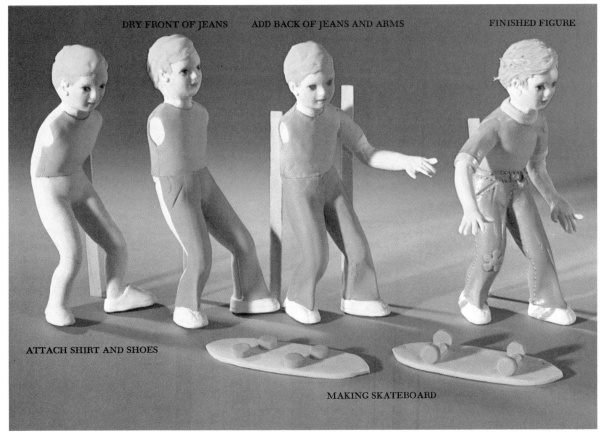

DRY FRONT OF JEANS   ADD BACK OF JEANS AND ARMS   FINISHED FIGURE

ATTACH SHIRT AND SHOES

MAKING SKATEBOARD

MAKE THE BOY AND HIS SKATEBOARD

Mold figure in the ten year old child molds, following the molding instructions on pages 172 through 178. Position carefully so figure is balanced and will stand. Dry 24 hours. Apply make-up as shown on page 178. Paint in hairline with royal icing and pipe ears with tube 1. Roll gum paste for clothing 1/16″ thick. Patterns needed are in The Wilton Way Pattern Book.

BEGIN TO DRESS FIGURE. Cut shoes from pattern and attach to feet with egg white. Trim excess from bottom and seam at back and smooth. Gently press in details on sneakers with a knife blade.

Cut a 1⅞″ high x 2⅛″ wide rectangle for shirt front and attach to figure with egg white. Cut a second rectangle the same size for shirt back and attach the same way. Trim neckline to a rounded shape and cut armholes with an X-acto knife. Dry.

ADD JEANS. Cut one front of jeans using pattern (this is half of the front). Score lightly on dotted line, then attach to leg with scored line falling in the middle of the toe of the shoe. Fold on scored line only near ankle. Make a second front piece in the same way as the first and attach to leg. Press in diagonal lines for front pockets. Trim at waist, cuffs and leg seams, then dry before doing back.

Cut back pieces of jeans using pattern and attach to legs with egg white. Trim to fit and dry. Attach a ⅛″ wide strip as waistband. Add back pockets and belt loops from small pieces of gum paste, attaching them with egg white.

FINISH FIGURE. Cut a strip of gum paste ⅛″ wide and attach around neckline with egg white. Cut a 1″ square and attach it smoothly on upper arm as sleeve, trimming excess at underarm seam. Cut a strip ⅛″ wide and attach at bottom edge of sleeve. Dry. Attach arms with pieces of wet gum paste brushed on both sides with egg white. Prop until thoroughly dry.

Pipe tube 1s trims on jeans and attach a gum paste flower cut with the forget-me-not cutter on the knee with egg white.

MAKE SKATEBOARD. Cut skateboard from ⅛″ thick gum paste using pattern. Cut wheels from ¼″ thick gum paste using tube 12. Dry pieces. Attach wheels to skateboard using tiny pieces of wet gum paste and egg white. Let dry, then attach completely dried figure to skateboard with pieces of wet gum paste brushed on both sides with egg white. Dry, then spray with two coats of acrylic spray glaze.

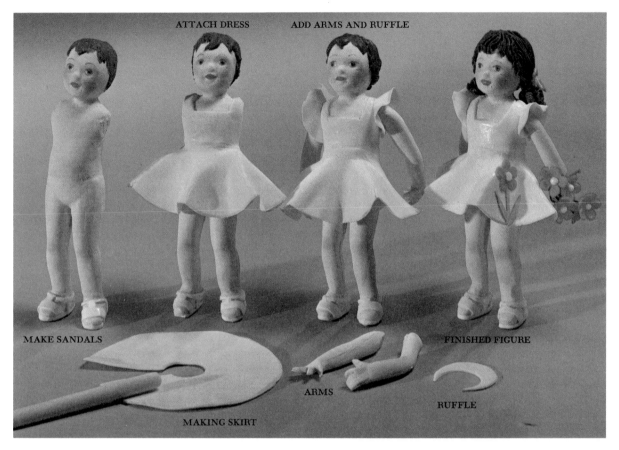

MAKE SANDALS

ATTACH DRESS

ADD ARMS AND RUFFLE

FINISHED FIGURE

MAKING SKIRT

ARMS

RUFFLE

MOLD HIS ADMIRING FRIEND

Mold figure in the five year old child molds using the molding directions on pages 172 through 178. Dry 24 hours, then fill seams with royal icing. Dry and apply make-up as described on page 178. Paint in eyebrows with thinned copper food color. Blush knees with dark flesh-colored powdered pastel using the same method as for blushing the cheeks. Define hairline by painting on royal icing. Dry. Roll gum paste for clothing 1/16″ thick unless otherwise stated. All clothing patterns needed are in The Wilton Way Pattern Book.

ATTACH SANDALS. Roll a piece of gum paste ⅛″ thick. Brush bottom of feet with egg white, stand figure on gum paste and cut around feet with an X-acto knife for sole of sandal. Roll gum paste for top of shoe 1/16″ thick. Cut a ¼″ wide strip for strap over toes. Cut strips for other straps ⅛″ wide. Attach with egg white.

MAKE DRESS. Cut bodice from pattern. Attach smoothly around figure with egg white, seam in back. Trim excess and match shoulder seams.

Cut skirt from pattern. Place on a piece of foam toweling and roll with modeling stick 2 to ruffle. Brush waist and one edge of seam with egg white and attach to figure. Prop skirt in position with cotton balls until dry.

Cut flower with forget-me-not cutter and attach to skirt with egg white. Cut center of flowers with tube 5 and attach. Stem and leaves are cut with an X-acto knife and attached with egg white.

ADD ARMS AND RUFFLE. Attach arms with pieces of gum paste brushed on both sides with egg white. Be sure they curve to the back. Prop until dry.

To make ruffle, cut a circle with the large end of tube 122. Cut a piece out from the edge using the large end of a standard decorating tube to form the crescent shape. Place on a piece of foam toweling and roll with modeling stick 2 to ruffle. Attach with egg white to shoulder. Dry.

FINISH FIGURE. Pipe hair and hair ribbons with tube 1. Cut about five flowers with the forget-me-not cutter. Curl petals by pressing from edge to the center of the flower with modeling stick 5. Dry. Pipe tube 2 centers and mount on wires as described in Chapter Twenty. Tape flowers into a bouquet and attach in the little girl's hand with a dot of royal icing. Dry, then spray the figure with two coats of clear acrylic spray glaze.

Two young lovers, members of feuding families, defy their parents and marry, yet their story is destined to end tragically. Shakespeare's immortal story of Romeo and Juliet has been presented countless times in drama, music, ballet and on film.

The gum paste figures of Romeo and Juliet that we created are shown on the opposite page, posed against a painting of their native Verona. If you wish to make an arch to enclose the couple, Chapter Thirteen will give you some ideas about building with pastillage and gum paste.

HOW TO MOLD ROMEO

Mold Romeo in the man molds, following the directions on page 177. Use brown gum paste to mold

COMPLETED FIGURE

BEGIN TO CLOTHE FIGURE

the legs and flesh-colored for the torso and arms. Finish the hands as on page 178. Allow the figure to dry for 24 hours before applying the make-up as described on page 178.

ATTACH BOOTS. Cut the boots from the Wilton Way pattern and attach to the feet with egg white, the seam in front. Trim excess in front and trim evenly around top of boot. Smooth front seam with fingers. Cut boot cuffs using pattern. Fold in half lengthwise, but do not crease. Attach them around the tops of the boots with the seam at the outside of the leg and fold down the cuffs so they are even. Dry. Attach medallions to the cuffs made by rolling a small ball of gum paste and pushing in the pattern with tube 24.

MAKE JERKIN. The jerkin is made in two pieces. Cut the back from the pattern and attach with egg white. Cut front from the same pattern and attach. Trim rounded neckline and armholes with an X-acto knife. Flare edges at side seams. Dry.

Cut strips of thin gum paste about ⅛" wide. Attach them with egg white around the bottom edges of the jerkin and in three vertical stripes on the front and back. Cut a ¼" wide strip for the belt and attach with egg white. Cut a buckle in proportion to the belt and attach.

DRAPE ARMS AND ATTACH. Cut a rectangle from green gum paste rolled thin and attach tightly around left arm as sleeve. Cover top of right arm with orange gum paste and lower part of arm with green. Attach arms with gum paste brushed on both sides with egg white. Prop until dry.

MAKE CAPE. The swinging cape Romeo wears gives dashing movement to the figure. Cut the cape from the pattern and roll long curved edge with modeling stick 2. Attach the cape to Romeo's shoulders by the corners of the short edge with egg white. Cut a ¼" wide strip to finish top of cape and attach around shoulders, then add a decorative gum paste buckle. Dry thoroughly.

ADD FINISHING TOUCHES. Cut strips of gum paste ¼" wide and attach on Romeo's right shoulder over the orange portion to form a puffed upper sleeve. Add ¼" wide band to hold the strips in position. Dry.

Cut a strip ⅛" wide and roll with modeling stick 5 to ruffle it. Attach as collar around neckline with egg white. Cut two strips ¼" wide, ruffle as for first strip and attach as cuffs around bottom edge of sleeves. Pipe hair with tube 1. Dry thoroughly, then spray with two coats of acrylic spray glaze to protect from moisture.

Mold Juliet in the woman molds, following the directions on page 177. The position of this figure is important in that it should reflect her youth, shyness and grace. Dry the figure 24 hours and then apply the make-up as described on page 178.

BEGIN TO DRESS THE FIGURE. Roll a piece of gum paste as thin as possible and cut a 2¼" square for bodice. Brush upper figure with egg white and attach square, wrapping it smoothly and meeting in the back. Trim the excess in the back, then trim the neckline straight across. Cut the lower part of the bodice diagonally below the waist. Cut out armholes with an X-acto knife.

Cut ¼" strips of gum paste for slippers and attach with egg white. Trim and shape with an X-acto knife. Dry clothing at this point.

ATTACH SKIRT. Cut the skirt from the Wilton Way pattern. Place on foam toweling and roll lower part with modeling stick 2 to form soft folds. Paint hips with egg white and wrap skirt around figure, meeting in back. Trim along the diagonal line of the bodice. Trim the hem and dry.

Cut ⅛" wide strips of gum paste and attach along hem and neckline. Also attach a strip as a belt, fol-

lowing the diagonal line of the bodice. Cut streamers, 3" x ⅛", and dry in fluted position.

Pipe free-hand embroidery on the dress with tube 1s. Start at the hem and work up. Dry.

MAKE SLEEVES from a 2¾" x 1½" rectangle. Brush the arms with egg white and cover smoothly with seam on underside. Trim excess and dry.

Attach arms with small gum paste pieces brushed on both sides with egg white. Prop to dry.

Cut the shoulder puffs from pattern. Attach smoothly at shoulder and gather straight edge around arm. Add a ¼" wide band. On left arm, attach ⅛" wide strips to form loops and streamers. Dry.

FINISH FIGURE. Pipe hair with tube 1 and add a net at back with the same tube. Attach ⅛" wide loops and dried streamers to belt. When figure has dried, spray with two coats of acrylic spray glaze.

AT RIGHT, a beautiful crèche takes the place of honor at Christmas. Directions for the figures are found on pages 202 through 205.

POSITION OF FIGURE

BELT STREAMERS

FIGURE PARTIALLY FINISHED

DISPLAY THE JOYFUL CHRISTMAS STORY

This reverent portrayal of the Nativity will become more precious as the years go on and it is brought out to take the place of honor in your home as Christmas approaches.

The simplicity of the figures demands careful attention to positioning limbs and heads in expressive poses and in draping the graceful garments.

You might want to start a tradition in your family and create new figures each year to enlarge the scene. Build a stable similar to the house on page 207. Make shepherds in rustic costumes with the man and ten year old child molds. Add the figures of the three kings in colorful royal attire. Even animals can be hand-modeled of gum paste.

Spray all the figures, when finished and thoroughly dry with two coats of acrylic spray glaze. This will bring out the colors and seal them from moisture. Store in a sturdy box, carefully wrapped and padded with soft tissue, in a cool dry place. Then bring them out each year to tell the joyful Christmas story anew.

MAKE THE ANGEL FIGURES

These charming little figures hold music scrolls as they sing the joyful message.

FIRST ANGEL. Mold the figure in the five year old child molds, following the instructions on page 177. Position it so it is leaning to the right. Positioning the legs is very important. The figure should be standing flat-footed with the body directly over the feet and legs. If done properly, the angel will stand firmly and will need no extra support. After attaching the torso, bend the body to the right, but not enough to throw the figure out of balance. Tilt the head to the side and up. Carefully open the mouth, using a small pointed stick and an X-acto knife. Dry figure 24 hours. After molding the arms, trim the hands carefully as shown on page 178. Bend the arms at the elbow and slightly at the wrist so they will be in the proper position to hold the scroll and prop on cotton balls to dry.

Apply make-up to the face, using the method on page 178. Blush the cheeks pink, do the eyes looking upward and paint the lips a peach color.

BEGIN TO DRESS FIGURE. When cutting and draping the robe on the angel, be sure to work very quickly so it will fall into soft folds and not crack.

MOLD FIGURE   ADD CLOTHES AND ARMS   BACK VIEW AND SCROLL

Tint a piece of gum paste cream-colored. Roll it as thin as possible and cut the angel robe using the Wilton Way pattern. Brush torso of figure with egg white and attach robe, "gluing" back seam with egg white. Keep the soft folds of the lower portion of the robe in position with cotton balls. If the robe is too long, trim with a pair of small scissors. Cut armholes and trim neckline with an X-acto knife. Dry 24 hours.

DRAPE ARMS AND ATTACH. Cut the sleeve of the robe from the Wilton Way pattern. Brush the arm with egg white, then drape the sleeve over it with the widest edge at the wrist and the two cut edges meeting below the arm to form a wide sleeve. "Glue" the lower edges together below the arm with egg white. Trim at the shoulder if necessary. Attach a small piece of gum paste to the arm where it attaches to shoulder with egg white. Brush more egg white on the piece and attach arm to figure, smoothing sleeve to shoulder for an inconspicuous seam. Prop until dry, about 24 hours. Drape and attach the other arm the same way.

MAKE WINGS using the Angelica Baroque gum paste mold. Carefully follow the directions that accompany the molds. After removing from the mold, gently trim off the face portion, leaving a flat piece of gum paste between the wings to attach to figure. Bend the wings back at the point where they meet the flat piece, then prop with cotton until dry. Attach wings to back of figure with a piece of gum paste brushed on both sides with egg white. Prop in position until dry.

Paint a stripe around the hem, neckline and sleeves of the robe with royal icing. Pipe hair with tube 1, creating waves and pulling out wisps.

MAKE SCROLL. Roll gum paste as thin as possible and cut scroll using the Wilton Way pattern. Working very quickly so the gum paste doesn't dry out, draw a line around the edge with a fine-line felt tip marker. Brush the angel's hands with egg white and drape the wet scroll gracefully over them. Dry thoroughly.

MAKE SECOND ANGEL. Make the second angel the same as the first, but position it so it is leaning to the left. Make the hair in soft curls rather than in wisps when piping.

BRUSH OFF any cornstarch that is on the angels with a soft, dry brush. Then spray each with two coats of clear acrylic spray glaze.

The Holy Family, the central focus of the crèche, should be molded with great care. The positions of the figures of Mary and Joseph and their facial expressions create the reverent mood. The Baby is hand-modeled and the features are only suggested. The simplicity and perfection of these figures give beauty to this Christmas crèche. Patterns needed are in The Wilton Way Pattern Book.

MOLD THE FIGURE OF MARY in the woman molds. Mold the legs using the method for the seated figure on page 172, inserting toothpicks above and below each knee. Make a cut at the top of the legs in front and back and at the back of the knees so the legs will bend easily. Insert a toothpick into the waist to support the torso. Place in a seated position on a 2⅜" high, 1" wide block of styrofoam, propping the legs with cotton. Dry 24 hours. Mold the upper body, inserting a piece of cloth-covered wire between the two halves. Attach to the legs, bending the torso forward slightly. Incline the head. Dry 24 hours. Mold the arms, position and dry, propping with cotton balls.

Apply the make-up as on page 178, but do the downcast eyes by making a faint red pencil line at the top of the eye socket. Paint in a thin line of copper color at the bottom of the eye socket and add tiny lines for lashes.

Cut the shoes from the Wilton Way pattern and attach with egg white. Cut a 1⅞" x 1¾" rectangle for the bodice and attach it to the front of the body (the back will be covered by the cape). Trim the neckline and armholes. Stack cotton balls around the legs to hold the skirt in position. Cut the skirt from the pattern, roll the lower portion with modeling stick 2 and attach it around the waist with egg white. Trim to fit, using a pair of thread scissors to shorten the skirt if necessary. Attach a gum paste "string" around the waist for a belt. Dry.

Cut 2¾" x 1½" sleeves and attach loosely around the arms, "gluing" the seam at the bottom. Attach the arms to the body with a small piece of gum paste brushed on both sides with egg white as described on page 176. Prop with cotton until dry. Cut cape from the pattern and drape it around the figure, attaching only to the neck area and positioning the bottom of the cape gracefully around the figure. Pipe the brooch with tube 1. Dry.

Pipe the hair with tube 1 and dry. Cut veil from pattern, stretching it in the center of the straight edge with stick 5. Attach it to the head with egg white with the straight edge framing the face. Mold it with the fingers to fit the top of the head. Dry.

MODEL THE BABY. Make a ½" ball for the head and press in a groove on one side of it with modeling stick 5. Dry. Model a 1½" long cone shape, ½" at the widest point. Flatten the wide end, then press the handle of an artist's brush down the length of the cone to form a seam. Attach the head to the flattened end of the cone with egg white. Dry. Pipe the ears and hair with tube 1.

Make the blanket from a 2" square of gum paste and roll it with modeling stick 5. Drape the blanket over Mary's arms, attaching it with egg white, then attach the Baby to the blanket with egg white. Dry.

MOLD THE FIGURE OF JOSEPH in the man molds. Mold the legs the same as for the standing figure on page 177. Position the legs carefully so the figure is balanced, prop and dry. Mold the torso and insert a cloth-covered wire between the two halves. Attach to the legs, incline the head and dry. Mold the arms and dry. Apply the make-up as for the man on page 178. Do the downcast eyes by drawing a faint red pencil line at the top of the eye socket, then add a line and tiny lashes at the bottom of the socket with a sharp black pencil. Paint the eyebrows with copper color. Cut shoes from pattern and attach to

SEATED FIGURE   CLOTHED FIGURE

ASSEMBLE THE BABY

feet with egg white, smoothing with fingers to fit. Trim excess gum paste.

Cut a 1½″ x 2″ shirt back and attach with egg white. Cut a second piece and attach it as the shirt front. Trim the shoulders, neckline and armholes with an X-acto knife.

Cut the skirt using the pattern and roll the lower portion with modeling stick 2. Attach it at the waist with egg white, allowing it to fall in soft folds. Dry.

Cut a 9″ x 2¼″ rectangle for the green stole. Gather it 4″ from one end and attach the gathers at the shoulder with egg white, the longer portion in front. Gather it slightly at the waist and add a gum paste "string" for belt. Pipe the hair and beard with tube 1.

Cut 2¾″ x 1½″ sleeves. Drape them on the arms and attach the arms to the body the same as for Mary. Prop them in position with popsicle sticks and cotton until dry.

SPRAY BOTH FIGURES with acrylic spray when the gum paste is completely dry. Allow the first coat to dry, then spray again to seal out moisture.

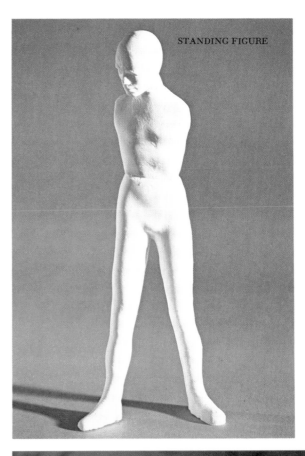

STANDING FIGURE

CHAPTER THIRTEEN

Building with Pastillage and Gum Paste

Explore the possibilities of gum paste, and its stronger cousin, pastillage, for a whole new world of decorating effects. These pliable materials can make a Victorian village, shape decorative vases and compotes, create unique wedding cake ornaments or build a fairytale doll's house like this.

POINTERS ON PASTILLAGE WORK

In building the Three Bears' house or any comparable structure, the walls, floor and roof are constructed of pastillage, chosen for its strength. Use gum paste for furniture, curtains and dishes.

MIX THE PASTILLAGE, using the recipe on page 112. This recipe will yield five pieces, each about 11½" x 7½", super thick. Make one batch at a time. You may, however, mix several batches, one at a time, and store several weeks. Keep wrapped in plastic in a covered container. Pastillage crusts quickly.

TINT THE PASTILLAGE by kneading paste color into one or more batches, until desired color is reached. Pastillage will be several shades lighter when dry. You may tint a larger amount than needed of one pale color, such as beige. Then add more color to the remaining pastillage for a deeper tint.

ROLL OUT THE PASTILLAGE on a smooth surface such as glass, plexiglas or a formica-covered board. Dust surface and rolling pin with cornstarch to prevent sticking. Roll to the thickness needed for the pattern piece you plan to cut. Check by trimming off an edge and comparing it with this chart.

SUPER THICK PASTILLAGE, FOR WALLS, ROOF AND SUPPORTS	
THICK PASTILLAGE FOR TRIM AND WINDOW FRAMES	
THICKNESS NEEDED FOR GUM PASTE FURNITURE	

CUT SMALLER PIECES with a very sharp X-acto knife. A pizza cutter is convenient for larger pieces. Keep cutting instrument perpendicular to pastillage. Be-

Continued on next page

GOLDILOCKS peeps in the open door of the Three Bears' house to admire their pretty supper table.

fore starting to cut, assemble all pattern pieces which require uniform thickness and color. Transfer accurately to thin cardboard and cut out. Label each pattern piece to avoid confusion. Lay cardboard pattern on rolled pastillage to cut. Large pieces should be cut, excess pastillage removed, then allowed to dry on the same surface.

DRY PASTILLAGE 24 hours on one side, then turn over and allow to dry another 24 hours on a sheet of styrofoam. This allows air for additional drying to come from below. After drying, lay pattern piece on pastillage. If pastillage has spread, very carefully sand or shave to original pattern shape.

To JOIN TWO PIECES of dried pastillage, use royal icing, tinted to match. A wet piece of pastillage may be joined to a dried piece with egg white.

MOLD AND DRESS GOLDILOCKS

Mold figure in five year old child molds as described on pages 172 through 178. Use white gum paste for legs and flesh-colored for torso and arms. When dry, trim instep of foot with an X-acto knife to form heel and fill seams with royal icing. Then apply make-up as shown on page 178. Roll gum paste 1/16″ thick for clothes.

ATTACH SHOES AND BODICE. Cut a ¼″ x 2½″ strip for shoe. Wrap around foot, attaching with egg white. Then cut away excess at back with an X-acto knife. Add a ⅛″ wide strap. Cut a 1½″ x 3″ rectangle for bodice. Attach to upper body, meeting in back. Trim excess and cut neckline and armholes. Dry.

ADD SKIRT. Cut a 1½″ x 6″ rectangle for skirt. Attach above waist with egg white, gathering as you attach it. Trim top evenly with an X-acto knife. Cut a ¼″ x 2½″ strip for waistband. Attach to skirt. Cut collar

from pattern and attach around neckline. Dry, then attach a small, very thin triangular piece and a small square to skirt with egg white for pocket and handkerchief. Cut a long ¼″ wide strip and attach around hem of skirt. Pipe tiny flowers on skirt with tube 1s. Dry.

ATTACH ARMS. Cut a ⅝″ x 1½″ strip for sleeve. Ruffle one long edge by rolling with modeling stick 2 on foam toweling. Attach sleeve around arm with egg white and dry. Attach arms to figure with a piece of gum paste brushed on both sides with egg white. Prop until dry.

FINISH FIGURE. Cut ½″ x 2½″ strips for straps on skirt. Ruffle edge by rolling with modeling stick 2 on a piece of foam toweling. Trim the ends into points. Trim ruffle with small scissors so it is narrower at the ends than in the middle. Attach straps over

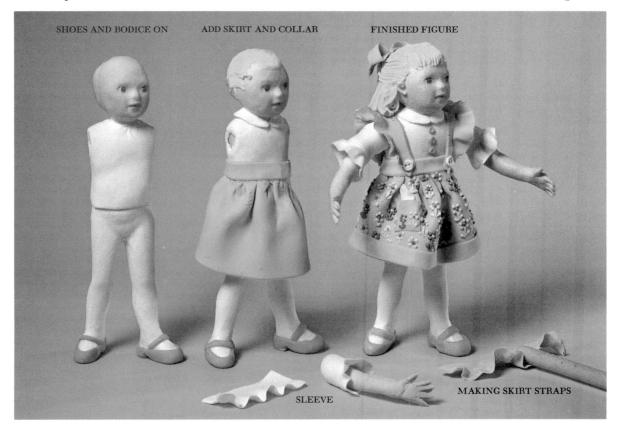

SHOES AND BODICE ON   ADD SKIRT AND COLLAR   FINISHED FIGURE

SLEEVE   MAKING SKIRT STRAPS

shoulders with the ruffles extending out over arms to conceal shoulder seam.

Cut buttons for bodice with tube 4 and buttons for skirt with tube 6 and attach. Pipe hair and ears with tube 1. Cut a ¼″ x 2″ strip for bow. Fold ends of strip to center to make loops, then attach two other strips, ¼″ x ½″, as streamers. Dry, then attach to hair with royal icing.

PREPARE GUM PASTE AND PASTILLAGE

To make the Three Bears' house, you will need four batches of gum paste (recipe on page 142) and six and a half batches of pastillage. Keep each batch separate and well-wrapped until ready to tint. Three batches of gum paste are used for the shingles on the roof and one for the fireplace, furniture, curtains and dishes. The following amounts of pastillage are needed for the building sections and should be tinted the appropriate colors: walls, three batches; roof, one and a half batches; floor, one batch; beams, door, window frames and shutters, one batch. Color the entire amount needed of a color at one time to insure an exact match. When working with pastillage, be sure to follow the instructions on pages 206 and 208 carefully to avoid problems when beginning to assemble. Make all the furniture and other small pieces first, then make the sections of the building itself. All patterns are in The Wilton Way Pattern Book.

CONSTRUCT THE FIREPLACE

CARVE a piece of 1″ thick styrofoam to form the support for the fireplace, using the pattern for the fireplace front. Paint with royal icing and dry.

CUT PIECES for fireplace from furniture-thickness gum paste using patterns. Cut mantel from thick gum paste using thickness chart on page 206 as a guide. Dry, then paint soot on hearth and back wall with black paste color on a dry brush.

MODEL THREE LOGS, ¼″ x 1¼″. Assemble with egg white and dry. Cut flame shapes from clear acetate and pipe flames with piping gel. Let set, then push in between the logs to secure.

ASSEMBLE FIREPLACE with royal icing. Attach back wall to styrofoam, then add sides. Secure front, then paint back, sides and front with cream-colored royal icing. Dry. Attach to hearth. Pipe rocks with tube 3 and gray icing, flattening them with a wet fingertip. Attach mantel and secure fire in position. Set aside to dry thoroughly.

MODEL DISHES AND CANDLESTICKS FOR THE THREE BEARS

The dishes and candlesticks are hand-modeled from gum paste (recipe on page 142). Designs are painted on dried gum paste pieces with food color thinned with a small amount of kirschwasser.

PITCHER. Roll a 1″ ball of gum paste. Model to pitcher shape and make a hole in top with modeling stick 4. Pitcher should be 1¼″ high and 1″ wide at the widest point. Dry, then add a gum paste "string" as handle. Dry again and paint design.

SUGAR BOWL. Form a piece of light cardboard into a ½″ diameter cylinder. Roll a piece of gum paste into a ¾″ ball and press the cylinder into the top of the ball to create the lid. Attach a small ball of gum paste to the top of the lid. Add gum paste "string" handles. Finished sugar bowl should be ⅝″ high and ⅞″ wide. Dry, then paint design.

MUGS. Make cylinders from light cardboard—¾″, ½″ and ⅜″ in diameter. Wrap a piece of tape completely around outside of cylinders so they will hold their shape. Press a ball of gum paste into each cylinder with modeling stick 2 to form mug shape. Largest mug should be ¾″ tall, medium ⅝″ tall and smallest ⅜″ tall. Remove from cylinders and dry. Lightly sand top edge to smooth. Add handles and paint designs.

CANDLESTICKS. To make large candlestick, cut a 1¼″ circle using the end of tube 234. Place it on a thick piece of soft foam. Use the end of tube 504 to press in a ¾″ circle in the center to form a dish shape. (When pressing the gum paste on the foam,

the edges will bend up to form the dish.) Attach a gum paste "string" as the handle. Dry. Model a 1″ high x ½″ wide gum paste candle around a piece of heavy florists' wire. Dry. Wrap a thin gum paste strip around the base of the candle and attach the candle to the dish with a piece of gum paste brushed on both sides with egg white. Pipe wick and candle drippings using tube 2 and royal icing. Medium candlestick is made the same way, using the end of tube 2A to cut a 1″ circle and the end of a standard tube to press in to form the dish shape. Medium candle is 1″ high x ¼″ wide. Baby bear's candlestick is made by cutting a ¾″ circle with the end of tube 504 and pressing in with a ½″ cardboard cylinder to form the dish shape. Small candle is ⅝″ high and 3/16″ wide.

SPOONS. Make a "string" of gum paste, lay on a piece of foam toweling and press in bowl of spoon with the round end of modeling stick 4. Dry. Large spoon is 1⅛″ long, medium spoon ⅞″ long and small spoon ⅝″ long.

BOWLS. To make large bowl, cut a 1″ circle with the end of tube 2A. Place on a thick piece of foam and press in center with modeling stick 2. Dry and lightly sand top edge. Paint line on inside of bowl. Make medium and small bowls the same, cutting a ¾″ circle with tube 504 and a ⅝″ circle with the end of a standard tube. Fill bowls with beige-tinted granulated sugar to resemble porridge.

BUILD THE DINING TABLE

The rustic style furniture for the Three Bears' house is made of gum paste (recipe on page 142). The furniture described on this page and on pages 212 and 213 adds a quaint, homey touch to the finished scene. Follow the directions carefully when cutting and assembling. The furniture is quite easy to make, but care must be taken when cutting the pieces to be sure they are exactly the same size and shape as the patterns, and when assembling so the finished furniture will stand without leaning. Be sure to *completely* dry the individual pieces and the partially assembled furniture. Otherwise, the pieces may crack, or the furniture may collapse.

When furniture is finished and completely dry, brush off any cornstarch with a soft brush and spray with two coats of clear acrylic glaze.

CUT PIECES. Trace the patterns onto light cardboard and cut them out. Roll gum paste ⅛" thick for all pieces (see the thickness chart on page 206). Lay the light cardboard patterns on the gum paste and cut around them with a very sharp X-acto knife. (You will have to change blades frequently as the sugar in the gum paste will dull them quickly.) Be sure the gum paste does not stretch out of shape as you cut it. Cut one each of the two circles for the table top and three pieces for the pedestal —one double leg and two single legs. Dry flat for at least 24 hours. When dry, lay the patterns on the gum paste pieces to be sure they are the same. If the gum paste pieces have spread, trim very carefully with an X-acto knife or sand lightly.

ASSEMBLE PEDESTAL. Mark center of double leg and attach one single leg in center with royal icing tinted the same color as the gum paste. Be sure it is at a 90° angle to the double leg. Prop in position with cotton balls until completely dry.

Stand pedestal up and attach other single leg with tinted royal icing. Adjust it so the leg is at a 90° angle to the double leg and so the pedestal is level. Dry. If the pedestal is still not completely level, lightly sand the bottom of it.

ATTACH TOP OF TABLE. Mark center of the smaller circle and attach pedestal to it, upside down, with tinted royal icing. Be sure pedestal is at a right angle to the circle and dry thoroughly.

Turn right side up and attach the larger circle on top of the smaller one with tinted royal icing. Level the top if necessary with icing when attaching. Dry thoroughly, at least 24 hours.

211

BABY BEAR'S CHAIR

MAKE CHAIRS AND BENCH

These darling little pieces of gum paste furniture brighten the quaint scene in the Three Bears' house. They are all quite easy to make, but precision is necessary when cutting and assembling the pieces to assure a proper fit.

Begin by tracing all patterns onto pieces of light cardboard and cutting them out. Sort the patterns, keeping those for each piece of furniture together. Roll gum paste ⅛″ thick (see thickness chart on page 206). Lay the patterns on the gum paste and carefully cut around them with a very sharp X-acto knife (see page 211 for procedure). Cut all pieces, keeping those for each piece of furniture together. Dry them flat. Lay the patterns on the dried gum paste pieces to be sure they are exactly the same size and shape. If not, trim very carefully with an X-acto knife or sand them lightly. Sand all edges to smooth.

The chairs and the bench are all assembled in a similar way, using royal icing tinted to match the gum paste.

BABY'S CHAIR. Attach the seat at a right angle to the back of the chair. Prop it in position with a small piece of styrofoam if necessary. Add the seat brace against the lower edge of the seat where it

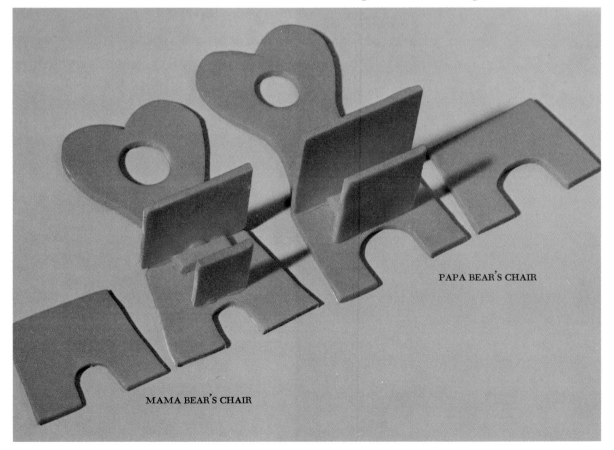

MAMA BEAR'S CHAIR

PAPA BEAR'S CHAIR

meets the chair back. Secure the lower brace to the back of the chair at a right angle. Prop if needed with a small piece of styrofoam. Dry thoroughly before proceeding.

Attach the front legs to the lower side of the seat and to the lower brace. Be sure this piece is at a right angle to both the brace and the seat. Dry. Add the arms of the chair and the footrest and dry again.

MAMA'S CHAIR. Attach the seat to the back of the chair at a 90° angle. Prop with a small piece of styrofoam to hold it in position if necessary. Add the seat brace on the underside of the seat where it meets the chair back, just as for the small chair. Attach the lower brace at a 90° angle to the chair back. Prop with a small piece of stryofoam. Dry.

Attach the front legs to the chair on the underside of the seat and on the lower brace, making sure that they are at a right angle to the seat and the brace. Dry at least 24 hours.

PAPA'S CHAIR. This chair is assembled exactly the same as Mama's chair. Let it dry thoroughly after it is assembled.

FIRESIDE BENCH. The bench is assembled upside down. Place stretcher piece in the center of the seat of the bench on styrofoam blocks, each ⅜″ high.

Attach one leg piece to the bench and to the stretcher at one end. Be sure the legs are at a right angle to the seat of the bench and the stretcher. Dry. Attach the other leg piece at the other end of the stretcher in the same way. Dry thoroughly, then carefully remove the styrofoam pieces. Turn the bench over to stand upright. Spray each piece of furniture twice with clear acrylic glaze.

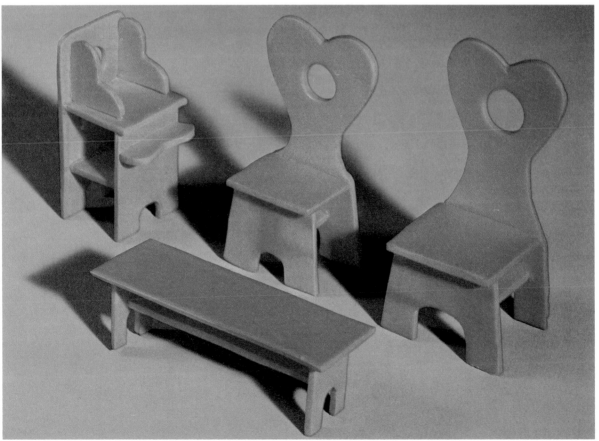

BUILD WINDOW BOX

Trace window box patterns onto light cardboard and cut out. Roll out pastillage about 1/16″ thick. Cut two pieces for the long sides of the box, two for the short sides and one for the base. Dry thoroughly. Cut a piece of ¼″ thick styrofoam using the pattern for the base of the box. Ice with green royal icing and dry.

Assemble window box with royal icing tinted the same color as the pastillage. Attach one long side and two short sides to the base. Dry. Secure styrofoam piece to the base with icing. Attach second long side and dry.

Cut gum paste flowers with the forget-me-not cutter and prepare them the same as the flowers on the top of the cake on page 195. Insert the wire stems into the styrofoam in the box. Set the finished window box aside until ready to attach to the outside of the wall.

MAKE LATTICE WINDOWS

These lattice windows add a very quaint look to the house. The window frames and the lattice are made separately and assembled later.

Trace patterns for the window frames onto light cardboard and cut out. Place on thick pastillage (see chart on page 206) and cut around them with an X-acto knife. Cut two window frames of each shape. One will be on the inside of the wall and the other will be on the outside.

To make lattice, tape grid pattern to a flat surface and cover with wax paper. Pipe with royal icing and tube 44. Dry thoroughly. To remove the lattice from the wax paper, slip a piece of parchment paper under the lattice. Handle very gently as it is extremely fragile. Set window frames and lattice aside until needed.

MAKE CURTAINS

To make curtain rod, roll a piece of pastillage into a piece 3/16″ in diameter and 3″ long. Flatten the ends and dry. Set aside.

For curtains, trace pattern onto a piece of light cardboard and cut out. Roll out a piece of untinted gum paste as thin as possible. Working quickly so the gum paste will not dry out and crack, cut curtain with an X-acto knife, using pattern. Lay it on a piece of foam toweling and roll bottom edge with modeling stick 5 to create soft folds. Roll top edges using the same procedure to make ruffled edge. Gather curtain just below the top ruffles, forming the lower part of the curtain into folds. Dry on a flat surface. Make the second curtain using the same procedure.

MAKE SHUTTERS

Transfer the shutter pattern to a piece of light cardboard and cut it out. Place the pattern on thick pastillage (see page 206 for chart) and cut around it with an X-acto knife. Cut out the heart-shaped opening with the X-acto knife. Mark the position of the score lines on the top and the bottom edges of the shutter. Score the lines by pressing in with the edge of a ruler. Dry thoroughly. Make the second shutter the same way.

Make four hinges from pastillage rolled thin. For each hinge, cut a small square piece and make impressions in it with tube 5. Set aside. Cut two circles with tube 11 and make impressions in them with tube 5. Cut a freehand triangular piece and press with tube 5. While wet, attach the two circles and the triangular pieces to the shutters with egg white as shown. Dry. Set aside.

EMBROIDER SAMPLER

Trace picture and frame patterns onto pieces of light cardboard and cut them out. Roll pastillage to furniture-thickness (see chart on page 206). Lay the patterns on the pastillage and cut around them with an X-acto knife. Press in lines at the corners of the frame to indicate the separate pieces of wood. Make impressions for the nails with tube 2. Dry thoroughly.

On the picture, score a line with the X-acto knife to indicate the inside opening of the frame (use pattern as a guide). Pipe heart with tube 1 and fill in with lines of icing using the same tube. Smooth them together with a damp artist's brush to form a flat surface. Dry. Pipe the message and design on the heart with tube 1. Dry, then secure picture in frame with dots of icing. Set aside to be attached to the wall later.

MAKE DOOR MAT

Trace the mat pattern on a piece of light cardboard and cut it out. Roll pastillage to furniture-thickness (chart on page 206). Lay the pattern on the pastillage, cut around it with an X-acto knife and dry. Transfer lettering to the pastillage piece. Beginning with the lettering, pipe dots with tube 1s to create a textured effect. Cover entire mat. Dry.

Make two flat rocks from balls of pastillage, rolling them out into free-form ovals about the same thickness as shown on the chart on page 206 for thick pastillage. One rock should be a little larger than the door mat and the other a bit larger than the first. Attach the smaller rock on top of the larger while wet with egg white, then attach the mat on top of the rocks. Dry.

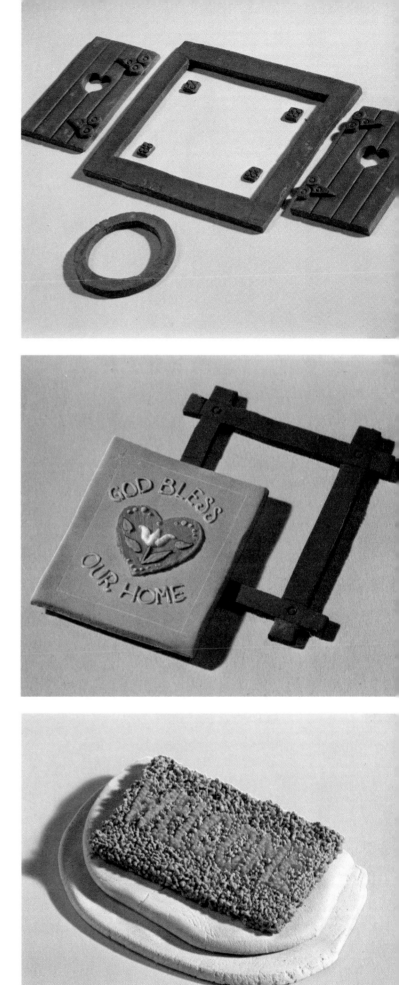

215

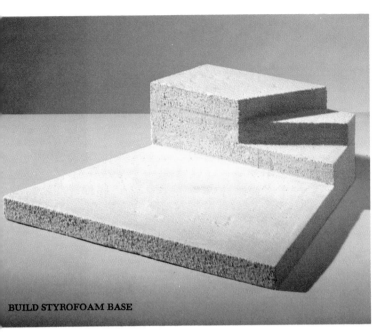

BUILD STYROFOAM BASE

COVER FLOORS

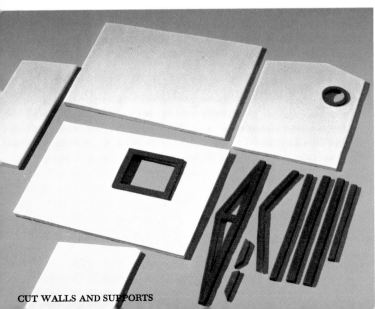

CUT WALLS AND SUPPORTS

BUILD HOUSE FROM THE GROUND UP

Precision in cutting the pieces of the house is extremely important—whether of styrofoam or pastillage. If all pieces are not accurately cut, they will never fit together properly. Before beginning, cut all pattern pieces from light cardboard.

When cutting the pastillage, be sure that the X-acto knife or pizza cutter is perpendicular to the pastillage to make a straight edge. Be sure you are thoroughly familiar with the general instructions on pages 206 and 208.

After the pastillage pieces are cut and dried, lay the patterns on top of them and check to be sure they have not spread. If the pieces are not exactly the same as the patterns, trim them gently with an X-acto knife or lightly sand them. Although trimming and sanding help to get the pieces to fit together better, do not depend on them for correcting more than a slight error.

MAKE STYROFOAM BASE. This is the base which will support the rest of the house and make it easy to assemble. Be sure all the pieces are of the correct size. Cut pieces from 1″ thick styrofoam using patterns. Assemble with royal icing, then push ¼″ dowel rods through the thickest part of the base (the stairway) to hold the pieces securely in position. Paint with thinned royal icing and dry. (Pastillage will not adhere to un-iced styrofoam.)

Cut another piece of 1″ thick styrofoam the same shape as the largest piece of the base, but 2¼″ larger at the sides and back and 4½″ larger at the front. Paint with thinned green royal icing. Dry.

Cut a piece of ½″ thick masonite so it is ½″ larger all around than the green styrofoam. Cover it smoothly with foil.

Use dowel rods extending up into the highest stair to hold the base of the house and the green styrofoam together. Use about four nails to hold the masonite to the two sections of styrofoam.

COVER THE FLOOR. Using pattern, cut the floor from furniture-thickness pastillage. Score the floorboard lines with the edge of a ruler. Cut pieces for stairs from pastillage the same thickness as that of the floor. Dry all pieces very thoroughly.

Attach the floor to the styrofoam base with royal icing. Attach the treads of the stairs the same way, then add the stair risers. Fill all seams with royal icing tinted the same color as the pastillage.

CUT THE WALLS and front support pieces from super thick pastillage (chart on page 206). Let all of the pieces dry very thoroughly. Attach the window frames to the inside walls with icing. Dry.

216

START TO ASSEMBLE

Now begin to attach the walls. The order in which they are attached is very important, so be sure to follow it carefully. Cut the gray shim strip and the overhead and upright support beams for the inside wall. Let them dry thoroughly.

How to attach walls. Pipe lines of royal icing on the exposed face of the styrofoam base where the wall will be attached. Place the wall in position and press it into the wet icing. Hold it in place for a few seconds. Fill the seams with royal icing tinted the same color as the pastillage and smooth with a damp artist's brush, then proceed to attach the next wall using the same method. It is not necessary to let each wall dry in position before adding the next, but care must be taken so you do not bump and knock them out of position.

Attach back and side walls. Attach the back wall first, using the method described above. Fill the seams between the wall and stairs with royal icing. Smooth with a damp artist's brush.

Secure the solid side wall in position next. Fill all of the seams with royal icing and smooth them with a damp brush.

Attach the side wall with the window to the styrofoam base and fill the seams with royal icing. Smooth with a damp brush. Be sure all the seams on all the walls are neatly filled before continuing.

Add beams. Cut back rafter beam and attach to top of back wall with egg white, while the beam is still wet. Cut the back rafter upright and mopboard. Attach them in position with egg white while they are still wet. Secure the dried gray shim strip in front with royal icing so you won't crack the floorboard extension.

Attach inside wall. Line up the inside wall and attach it to the styrofoam at the front of the stairs with royal icing. Attach the dried overhead beam behind the wall with royal icing, then secure the dried upright beam on the step for support. Fill the crack with royal icing and smooth.

Cut the upright beams for the inside wall and the corner and attach them in position with egg white while they are still wet. Cut the mopboards and attach them while wet using the same method.

Complete inside of walls. Secure the fireplace in position on the inside wall with royal icing. Attach the picture to the wall with royal icing. Pipe the nail and strings with tube 1.

Attach the curtain rod to the window frame with royal icing, then attach the curtains in position with royal icing. Dry.

BACK AND SIDE WALLS

ADD THIRD WALL
ADD BEAMS

ADD INSIDE WALL
COMPLETE WINDOW

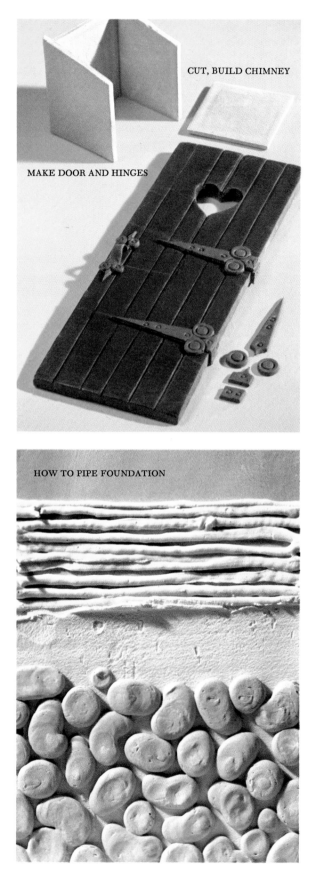

CUT, BUILD CHIMNEY

MAKE DOOR AND HINGES

HOW TO PIPE FOUNDATION

CONTINUE CONSTRUCTION

After the back and side walls are dry and the interior of the walls are finished, it is time to attach the front wall in position.

ATTACH FRONT WALL following the instructions for attaching walls found on page 217. Fill seams with royal icing and smooth with a damp brush.

FINISH WINDOWS. Working on the outside of the walls, paint the area with icing between the inside window frame and the outside of the wall on the square and round window. Insert the window lattice carefully into the windows and secure with royal icing. Attach the outer window frames, then the shutters and the square part of the hinges with royal icing on the square window. Secure window box in position with royal icing.

MAKE CHIMNEY AND DOOR. Trace the patterns for the chimney and door onto light cardboard and cut out. Cut pieces for the chimney from thick pastillage (see chart on page 206). Let pieces dry and assemble with royal icing. Set aside.

Cut door from super-thick pastillage (chart on page 206). Score the lines in the door with the edge of a ruler while the pastillage is still wet. Dry. Cut three hinges and one door handle from pastillage rolled very thin. Cut freehand triangles and circles and press in details on the pieces with tubes 4 and 11. The door hinges are made in a similar way to the shutter hinges on page 215. Attach them to the door with egg white while wet, then dry.

ATTACH BEAMS. First attach the beams to the front of the house, using the beams that were cut when the walls were cut. (See page 216.) Follow the order for attaching the beams shown in the diagram on page 219. Begin by attaching the beam on the right side with royal icing. Attach the beam on the left side in the same way, butting it against the front wall. Then attach the door support beam to the front wall. Secure the top beam section to the front wall and to the beams already in position. Measure the width of the door and mark this distance, beginning at the door support beam. Secure the last beam at this mark. Attach the two short supports with icing and hold in position for a minute to be sure they are secure. Fill all seams with tinted royal icing.

Next, cut and attach the beams to the sides and back of the house. Cut them using the same method as for the front beams (see page 216). Attach them while still wet to the corners of the house with egg white. See page 221 for positions. Dry.

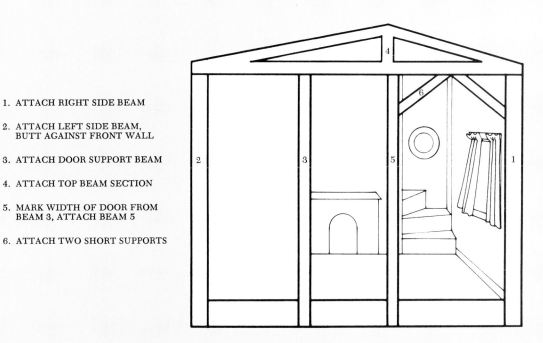

1. ATTACH RIGHT SIDE BEAM

2. ATTACH LEFT SIDE BEAM, BUTT AGAINST FRONT WALL

3. ATTACH DOOR SUPPORT BEAM

4. ATTACH TOP BEAM SECTION

5. MARK WIDTH OF DOOR FROM BEAM 3, ATTACH BEAM 5

6. ATTACH TWO SHORT SUPPORTS

ORDER OF SECURING BEAMS ON FRONT OF HOUSE

PIPE ROCKS on the foundation of the house. Mark a faintly visible line all around the bottom of the house, 1″ up from the base. This will be height of the foundation. With tube 3 and beige icing, pipe lines back and forth across the pastillage piece from the marked line to the bottom of the house. Smooth icing with a spatula. Pipe rocks with tube 3 and gray icing. Press flat with wet finger.

CREATE STUCCO EFFECT on the green styrofoam. With green icing and a damp sponge, pat the styrofoam to achieve a grassy stucco effect on the sides and the top, up to foundation of house. Dry.

ATTACH DOOR. To hang the door, pound two dowel rods into the styrofoam base so they are exactly 1″ above the stucco. Use the door to measure to be sure they are in the proper place. The bottom of the door will rest on these. Cover the dowels with gray icing to look like rocks.

Pipe a line of royal icing the same color as the door right next to the beam on the edge of the front wall (beam number 3). Place the door in position and wipe away any exposed icing. Make three square hinges from gray pastillage. Press in nail marks with tube 4. (See section on making the door hinges on the opposite page.) Attach the wet hinges to the beam with egg white, matching them up with the hinges on the door.

SECURE DOOR IN POSITION

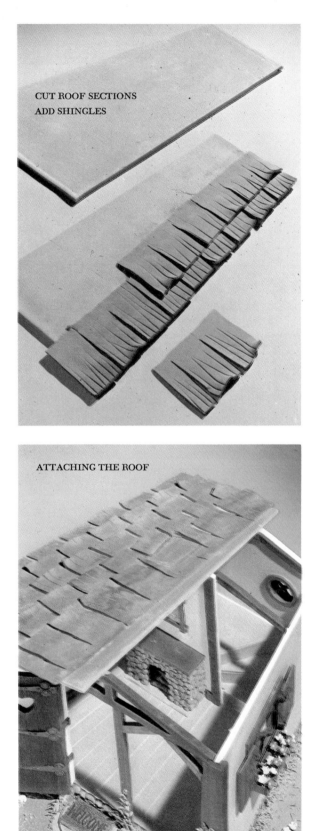

CUT ROOF SECTIONS
ADD SHINGLES

ATTACHING THE ROOF

BEGIN ROOF CONSTRUCTION

The house is now almost complete. All that needs to be added is the roof, gum paste shingles, the chimney and a few finishing touches to complete the charming woodland scene.

CUT ROOF PIECES. Trace roof patterns on light cardboard and cut them out. Place patterns on thick pastillage (chart on page 206) and cut out. Dry thoroughly, then scratch in lines on the roof sections to indicate the positioning of the top edge of each row of shingles. Mark the position of the chimney on the larger roof section.

Transfer shingle patterns to light cardboard and cut out. Roll gum paste to furniture thickness, then roll from center to one edge so it tapers down to half the original thickness. Work with a section of three shingles at a time for ease in handling. Place pattern on gum paste, the edge where the shingles are attached to each other on the thinner part of the gum paste. Cut out. Press in lines on each shingle with the edge of a thin ruler.

Brush underside of the top edge of the shingles with egg white and attach to the roof section. Bend the edges of the shingles to give them a natural look. Cut a second section of three shingles using the same method. Attach it next to the first section on the roof. Continue cutting sections of three shingles and attaching them until the first row is completed. Then begin on the second row. Continue making and attaching shingles as described above, leaving the space for the chimney uncovered. Do not attach the last row of shingles until the entire roof is in position.

ATTACH ROOF. Secure the larger roof section in position with royal icing on the beams and tops of the walls. Then attach the smaller roof section with royal icing in the same way. Fill the seam between the two roof sections with gray royal icing. Smooth with a damp brush. Cut the final row of shingles so they are shorter and attach them to each roof section, making sure that they meet in the center. Fill in the seam a bit by painting on some gray royal icing with a small artist's brush.

ADD CHIMNEY. Attach the chimney in position with royal icing. Then cover it with tube 3 lines of beige royal icing. Smooth with a spatula. Pipe rocks with tube 3 and flatten with a wet finger. This is the same method as for making the foundation on pages 218 and 219. Dry. See the next page for a picture of the completed chimney.

COMPLETE THE SETTING

Secure the door mat attached to the flat rocks in front of the doorway with royal icing. Pipe tube 3 rocks so they appear to be scattered around the house in a natural fashion.

To make the flowers, roll out gum paste as thin as possible and cut flowers using the forget-me-not cutter. Working with one at a time, place on a piece of foam toweling and curl the petals by pressing from the edge to the base of each with the rounded end of modeling stick 5. Dry, then pipe tube 1 center. You will need about 48 flowers for around the base of the house.

Pipe vines growing up the sides of the house and on the beams with tubes 1 and 2. Pipe leaves on the vines with tubes 65s and 65. Pipe tube 2 grass on the green styrofoam base. Then attach the gum paste flowers with dots of royal icing.

Now, using the gum paste furniture and dishes you made, furnish the house as shown on page 207, placing the bench near the fireplace. Position Goldilocks as shown and attach her to the styrofoam base with dots of royal icing piped on the bottom of her feet. The adorable little house is now finished and is ready to be displayed with pride.

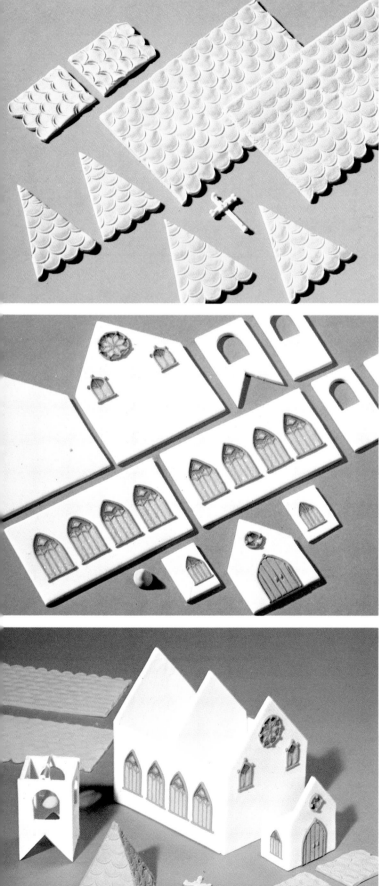

Each building is constructed on a block of stryrofoam to make assembling easy. Trace Wilton Way patterns onto light cardboard and cut out. Roll gum paste ⅛″ thick. (Recipe on page 142.)

CUT AND DECORATE CHURCH ROOF. Cut pieces one at a time and press in shingles with tube 401. Trim bottom edge into scallops.

Cut ⅛″ wide strips 1¼″ long and ¾″ long for cross. Attach with egg white. Pipe tube 1 designs. Dry.

CUT AND DECORATE CHURCH WALLS. Cut wall sections. Dry, then mark windows on pieces.

Pipe outside of side windows with tube 2 and inside design with tube 1s. Pipe outside of small windows with tube 1 and inside design with tube 1s. Fill with colored piping gel. Dry.

Cut door from thin gum paste. Press in vertical lines. Attach to entrance wall. Outline door and pipe door handles with tube 2.

Hand-model bell from a ½″ ball of gum paste. Make a hole through bell with a pin. Dry.

ASSEMBLE CHURCH. Cut two pieces of 1″ thick styrofoam, 3¼″ x 2⅛″ for the building support. Cut a piece 1¾″ x 1″ to support entrance.

Lightly sand edges of pieces. All parts are secured with royal icing. Secure inner brace between the two larger pieces of styrofoam. Attach the two side walls. Add front and back walls. Fill seams with icing. Dry. Assemble entrance, dry and attach.

Join pieces of steeple roof by attaching on the inside with wet gum paste brushed with egg white. Dry, then fill seams. Trim point on roof to attach cross. Assemble steeple walls and dry. Cut a toothpick the width of steeple and attach at top of walls. Dry. Insert thread through bell and tie around toothpick. Attach steeple roof.

Secure all roof sections in place. Dry. Attach steeple on roof of church and attach cross. Dry.

CREATE THE SCENE when buildings are finished. Construct leafless tree with florists' wire. Cover with icing and smooth. For pine trees, cover paper cones with icing. Pipe tube 16 upright shells, then tube 74 "foliage". Needles are tube 233. Make bushes using a mound of icing as base. Dry.

Build landscape using a 24″ square, 2″ thick piece of styrofoam. Build up back 5″ with styrofoam block. Cover with cheesecloth. Create a smooth slope, inserting crumpled tissue paper under cloth. Cover landscape with boiled icing, leaving building areas without icing. Position buildings, trees and bushes. Sprinkle lavishly with edible glitter.

BUILD A COUNTRY FARM HOUSE

Cut a piece of 1″ thick styrofoam 3¼″ x 2½″ for the support to build the house around. Roll gum paste ⅛″ thick for walls, porch and roof.

Cut pieces. Cut roof pieces one at a time and press in design with tube 326. Cut porch railing and cut out center portion with tube 8 squeezed into an oval shape. Make porch supports by wrapping toothpicks cut to 1½″ lengths with gum paste. Cut windows and doors from thin gum paste. Cut the rest of the pieces and dry.

Begin to assemble using royal icing. Attach door and windows to wall and outline with tube 1. Pipe clear piping gel onto windows. Dry.

Assemble house as shown in picture at left, using the method described for the church on page 222. Then attach roof on house. Secure porch roof in position and prop with a piece of styrofoam while attaching porch supports. Position porch railing and attach with royal icing.

Assemble chimney and dry. Roll a piece of gum paste as thin as possible. Cut a piece 3½″ x ⅞″. Gently score lines on it to look like bricks, then brush chimney with egg white and attach the piece around it. Trim to fit at bottom. Dry, then secure chimney to roof. See page 223 for finished house.

BUILD A GABLED TOWN HOUSE

Cut a piece of 1″ thick styrofoam 5″ x 2⅛″ to use to build the house around. Roll out gum paste ⅛″ thick for walls, roof and gables.

Cut pieces. Cut roof pieces one at a time and press in design with tube 353. Cut the windows, shutters and door from gum paste rolled very thin. Dry. Cut the wall pieces and dry thoroughly, then attach the windows, shutters and door in place with royal icing. Pipe window trim with tube 1 and pipe clear piping gel for "glass". Trim door with tubes 1 and 2.

Assemble the house with royal icing. Assemble the house as shown in the picture at left, using the method for the church on page 222. Attach the walls to the styrofoam and to each other. Fill the seams with royal icing. Attach the roof. Assemble the gables, dry and attach to roof. Attach gable roofs in position. Dry.

Assemble chimneys and dry. Roll a piece of gum paste as thin as possible and cut a piece 3½″ x ⅞″. Score lines on it to look like bricks, brush chimney with egg white and wrap piece around. Trim at bottom to fit. Dry. Cover other chimney the same, then attach both to roof. Dry. See page 223 for a picture of the finished house.

MAKE CHARMING CONTAINERS FOR
FLOWERS AND CANDY FROM GUM PASTE

Decorative containers made from gum paste give a special personality to lasting piped or gum paste flower arrangements—choose the design and color that best sets off the blossoms. A dainty gum paste box is a very pretty way to present a gift of home-made candy.

The flexible, plastic quality of gum paste makes it very easy to mold into clear-cut detailed shapes. Many objects found in your kitchen can be used as molds—bowls, saucers, baking dishes and gelatin molds are all suitable.

Baroque designs made of gum paste give sculptural trim to the finished pieces and serve to reinforce the basic shapes. Round cookie cutters are convenient to cut circles. You may also wish to experiment with small gum paste flowers and leaves and piped royal icing trims.

ABOVE, a molded gum paste compote and vase hold flowers, a little gum paste box contains candy.

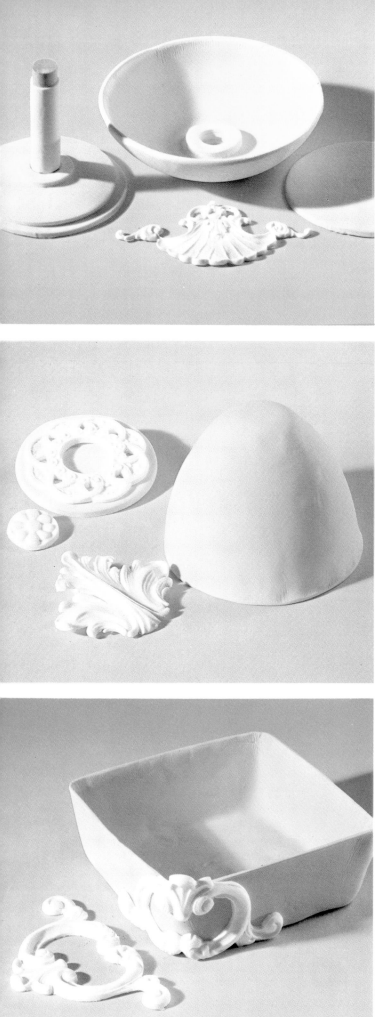

HOW TO MOLD THE CONTAINERS

MOLD THE COMPOTE on a one-quart stainless steel mixing bowl. Roll out gum paste to ⅛″ thickness and cut out a 6½″ diameter circle. Dust the bowl with cornstarch and lay the circle over it smoothing gently. Cut a hole in center with end of a standard tube. Cut a 3½″ diameter circle and drape over the back of a small saucer. Cut a hole in center with standard tube. Now cut a 4″ circle as base, and a 3½″ circle which will fit inside the bowl. Dry all pieces thoroughly.

Use a ½″ diameter dowel rod, 3⅜″ long for stem. Cover smoothly with gum paste, leaving ⅜″ at each end uncovered. Dry.

Cut a 1½″ gum paste disk and cut out center with end of standard tube. While still wet, attach to underside of gum paste bowl with egg white, lining up holes. Cut two more 1½″ disks, cut out centers and attach, still wet, to inside of bowl, one atop the other, lining up holes. Attach the 3½″ circle to inner disks with egg white. Dry.

Cut two more 1½″ disks, cut out centers and attach to gum paste saucer shape with egg white, one on top and one below, lining up holes. Dry. Attach saucer shape to 4″ circle with royal icing and edge with tube 2 beading. Fit stem into base and secure with icing. Pipe mound of icing on top of stem and fit bowl over it. Dry thoroughly. Now mold four Classic Shell Baroque designs and attach to bowl with egg white while still wet. Mold four small motifs from Regalia molds and attach to stem and base with egg white. Dry thoroughly.

MOLD VASE over small Wonder Mold, well-dusted with cornstarch. Trim off even with base. Cut 2¾″ circle of gum paste for base. Dry. Mold Rose Window design with Baroque mold, cut out center and attach to base with egg white while still wet. Dry, then secure bowl shape to base with royal icing. Mold four Acanthus designs and attach to vase with egg white while wet.

TO DISPLAY FLOWERS in vase or compote, trim a piece of styrofoam and insert in container, securing with royal icing. Cover with green icing, piped with tube 3, and insert wire stems of flowers.

MOLD CANDY BOX over a 5″ square pan well-dusted with cornstarch. Roll gum paste ⅛″ thick to a 9″ square. Smooth over corners and trim off even with rim with a pizza cutter or sharp knife. Dry, then gently smooth edges with fine sandpaper. Mold four Baroque Mantle designs and attach to box with egg white while designs are still wet, curving around corners.

A beautiful, handmade wedding ornament adds a personal touch to that special cake. Making the ornament shown here, or one of your own design, is not hard to do. It is made in parts and then assembled after each has dried. A handmade ornament looks its best when the trim on the cake reflects its design. It will be preserved by the bride as a personal treasure.

All patterns needed for the ornament are included in The Wilton Way Pattern Book.

MOLD CUPID FIGURE

MOLD GUM PASTE FIGURE using the five year old child molds and molding instructions on pages 172 through 178. Position figure carefully so it stands firmly. Open the mouth with a pointed stick and X-acto knife. Finish the hands as on page 178, then prop the arms on cotton balls. Dry 24 hours.

SMOOTH SEAMS carefully with an X-acto knife. Fill all crevices with royal icing and dry. Apply make-up as described on page 178. Attach the arms with a small piece of gum paste brushed on both sides with egg white. Prop until dry.

CUT RIBBON from gum paste rolled very thin, using the pattern. Drape over the figure, attaching with egg white. Dry. Pipe hair with tube 1.

CUT HEART from thin gum paste using pattern. Dry flat. Pipe message and beading with tube 1s. When dry, attach in cupid's hands with egg white.

MAKE FLOWERS FOR TRIM

Cut flowers to trim the ornament from very thin gum paste using the forget-me-not cutter. After cutting, lay flower on a piece of foam toweling and press from the edge of each petal to the center with modeling stick 5 to curl them. Dry. Pipe centers with tube 2. Make 24 white and 100 blue flowers. Attach about 30 blue flowers to white wire stems as described in Chapter Twenty.

CUT PIECES FOR ORNAMENT

MAKE BASE. Roll out gum paste ⅛″ thick. Cut one bottom plate and one top plate for base. Dry flat, twelve hours on each side. Cut the center insert for base from ¾″ thick styrofoam. Cover sides of insert with a ¾″ wide strip of 1/16″ thick gum paste, attaching it with egg white. Dry. Join the three pieces with royal icing, then fill the crevices between plates and insert with royal icing. Dry.

MAKE PILLARS from three ¼″ dowel rods 5½″ long. Roll gum paste 1/16″ thick and wrap smoothly around the dowel rods, leaving ⅛″ at top and bot-

tom uncovered and attaching with egg white. Dry. For the top and base of each pillar, roll gum paste 1/16″ thick and cut six circles with base of tube 2D and six with base of any standard tube. Attach smaller circles to larger with egg white while still wet and cut a hole in the center with tube 10. Dry.

MOLD DOME in the blossom pan using gum paste 1/16″ thick. Dust inside of pan with cornstarch before pressing in the rolled gum paste to prevent sticking. Dry dome twelve hours inside the pan, then remove and dry upside down twelve hours.

Cut the plate for inside the dome from gum paste rolled ⅛″ thick. Dry twelve hours on each side.

ASSEMBLE THE ORNAMENT

ATTACH PLATE inside dome with pieces of gum paste brushed with egg white. Secure three pillar tops to plate with egg white as pictured. Dry. Mark their position on tracing paper. Transfer markings to ornament base and attach pillar bases. Dry.

ADD PILLARS. Insert tiny pieces of gum paste, brushed on both sides with egg white, into pillar bases. Insert pillars. Place dome on top, attaching pillars in pillar tops same as for bases. Dry.

SECURE FLOWERS with royal icing. On each "petal" of dome and curve of base plate insert, attach white flowers and add tube 65s leaves. Add blue flowers at top of dome. Secure flowers on stems at base of pillars and fill in with more flowers.

Mark scallops around dome. Outline scallop with tube 2 stylized flowers, fleurs-de-lis and tube 1 dots. On the bottom edge of dome, pipe a series of tube 2 graduated dots in the indentations between the "petals", then complete edge with tube 1 dots.

Brush small pieces of gum paste with egg white and attach to cupid's feet. Brush again with egg white and set cupid in position.

DECORATE THE CAKE

MAKE GUM PASTE TRIMS. Mold three shapes same as dome, then while still wet, cut out bottoms. Cut each in half to form six baskets.

Make six Laurel Wreaths and six Angelica designs using Baroque gum paste molds. Dry Laurel Wreaths on an 8″ curve and Angelica designs on a 6″ curve. Pipe royal icing spikes on backs. Dry.

Make many gum paste flowers using blossom and sweetheart rose cutters. Curl petals as for flowers on ornament and dry. Pipe tube 1 spikes for centers. Mount most on white cloth-covered wires. Tape into clusters. Also make 80 forget-me-nots. Dry.

MAKE PILLARS from six ½″ dowel rods 8″ long. Roll gum paste 1/16″ thick and cut a strip 2¾″ wide. Attach smoothly around dowel, leaving ½″ uncovered at one end and 4¾″ at the other. Dry. Cut two circles, ¾″ and 1″, using tubes 506 and 124, from ⅛″ thick gum paste for pillar bases. Attach smaller circles to larger with egg white while wet and cut a tube 1A hole from center. Dry.

MAKE AND ASSEMBLE TIERS. Bake seven 6″ x 4″ cakes for bottom tier, 12″ x 4″ round for middle and 8″ x 3″ round for top. Ice tiers and assemble bottom tier on serving plate at least 22″ in diameter. (Seventh 6″ cake is unseen in center for support.) Insert clipped-off dowel rods for support. Place middle tier, set on cardboard cake circle, in position.

Place top tier on 9″ foil-covered cardboard cake circle with six stud plates glued to the bottom. Determine position of pillars on middle tier by marking lightly with top tier. Push a flower spike into center of middle tier. Insert a cluster of flowers into spike. Slip pillar bases over exposed dowel rods on pillars, then insert dowels down to cardboard beneath middle tier. Place top tier in position.

DECORATE BOTTOM TIER. Pipe tube 8 bottom ball border. Mark three scallops on each 6″ cake. Using tube 5, outline scallops with stylized flowers, petal designs and dots. Pipe tube 7 top ball border with stylized petals. Push Angelica Baroque designs into side of tier. Attach flowers at base of tier with icing.

DECORATE MIDDLE TIER. Attach half-baskets with royal icing, then insert flower spike inside each. Pipe tube 7 top and bottom ball borders with stylized petal designs. Mark scallops from top edge, extending down between baskets. Pipe tube 5 dots and stylized flowers to outline scallops. Place a cluster of flowers into spike in each basket.

DECORATE TOP TIER. Pipe tube 6 bottom ball border and tube 5 top ball border, each with stylized petal designs. Attach Laurel Wreaths to side of tier. Secure ornament to top of tier. Serves 210.

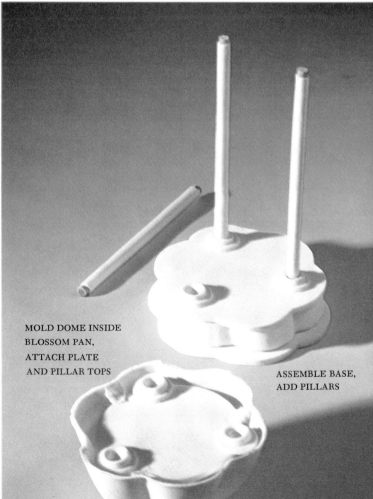

MOLD DOME INSIDE
BLOSSOM PAN,
ATTACH PLATE
AND PILLAR TOPS

ASSEMBLE BASE,
ADD PILLARS

CHAPTER FOURTEEN

The Shimmering Art
of Pulled Sugar

Pulled sugar is a very old art form and one that few practice to perfection. However, a decorator who likes a challenge can learn this art and produce cakes and centerpieces as breathtaking as those pictured in this book.

Just as in other techniques, *practice is essential.* Start by doing a 10″ or 12″ cake, perhaps the middle tier of the cake on the opposite page, or the birthday cake on page 267. Pulled sugar is so beautiful in itself that even the simplest cake trimmed with it becomes a masterpiece.

Only experience will teach you just how thin you can stretch the ribbons. Too thick, they will lack brilliance and gloss, too thin, they will break. Your hands will learn how warm the sugar should be to form ruffles, curve flower petals, make lustrous bows and other glistening trims.

Norman Wilton believes that the beautiful art of pulled sugar should be preserved and expanded —for the pleasure and satisfaction of the decorator, and the delight of all those who view the shining results. In this chapter, assisted by Manuel Lopez, he shows you, step-by-step, how to create White Satin, the fabulous wedding cake at right. In this one cake, all the traditional basic techniques of pulled sugar are represented. Study the directions carefully before beginning your own masterpiece.

A WORD OF CAUTION: dampness is the enemy of pulled sugar, and makes it droop and lose its gloss. Therefore, do not attempt a pulled sugar project unless the air is dry and clear. In the Northern states, October through March are the most favorable months for this work.

EQUIPMENT YOU'LL NEED

Some of the equipment for pulling sugar you probably have in your kitchen, none is very expensive.

A HEAVY ALUMINUM PAN, six-quart size, for boiling the sugar. This will be large enough to boil the sugar to cover and trim a 12″ two-layer cake. Sturdy pans are available in restaurant supply stores.

A CANDY THERMOMETER. Be sure it registers 312°F. or higher, as sugar must be cooked to this temperature.

A MARBLE SLAB, about 2′ x 3′, at least one inch thick. You might find a used one at a wrecking company (old marble is better than new for sugar work), or consult your directory for firms dealing in marble. This will be the surface on which you pour the cooked sugar. Marble is the only satisfactory material for this purpose.

A STURDY METAL SCRAPER. Purchase one in a housewares department.

A STRIP OF HEAVY CANVAS, four feet by 18″ wide.

TWO LARGE STRONG TABLES, one to hold the marble, and one to work on while pulling sugar.

A SCREEN of fine 40 to 60-gauge copper mesh, wood framed. This should measure about 36″ x 18″. Purchase at a well-stocked hardware store.

ONE OR TWO ELECTRIC HEATERS, guards at the front removed. It is often necessary to touch pieces of sugar directly to the heating element.

SCISSORS, a leaf mold, clean pastry brush and food colors. Dowel rods and coat hangers are used for basket handles.

WHITE SATIN, at right, is an outstanding example of a cake that displays the basic techniques of pulled sugar. The pages that follow show you how to cover the tiers and trim them with shining loops, ruffles and flowers.

HOW TO CREATE WHITE SATIN, A PULLED SUGAR WEDDING CAKE

Before beginning, be sure to read this chapter through in its entirety. Study the pictures well as Norman Wilton shows you, step by step, how to decorate this lovely cake. As you proceed with the work, your hands will become accustomed to the feel of the sugar.

The order of work is important. Start with pulling ribbons to cover the sides of the tiers and for the bows, while sugar is most pliable. Flowers and other small trims are made last. *Any sugar you are not working with should be kept on the screen in front of the heater.* Turn it from time to time to keep it evenly warm and pliable.

PREPARE THE CAKE

Bake the two-layer tiers—14″, 10″ and 6″, using a firm pound cake recipe. Fill the layers, then set each tier on a cake circle.

Now paint the tiers with hot apricot glaze (heat one cup of apricot preserves to boiling and strain). Let set, then cover the tiers with white rolled fondant. (Recipe is on page 92, method page 94.) Norman Wilton recommends this method of preparation, because the fondant makes a smooth background for the sugar and will not eat through it. All the pulled sugar cakes shown in this book were first covered in rolled fondant.

Another choice would be to ice the cake in buttercream, then cover it with poured fondant (recipe page 135). If you ice the cake in buttercream only, you will need to wrap the sides with ribbon twice, as the icing will eat through the pulled sugar.

Assemble the tiers on a sturdy cake board.

SET UP THE WORK AREA

Set the marble slab on a sturdy table near the stove. Near by, on one end of a long table, install the heater, guard removed, with the copper screen laid in front of it. Stretch the canvas strip over the remaining area of the table. Have your other equipment conveniently at hand.

Clean the marble well, dry it, then grease it thoroughly with lard or solid white shortening.

PULLED SUGAR RECIPE

10 cups granulated cane sugar
  (Beet sugar tends to boil over.)
2½ cups water
1 teaspoon, slightly mounded, cream of tartar
  (As you gain experience you may decrease this amount by one-third for more durable pulled sugar.)

Add water to sugar and mix by hand until mixture is smooth and all lumps have dissolved. Add cream of tartar and cook to 312° F., washing down the sides of the pan about ten times during cooking with a wet pastry brush to keep crystals from forming. The faster the sugar is cooked, the whiter the mixture. For tinted sugar—the whiter the batch, the truer the color. The recipe will take about 40 minutes to cook on a household range. Yield: five pounds, enough to decorate a 12″ cake. If you plan a cake as large as White Satin, this recipe will cover the tiers. Make a second batch for the trim. As you become proficient, you may double this recipe by using a candy-making stove that cooks sugar faster.

POUR THE HOT SYRUP on the marble as soon as it reaches 312° F. Slowly move the pan above the marble to achieve an even layer as Manuel Lopez shows above. As soon as a skin has formed on the syrup (about one minute) start flipping the edges in to the center with the scraper. As the syrup flows out again, continue scraping and flipping the sugar from the edges in. Have a spatula handy to remove any syrup that may stick to the scraper as you work.

As you flip the syrup repeatedly, it will start to cool somewhat, and begin to stiffen. Keep working it with the scraper until it forms a large ball in the center of the marble.

At this point, if you wish to tint a portion of the batch, cut off a piece and put the remainder on the copper screen in front of the heater to keep warm. If you need only untinted sugar, as for a cake like White Satin, the cut-off piece is now ready to pull.

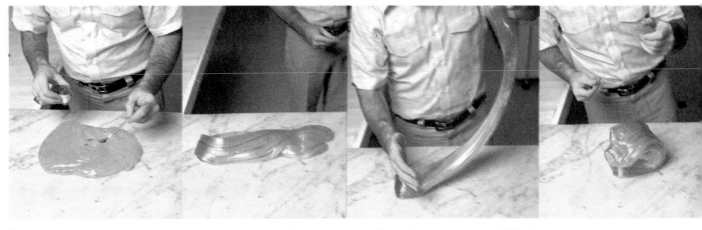

Place a little paste food color on the piece of sugar. (These pictures show the procedure with tinted sugar, but you will do the same with untinted sugar.) Stretch the sugar out and fold it over the color. Now begin to pull the sugar. Lift one end of the piece up and drop it down over the other, then lift the other end up and drop it in a pendulum-type motion, using alternate hands. Pull about ten to fifteen times for a small piece of sugar, 20 to 25 times for a larger piece. If the sugar is still trans-parent, pull until it is opaque. Fold the sugar over and put in front of the heater. It is now ready to stretch into a ribbon to cover the top tier.

Color note. If you need several colors of pulled sugar for a cake, cut off a piece for each color from the main batch and tint and pull it as described here before going on with the work. Keep the tinted sugar in front of the heater.

Start to stretch the ribbon to cover the top tier. Ribbons and bows are always made first while the sugar is most pliable. Cut off a piece of sugar about 6″ long, 2″ wide and 1″ thick. Lay it on the canvas and stretch it out into a thin ribbon. Hold end of the sugar with one hand and tug as you stretch and smooth with the other. Fold the ribbon in two, making fold at an angle so ribbon almost doubles in width. As you stretch the sugar, it will take on a satiny whiteness.

RUN YOUR HAND over the folded ribbon to join the two lengths together and stretch the ribbon longer. Continue to stretch, smooth and fold until the ribbon is about 22″ long and 4½″ to 5″ wide. (If you are new at pulled sugar, it is handy to lay a yardstick on the table.) Work quickly so sugar remains warm and pliable. Now cut off the rough end of the ribbon with a scissors, pick it up by both ends and very quickly wrap it around the top tier, tucking the ends together to fasten. NOTE: the side of the sugar that has been next to the canvas should always be on the outside of the cake, as it is the smoothest and shiniest.

GENTLY TOUCH the top edges of the ribbon with your fingers to ripple it on the top of the tier. Do this on each tier after you have wrapped it in ribbon. Now prepare another ribbon to cover the middle tier. You will need a ribbon about 36″ x 5″. Cut off a piece of sugar about 9″ x 2″ x 1″. Stretch, smooth and fold it just as you did the ribbon for the top tier. The greater length requires you to work very quickly so the ribbon remains flexible. Wrap the ribbon around the tier and tuck together at back, just below the fastening on the top tier.

Finally, cut off a piece of sugar about 12″ x 2″ x 1″ and stretch a ribbon to cover the base tier. Stretch, smooth and fold for a ribbon about 5″ x 45″ long. Quickly wrap the tier and fasten. The cake is now completely covered in pulled sugar.

MAKE RUFFLES TO EDGE TIERS. If you have made the five-pound recipe on page 232, repeat it for trim and prepare as shown on pages 232 and 233. Pull out a long ribbon about 2″ wide x 24″. Turn the ribbon over so smoother side is on top. Ruffle by gently pinching between thumb and forefinger, using both hands as shown above. Attach small pieces of sugar to base of tier to hold ruffle to cake. Do this by pulling off a small piece of sugar from the batch, touching to heater, then to tier. Pick the ruffle up and slide it onto your forearm, then attach it to bottom of base tier. Make more lengths of ruffle and attach until tier is completely edged. Now add ruffle to bottom of the middle tier the same way.

START TO MAKE BOWS. Each bow is composed of individually-made loops. For a big bow, like those on White Satin, you will need about six loops for outer part of bow, three or four for the center. Pull out a ribbon about 3½″ wide as described on opposite page. Starting from right hand side, cut ribbon in 8″ lengths. Fold into loops and let cool and harden *on edge*. (This keeps the loops in shape.) It is wise to have a helper form the loops as you cut ribbon, as work must proceed quickly.

Twist off a piece of sugar from the batch and flatten with a rolling pin to a diameter of about 4″.

TOUCH PLAQUE TO HEATER, then attach to side of cake. Test if loops are completely cool by touching to your cheek or wrist. Both areas are more sensitive to heat than your hand. If loops are warm, they will droop when handled. Touch loop to heater, then attach to plaque, working from outside in. Attach six loops to outer edge of plaque, then fill center with three or four loops. Bows made directly on the cake in this fashion will have a very graceful appearance. Make two more bows the same way on cake.

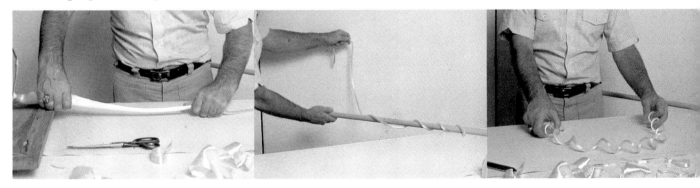

MAKE TWINING VINE that circles top tier. Round out a piece of sugar from the batch (still under heater) to a club shape. Hold the "club" with one hand as you pull out a strand with the other. Diameter of strand should be about as thick as a pencil. When you have pulled out a strand about five feet long, clip it off with the scissors. Let it lie on the canvas a few minutes to cool, then wrap it around a clean broomstick as Norman Wilton shows above. Just before the sugar hardens, and it is still warm to the touch, pull the spiral vine off the broomstick and twist it into a wreath shape.

WRAP THE VINE around the base of the top tier. Now attach it to the tier with small pieces of sugar taken from the batch, touched to heater, then to tier, just as you attached the ruffles (page 234). Trim the vine with wild flowers and leaves that you have made ahead of time. Directions for leaves are on page 240, flowers on page 242. Touch the base of the flowers to heater, then stick to vine. Attach the leaves in the same way. Your glistening pulled sugar wedding cake is nearly finished!

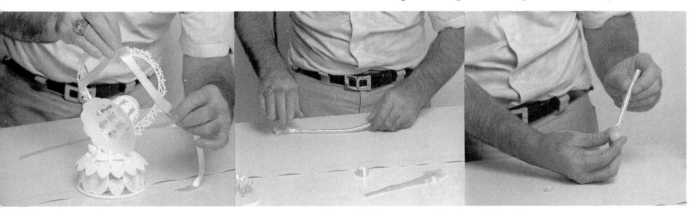

START TO DECORATE THE ORNAMENT with pulled sugar. This will add a beautiful finish to your cake. Use any simple ornament and remove tulle and flower trim. This bell ornament is ideal. Pull out a ribbon about 15″ long, ¾″ wide (see page 233). Touch a tiny piece of sugar to heater and stick on top center of heart background. Attach end of ribbon to this and drape on side of heart, folding around heart at center and letting end rest on ornament base. Pull out a second ribbon and drape around other side of heart.

Now make "dong" for bell. Pull out a strand about 12″ long just as for twining vine, above. Fold strand in two, twist, roll on canvas and clip off to 4″ or 5″ length. Make ball for end of dong just as you would a meat ball, rolling a small piece of sugar on the canvas. Let dong and ball *cool completely*. (Test by touching to your cheek or wrist.) Now touch end of dong to heater and fuse to ball. Touch other end to heater and insert in bell.

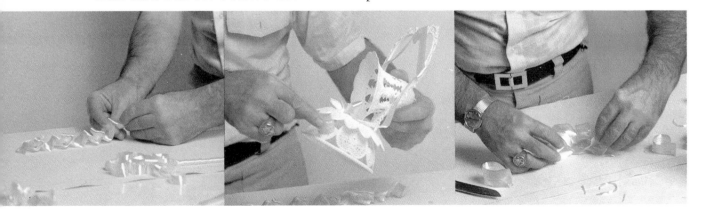

CONTINUE ORNAMENT TRIM. Pull out a ribbon about 1½″ wide and ruffle it (see page 233). Touch small pieces of sugar, from the batch, to heater and fuse to ornament base. Wrap ruffle around base.

Now make little bow for top of ornament. Technique is same as for large bow, page 235. Pull out a ¾″ wide ribbon, cut into 4″ lengths and fold into loops. Work very quickly. Use a rolling pin to flatten a 1″ piece of sugar from batch into plaque. Touch plaque and loops to cheek or wrist to be sure they have cooled completely. Touch end of loop to heater, then to plaque to fuse.

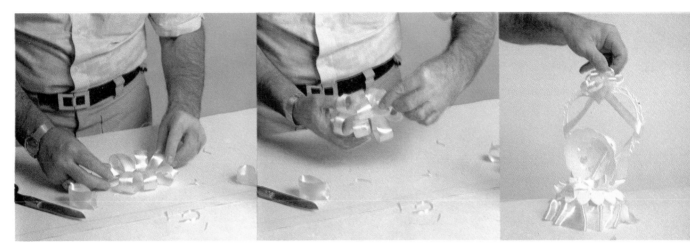

FINISH BOW by completing circle of loops around outside edge of plaque. Now pick plaque up and add loops in center. This gives bow a full, rounded look. Allow to cool completely (check by touching to cheek). Fuse to top of heart with a small piece of sugar touched to heater.

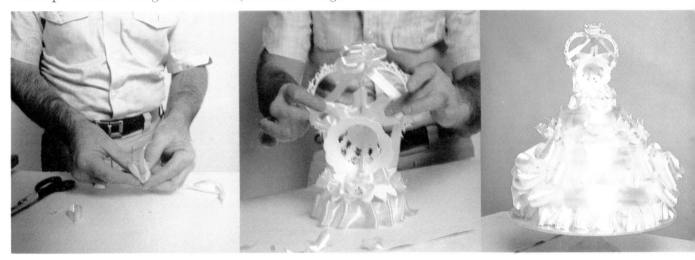

MODEL TWO LOVE BIRDS, each about 2½″ long, by pulling off a small piece of sugar and forming into curved neck and beak shape with your fingers. Model two leaf shapes, cool completely and fuse to neck for body. Model two more leaf shapes, cool completely, and fuse to body for wings. Paint beaks and eyes with food color. Attach love birds to top of bell on two pieces of sugar touched to heater and then to bell. Set the lovely ornament on your pulled sugar masterpiece cake.

As you continue your adventures in pulled sugar, be sure to refer to this chapter. It is a primer in the basics of pulled sugar—ribbons, ruffles, bows and twining vines.

CHAPTER FIFTEEN

More Pulled Sugar Techniques

Continue your adventures in pulled sugar by learning the advanced techniques in this chapter. The sugar will form the prettiest dessert shells and rose cups to hold ice cream. It can be pulled into shining ribbons, with alternate stripes of clear and satiny colors. Pulled sugar will make fantastic flowers, the petals gleaming like glass, graceful swans and shimmering basket centerpieces to fill with candy or to use as table decorations.

If you are not experienced in pulled sugar techniques, it is wise to review pages 230 through 237 to refresh yourself in the basics of this art. Remember to keep your batches of variously tinted sugar in front of the heater at all times. Be sure to turn them as you work so all sides are kept evenly warm.

DAINTY DESSERT SHELLS filled with ice cream provide a festive finale to an important dinner. After the shells are made as described on the next page, trim them with tiny pulled sugar wild flowers as explained on page 242. Touch the base of the flowers to the heater, then to the shells to fuse together.

Form balls of ice cream and freeze till very hard. Just before serving time, set the shells on dessert dishes and place an ice cream ball in each shell. Add a few drops of oil of peppermint to the batch of sugar that you will use, just after it is poured on the slab. Your guests will enjoy the flavor and texture of the candy shells.

238

To MAKE DESSERT SHELLS, work the sugar to the stage described on page 233 and tint it to your taste. Place the candy in front of the heater to keep warm and pliable. Pull off a piece about 4″ in diameter and work and stretch it with your hands into an even circle. Make several of the circles and lay them on the canvas to cool. When still warm, press the circles into a cupcake pan to form cups. Repeat this procedure until you have formed as many shells as needed. Allow the shells to cool completely in the pan before trimming them with wild flowers. (Test by touching to your cheek or wrist.)

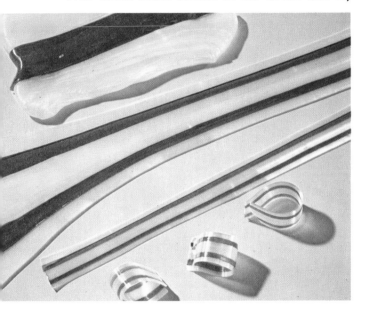

MAKING COLOR-STRIPED RIBBON IN SUGAR

Here is the method for forming ribbons and loops with alternating clear and satiny stripes. These gay ribbons give a very perky look to a pulled sugar cake.

Prepare clear red candy by placing a few dots of paste color on a piece of sugar after it has been flipped and formed into a ball (page 233). Fold the sugar over a few times to distribute the color—do not pull. Place in front of heater to keep warm.

Cut off a piece of untinted sugar and pull it ten or fifteen times as shown on page 233. Pull just enough so sugar loses its transparency. Now cut off two pieces of this candy and form two strips, each about 6″ x 2″. Cut off a piece of the clear red sugar, form it into a 6″ x 2″ strip and lay between the two white strips on the canvas, sides touching. Press the pieces together with your hands—their warmth will make them stick together.

Stretch and pull out the joined piece to twice its length. Cut in half and place the two pieces side by side. Press to join, then stretch and pull out again to the width desired. You must work very quickly. Clip off lengths of the striped ribbon, and fold into loops as demonstrated on page 235. It is helpful to have someone else form the loops as you clip. Set the loops *on edge* to cool (if laid on their sides they will lose their shape). Now you may use the red and white striped loops to form a bow as shown on pages 235 and 237.

CLEAR AND PULLED UNTINTED CANDY makes very dainty, sparkling striped ribbon. Follow the procedure above, but do not tint the unpulled candy.

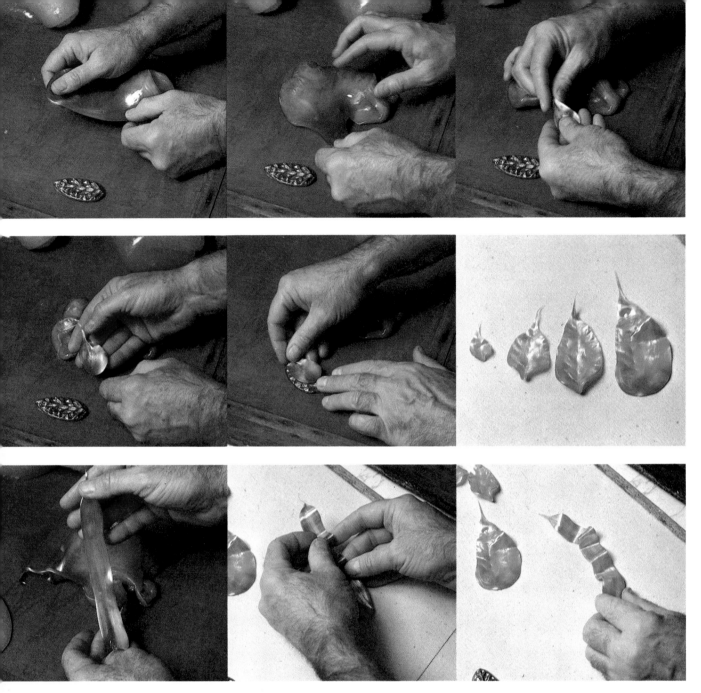

MAKING PULLED SUGAR LEAVES

It is very important to learn to make a leaf properly. This skill will make it easy to make a variety of pulled sugar flowers, since almost all petals resemble leaves before they are assembled. For leaves and all flowers, *work directly before the heater* to keep the sugar soft and pliable.

Tint all the colors you will need for flowers, leaves or other work at one time. Divide the main batch into portions and tint each a different color. Place a few drops of paste color on the portion, fold over and pull and stretch a few times to distribute color. (See page 233) Place all portions under the heater to keep warm. Turn from time to time to keep evenly heated.

STRETCH GREEN SUGAR to thin it by grasping with both hands and pulling it out. Place your thumb in the sugar and pull it out to form the leaf. Squeeze between thumb and forefinger and twist to snap off, or cut off with scissors.

To VEIN THE LEAF, press it into a greased leaf mold with your thumb. Make different sizes of leaves by pulling out varying amounts of sugar.

To MAKE A LONG NARROW LEAF, pull out a long ribbon-like leaf in the same way as above. Ruffle the leaf by grasping between thumbs and forefingers, using both hands.

Before attaching to flowers or cake, *leaves must be completely cool.*

HOW TO MAKE A CALLA LILY

This regal flower is very easy to make—it consists of two leaf shapes and a stamen. *Work directly in front of the heater.*

PULL OUT A LARGE LEAF, about 3½″ x 2″ wide, just as shown on opposite page. Roll the leaf to a curved form between thumb and forefinger. Roll the tip to curve it down. Allow to cool completely.

MAKE A STRAND of sugar from the batch just as you did for the vine on page 235. Form a small piece of sugar into a cylinder. Hold with one hand while you pull out a strand with the other. Clip the strand into 2″ lengths and set them aside to cool completely. Moisten the 2″ strand with a damp cloth and dip it into yellow-tinted granulated sugar. Touch the end of this stamen to the heater and insert it into the petal to attach.

PULL OUT A LEAF about 3½″ long from green-tinted sugar. Now wrap the leaf around the base of the lily, overlapping at the front. Set the completed flower aside to cool completely.

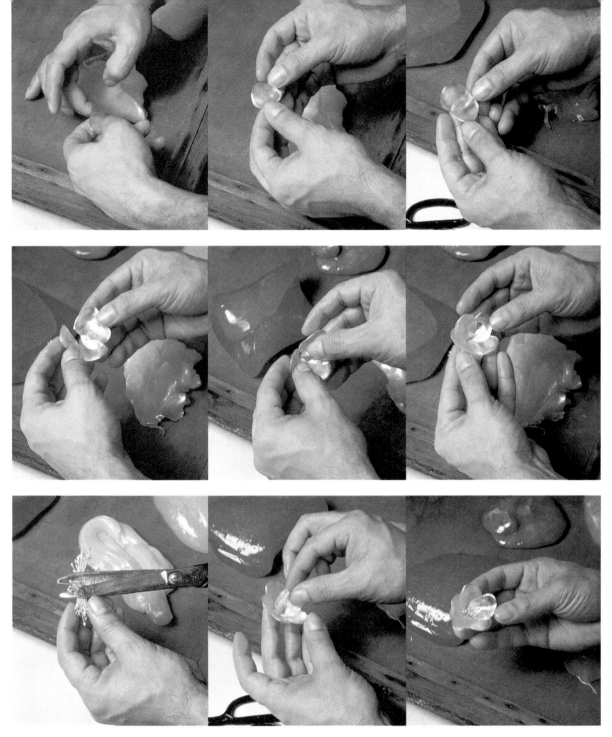

MAKE A FIVE-PETAL WILD FLOWER

This pretty little flower is easily made and is the one most often used for cake trims and flower arrangements. Start by thinning a small piece of tinted sugar by stretching with both hands. *Work directly in front of the heater* to keep the sugar soft and pliable.

PULL OUT A PETAL by placing your thumb in the sugar, pulling, then snapping off by pinching the tip of petal and giving a sharp twist. Make another petal and press to join to the first. They will stick together because they are still warm.

CONTINUE TO MAKE PETALS and join them in a fan

shape by pressing until you have joined five petals. Curve the fan shape with your thumb and forefinger into a flower shape with all petals joined. Set the flower shape upside down on the canvas to completely cool.

MAKE FLOWER CENTER by trimming off the stems of several artificial stamens to about ½″ length. Pinch off a small piece of sugar and wrap around the stamens. Touch wrapped sugar to the heater and insert in flower shape. Set completed flower aside to cool before attaching to cake.

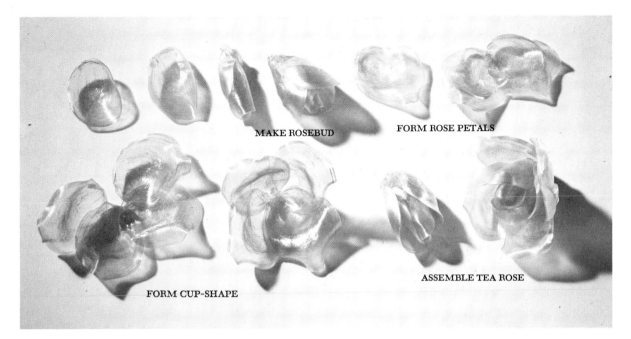

MAKE ROSEBUD   FORM ROSE PETALS

FORM CUP-SHAPE   ASSEMBLE TEA ROSE

FORMING THE ROSEBUD AND THE ROSE

This lovely flower starts by forming petals just as you did for the wild flower on opposite page. First stretch a piece of sugar to thin it. *Work directly in front of the heater.*

Follow the steps to assemble the flower as shown in the picture above. The pictures at the bottom of the page show you how the petals are formed.

MAKE ROSEBUD FIRST. Pull out two petals and snap off, just as you did for the wild flower. Curl the side of one petal, then place the other petal within it and roll the two together so they are interlocked. Pull out three more petals and press around the interlocked center of the bud.

MAKE ROSE PETALS. Put your thumb in the candy and push it down as you pull out and snap off to form a cupped petal. Now, with both thumbs and forefingers, curl the outer edges of the petal under

for a true rose petal effect. Make three more petals in the same way. Press each petal to the next as they are made to form a half-circle shape.

Join the half-circle into a cup shape by pressing the two outer petals together. Cool completely.

ASSEMBLE THE TEA ROSE by touching the base of the completed rosebud to the heater and then inserting it into the cup-shaped outer petals. Your beautiful tea rose is now complete.

MAKE A FULL-BLOWN ROSE (not shown). For a very showy rose, make six rose petals as described above, furling the outer edges of each petal. Allow the individual petals to cool completely. Now touch the base of each petal to the heater and fuse to the base of the tea rose, circling the entire flower for a lavish, full effect.

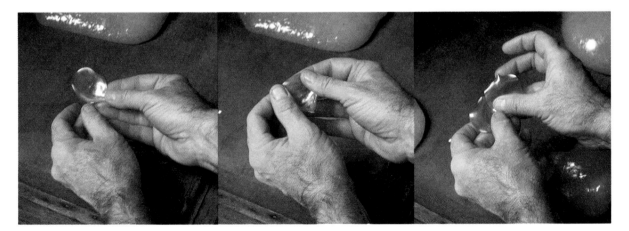

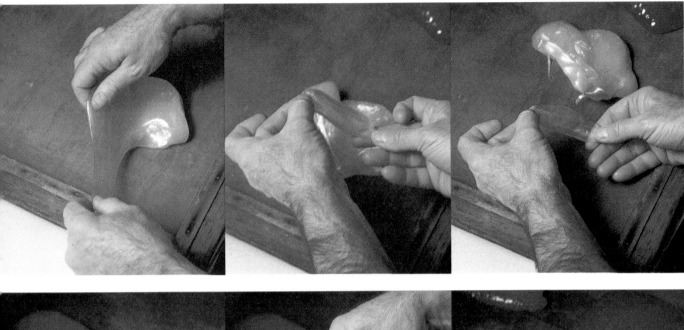

You must work quickly to make this imposing flower, and always in front of the heater. Like most flowers, its petals are formed in the same way as for a leaf (page 240). Thin a small piece of sugar by stretching it with both hands, then begin.

FORM SIX LONG PETALS, each about 2½″ x ½″ by putting your thumb into the sugar and pulling out, then clipping off. A quicker way is pinch base of petal and twist to snap off. Point the tips with your fingers. As each petal is made, press it to a completed petal to form a fan shape.

WRAP THE FAN SHAPE into a cone, pressing together the end petals. If the flower becomes too stiff to work, place it in front of the heater to soften.

Holding the base of the cone, curl each petal by pulling outward then down to form the lily shape. Set upside down on canvas to cool completely.

MAKE PISTILS FOR THE LILY. Pull out a very thin strand of sugar. First form a little sugar into a cylinder, then pull it out into a strand, holding cylinder with one hand and stretching with the other.

Clip the strand into 2″ lengths with a scissors and cool them completely. Moisten each strand with a damp cloth and dip into a bowl of yellow-tinted granulated sugar.

PLACE PISTILS IN FLOWER. Touch each strand to the heater and insert into center of lily to fuse. Place three pistils into each lily.

MAKE CALYX FOR LILY by pulling out a large leaf about 3″ long from green-tinted sugar that has been stretched to thin. (See page 240.) Wrap the leaf around the base of the lily, stretching and twisting to form a stem. Lay completed flower on its side to cool.

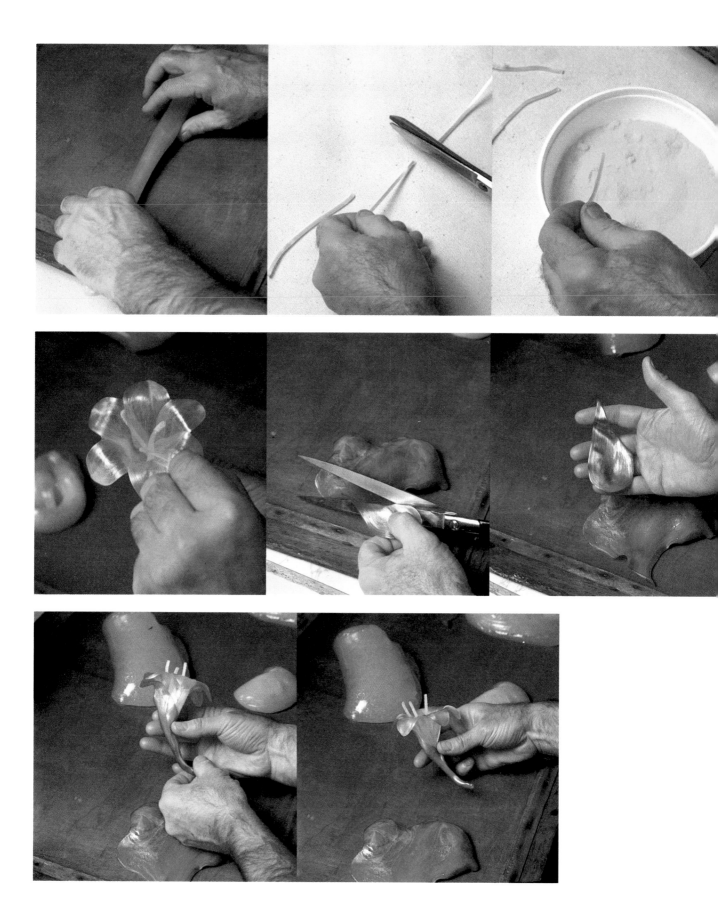

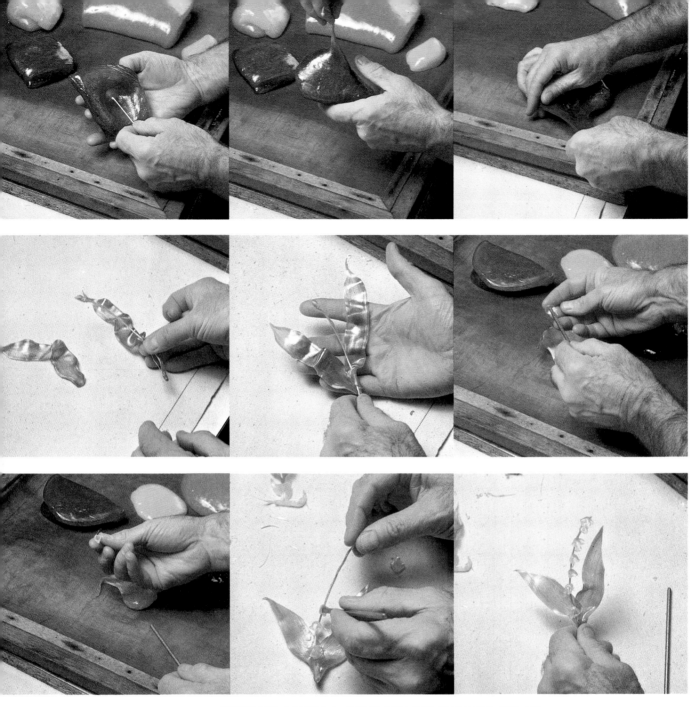

HOW TO MAKE A LILY-OF-THE-VALLEY SPRAY

To make this dainty springtime cake trim, you will need 18- or 22-gauge, cloth-covered florists' wire for the stem and a small metal rod of 3/16″ thickness to form the flowers. The end of a metal crochet hook will serve. *Work in front of the heater.*

FIRST COVER STEM. Cut the wire into 3½″ lengths. Pull a small piece of green-tinted candy with your hands to thin it. Push a length of wire into the candy. As it protrudes on the other side, reach around and pull it through, using a twisting motion so the candy adheres to the wire. Curve the candy-covered stem.

MAKE TWO LONG LEAVES. Pull out a leaf about 3½″ x 1½″ as described on page 240. Ruffle both edges

with thumb and forefinger. Wrap leaf around the base of the stem, pinching to attach. If the leaf is too stiff, soften it in front of the heater. Make another leaf and wrap around stem. *Cool completely.* (Test by touching to cheek or inner wrist.)

MAKE FLOWERS. Thin a small piece of untinted candy by stretching it with both hands. Pinch off a little piece of the candy about ¼″ in diameter and place it on the end of the metal rod, wrapping it around the tip. Touch the candy-covered end of the rod to the heater, then to the flower stem. Repeat for seven to twelve flowers, fusing them to alternate sides of the stem.

246

MAKE A GOLDEN DAFFODIL IN PULLED SUGAR

Before starting, thin a small piece of yellow-tinted sugar by stretching it with both hands. Always work in front of the heater to keep the candy soft and pliable.

MAKE SIX PETALS, each about 1½″ x ¾″. Put your thumb in a piece of thinned candy, pull out and snap or cut off with scissors. Pinch the tip with your fingers and pull out to point. As each petal is made, press it to a completed one, points facing away from you.

When all six are completed and arranged in a fan shape, bring the end petals of the fan together and press to join. Shape and curve the petals with your hand. If they are still too soft to hold their shape, gently blow on them to cool. Set the flower on its face to cool completely.

FORM DAFFODIL CENTER CUP. Pull out a 1″ wide ribbon from thinned candy and clip to 2″ length. Fringe the ribbon by making many short cuts with scissors on one long side. Roll the ribbon around your finger to form a bell shape and press to join edges. Immediately touch the base of the bell to the heater and fuse in the center of the cooled petals. Cool flower completely.

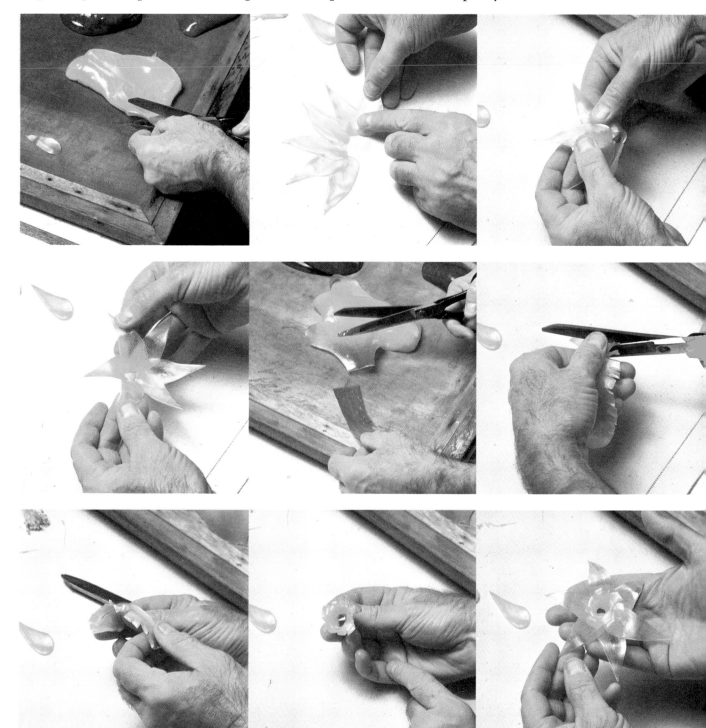

HOW TO MAKE A SPARKLING CHRISTMAS POINSETTIA

The poinsettia is an assembled flower. Outer and inner petals are made and cooled, a small ball for the center is formed, then the flower is put together and finished. Follow the pictures to create this holiday flower.

FORM PETALS. First make the six longer outer petals, each about 2½″ x ⅝″. Pull out a petal from thinned candy just as you did for the leaf on page 240. Stretch the edges between thumb and forefinger to ruffle and pinch and pull the tip to a point. Hold the base of the petal and pull the tip end down to curve. Let long petals cool completely.

Now make four or five shorter petals, each about 2″ long. Do them the same as the long petals.

ROLL A BALL for center from a small piece of candy. It should be about ½″ in diameter. Make sure petals are cool by touching them to your cheek or inner wrist. Attach longer petals first by touching bases to heater, then to ball to fuse. Attach shorter petals to ball in the same way, fusing to the ball above the longer petals.

MAKE STAMENS from bright yellow sugar. Form a small piece of sugar into a cylinder. Hold cylinder in one hand and pull and stretch with the other to form a very fine strand. Clip the yellow strand into tiny ¼″ lengths.

FINISH FLOWER. Pick up each yellow stamen with a tweezer, touch to heater, then fuse to center ball of flower. (Stamens are too small to hold with fingers.) You will need about four stamens for each poinsettia blossom.

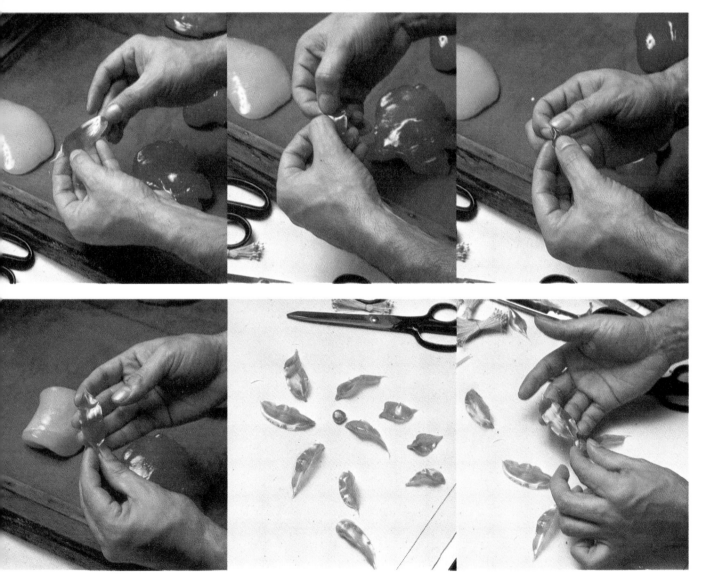

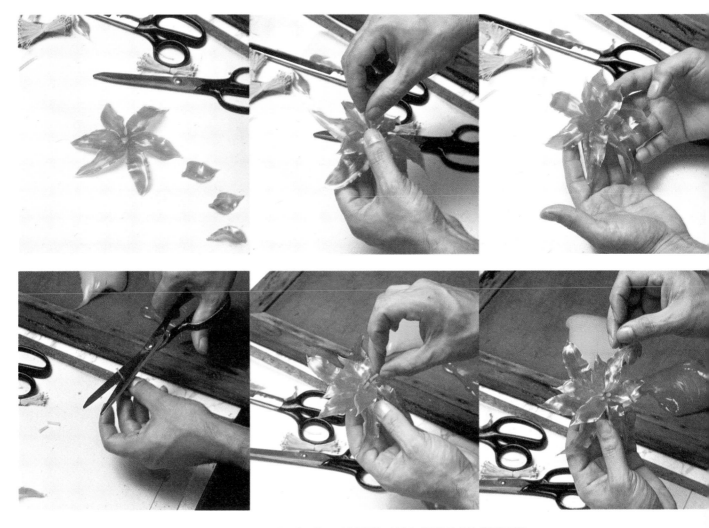

HOW TO MAKE PULLED SUGAR DAISIES AND BELL FLOWERS

FORM THE DAISIES. Pull out about 13 petals each about 1½″ x ⅜″, from thinned sugar. Keep the tips rounded. As each petal is formed, overlap and press it to a completed one. Final petal will make almost a full circle. Pick up the joined petals and press the two end petals together to complete the circle. Work quickly—if petals become too stiff, place in front of heater. Cool flower upside down.

Form a ⅜″ diameter ball from yellow candy. Press in yellow-tinted granulated sugar, touch to heater, then fuse in center of petals. Flatten ball with your thumb.

MAKE BELL FLOWERS. You will need a slim metal rod, or use a blunted nail, to form this flower. Press a small piece of sugar to a ½″ disk. Hold the disk on your forefinger and press the rod into it. Remove the rod and set aside to cool. Clip off stems of artificial stamens to ½″. Wrap a little piece of candy around base of a few stamens, touch to heater, then insert into flower.

SERVE DESSERT IN SHINING ROSE CUPS

These dainty, flower-like cups look very impressive, but they are not as difficult to make as your guests at a gala dinner might think! To capture a bit of the artistry of the nineteenth century, when such a fitting climax to a memorable dinner was a part of elegant living, is something you will find immensely rewarding, a truly gourmet touch even in that golden age of the culinary arts. Start these conversation pieces in a similar manner to the way you begin the dessert shells on page 238. Divide cooked sugar into two portions. Tint one a delicate green for the "calyxes". Tint the other rose, peach or yellow for the petals.

MAKE GREEN BASES or "calyxes". From green-tinted sugar under the heater, pull off a piece about 3½" in diameter. Work it with your hands into a circle, extending it to about 4". Allow the circle to cool a little on the canvas. While still somewhat warm, press the circle into a cupcake pan, letting edges ruffle at the top. You can work with four or five circles at a time—while several are cooling, work out another circle.

MAKE ROSE PETALS. These are made in exactly the same way as the rose petals on page 243, but larger. Thin a small piece of tinted sugar by stretching it with both hands. Grasp a piece of the sugar with thumb and forefinger. Pressing thumb down to form a cupped shape, pull out a petal about 2" wide. Snap off by pinching base of petal and giving a twist, or cut off with scissors. Work under the heater.

Furl the two sides of the petal under at the tip and place in the green calyx. It will adhere because it is still quite warm. Repeat making and attaching petals in the calyx, each slightly overlapping, until you have five in the shape of a rose. Let the rose cups cool completely before lifting out of pan.

FORM ICE CREAM BALLS and freeze very hard. At serving time, place each rose cup on a doily and add an ice cream ball. Garnish each with a cherry, or a piped swirl of whipped cream. Serve at once, before ice cream melts.

AT RIGHT, A GREEN CRYSTAL BASKET, draped with satiny ribbons and trimmed with dainty bell flowers. Directions start on page 252.

250

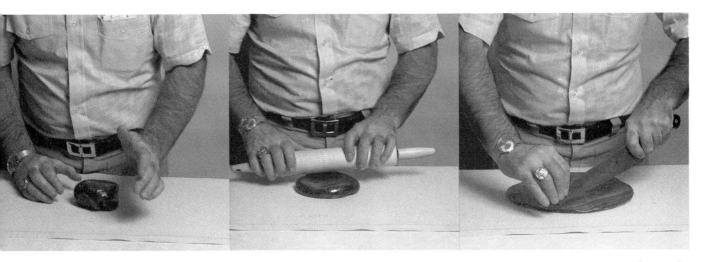

To achieve the sparkling, glass-like look of this basket, the sugar is not pulled at all. Use the recipe on page 232. As soon as the cooked syrup is removed from the heat, add paste food coloring, stir just to blend, then pour it out on the greased marble slab. (Use *only* paste color for sugar work.) Work and flip the syrup into a ball as shown on pages 232 and 233, then place it on the screen under the heater.

FORM THE BASKET BASE. Take a piece of candy about 4″ in diameter and 2″ thick from the batch and place it on the canvas. Press it into a rough circular shape, then use a rolling pin to thin it out further. Keep rolling and working the candy with your hands until it becomes an 8″ circle.

Now take a long knife and make parallel cuts in the circle about 1½″ apart. Press lightly so as not to cut through sugar. Make a second series of parallel cuts perpendicular to the first, crisscrossing the indentations. Since the circle is still soft it will retain the design, which appears like cut glass.

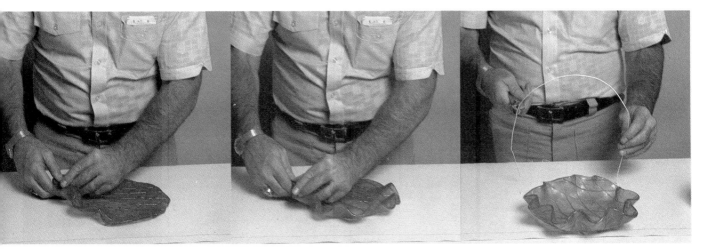

RUFFLE THE EDGES of the basket. Leave the cuts right side up. Lift up the edge with thumb and forefinger, then with finger of other hand, push edge down. Continue around entire circumference of circle until edge is completely ruffled.

CURVE BASE OF BASKET. Set a small bowl about 6″ in diameter upside down. Turn the circle over so crisscross surface is down, and lay it on the bowl. Re-shape the ruffled edges with your hands, and set aside to cool completely, five minutes or more. Since the base is still warm and soft, it will assume the curved shape of the bowl.

PREPARE THE BASKET HANDLE. Clip off the hook of a white-painted coat hanger and shape it to an arch, using the basket base as your guide. You will need a pliers and snippers. Check to be sure the ends of the handle will fit inside the base.

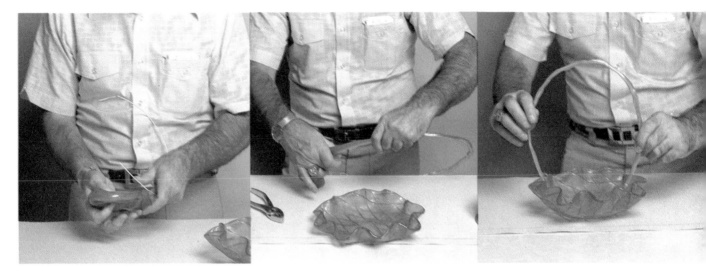

COVER THE HANDLE with sugar. Take a small piece of candy from the batch under the heater. Thin it out a little by stretching with both hands. Push one end of the handle into it. As it protrudes from the opposite side, reach around and pull. Continue pulling very slowly until entire handle has passed through the candy and is completely covered. Check again with the base to make sure handle has correct curve.

ATTACH HANDLE TO BASE. Cut off a piece of soft candy from the batch under the heater. Wrap it around one end of the handle. Do the same to wrap the other end. These pieces of candy will form a strong base for the handle. Touch the ends of the handle to the coil of the heater and set the handle into the basket base. It will fuse immediately. Set two cups inside basket so bases of basket handles rest against cup handles. This will steady handle until it is completely cool.

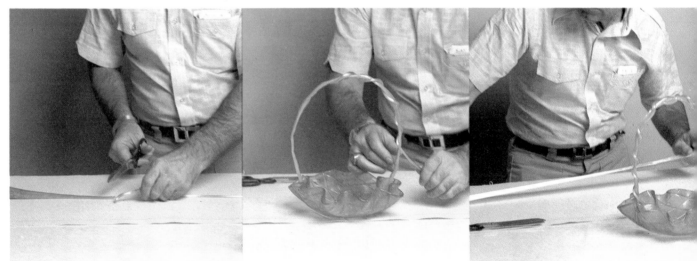

MAKE A VINE to wrap around the handle. Cut off a piece from the soft green candy under the heater and roll it into a club shape. Hold it with one hand while you stretch and pull with the other, keeping the strand within your closed fist. Pull it until it is about ¼″ thick and about four feet long. Cut strand in two.

TWINE THE VINE around the handle. Take one sec-tion of vine and stick it to the top center of the handle. It will adhere because it is still soft. Wrap it around one side of the handle, ending at the base. Take the other vine section, attach to top center of handle and wind around other side of handle. You must work quickly so vine does not harden. Our next step is to drape a ribbon around the handle.

Finish the basket with draped ribbons, a full bow and dainty flowers and leaves.

Make the ribbons. For this we are using untinted candy. Start with a piece of candy from the batch under the heater about 6″ long and 1″ thick. Stretch and pull the candy just as is shown on page 233. Pull out the piece, stretch it on the canvas, fold over and stretch and pull again. Do this until ribbon is three feet long and 2″ wide. Cut in half with scissors. Touch an end of one section of the ribbon to heater and attach to center of handle. Drape ribbon down and twirl it around the base of handle, so it comes out the other side. Arrange the remaining ribbon in folds on the basket base.

Turn the basket around and drape second section of ribbon around handle in the same way.

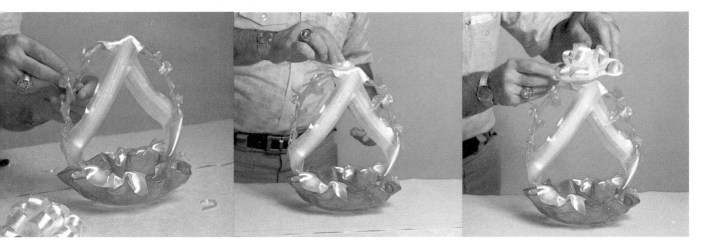

Make a bow for the handle just as described on page 237. Pull and stretch out ribbon from untinted candy to about 1¼″ width. Cut the ribbon in 3″ lengths. Make loops by folding cut pieces of ribbon over your finger and set *on edge* to cool. (If laid on their sides they may flatten out.)

Form a plaque of candy about 3″ in diameter by pressing and shaping with your fingers. Touch a cooled loop to heater and fuse to edge of plaque. Add six or seven more loops until plaque is circled. Pick up the plaque, allowing loops to fall down over your hand and fill center with four or five more loops. Let bow cool completely.

Make flowers and leaves. The little bell flowers are made of untinted sugar. Pull off a piece of candy and flatten to a ½″ circle. Push a metal rod into it to form flower shape. (Use the end of a metal crochet hook, or a piece of thick coat hanger.) Touch rod to heater, then to handle to attach. Make four or five flowers for each side of handle, attaching as they are made.

Pull out twelve or more small leaves as described on page 240 and press into greased leaf molds. Cool the leaves, then touch base of each to heater and fuse to handle.

Finish basket by attaching bow, now completely cooled. Pull off a ½″ piece of candy from the batch, touch to heater and fuse to top of handle. Fuse another piece of candy to bottom of plaque. Immediately set bow in position. Your beautiful crystal basket is now completed and ready to fill with candy or just serve as a lovely table decoration.

A DAINTY LITTLE SWAN
Directions start on page 256

A RIBBONED CANDY DISH
Directions page 258

HOW TO MAKE A GLISTENING LITTLE SWAN

When finished, this little pulled sugar swan will be about 4½" high and 4" long—just the right size to set on a tray heaped with candied almonds. START BY FORMING THE NECK. Take a piece of candy from the batch under the heater. It should be 4" to 5" long and about 1" in diameter. Round it into a pear shape by rolling it on the canvas. Stretch it out by running it through your hands until it forms a thick, even strand.

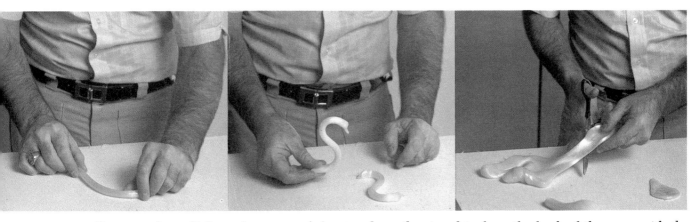

CLIP OFF about 6" from the center of the strand. This will eliminate the rough ends which are somewhat thicker. Roll this piece back and forth on the canvas, just like a pencil. This action will keep the strand evenly round as it cools a little. Now with your fingers, turn, pinch and squeeze one end of the strand to form the beak of the swan with the rounded head behind it.

Lay the strand back on the canvas and form it into a figure "S". Let the completed neck and head cool completely, about seven or eight minutes.

To MAKE A WING, pull out a large leaf, just as you did for the calla lily on page 241. Round out the broader end with your thumb into a saucer-like shape which will attach to the neck. Turn up the pointed end. Make a second wing just as the first, but opposite facing. Now make a third leaf, thicker than the others, for the base of the swan. Lay this base on the canvas and move up the pointed end about an inch to form tail portion. Keep the rest of the base flat so you can attach the neck.

Test all pieces to make sure they are totally cool. Now touch the bottom of the swan neck to the heater, and fuse it near the front of the base.

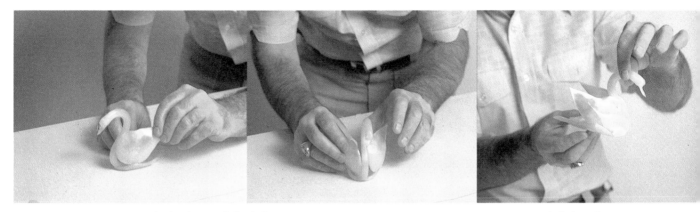

ATTACH THE WINGS. Touch the front of the left wing to the heater, rolling it back and forth so entire front portion is melted, then fuse it to the neck and base. Do the same for the opposite wing. Don't worry if the fused edges of the wings appear brown and scorched—they will be covered up. Be careful not to burn your fingers as the candy is very hot.

PULL OUT ANOTHER LEAF, just as you did for the calla lily on page 241. Attach it to the front and one side of the swan, pointed end to the rear. Make a second leaf and attach to the other side of the swan. Now make a third leaf and fuse to the front. The swan is complete.

TRIM THE SWAN with pink ribbons. Take a little piece of pink candy from the batch under the heater and stretch and pull it just as shown on page 234, but this ribbon should be only about ½″ wide. Clip off 1½″ pieces and fold them over your finger to make two loops. Cool on edge to preserve shape. Cut off a piece about 2″ long and wrap it around the swan's neck, ends meeting at the top. The

warmth will make it stick. Now take a ribbon about 6″ long, fuse to ribbon on neck, and drape it back along one wing. Do the same on the other side of the swan. Touch the ends of the loops to the heater and set them in position to form a bow.

Your fairytale little swan is now finished and ready to adorn a reception or dessert table.

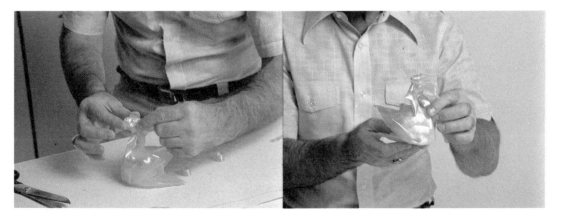

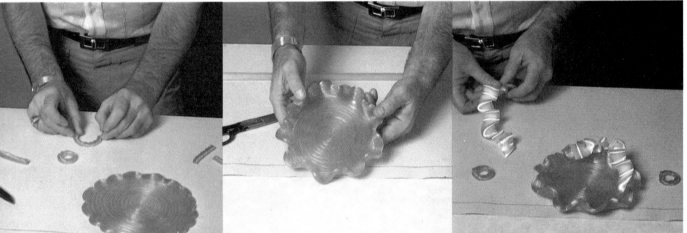

HOW TO MAKE A CANDY DISH FROM COILED SUGAR

This pretty little candy dish is formed by coiling an even strand of sugar into a flat circle. This is a good technique to master—with it you can make many decorative dishes and baskets.

TAKE A LARGE PIECE OF CANDY from the batch under the heater and roll it on the canvas into a pear shape about 7″ or 8″ long. Hold the end of this with one hand while you stretch and pull it through the other to form an even strand about ¼″ thick. (See bottom, page 235.) Coil the strand. Lay the end on the canvas and wrap the strand around in a spiral fashion from the center out. As you wrap, keep pulling out the strand, never allowing it to break off. Keep turning and wrapping the strand until the circle is about 7″ in diameter—then cut off the strand. If you are new to this technique, it's helpful to have someone else pull out the strand while you turn and wrap the circle.

INDENT THE EDGES of the circle about every ¾″ with a scissors. Turn the circle over so the smooth side is on top. Now begin to flute the edge about every 2″, just as you did for the green basket on page 252. Make sure the circle is still somewhat soft as you do this. Cool completely.

MAKE ROUND HANDLES by pulling out a strand of candy and clipping it off. Double the strand and twist and roll it along the canvas. Cut off two pieces about 2″ long and shape into circles. Cool.

TRIM THE DISH with ruffled ribbons and bows. Stretch out a ribbon about 1″ wide, ruffle it between thumb and forefinger, using both hands, and drape it on one side of the dish. Add a second ruffled ribbon to the other side. Fuse handles to dish by touching to heater, then to edge of dish. Make a bow (see page 237) with 10 or 12 loops about ⅝″ wide and fuse to the candy dish.

A BEAUTIFUL BASKET trimmed with ribbons, flowers and loops. Directions start on page 260.

THIS BASKET BEGINS the same way as the candy dish described on page 258—with a coiled base. Pull out a ¼″ strand of candy, and starting in the center, coil it into a circle, wrapping and turning until it is 9″ in diameter. Indent the edges every ¾″ with the blade of a scissors, then flute the rim just as you did for the green basket on page 252. While the base is still somewhat warm and soft, place it over the outside of a bowl about 7″ in diameter to give it a rounded shape as it cools completely.

MAKE BASKET HANDLE. You will need three lengths of ¼″ dowel rod—two 11″ long and one 9″ long. Thin a small piece of soft candy by stretching, and insert the end of a dowel into it. As it comes through the other side, reach around with your other hand and pull the rod slowly through the candy. A little thread of candy will still be attached to the rod. Turn the candy-covered rod and rotate it between your fingers as the thread wraps itself around the rod from top to bottom. Now hold the other end of the rod and rotate it between your fingers again as the still-unbroken thread of candy wraps around it, creating a crisscross design. Should the thread break, pull out another from the soft candy, attach to rod and twirl again to complete design. Cover and trim other two rods the same way.

ATTACH HANDLE TO BASE. Take a small piece of candy and wrap it around the end of an 11″ covered dowel. Touch it to the heat element and fuse it to the side of the basket base. Ask a partner to hold the rod in position until it cools. Add another 1″ piece of candy to base of the handle to reinforce it. Secure a 9″ covered dowel to the other side of the base the same way.

Hold the 11″ crosspiece in position against the side handles. Touch a small piece of candy to the heater, then to the juncture of the crosspiece and one side dowel. Do the same on the other side of the crosspiece. When these have cooled, take small pieces of warm candy and wrap around the points where the crosspiece meets the two side handles. This will give more stability. Let the handle cool completely.

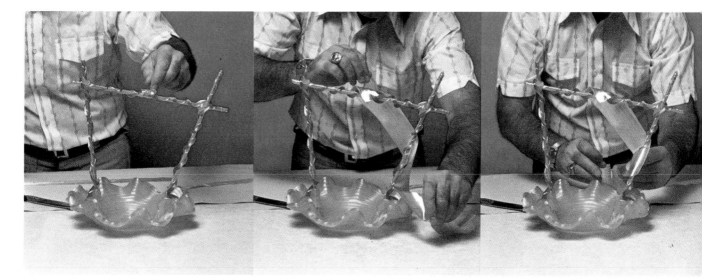

ADD A TWINING VINE. Form a piece of soft green candy from the batch under the heater into a pear shape. Holding in one hand, pull out a ¼″ strand about five feet long with the other, letting it pass through your fist for even diameter. Cut strand in two. Touch a small piece of candy to heater, then to top center of handle. Touch end of one strand to the heater, then to this piece and wind around top handle and down to base of basket. Do the same on the other side of the handle. You will use the vine as support for flowers and leaves.

MAKE RIBBON. Take a small piece of untinted candy from the batch under the heater, and stretch and pull out a ribbon about 1¾″ wide, three feet long. (See page 234.) Cut the ribbon in half. Touch end of one ribbon to heating element, then to top center of handle to fuse. Then wrap the ribbon around side handle and drape it on the side of the basket base.

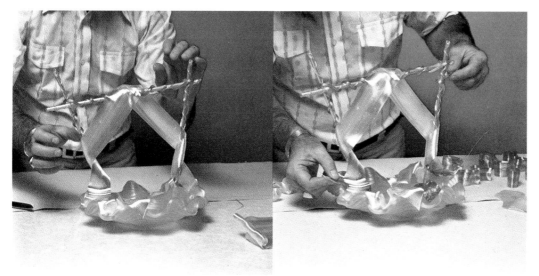

CONTINUE TRIMMING THE BASKET. Attach the other ribbon to the basket handle and wrap and drape it just as you did the first. Take a small piece of green candy from the batch under the heater and thin it by stretching with both hands. Put your thumb into the candy and pull out a small leaf, twisting and pinching to snap off. Press leaf into greased leaf mold to vein. (See page 240). Make about 16 leaves. Cool leaves completely. Now begin to attach leaves to handle. Touch base of each leaf to heater, then to candy-covered handle.

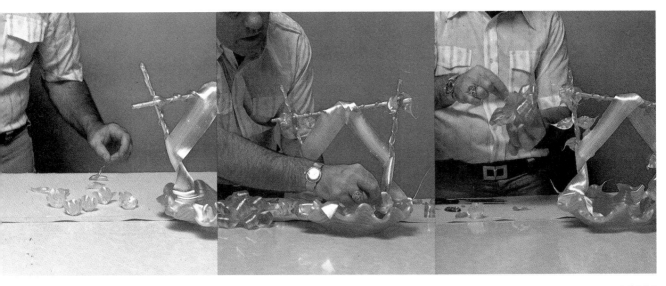

MAKE STRIPED BOW. The clear striped ribbon is made just as described on page 239. Form a piece of pink candy into a shape about 5″ x 2″ x 1″ thick. Form a piece of untinted candy into the same shape and lay on the canvas beside the pink candy, sides touching. Press to join the pieces. Stretch and pull out to about 12″. Cut in two, lay the pieces side by side and press to join. Now stretch and pull out until the ribbon is about 1¼″ wide. Working very quickly, clip into 4″ lengths and form loops by folding over your finger. Set on edge to cool. Assemble bow on a 2″ plaque of candy just as described on page 237. Set the sparkling bow aside to cool completely.

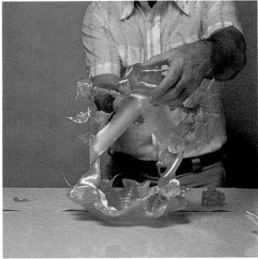

MAKE WILD FLOWERS as shown on page 242. You will need about eight. Make four or five white rosebuds as described on page 243. To attach the flowers to the handle, first stick a tiny piece of soft candy to the base of each flower, then touch to heater and then to handle. Since the flowers are very thin, this will prevent the heater from burning a hole through them. Attach a few more leaves to frame the flowers.

FINISH BY ATTACHING BOW. Stick a soft piece of candy to the back of the plaque, touch to heating element, then place bow on handle to fuse. Your beautiful basket is ready to decorate the table.

HOW TO MAKE A COMPOTE

This lustrous fluted compote can hold mints or candy to adorn the most festive reception table. It is easier to make it over a base. This one is made by gluing a plastic pillar to two ornament plates.

FIRST COVER THE STEM. Pull out a yellow ribbon about ¾″ wide and 8″ long. Touch a small piece of candy to the heater, and stick it to the base of the stem. Now attach the end of the ribbon to this piece and wrap it around the pillar to the top. Attach to top of pillar with a piece of hot candy.

MAKE LOOPS FOR BOW. Pull out a long ribbon about 1″ wide. Clip into 4″ or 5″ lengths and fold the lengths over your finger, working very quickly. Set aside *on edge* to cool completely.

MAKE RUFFLE FOR BASE. Pull out a ribbon, 1″ wide and about 9″ long. Ruffle it with your thumbs and forefingers, using both hands. Circle the base with it. To secure it to the base, take a tiny piece of soft candy, hold it with scissors or tweezer and touch to heat element. Place it on the plastic base, under the ruffle, and the two will fuse together. Attach ruffle in two more places to base.

MAKE THE PLATE for the top of the compote. This is made in exactly the same way as the candy dish described on page 258. Wrap and coil a ¼″ strand until you have a circle 8″ in diameter. After it has cooled somewhat, but is still soft, crimp the edge with the blade of a scissors. Turn the circle over so the smooth side is up and flute the rim about every 2″. Set aside to cool completely. If the fluting tends to fall down as it cools, move it back to shape.

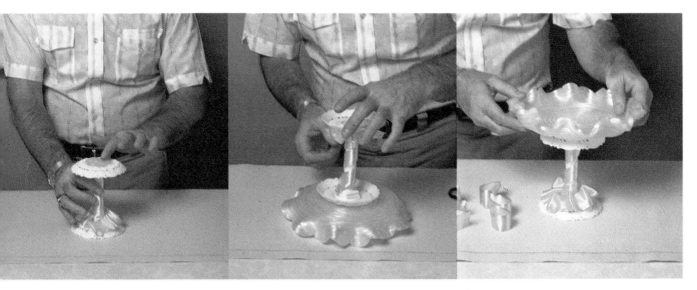

ATTACH PLATE TO COMPOTE. Flatten a piece of soft candy to about 2″ diameter and touch it to the heating element and fuse it to the plastic plate. Turn the fluted candy plate upside down. Make sure it is completely cooled. Now pick up the compote, touch the candy on top to the heater and place it in the center of the candy plate. This will attach the plate firmly to compote. Turn it right side up.

MAKE TWO ROUND HANDLES as described on page 258. When these have cooled, touch each to the heater, then to the sides of the plate to fuse.

ASSEMBLE THE BOW on a candy plaque about 1½″ in diameter. Do this just as shown on page 237.

PULL OUT A RIBBON about 1½″ wide and 20″ long. Cut it in half. Ruffle the ribbons with your thumbs and forefingers, using both hands, then drape them on both sides of the compote plate.

ATTACH BOW. Make sure it is completely cool. Touch a small piece of candy to the heater, then to the plaque on the bottom of the bow. Now touch the bow to the heating element and set it on the compote.

CHAPTER SIXTEEN

A Gallery of Sugar Showpieces

Browse through this chapter to see how the sugar techniques in Chapters Fourteen and Fifteen can be used to create cakes and centerpieces of breathtaking beauty. Some are quite simple, others more time-taking—all are spectacular.

This chapter will also introduce you to the arts of sugar basket-weaving and spun sugar. Page 268 tells how to transport and serve a pulled sugar cake.

When you are planning to decorate a cake in pulled sugar, add a few drops of oil of peppermint to the cooked sugar after you have poured it on the marble slab. Your guests will appreciate the flavor.

CHRISTMAS SPARKLE, a cake just as joyous as the season, crowned with scarlet poinsettias. Directions are on the next page.

CHRISTMAS SPARKLE (shown on page 265)

To make this gay holiday cake you will need one recipe of pulled sugar and a 12″ two-layer cake, fondant-covered. See page 232. Tint small amounts of sugar red and green, a tiny portion yellow.

STEP ONE. Pull, stretch and fold a ribbon 38″ long by about 5″. Wrap this around the cake.

STEP TWO. Pull out a 1½″ ribbon from red candy. Ruffle it with your thumbs and forefingers, using both hands. Place it around the base of the cake, and attach it with little pieces of candy touched to heater, then to cake. Add more ruffles until entire cake is circled.

STEP THREE. Make striped ribbon about 1″ wide. (See page 239.) Clip to 9″ lengths and attach in four swags to side of cake by touching ends to heater, then cake. Make a dozen small loops for bows. Cool completely, on edge. Attach three loops to each point of swag by touching ends to heater, then *directly to cake.*

STEP FOUR. Make a twining vine from green candy just as on page 236. Pull it off the broom handle and lay it on the cake in a curve. Make about 18 long ruffled leaves about 4″ or 5″ long and three poinsettias. When completely cooled, attach leaves to vine by touching base to heater, then to vine. Fuse poinsettias to vine and fill in with more leaves. Your Christmas vision is complete!

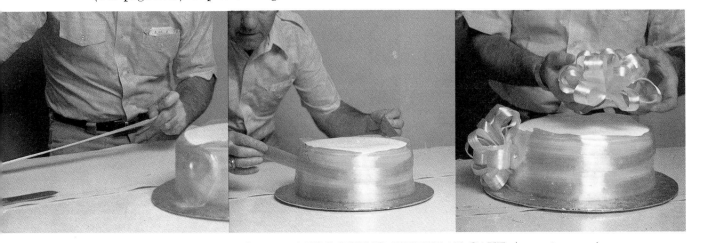

CHAMPAGNE, A SHIMMERING BIRTHDAY CAKE (opposite page)

A very simple cake made spectacular by the color and shine of pulled sugar. With Champagne centering the table, any birthday will become a gala celebration. You will need a 10″ two-layer cake covered with fondant and one recipe of pulled sugar, page 232. Tint about two-thirds of the sugar yellow, the rest pink.

STEP ONE. Stretch and pull out a yellow ribbon about 33″ long and about 5″ wide. Wrap it around the cake. Now stretch out a pink ribbon the same length and about 1¼″ wide. Wrap this around the base of the cake. The warmth will make it stick. Wrap another pink ribbon around the cake about 1″ higher. This creates the unique striped effect.

STEP TWO. Stretch out pink and yellow ribbons about 1″ wide and cut off about 5″ lengths to form loops. You will need about 24 of each color. Roll out two sugar plaques, one about 3″ in diameter for the top of the cake and the other 2½″ for the side. Attach plaques to top and side of cake by touching to heater, then to cake. Assemble bows with loops as shown on page 235, alternating colors. Insert the candles.

You can adapt this cake for many occasions by varying the color and adding script messages.

AURORA'S WEDDING, A FAIRYTALE BRIDAL CAKE

This rosy fanciful cake is fit for the wedding of a princess! The shining pink tiers are adorned with ruffles, bows and dainty white roses.

Prepare three tiers, 16″, 12″ and 8″, each two layers. Cover with rolled fondant (page 232) and assemble on cake board with two 10″ separator plates and 5″ square filigree pillars. You will need two recipes of pulled sugar (page 232). Tint most of it pink, a small amount green, leave remainder untinted. Review Chapter Fourteen for techniques.

STEP ONE. Wrap the tiers with ribbons as shown on page 234. Pull and stretch out ribbons about 1½″ wide, ruffle them between your thumbs and forefingers, and attach to the bases of the two lower tiers. Do this by touching a small piece of candy to the heater, then to the base of the tier.

STEP TWO. Make three large bows. Roll out pieces of green candy to about 3½″ in diameter. Touch to heater, then to cake, against two lower tiers. Make many loops from 5″ lengths of ribbon about 1″ wide. Cool on edge. Assemble the loops on the plaques, working from outside in as shown on page 235.

STEP THREE. Decorate top tier. Make pink and white striped ribbon, about 1″ wide as shown on page 239. Cut it into four 7″ lengths and attach in swags to top of tier. Touch ends of ribbon to heater, then to tier. Make loops of the striped ribbon and cool. Attach four loops to each point where swags meet. Touch ends to heater, then to tier.

STEP FOUR. Set two White Birds within pillars. Pull out a long strand of green sugar, spiral it around a broomstick and place on top of center tier. Page 236 shows how to do this. Pull out another green strand about 10″ long and attach vertically from top of middle tier to base of cake, between two bows. Secure with small pieces of hot candy. Repeat for two more vertical vines, centering between large bows. These will hold the flower cascades.

STEP FIVE. Make about 20 white tea roses and 20 wild flowers. Pull out a large number of green leaves. Pages 240, 242 and 243 give directions. Attach a tiny piece of hot candy to the base of each flower. Now attach leaves and flowers to the green vines and to the top of smallest tier. Touch each to heater, then to vine or tier. The pillars will be circled with flowers and three flower cascades will run down the lower part of the cake.

STEP SIX. Decorate ornament. Almost any ornament can be easily trimmed with pulled sugar to blend with the cake. This whimsical ornament is trimmed with ½″ pink ribbon, a full bow and wild flowers and leaves. See pages 236 and 237 for techniques.

Aurora's Wedding is ready to shine at a brilliant bridal reception!

HOW TO CARRY AND SERVE A PULLED SUGAR CAKE

Since moisture and humidity will cause the sugar to dull and soften, *never* put the cake in the freezer or refrigerator. The drier the room, the longer the sugar will shine.

To carry a pulled sugar cake, slide it into the open side of a large corrugated cardboard box. Crumple wax paper and place it all around the sides of the cake to keep it from shifting. Tape sheets of newspaper over the top of the box, then cover it. If the box doesn't have a cover, stretch a large cloth over it to keep all the moisture out. You may take the top tier off to pack separately, just as for any other tier cake.

Make sure that you unpack and assemble the cake yourself at the reception hall. Pulled sugar is very fragile!

To serve a pulled sugar cake, first slip a knife behind the plaque that holds the bow. The whole bow will come off almost intact. Then lift off the vines and flowers. As you cut through the cake, the ribbon will shatter. Place these delicious mint-flavored pieces on the cake slices.

FLOWER SHOWER FOR A LUCKY BRIDE-TO-BE

The feature of this glowing shower or announcement cake is a golden sugar umbrella. You will need two recipes of pulled sugar, page 232. Tint most of it yellow and small amounts green and pink. Prepare two fondant-covered tiers, 6″ x 3″ and 12″ x 4″. Cover the tiers with ribbon and secure ruffles at base. See Chapter Fourteen for techniques.

STEP ONE. Flatten a piece of candy and roll out to a circle about 3″ in diameter. Press it over a greased plastic 4″ ball mold. Cool completely on mold. Pull out three little strands of candy about 7″ long. Moisten the umbrella with a damp cloth and crisscross the strands to resemble ribs. Edge the umbrella with a twisted strand. For the handle, cover a ¼″ dowel rod, 5″ long, by pushing through a small piece of sugar. Trim it with a criss-cross thread as shown on page 260. Wrap a small piece of soft candy around end of handle, touch it to the heater, then fuse to the inside of the umbrella.

STEP TWO. Make a coiled circle 4″ in diameter, just as described on page 258. Place on top of cake, and fuse umbrella to it.

STEP THREE. Pull out green leaves about 4½″ long (page 240). Attach to cake to outline shape of flower spray. Cover two curved coat hanger wires, each about 8″ long, with candy (page 253). Fuse these to the leaves. Secure with small pieces of candy touched to heater, then to leaves. Make wild flowers and rosebuds (pages 242, 243), attach a tiny piece of green candy to base of each, and fuse to wire. Fill in with more leaves. Clip a green strand to 3″ lengths and fuse to wire for stems.

STEP FOUR. Pull out a ribbon about ¾″ wide and 20″ long. Cut in half, ruffle it, and attach to back of umbrella, then drape around cake. Add a bow by fusing loops directly to umbrella.

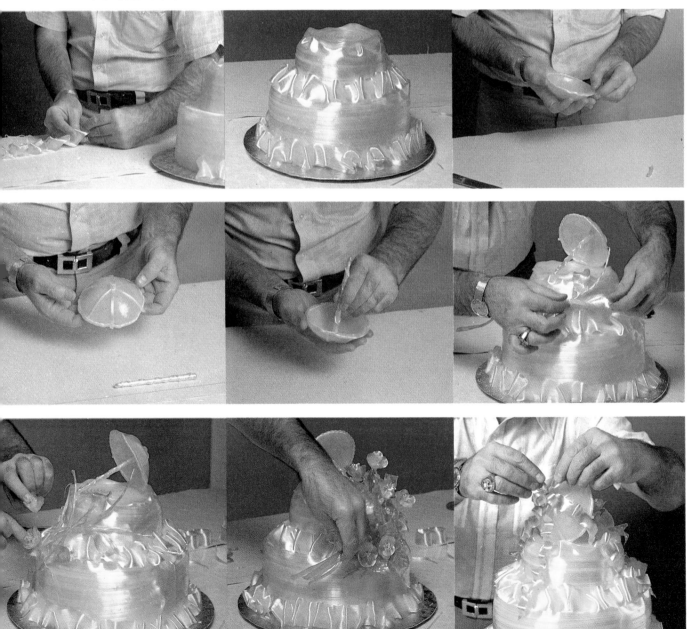

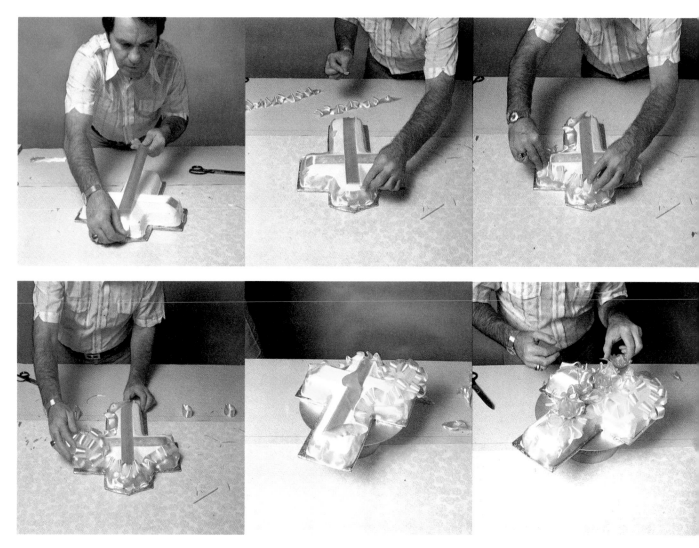

SUNRISE, A GLOWING EASTER GREETING

This unique and joyful cake expresses all the hope and fresh beauty of spring. You will need one recipe of pulled sugar, page 232, and a cross-shaped cake covered with rolled fondant. Set cake on cross-shaped cake board. Tint about two-thirds of the sugar yellow. Equal portions of the remainder are pink, green and untinted.

STEP ONE. Stretch out yellow ribbons about 1½″ wide and lay them in a cross shape on top of the cake. Stretch out more ribbon about 2½″ wide and cover the sides of the cake, pleating the ribbon at inner corners.

STEP TWO. Pull out another ribbon 1½″ wide, about 20″ long. Cut it in half and ruffle it. Place end of one ribbon on the side arm of the cross and drape it across the top of the cross and over to other side arm. Drape the other ruffled ribbon down to the base of the cross. Secure to cake with small pieces of candy touched to heater.

STEP THREE. Pull out a 1″ wide yellow ribbon, clip to 4″ lengths and form loops. Set on edge to cool, then assemble on a 2″ candy plaque. (See page 237.) Cool bow completely. Touch a small piece of candy to heater then to bottom of plaque. Touch plaque to heater, then lay bow on cake.

STEP FOUR. Make a number of green leaves about 2½″ long. Touch to heater, then to top of cake to form a base for the flowers. This is needed to support the flowers, as the ribbon on top of the cake is very fragile.

STEP FIVE. Make five roses, three or four Easter lilies and several calla lilies as described in Chapter Fifteen. When the flowers are totally cool, put a large warm leaf on the base of each. Cool again, then touch each to heater, and place on cake in a spray. Fill in with more leaves.

CONNIE, A CRYSTAL BIRTHDAY CAKE

This glistening feminine cake will make her birthday very memorable! The two-layer cake is 10″ round, covered in rolled fondant. You will need one recipe of pulled sugar. Tint small amounts pink and green, about half the remainder yellow.

To MAKE "BASKET WEAVE", stretch out yellow and white ribbons about 1″ wide. Clip and lay across top of cake, yellow going in one direction and white at right angles. Let the ends hang down side of cake. Now pull out a yellow ribbon about 5″ x 33″ and wrap around cake. Pull out a long ribbon about 1½″ wide, double it, and stretch again to give more thickness. Twist it to give a corkscrew effect, then wrap around the base of the cake.

MAKE STRIPED RIBBON from clear and pulled candy, about 1½″ wide (see page 239). Clip to 7″ lengths and ruffle. Fuse two of these ruffled streamers at four places on top edge of cake by touching to heater, then to cake. Cut 4″ lengths of the striped rib-

bon and form loops. When cool, fuse four loops to the top of each set of streamers.

PULL OUT A NUMBER OF LONG GREEN LEAVES and place on top of cake to form a base for the flower spray. (See page 240.) Their heat will make them stick. Now cover five or six curved cloth-covered florists' wires with green candy as shown on page 246. Their lengths should be about 4″ to 8″. Attach these stems to the leaf base with small pieces of hot candy. Make Easter lilies, roses and buds as explained in Chapter Fifteen. Fuse a small piece of candy to the base of each flower, touch to heater, then to stems. Make leaves and fuse to stems.

FORM SCROLL from a 3″ white ribbon. Fold it over twice to give it more thickness and clip to about 9″. Roll the ends of the ribbon and cool. Attach two pieces of soft candy to the back of scroll, touch these to heater, then to the side of the cake. Pipe the name in royal icing.

274

SWAN LAKE, A POETIC CENTERPIECE

This imposing Swan makes a beautiful centerpiece for a lavish buffet or reception and is a reminder of the dedication and care that went into the preparation for elegant 19th century parties. This majestic swan is 19″ high and 13″ long.

Before making it, review the directions for making the small swan on pages 256 and 257. This one is made in a similar fashion. You will need one batch of the sugar recipe on page 232. Tint a very small amount pink.

STEP ONE. Take a big piece of candy from the batch under the heater. Pull it to cool it down and become shiny. Page 233 shows how to do this. Fold it up into a ball and shape into a rough cylinder about 3″ in diameter. Roll it on the canvas with your hands, just like a big pencil, stretching as you roll. The rolling keeps it an even, round diameter. When the cylinder is about 2″ in diameter and about 17″ long, clip off the two ends.

STEP TWO. Pinch, squeeze and turn one end of the cylinder to form the beak and head. Continue until the beak, with the rounded head behind it, is clearly defined. Now lay the neck on the canvas and shape it into a figure "S". Let it cool completely.

STEP THREE. Now make three big leaf shapes, one for the base and the others for the wings. Stretch and shape on the canvas. Roll each with a rolling pin to about ¾″ thickness. Turn up the tip of the base. Round and hollow out the wing sections. Let all pieces cool *completely*, testing by touching to cheek or inner wrist.

STEP FOUR. Touch the base of the neck to the heater, then set it on the base, holding until secure. Roll the rounded edge of each wing on the heat element and place against neck and base. For further stability, touch two pieces of candy to the heater, then fuse to juncture of base and neck.

Continued on next page

THE SHAPE OF THE SWAN is now complete. "Feather" the wings and add a graceful bow.

STEP FIVE. Pull out white leaves as shown on page 240. Dampen a wing section with a moist cloth and attach the leaves, starting at rear tip of each wing. The dampness causes the leaves to stick to the wing. Overlap the leaves as you move forward to the neck. Do the same on the other wing.

STEP SIX. Pull out a 1″ pink ribbon and clip to 7″ length. Wrap around the neck of the swan, fasten-ing at top. Pull out a ribbon about two feet long. Cut it in two and ruffle each piece with your thumbs and forefingers. Attach to neck ribbon and drape to wing tips. Secure with small pieces of candy touched to heater. Paint beak and eyes with food color.

STEP SEVEN. Make a bow with ¾″ ribbon loops and a 1½″ sugar plaque. Fuse a piece of candy on back of plaque, touch to heater and set bow on swan's neck. Place the beautiful swan on a crystal tray.

PRIMAVERA, A LUSTROUS SPRINGTIME CAKE

This is the daintiest of confections, simply trimmed with a "basket weave" effect, a full bow and a spray of spring flowers. You will need a 10″ two-layer cake covered with rolled fondant and one recipe of pulled sugar, page 232. Tint small amounts of the sugar yellow, pink and green.

STEP ONE. Criss-cross the top of the cake with ¾″ yellow and white ribbon, as described on page 274. Wrap the side with a 5″ ribbon. Make a bow with 1″ yellow and white loops on the cake (see page 235).

STEP TWO. Before placing a floral spray on the fragile ribbon, you must make a base. Do this by pulling out 4″ to 5″ leaves and placing them on the cake where you plan to put your spray. If soft the leaves will stick, otherwise touch ends to heater.

Cut six or seven lengths of stiff cloth-covered florists' wire, about 3″ to 5″ long. Curve the wires and cover with green candy for stems (page 246). Wrap a small piece of soft candy around end of each cooled wire and fuse to leaf base.

STEP THREE. Make a spray of lily-of-the-valley, two roses, two daisies and a few rosebuds (see Chapter Fifteen). Fuse a small piece of candy to back of each flower. Place the lilies-of-the-valley in position, then touch each of the other flowers to the heater, then to wire stems. Pull out a thin strand of green candy and clip to 3″ lengths to make stems. Fuse to base. Fill in with more leaves. By sliding a knife under the base of the spray, you can lift it off almost intact at serving time.

SPUN SUGAR, THE LIVELY ART

Glistening nests of spun sugar are easy and fun to make and add an impressive touch to dessert. Spun sugar is as fragile as it is beautiful, so plan to make it from October through March, when the humidity is low. It will deteriorate rapidly in the spring and summer months.

First make a "shaker". Start with a 4″ square of hard wood, 1″ thick. Drive about 40 3″ nails through it, arranging in rows. Screw on a convenient handle. You will also need two clean sticks about 5 feet long. Broom sticks are fine.

SPUN SUGAR RECIPE

2 pounds granulated sugar
1 pound corn syrup
1¼ cups water
A few drops oil of peppermint

Combine ingredients in a large heavy saucepan. Cook to 290° F. As sugar cooks, wash down sides of pan frequently with a brush dipped in warm water to prevent crystallization. Remove from heat, add flavoring and tint with a little paste color. Let the syrup cool just a bit before spinning.

To SPIN SUGAR, place the ends of the two sticks on the table, about two feet apart. Hold them steady with a weight. Cover the floor with paper. Keep people away as the sugar is very hot.

Stand on a chair or stepstool, hold the pan in your left hand and the shaker in the other. Dip shaker into syrup and let drain into pot. As it starts to thread, swing your arm over the sticks. When the thin strands build up to 6″ or 7″, lift the sugar gently and place it on the table. Repeat until all the syrup is used. If the syrup gets too stiff, gently reheat, stirring it with the shaker.

STORE SPUN SUGAR in a large covered can in a dry place. Handle gently—even dropping the can an inch or two will break the delicate strands and cause the sugar to collapse.

To MAKE A NEST, cut off a portion with the spatula, and gently shape it into a circle, depressing the center. Little nests make charming settings for chocolate or summer coating Easter eggs.

THE FABULOUS DESSERT on the opposite page starts with a large spun sugar nest. Stretch out a 4″ ribbon from pulled sugar, wrap the nest and fuse a pulled sugar bow to the side. Freeze ice cream balls till *very* hard. Just before serving, put the ice cream balls in the nest. (If the ice cream melts, it will soften the spun sugar.)

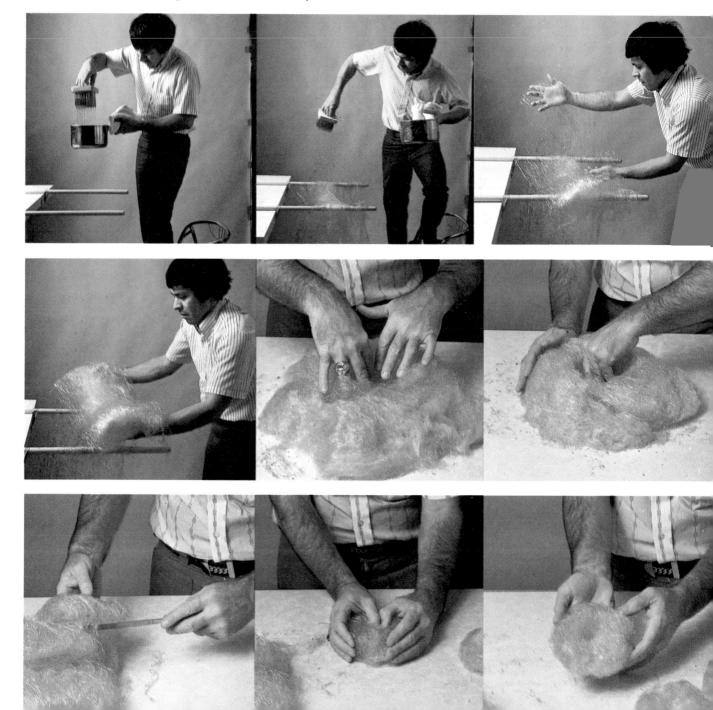

FESTIVAL, A SHINING FLOWER BASKET

This elaborate centerpiece is a supreme example of the beauty that skilled hands can create with pulled sugar. The basket is woven just as a straw basket would be, but in this case the material is a shimmering strand of candy.

To weave the basket you will need a weaving board. You may obtain one by writing Customer Service, at Wilton Enterprises, Inc., 833 West 115th Street, Chicago, Illinois 60643.

WEAVE THE BASKET. Set rods in position on the weaving board, defining a 4″ circle. Make sure you use an odd number of rods. Take a large piece of candy and knead it on canvas to cool. If too stiff, work in front of heater. The most important thing in weaving is to have the candy strand cool enough so that the loops will not fall down because the candy is too soft. Roll the candy into a pear shape, 12″ long and 4″ or more in diameter. Pull out a pencil-thick strand, then start weaving the strand—in front of one rod, behind the next. Push the strand down with your finger as you work and hold enough tension on the strand so it won't sag. If you are not experienced in weaving, it is wise to have someone else pull out the strand as you weave. If the strand breaks, wrap it around the rod and attach a new strand.

When the basket is woven, pull out five or six strands of candy 5″ long, the height of the basket, and ⅜″ in diameter. Place them inside the basket from bottom to top, touching all the ribs. The soft strand will adhere to the basket. This reinforcing will hold the fragile, brittle basket together. When the basket is almost cool, begin to take out the rods. Carefully wiggle them back and forth as you pull them out. This basket, turned upside down, will be the base of the double basket.

Now make a second basket, just like the first. Reinforce as before. Roll out a piece of candy to 4″ diameter and fuse it to the base of this basket by touching pieces of candy to the heater, then to the reinforcing strands. Fuse the two baskets together with small pieces of hot candy, always fusing at the point of the reinforcing strands.

MAKE THE COILED COLLAR. Do this exactly as shown on page 258, but leaving the center empty, starting at the outside of a 5″ circle. Coil the strand until the collar is about 3½″ wide. Indent with a scissors and flute. Shape to an up-turned position and cool. If it falls while cooling, pull back to position.

STRETCH A RIBBON 2″ wide and wrap around the basket where the two halves meet. Let the ends hang down in a casual drape.

Continued on next page

ATTACH COLLAR by fusing to reinforcing strands with small pieces of hot candy.

COVER AND TRIM THE HANDLE, just as shown on page 260. You will need two ¼″ dowel rods, 27″ and 24″ long for the sides and a 15″ crosspiece.

ATTACH A SIDE HANDLE to the base of the basket by wrapping a piece of soft candy around end of one rod. Touch to heater, then to base of basket. Attach to edge of collar the same way. Hold to steady, then fuse other side handle. Cool completely. Attach the crosspiece by wrapping soft candy around the side handle and crosspiece. Attach to other side piece the same way.

TRIM HANDLE with a vine and draped ribbon just as shown on page 261. Make a full bow as described on page 237 and fuse to handle.

MAKE STEMS FOR FLOWERS. First cover two 5″ lengths of coat hanger wire with green candy (see page 246). Criss-cross these two wires on inside of top of basket and fuse with small pieces of hot candy. These wires will give support to stems.

Now cut coat hanger wire to various lengths from 6″ to 11″ and curve them. Cover with green candy. Wrap ends of some wires with soft candy, then fuse to inside base of basket. Fuse again at crossed wires or side of basket. Make roses, wild flowers, Easter lilies and buds (Chapter Fifteen) and fuse a small piece of candy to back of each.

ADD FLOWERS TO STEMS. Wrap soft candy around end of stems, touch to heater, then to back of flower. Most flowers were fused to stems, then fused inside the basket. Some were fused to stems already in place in basket. Add some flowers to vine on handle. Try to create a natural, lifelike effect. Make a lot of green leaves ahead of time, and fuse to flowers, stems and handle. This will disguise any rough spots where flowers are fused, and give a full natural look to the arrangement.

Your spectacular flower basket is finished!

CHAPTER SEVENTEEN

Fine Candy Making

Nothing expresses the good life so well as a tray or pretty box of fine, home-made candy. The fresh, refined flavor of candy made at home is far superior to any purchased confection, and reflects the care and quality ingredients that go into its making.

Candy can serve as the luxurious finale of any important party, whether a children's birthday celebration or a lavish reception. Well wrapped, candy is an always-welcome gift.

In this chapter we present an array of recipes that will enhance any cook's reputation. The tech-niques of decorating candy are already in your repertoire, so the finished product will look as spectacular as it tastes.

If you would like to add an extra touch to your home-made confections, present them in a pretty compote or box you made yourself from gum paste. See page 225 for ideas.

BELOW, DECORATED MINTS for a shower or bridal reception. Directions are on the next page.

HOW TO MAKE MINT PATTIES

A tray of daintily decorated homemade mints makes a delicious after-dinner treat and is a festive addition to a sweet table. Mints may be made of fondant, chocolate or summer coating. Don't attempt the chocolate or fondant varieties in warm humid weather.

FONDANT MINTS

Make a recipe of Wilton Quick Fondant (page 135) or if you wish, make traditional fondant using the recipe and instructions in *The Wilton Way of Cake Decorating, Volume One.* One recipe of Quick Fondant makes five dozen or more mints.

Heat the fondant to 100°F in the top of a double boiler, stirring occasionally. Add food color and flavoring while heating. Drop the mints on wax paper or fine-ribbed rubber matting.

Form mints with a mint patty funnel. Put the stick in the funnel so the pointed end closes the opening in the small end of the funnel and pour in the warmed fondant. Holding the funnel over the wax paper or ribbed matting, lift the stick briefly so fondant runs out and forms a patty, then drop stick to stop the fondant from flowing out. Continue, moving along briskly with an even rhythm.

CHOCOLATE AND SUMMER COATING MINTS

When making chocolate mints, the chocolate must first be tempered (see page 127). Reheat to the appropriate temperature and add desired flavoring. Pour the chocolate into the funnel and use the same procedure as for fondant mints.

To make summer coating mints, cut up the summer coating and heat until just melted in the top of a double boiler. Add flavoring while heating. Pour into a mint patty funnel and use the same method as for making fondant mints.

DECORATING MINTS

The decorated mints shown on page 285 were inspired by Pennsylvania Dutch designs. Using the picture as a guide, pipe designs on the mints with tube 1 and slightly thinned royal icing.

Your imagination will guide you in piping these tiny masterpieces. Stylized flowers, initials, geometric designs and swirls are all effective. Choose a color scheme that complements the party decor.

MOLDED CHOCOLATE CANDY

To mold chocolate candy in plastic candy molds, temper chocolate and reheat to the appropriate temperature. Fill a parchment cone with chocolate, cut the tip and fill the indentations of the molds. Tap molds to release any air bubbles. When completely hardened, invert molds and release.

BELOW, sparkling molded hard candy is easy to make. See the next page for instructions.

HOW TO MAKE HARD CANDY

Dazzling hard candy treats are always a delight and are quite easy to make. Use the recipe below. If you need more candy syrup than what this recipe makes, make a second batch rather than doubling it. Too big a batch makes the pan too heavy for easy pouring and the candy tends to solidify before it can all be poured.

HARD CANDY RECIPE

2 cups granulated sugar
⅔ cup water
¼ teaspoon cream of tartar
Food coloring (by drop as needed)
1 teaspoon Hard Candy Flavor

Combine water, sugar and cream of tartar in a straight-sided 3 quart saucepan and bring to boil over high heat, stirring constantly. When it begins to boil, stir in coloring, insert candy thermometer and stop stirring. Continue cooking over high heat, occasionally brushing sides of pan and thermometer with a wet pastry brush to prevent crystals from forming.

When temperature reaches 280°F, turn to low heat or candy will burn. At this point, stir in flavoring. If added sooner, the flavor will evaporate. When candy reaches 300°F remove from heat and pour into greased molds.

MAKING SMALL MOLDED CANDIES

Lightly grease hard candy molds with vegetable oil. Place them on foil-lined baking sheets. Pour hot syrup into molds. Place candy in the refrigerator for 15 minutes or until hardened. To remove, turn molds upside-down and pop candy out by pressing back of molds lightly with thumbs.

If you wish to attach wires to back of the molded candies, take a piece of medium thickness florists' wire and bend a small loop in one end. Dip loop in hard candy syrup and immediately press to back of molded candy. Let harden.

MAKING LOLLIPOPS

Make one recipe of hard candy. While cooking, prepare large cookie cutters to use as molds. Place heart cutter in the middle of a square of foil. Crumple the foil around the outside of the cutter, keeping the part inside the cutter smooth and flat. Brush inside of cutter and foil with vegetable oil. Place on a baking sheet.

When hard candy syrup is cooked, pour it into the prepared cutters to a depth of about ⅜". Cool, then place in freezer for about ten minutes for them to harden.

When hardened, remove cutters and peel off foil

from back of candy heart. To attach stick to back, dip one end of stick in hard candy syrup and place on back of lollipop. Brush on more syrup to help secure stick. Let harden about ten minutes. Pipe freehand tube 2 trim. Let dry, then attach ribbon bows to sticks.

ABOVE, sparkling lollipops and molded hard candies mounted on wires make a colorful party centerpiece. To create it, take a gelatin mold or vase and attach a piece of styrofoam in it with royal icing. Fill container with more icing so there is a flat surface. Push sticks on lollipops and wires on candies down through icing into styrofoam. Let icing dry.

Chocolates made in the Continental manner are very luxurious and make marvelous gifts for friends, relatives, or even for yourself. Making fine chocolates is time-consuming, but the results are very rewarding. The European recipes given here are for candies that are not obtainable in even the most expensive shops in the United States.

For the best results, be sure to use only high-quality ingredients. We recommend using Swiss chocolate for these candies. Fondant is an ingredient in several of the candies, and for these fine chocolates, the refined flavor of homemade fondant is essential. You should use traditional fondant rather than quick fondant for the proper results. Complete directions for making traditional fondant can be found in *The Wilton Way of Cake Decorating, Volume One*.

Many of the chocolates have liqueur as an ingredient. Besides adding a delicious flavor and perfume, the liqueur serves as a preservative so the candies can be stored in a cool, dark place for a long period of time.

MAKING CHOCOLATES. It is almost impossible to make chocolates during the summer months and have them turn out properly. It is also very difficult to store them during the summer. It is best to make chocolates in cool, dry weather.

TEMPER CHOCOLATE. Before dipping the candy centers or molding chocolate cups to be filled, the chocolate being used must be tempered. Complete directions for tempering dark and milk chocolate are found on page 127.

To DIP CANDY CENTERS, place tempered chocolate in a small, deep pan and reheat to 90°-92°F for dark chocolate, 86°-88°F for milk chocolate. Place a candy center on a bent fork, dip into chocolate, then place on wax paper to cool and harden.

To PIPE CHOCOLATE TRIMS, put a small amount of prepared piping chocolate (page 134) into a parchment paper cone either fitted with a decorating tube or with the tip of the cone cut.

KARAMELMARZIPAN
(Caramel Marzipan)

8 ounces sugar
6 ounces sweet butter
4 ounces whipping cream
1½ pounds almond paste
Maraschino liqueur
8 ounces almond paste
2 pounds tempered milk chocolate
Chocolate shot

Melt sugar with butter over low heat. Mix in cream and remove from heat. Crumble 1½ pounds of almond paste into small pieces, then add to mixture. Mix well to a consistency similar to mashed potatoes. Add enough maraschino liqueur to thin the mixture so it can be dropped from a cone.

Make marzipan bases by rolling 8 ounces of almond paste about ⅛" thick. Cut with a ¾" to 1" plain round cutter to form a base for the soft filling and provide ease in dipping the candies in the melted chocolate.

Place filling mixture in a parchment cone fitted with tube 6 and drop it out onto the marzipan bases forming mounds with a pointed tip. Place in the refrigerator to stiffen before dipping in tempered milk chocolate and sprinkling with chocolate shot. Recipe makes 80 to 100 candies.

NUSSKREM
(Nut Creme Cups)

2 pounds tempered dark chocolate
8 ounces sweet butter
8 ounces fondant
3 ounces confectioners' sugar
16 ounces whipping cream
1 pound tempered milk chocolate, reheated
5 ounces toasted, ground hazelnuts
Whole roasted hazelnuts
Milk chocolate, prepared for piping (page 134)

Make dark chocolate cups in Flute Candy Mold. Place tempered chocolate in parchment cone, cut a small opening and fill molds. Turn molds over and drain out excess chocolate. Place in refrigerator. After eight to ten minutes, the cups can be removed from molds.

Beat butter, fondant and confectioners' sugar together with an electric mixer until well-mixed and slightly fluffy. Set aside.

Boil cream, then add melted milk chocolate. Remove from heat. Stir well to form a creme-like substance, then add ground hazelnuts. Let cool, then fold in first mixture.

Lay a roasted hazelnut in each chocolate cup. Fill cups with nut creme mixture to just below the rim of the cup. Shake a little to settle and place in refrigerator. Remelt chocolate left from making cups and place in a parchment cone. Remove cups from refrigerator and cover tops with chocolate to seal. Decorate with prepared milk chocolate and tube 16, making an "S" shape. Yield is approximately 80 to 100 candies.

KROKANTSTAEBCHEN
(Krokant Sticks)

These crisp and crunchy, chocolate-covered candies have a flavor and texture very similar to that of English toffee. Excellent taste.

2½ pounds granulated sugar
3 ounces glucose
2½ ounces sweet butter
1 pound 4 ounces white slivered almonds
2 pounds tempered milk chocolate
Dark chocolate, prepared for piping (page 134)

Melt sugar evenly in a heavy pan (copper preferred) over low heat until light brown in color. Add glucose and butter, stirring until well-mixed. Add almonds and stir. Turn out of pan onto a greased baking sheet. Working quickly, roll out fairly flat and even to a thickness of ½″ with a greased rolling pin. While still warm, cut into strips. Cool.

Dip in tempered milk chocolate and place on wax paper to cool and harden. Make four or five decorative fork marks on each one, beginning on the first one after the third candy has been dipped. Decorate with tube 16 prepared dark chocolate rosettes at the ends of each candy. Makes 80 to 100 Krokant Sticks.

ZITRONENMARZIPAN
(Lemon Marzipan)

The tangy taste of lemon in these candies, combined with the summer coating, gives them a refreshing and distinctive flavor. A real treat!

1 pound almond paste
2 ounces fondant
2 ounces confectioners' sugar
1 ounce lemon fruit powder (lemon-flavored powdered fruit drink mix may be substituted)
Lemon liqueur
2½ ounces white raisins
2 pounds white summer coating
White raisins for trim

Mix almond paste, fondant, confectioners' sugar and lemon fruit powder with 2 tablespoons lemon liqueur, forming a dough-like mixture. Let raisins soak for one hour in enough lemon liqueur to cover them, then add raisins and liqueur to mixture. Mix well and form into balls, incorporating one to two raisins into each ball. Flatten bottoms of balls, dip in white summer coating and decorate with a white raisin on top. Makes 80 to 100 pieces.

PICTURED ABOVE, from top to bottom, *Karamelmarzipan, Nusskrem,* and *Krokantstaebchen.*

KURKONFECT
(Fruit-nut Candies)

The sunny flavors of chopped fruits and nuts are enhanced with brandy and honey and set off by a rich chocolate coating. These European treats are both delicious and healthful.

    1 ounce pitted prunes
    1 ounce pitted dates
    1 ounce figs
    1 ounce sun-dried apples
    1 ounce sun-dried pears
    1 ounce sun-dried apricots
    1 ounce sun-dried peaches
    1 ounce sliced, slivered almonds
    1 ounce chopped pistachios
    2 ounces honey
    3 ounces brandy
    Corn syrup for glaze
    2 pounds tempered dark chocolate
    Dark chocolate, prepared for piping (page 134)
    Pieces of pistachio for garnish

Chop dried fruits to a medium coarse consistency. Add nuts, honey and brandy. Mix thoroughly and let soak at least one hour. Shape into spoon-like oval pieces. Place on wax paper and let dry one hour. Glaze with hot corn syrup, then cool. Dip into tempered dark chocolate, but do not completely submerge, leaving an opening on top to see the fruits and nuts. When chocolate has set, pipe

a tube 16 prepared chocolate scroll on one edge and top with a piece of pistachio. 80 to 100 candies.

ZURICHER BIRNEN BECHER
(Zurich Pear Cups)

Little chocolate cups hold a creamy chocolate mixture with the subtle flavor of fresh pears. Like most Continental candies, these are not too sweet and very satisfying.

    2 pounds tempered dark chocolate
    2 cups tempered semi-sweet dark chocolate, reheated
    1½ cups whipped cream
    2 tablespoons pear liqueur
    Dark cocoa powder

Make dark chocolate cups in plastic Flute Candy Molds. Fill molds with tempered chocolate, tip molds to drain excess chocolate. Place in refrigerator for eight to ten minutes, then remove them carefully from molds.

Fold whipped cream into semi-sweet chocolate. Add pear liqueur. Place mixture in a parchment cone, cut tip and fill chocolate cups. Smooth top with a spatula until it is very flat. Cool in refrigerator about one hour, then dust top with dark cocoa powder. Yield is 80 to 100 Pear Cups.

ON TRAY ABOVE, from left to right, *Orangemarzipan, Walnusstrueffel* and *Kurkonfect.*

WIECHKROKANT
(Soft Krokant)

The flavor of these candies is similar to that of *Krokantstaebchen*, but instead of being crunchy, these luscious chocolates are chewy. You'll love the smooth toffee taste.

   1 pound 10 ounces granulated sugar
   6 ounces glucose or corn syrup
   5 ounces sweet butter
   Dash of vanilla
   1 pound 4 ounces toasted, chopped almonds
   2 pounds tempered dark chocolate
   Milk chocolate and dark chocolate,
     prepared for piping (page 134)

In a heavy pan (copper preferred) melt sugar to a light brown color. Add glucose, butter and vanilla, mixing well. Stir in almonds. Let mixture cool a bit, then roll out ½″ thick and cut it into squares. Cool. Dip in tempered dark chocolate. Decorate each with two prepared milk chocolate ribbons piped with tube 46. Add a tube 16 prepared dark chocolate star on top. 80 to 100 candies.

ORANGEMARZIPAN
(Orange Wedges)

The delicate, tangy-sweet flavor of oranges permeates these candies. The flavor improves if allowed to sit a few days in a cool, dark place before eating.

   2 pounds almond paste
   3 ounces confectioners' sugar
   ½ cup grand-marnier liqueur
   2 ounces orange fruit powder (orange-flavored
     powdered fruit drink mix may be substituted)
   5 ounces finely chopped candied orange peel
   2 pounds tempered milk chocolate
   Milk chocolate, prepared for piping (page 134)
   Thin pieces of candied orange peel

Mix first five ingredients together well on a clean table surface into a dough. Roll out to about ½″ thickness on a surface dusted with confectioners' sugar. Cut into strips 1″ wide, then into wedges. Dip wedges in tempered milk chocolate. Pipe prepared milk chocolate scroll on thicker part of wedge with tube 16 and add a very thin piece of candied orange peel. Yield is 80 to 100 wedges.

WALNUSSTRUEFFEL
(Walnut Truffle)

The soft, creamy centers of the Walnut Truffle have a sweet, nutty flavor that is enhanced by the walnut halves placed on top.

   8 ounces almond paste
   12 ounces sweet butter
   3 ounces confectioners' sugar
   6 ounces rum

   1 pound 12 ounces tempered milk chocolate,
     reheated
   Walnut halves
   2 pounds tempered milk chocolate
   Milk chocolate, prepared for piping (page 134)

Make marzipan leaves by rolling almond paste about 1/10″ thick. Cut with a ¾″ to 1″ plain round cutter to form a base for filling.

Beat butter with confectioners' sugar. Add rum and beat well. Fold in melted chocolate to form a creme-like mixture. (Chocolate must be lower than body temperature or it will destroy the butter.) Cool until thickened enough to be dropped from a parchment cone. Place filling in parchment cone and drop out in mounds onto marzipan leaves. Top each with a walnut half. Dip into tempered milk chocolate up to, and slightly covering, the edge of the walnut. Decorate with prepared milk chocolate in the center of each walnut half. Recipe makes about 80 to 100 truffles.

On tray above, from left to right, *Zitronenmarzipan* and *Wiechkrokant*.

291

SCHWIEZER SAHNE TRUEFFEL
(Swiss Truffle—Dark and Light)

The centers of these European candies have a smooth, satiny texture and a subtle delicious flavor imparted by rum or orange liqueur.

8 ounces whipping cream
1 pound 6 ounces dark semi-sweet chocolate
3 tablespoons 80 proof rum
2 pounds tempered dark chocolate

Bring cream to a boil, remove from heat and add semi-sweet chocolate, stirring until chocolate is completely melted. Mix in rum. Cool mixture in refrigerator until it is firm enough to be formed into balls. Cool again in refrigerator. Dip in tempered dark chocolate twice. When dipping the second time, try to form the typical truffle "noses". This can be done with your fingers or with a spoon by lifting up and off sideways. Recipe yields 80 to 100 truffles.

For light truffles, replace the rum with grand-marnier liqueur and a little finely chopped orange peel which has been cooked for a few minutes with a little sugar to insure sterility. Handle them the same as the dark truffles, but dip twice in tempered milk chocolate.

NUSS KONFECT
(Pecan Delights)

2 pounds tempered dark chocolate
3 ounces egg yolks
6 ounces granulated sugar
16 ounces whipping cream
2 pounds dark chocolate, coarsely chopped
3 ounces nut liqueur or cognac
Pieces of well-toasted pecans
Tempered milk chocolate for trim
Dark chocolate, prepared for piping (page 134)

Make dark chocolate cups in plastic Ruffle Candy Molds. Fill molds with chocolate, then tip to empty excess chocolate from mold. Place in refrigerator for eight to ten minutes and carefully remove the cups from the molds.

Beat egg yolks and sugar. Boil whipping cream, remove from heat and add sugar and egg mixture and chopped dark chocolate. Stir until chocolate is melted and the mixture is a thick cream-like consistency. Stir in nut liqueur. Let cool.

Place a piece of pecan in each chocolate cup. Fill cups with creme. Place in refrigerator for one hour, then seal with dark chocolate. Fill a parch-

SHOWN AT TOP, *Zuricher Birnen Becher;* in middle, *Schwiezer Sahne Trueffel;* at bottom from left to right, *Nuss Konfect* and *Teezungen.*

292

ment cone, tip cut, with the melted chocolate and cover tops thoroughly. Allow to harden. Turn upside down. Dip the tip of each candy into milk chocolate and decorate with a tube 16 circle of prepared dark chocolate. Makes 80 to 100 candies.

TEEZUNGEN
(Tea Tongues)

You'll enjoy the subtle tea flavor of these candies.

    1 ounce best quality tea
    16 ounces whipping cream
    7 ounces finely chopped dark chocolate
    1 pound 10 ounces finely chopped milk chocolate
    2 pounds tempered milk chocolate

Milk chocolate, prepared for piping (page 134)

Put cream in a small sauce pan, add tea and bring to a boil. Remove from heat, strain, and let cool slightly. Add chopped dark and light chocolate and mix well to a cream-like consistency. Place in refrigerator, stirring occasionally until it is thick enough to drop from a parchment cone.

Place mixture in a parchment cone fitted with tube 9. Drop out onto wax paper in long oval shapes. Place in refrigerator about one hour to harden. Dip in tempered milk chocolate. Decorate with prepared milk chocolate. Pipe a tube 46 band across the middle and top with a tube 16 star. Recipe makes 80 to 100 candies.

CHOCOLATE-COVERED MARSHMALLOW EGGS

This delectable candy is light, not too sweet and has a tender, cloud-like texture. A favorite Easter treat with a fabulous flavor. Tint the marshmallow in delicate spring colors to delight the children.

MARSHMALLOW

    2 tablespoons unflavored gelatin
    ½ cup cold water
    2 cups granulated sugar
    ¾ cup hot water
    1 cup light corn syrup
    2 teaspoons vanilla
    Food coloring

Combine gelatin and cold water. Let stand until thick—five minutes or more.

Combine sugar, hot water and ½ cup corn syrup in a saucepan. Cook over high heat to 240°F (238°F for softer marshmallow). Remove from heat, add rest of corn syrup and stir gently.

Pour mixture into a 9″ heat-proof bowl and add vanilla. Beat with electric mixer at high speed, adding 1 teaspoon of gelatin mixture at a time until marshmallow is heavy, white and lukewarm

(about ten minutes). Add food coloring before marshmallow is fully beaten and at a medium consistency. If using green coloring, substitute a small amount of peppermint flavoring for vanilla. Use strawberry or raspberry flavoring if using red food coloring.

Molding eggs. Lightly butter small egg molds or egg cupcake pans. Pour in the lukewarm marshmallow. Refrigerate for several hours until firm. Dust exposed marshmallow with a mixture of one-third cornstarch and two-thirds confectioners' sugar. Turn out onto table or board.

Coating with chocolate. Dip half-eggs into tempered chocolate, fondant or pastel summer coating. Place on wax paper to harden. Makes about two pounds marshmallow eggs.

If you do not wish to coat the eggs with chocolate, dust them thoroughly with the cornstarch-confectioners' sugar mixture after turning them out of the molds to prevent them from sticking to each other. Store the uncoated eggs in an airtight container in a cool, dry place.

CREME CARAMELS

Caramels are easy to make, but must be watched closely while cooking to prevent scorching. Their flavor is creamy and absolutely delicious.

    2 cups granulated sugar
    1 cup light corn syrup
    2 cups warm whipping cream
    ⅛ cup butter
    ½ teaspoon salt
    1 teaspoon vanilla

In a large saucepan, cook sugar, corn syrup and 1 cup cream for ten minutes over medium heat. Add rest of cream very slowly and cook five minutes. Add butter a little at a time. When mixture

reaches 230°F, lower heat and cook slowly to 242°-244°F. For firmer caramel, cook to 244°-246°F. Remove from heat, add salt and vanilla and mix gently but thoroughly.

Pour into well-buttered 8″ square pan and refrigerate until firm enough to cut. Remove from pan, wipe butter from candy and cut into desired size pieces. If caramel is difficult to remove from the pan, hold pan over low heat a few seconds and turn out at once. Wrap individually in wax paper to prevent spreading. Makes about two pounds. Store caramels in a cool, dry place.

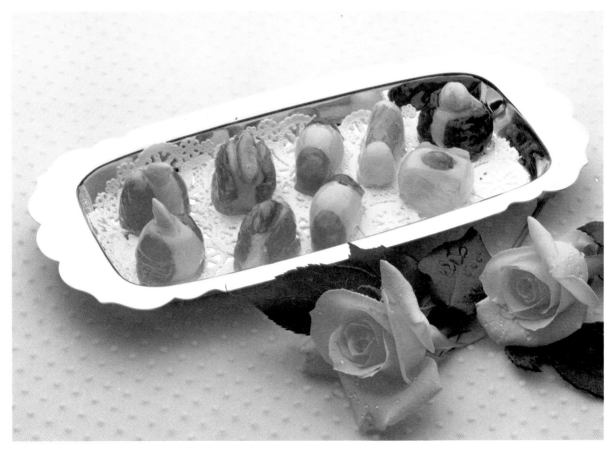

Luscious fruit confections, such as those shown and described here, are made with dried, fresh or frozen fruit. Each is a wholesome, delightful treat.

KARAMELIERTE PRALINEN
(Caramelized Candy)

These delicious candies are made in a variety of tantalizing shapes. Do not attempt these candies in warm humid weather.

　　Candied and dried fruit (red and green cherries,
　　　　pears, apples, peaches, apricots and prunes)
　　Nuts (walnuts, almonds and pecans)
　　10 ounces almond paste
　　1 ounce confectioners' sugar
　　Maraschino liqueur

Cut about 1 ounce of each fruit and nut into medium size pieces and set aside.

　　Mix almond paste with confectioners' sugar. Add maraschino liqueur to form a soft dough. Form centers from this dough in a variety of shapes. Cover the tops and sides of the centers with the pieces of the fruit and nuts, letting your imagination go wild. Dry candies one to two hours so the fruit and nuts will adhere to the centers, then carefully dip them in caramel glaze (recipe below).

Set dipped candies on a greased baking sheet to cool. Store in a candy tin. Recipe makes between 80 to 100 candies.

WILTON CARAMEL GLAZE

This sparkling clear glaze is used for coating candies and fresh fruit.

　　4 cups granulated sugar
　　1⅓ cups water
　　½ teaspoon cream of tartar
　　Lemon extract

Mix the sugar, water and cream of tartar together in a heavy pan (preferably copper). Do not use an aluminum pan or it will discolor the mixture. Bring to a boil over high heat, stirring constantly. When it begins to boil, stop stirring and cook to 305°F. Remove from heat and stir in a few drops of lemon extract. Dip candies or fresh fruit in the glaze. Caution: mixture is extremely hot. Be sure to keep a bowl of cold water nearby in case you accidently drip some of the glaze on your hand.

ABOVE, an assortment of sparkling *Karamelierte Pralinen* is shown on a silver tray.

GLAZED FRESH FRUIT

These sparkling fruits gleam like jewels and always bring exclamations of delight from your guests. The crisp brittle coating accents the fresh tart flavor of the fruit.

Skewer dry, perfect fruit (not over-ripe) with drink mixers or thin wooden or bamboo sticks. Be sure there are no breaks in the skin except where the stick is inserted. We used grapes, strawberries and cherries. You will need about 40 pieces. Puncture a medium grapefruit so you can insert the sticks into it. Using the glaze recipe on page 294, dip the skewered fruit quickly and insert the sticks into the grapefruit. If the syrup gets too hard to dip the fruit into, reheat it a little. Attach mint leaves with hot syrup and serve immediately. Glaze fresh fruit only in dry weather.

RASPBERRY TURKISH DELIGHTS

This candy is a favorite of many people who like sweets with a tangy taste.

    2 tablespoons unflavored gelatin
    ½ cup puréed thawed frozen raspberries
    1 tablespoon lemon juice
    2 cups sugar
    ¼ teaspoon salt
    ⅔ cup water
    Food coloring

Sprinkle gelatin over a mixture of thawed raspberry purée and lemon juice.

Combine sugar, salt and water in a heavy saucepan. Stir over low heat until sugar is dissolved. Cover tightly and cook over medium heat until mixture comes to a boil, then boil two minutes. Uncover, insert candy thermometer and cook to 236°F without stirring. Remove from heat. Add gelatin mixture and food coloring, then return to heat and cook to 224°F, stirring constantly.

Pour into a lightly buttered 9″ x 5″ loaf pan to a depth of ½″. Let stand until firm or overnight.

Dust top of jelly with confectioners' sugar. Using spatula coated with sugar, loosen jelly from pan. Invert onto board dusted with confectioners' sugar. Cut into rectangles with sugar-coated knife. Dust pieces with more confectioners' sugar. Makes about 1¾ pounds.

ABOVE, glazed fresh fruit makes an elegant and delightfully different dessert.

295

CHAPTER EIGHTEEN

The Decorator as Painter

Since color and form are the strongest elements in cake decorating, adventurous decorators are intrigued with the art of creating pictures as cake trims. This form of decorating is commonly called scenery painting, but the subject may be a portrait, a representation of a figure or a still life, as well as land or waterscapes. In this chapter are modern, time-saving techniques for practicing the centuries-old art of decorative painting.

Before starting your edible painting, study a favorite picture for inspiration for color and technique. Keep your painting simple—often just a small portion of a picture will be ideal to reproduce for a cake trim.

TYPES OF DECORATIVE PAINTING

There are five methods of edible painting, although two or more are often combined in the same painting.

PAINTING ON WAFER PAPER. This is probably the best method to begin with, as you can transfer a scene directly to translucent, edible rice paper. Apply the paper to a freshly-iced cake and fill in the areas with thinned food colors. The moisture of the colors and icing cause the wafer paper to almost become part of the cake. Wafer paintings like the one at right have a fresh look, like that of a water color.

CLASSIC PAINTING is most easily done on a pastillage or gum paste plaque. Tinted royal icing is applied with tubes and a spatula or palette knife.

GEL PAINTING is similar to Color Flow, but the outlines are piped on wafer paper, the paper applied to the cake, then the areas filled in with tinted piping gel. Results are brilliant and sparkling.

SPATULA PAINTING is much like Classic Painting, but the painting is executed almost entirely with a spatula or palette knife and royal icing. These paintings give a strong, impressionistic effect.

COCOA PAINTING uses cocoa for the pigment, cocoa butter for the mixing medium, and marzipan for the canvas. Cocoa paintings have a warm, mellow look in varied shades of brown.

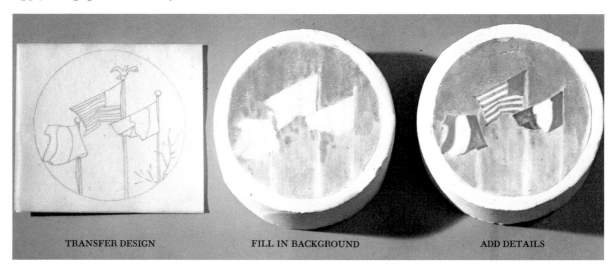

TRANSFER DESIGN   FILL IN BACKGROUND   ADD DETAILS

TRIM A CAKE WITH A WAFER PAPER PAINTING

First select a design for your cake top. This one is a Wilton Way Pattern, but you may choose any simple scene. If the scene is not the right size for the cake you plan, enlarge or reduce it by means of a photostat. If you are accomplished in drawing, you may sketch your own. Just before you start your painting, ice an 8″ two-layer cake with boiled icing. The icing should be moist when you apply the wafer paper. You will need small and medium water color brushes.

TRANSFER DESIGN. Tape a piece of wafer paper over your design. Outline main lines with yellow or pale beige thinned food color (the lines in the picture are darker for visibility). Trim the paper to a circle, brush clear piping gel over the back, and set on the cake top. Press gently to adhere.

FILL IN BACKGROUND FIRST. Small containers or a plastic or china palette are convenient for mixing your colors. Dilute paste food colors with water and brush in the sky area. Brush over the upper area to create a darker blue. Keep the wafer paper evenly damp.

PAINT DETAILS. Using colors diluted in separate containers, brush in the colors on the flags. Paint tree branches and cords with a smaller brush. Using a larger brush, paint the leaves in varied tints of green.

FINISH THE PAINTING. Pipe the flag staffs, eagle and balls with tube 4. Frame the painting with tube 14 shells, then add a second circle of shells at the top edge of the cake. Pipe tube 16 shells for base border. Your flag cake serves ten.

PAINT A WATER SCENE IN ICING
USING THE CLASSIC TECHNIQUE

Almost any picture can be used as a model for a Classic decorative painting—a photograph, post-card or your favorite painting. Study the picture carefully to decide which details to eliminate and what area of the model you wish to use. Determine your color scheme, always remembering the fewer the colors, the stronger and more pleasing the final effect will be. It's a good idea to tint the icing and put small amounts side by side on a piece of white cardboard to judge the effect of one color on another.

The painting at left was inspired by a modern oil painting, then greatly simplified. After studying the painting a simple sketch was drawn on parchment paper showing the shapes of the mountains, hulls and masts of the sailboats. Roll out pastillage about 3/16″ thick and trim to 7½″ x 11″. (Recipe on page 112). Dry thoroughly. Gumpaste may also be used for the plaque.

TRANSFER THE SKETCH by laying the paper drawing over the plaque and tracing with a hard pencil. Tint royal icing light blue for sky, two shades of green for mountains, deep blue and medium blue for the water.

STROKE IN BACKGROUND COLORS. With a spatula, apply the tinted icing to the sky, mountain and water areas. Add white icing for the clouds. Work quickly so icing does not crust. Now dampen a paper towel, lay over the painting, and roll very lightly with a rolling pin to smooth and generalize the colors. Remove towel and let the painting dry.

PROCEED WITH THE FOREGROUND. Cut out the shapes of the boats from the sketch and mark the hulls and masts again on the plaque. Outline, then fill in the white hull with tube 5 and a zigzag motion. Smooth with a spatula. Do the red and blue hulls the same way. Pipe each mast with tube 4 lines.

PIPE DETAILS. Pipe the rigging with tube 2, doing the blue boat first, then the red and last the white. Add a "forest" to the nearer mountain by piping vertical squiggles with tube 4. Do the same on the second mountain with tube 2. With a small spatula or palette knife add the texture to the water area. Pipe the gay flags and banners with tube 44 and tube 2. Add tube 2 birds.

BAKE AND ICE a 9″ x 13″ sheet cake and center the painting on top. Frame the painting and do the borders with tube 17. Your sailboat cake will serve 24. At serving time, slide a knife under the plaque to remove.

STROKE IN BACKGROUND COLORS

DEFINE SHAPES OF HULLS

PIPE DETAILS

A SHINING SCENE IN PIPING GEL

Three cheerful children smile under a big umbrella in this scene done with the Piping Gel technique. This cake uses a Wilton Way pattern, but you will enjoy exploring this method with any simple Color Flow pattern.

TAPE PATTERN to smooth surface and tape wafer paper over it. Outline pattern with tube 2 and a mixture of royal icing combined with an equal amount of piping gel. Dry.

BAKE AND ICE a 10″ two-layer cake with boiled or buttercream icing. Trim edge of outlined wafer paper with a sharp X-acto knife, brush clear piping gel over entire back and place on cake. Press light-

ly to secure and flatten. Icing should be moist when you attach wafer paper.

FILL IN AREAS with piping gel mixed with an equal quantity of water, and tinted. Use a cut cone. Let stiffen, then add eyes, mouths and buttons. Finish the cake by piping a tube 8 bulb border at base, tube 6 at top. We added a daisy and "Rain, rain, go away" done with tube 2 on the side. A brightly attractive cake, quickly done, that serves 14.

A BOUQUET OF SUNFLOWERS is executed in the Spatula technique. Directions are on page 302.

A VIVID FLOWER PAINTING IN THE
SPATULA TECHNIQUE

A French impressionist painting inspired this bold bouquet of sunflowers. Like the original painting, it was done almost entirely with a palette knife, giving it a depth and texture descriptive of the flowers. A palette knife is very useful in decorative painting because of its small size and very flexible blade. You will find it convenient for other decorating tasks also. The painting is done on a gum paste or pastillage plaque. (Recipes are on pages 142 and 112.)

Just as in Classic decorative painting, it is most convenient to paint on a plaque. Any mistake can be scraped off the plaque immediately and a new attempt made. And since these paintings are truly little works of art, they may be removed from the cake before serving, and saved to grace another confection.

Spatula painting is done very quickly once the plaque is prepared. Study the painting you are using as a model, and decide which areas and details you wish to eliminate. Use a minimum number of colors—as you work the colors will blend to create interesting new hues. It's a good idea to make a trial painting on cardboard—then you can correct any errors of color or composition before doing the final painting.

PREPARE PLAQUE. Prepare an oval pattern, 6″ x 8″, using the proportions of the oval pan. Roll out the gum paste or pastillage to 3/16″ thickness, cut according to pattern and dry thoroughly.

TINT ROYAL ICING for "paint". Using a cardboard cake circle as a palette, heap portions of royal icing on the cardboard. Mix with paste color, using the palette knife. Don't mix thoroughly, leave the color somewhat streaky for a painterly effect. You will need gold, green, copper, red, blue and light blue.

STROKE IN BACKGROUND on the plaque with a spatula. While the icing is still wet, mark position of flowers and vase with a toothpick. As is true with most decorative painting, the original picture was greatly simplified.

ADD VASE with the palette knife. Use the same tool to indicate the centers of the sunflowers and background leaves.

PAINT PETALS, starting with flowers in the rear. Gradually work to foreground flowers, using palette knife for all petals. Fill in with more leaves. Finish the painting by piping tube 2 stamens.

PREPARE CAKE. Bake, fill and ice a two-layer 9″ x 7″ oval cake. Center plaque on top and edge with tube 17 shells. Pipe shells with same tube for top and base borders. Your sunflower cake serves 12. Slide a knife under the plaque and remove it before slicing.

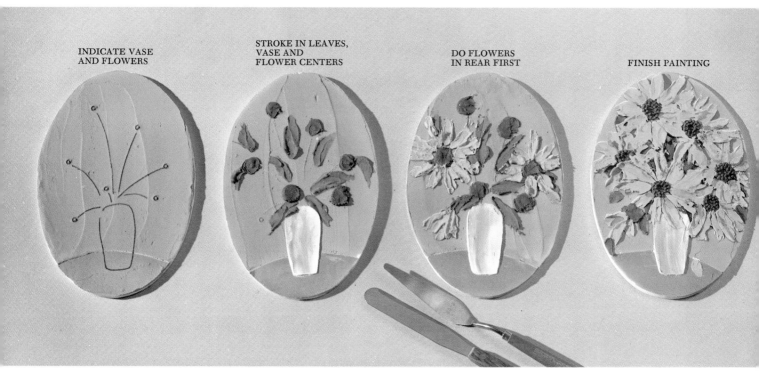

INDICATE VASE
AND FLOWERS

STROKE IN LEAVES,
VASE AND
FLOWER CENTERS

DO FLOWERS
IN REAR FIRST

FINISH PAINTING

THE VENERABLE ART OF COCOA PAINTING

This art form, practiced by chefs for centuries, uses a technique very similar to oil painting to create pictures with a warm appeal. Cocoa paintings may be placed on cakes decorated for very important occasions, or framed for lasting wall decorations. Unless you are skilled in drawing and painting, it is wise to choose a favorite piece of art to render in cocoa. This picture is adapted from a drawing by Thomas Nast, first published in 1881.

The materials are simple and all edible. Powdered cocoa is the pigment, cocoa butter, purchased at a pharmacy, the mixing medium, and rolled marzipan the canvas. You will need water color brushes, stiff cardboard, and an inexpensive frame.

PREPARE BASE FOR PAINTING. Cut a piece of stiff cardboard to size and shape required for your frame. We used a discarded oval frame with an opening 11″ x 9″, but the picture may be set in a rectangular frame. Adjust the mat to fit.

Make a recipe of marzipan (page 76) and roll out between sheets of wax paper to an even ¼″ thickness. Trim the marzipan to an oval 1″ wider on

Continued on page 304

all sides than the area of the image. Dry the scraps for practice. Apply royal icing *very thinly and smoothly* to the cardboard, then transfer the marzipan oval to the center of the cardboard. Press lightly to attach. Dry several days to a hard surface.

TRANSFER PATTERN TO MARZIPAN by rubbing the back with a soft pencil, making sure to cover all lines. Place pattern right side up on dried marzipan oval and trace over all lines with a sharp pencil. If pattern does not transfer easily, allow marzipan to dry longer.

MIX PAINT. Divide two ounces of cocoa butter into thirds and place each in a small container. Set containers into a pan of very hot water until butter melts. Tint the melted butter with varying amounts of cocoa into three distinct shades—light, medium and dark. Test by brushing a little of the paint on dried marzipan scraps. As you paint, keep the containers in a pan of warm water to maintain a smooth consistency. Reheat as necessary. Too hot, and paint is runny and hard to control, too cool and consistency is too stiff. Stir the paint frequently so colors won't separate. If you must leave your work before finishing the painting, let paint harden, then re-heat and stir.

START PAINTING by laying in background area. Light and medium tints were used for this painting. Then proceed to a clearly defined area—here Santa's head. Work from dark to light, blending paint by adding more color with brush. Then proceed to next area. When entire picture is painted, you may go back to sharpen details with a small brush. Add highlights by scraping away small areas of paint with an X-acto knife.

MAKE MAT AND FRAME. Roll out another recipe of marzipan to ⅛″ thickness and cut mat, using pattern for inner opening. Outside shape will be same as base cardboard. Dry one or two days until hard, then attach to painting with royal icing.

Tint a recipe of marzipan by kneading in cocoa and roll out to a long strip, 4″ wide. Lay strip over frame and mold it to contours by smoothing with hands. Cut out flowers from same marzipan with blossom cutter, curl petals by rolling from edge to center with stick 5 and dry. Attach with egg white.

When frame is dry, insert matted picture and secure with heavy tape. Spray with acrylic spray glaze. Keep away from direct heat or sunlight.

As you gain experience in this technique you'll enjoy translating your own favorite scenes to attractive cocoa paintings.

CHAPTER NINETEEN

A Gallery of Outstanding Cakes

Here is a picture gallery of cakes, each planned for a very important party. Each displays an interesting technique used in a new and unusual way.

Several show how even a simple cake becomes a showpiece through the use of delicate gum paste flowers as trim. See how Color Flow can set a scene, marzipan can create a lifelike rose and icing can pipe realistic figures. Included is a new way of painting on marzipan—a technique you'll want to explore and expand.

SANTA AND HIS SLEIGH

This Christmas sheet cake makes a cheerful centerpiece for a buffet table or Christmas party.

Make sleigh from rolled gum paste, ⅛″ thick, using recipe on page 142 and patterns in The Wilton Way Pattern Book. Let the sleigh sides dry flat, then cut underside. Pipe a line of royal icing ⅛″ in from lower edge of one side. Set underside of sleigh, still wet, in position and prop until dry. Attach second side of sleigh with icing. Dry. Pipe runners with tube 10, following pattern. Dry, then turn over and pipe again for rounded look. Attach sleigh to a 2¼″ x 3½″ piece of iced styrofoam, 1″ thick. Secure runners to sleigh and styrofoam with royal icing. Trim sleigh with Color Flow hearts, tube 225 drop flowers, tube 1 vines and tube 65s leaves. Cover seams in sleigh with tube 14 zigzags and pipe tube 4 beading around edges. Pipe tube 1 lettering and dots around hearts.

Make santa from marzipan using recipe on page 76. Model by hand so he is 4½″ tall. Join body sections with egg white. Pipe beard with tube 14.

Model sack and toys from marzipan. Make the sack 2½″ tall and the toys ¾″ to 1″ long. Paint sugar cubes with royal icing for packages and pipe tube 1 ribbons and bows.

Bake and decorate cake. Bake a 9″ x 13″ two-layer cake. Ice and set on a foil-covered board. Pipe tube 12 bottom ball border. Spread boiled icing on top of cake and sprinkle with edible glitter. Create "icicles" with icing and piping gel. Set sleigh and Santa on cake and arrange gifts. Serves 24.

TENDER VIOLET

This dainty springtime cake is trimmed with gum paste baroque scrolls and realistic violets.

MAKE 30 GUM PASTE VIOLETS and a dozen leaves as directed on page 149. Arrange into spray for top and clusters for sides, binding with floral tape. Make Mantle designs using Baroque Gum Paste Molds. Follow instructions that accompany molds for general molding directions. Make two designs for sides and dry on 6″ curve. For top ornament, dry one design flat. Attach back to back on second design, still in mold, with egg white, first laying toothpicks on two outer curls of design. Invert mold to release. Dry thoroughly.

BAKE CAKE. Bake a 9″ oval, two-layer cake. Ice and set on serving tray. Pipe tube 7 bottom bulb border. Divide cake side into twelfths. Drop a tube 2 guideline from point to point. Pipe a tube 7 zigzag garland then a tube 104 ribbon above it. Top points of garlands with a trio of tube 4 bulbs. Pipe a tube 7 curved bulb top border.

ATTACH SIDE DESIGNS with icing and add clusters of violets. Attach spray to cake, then push toothpicks on top ornament into cake. Serves twelve.

EASTER LILY, A REGAL WEDDING CAKE

This towering wedding cake will be spectacular at a springtime wedding.

MAKE GUM PASTE EASTER LILIES as directed on page 146. Prepare five vases. Attach half a styrofoam ball in Heart Bowl and fill with royal icing. Dry. To insert flowers, poke hole with ice pick and insert stem into styrofoam.

BAKE TIERS—6″ x 3″, 10″ x 4″ and 18″ x 4″ round. Ice and assemble on tray or foil-covered board. Use four 10½″ Roman columns, four 5″ Grecian pillars, two 12″ and two 8″ round separator plates.

DIVIDE 18″ TIER into sixteenths and pipe a tube 32 column at each division. Pipe tube 16 zigzag around base of cake. Make tube 16 "C" shapes on either side of column and star at top. Trim separator plate with tube 17 scallops. Pipe tube 16 shells and upright stars for top border.

DIVIDE 10″ TIER into sixteenths. Pipe tube 17 bottom shell border. Drape tube 16 swags from point to point. Pipe tube 15 curls and stars where swags meet. Trim separator plate with tube 17 scallops. Pipe tube 16 top shell border.

DIVIDE 6″ TIER into twelfths. At each division pipe a vertical tube 14 line about 1½″ long. Top each with a tube 15 fleur-de-lis. Then pipe tube 16 curl on each side of bottom of line. Add tube 15 stars at points where fleur-de-lis and curls meet line. Pipe tube 16 stars where curls meet at separator plate. Pipe tube 15 top shell border.

SECURE FOUR VASES of lilies between Roman columns and one vase on top of 6″ tier. Add bridal couple between Grecian pillars. Serves 210.

EASTER LILY
Directions on opposite page

BRIAR ROSE
Directions on page 310

SPRINGTIME
Directions on page 310

Happy Birthday

MAKE CENTER

CUT PETALS, ATTACH WIRE

TAPE TO STEM

COMPLETED FLOWER

CHRISTMAS CHEER *(shown at right)*

Create this handsome cake to grace your holiday table. Adorned with poinsettias, holly leaves and pine, it's as pretty as a Christmas card.

MAKE THREE POINSETTIAS. Take ten 5″ pieces of 28-gauge wire and make a small loop at one end of each. Tape them around a 6″ piece of 20-gauge wire, spreading the tops. Pipe a tube 2 ball of green icing over each loop. Using tube 1, pipe a red dot on seven of the balls, then top all ten with tube 1 yellow dots.

Make gum paste using recipe on page 142. Roll as thin as possible, then using The Wilton Way patterns, cut the smallest petals first. As you cut each petal, immediately attach a 28-gauge wire to the back with egg white and fold base of petal gently around wire. Bend wire at 90° angle about ¼″ to ½″ from petal—the bigger the petal, the farther away. It is not necessary to let each petal dry completely before attaching to the stem. Just allow them to set for a few minutes—it is possible to do about eight petals and then tape them to stem. Space smaller ones evenly around blossom center and tape to stem as close to center as possible.

Continue wiring and taping petals to stem, layering tightly. Finish with largest petals.

MAKE GUM PASTE HOLLY LEAVES and berries as directed on page 157. Also make several pine cones as shown on page 17.

MAKE PINE BRANCHES. Bend a 22-gauge wire into a "V" shape and tape with floral tape to an 18-gauge wire forming "Y" shape. Cover "V" with icing by pushing into bag filled with green icing and fitted with tube 2, then pull out many tube 1 needles. You will need four branches.

BAKE A 10″ x 4″ SQUARE CAKE. Ice with boiled icing, swirling sides. Place on foil-covered board. Pipe tube 18 stars around base of cake and pipe tube 17 stars between the tops. Pipe tube 16 top star border. Insert a taper into top of cake and arrange sprays of poinsettias, holly, cones and pine branches on top and side of cake. Serves 20.

BRIAR ROSE *(shown on page 308)*

Trimmed with delicate gum paste flowers, this lovely cake could be a dainty shower centerpiece cake or a petite wedding cake.

MAKE GUM PASTE BRIAR ROSES, buds and leaves as directed on page 150. Tape into two large and two small sprays. Use The Wilton Way pattern, then roll out and cut a gum paste heart. Dry on 10″ curve. Pipe tube 1 lettering and tube 2 beading.

BAKE TIERS. Bake 10″ and 6″ round two-layer tiers. Ice and assemble on tray or foil-covered board. On bottom of 10″ tier, pipe tube 20 upright shells topped with tube 16 stars. Circle top of tier with tube 17 stars. On 6″ tier, pipe tube 17 bottom star border and tube 16 top star border.

SECURE BIRD ORNAMENT to top of cake. Insert flower spike behind ornament. Insert one large spray into spike. Insert flower spikes into sides of 6″ and 10″ tiers. Position other large spray in flower spike on 6″ tier to drape over edge of tier below, and position small sprays in spikes on side of 10″ tier. Serves 20 party-style or 60 wedding guests.

SPRINGTIME *(shown on page 309)*

Honor a special birthday with this sunny spring-like cake trimmed with crocuses and daffodils.

MAKE GUM PASTE CROCUSES as directed on page 144 and daffodils as directed on page 147. Use The Wilton Way pattern to cut two gum paste stylized tulip motifs. Dry flat and pipe tube 1 message.

BAKE TIERS. Bake a 6″ x 4″ round and a 10″ x 4″ square tier. Ice and assemble on foil-covered board. On 10″ tier, pipe tube 17 bottom shell border and tube 16 top shell border. Pipe tube 16 shells around top and bottom of 6″ tier.

INSERT THIN TAPERS into top of 6″ tier. Then insert stems of daffodils and crocuses into top of 10″ tier. Attach gum paste tulip motifs to sides of 10″ tier with dots of icing. Poke small holes in board and insert crocus stems at corners of cake, using tiny dots of icing to steady. Serves 26.

CHRISTMAS CHEER
Directions on opposite page

ART NOUVEAU
Directions on page 314

CINDERELLA
Directions on page 314

EXPLORE THE DECORATIVE OPPORTUNITIES the Color Flow technique offers. This method of drawing in icing can create an intriguing openwork cake top, dramatize a fairy tale with the cake as stage, or give a picture a layered, dimensional look. Your own imagination will discover many more variations of this versatile technique.

ART NOUVEAU *(shown on page 312)*

The openwork Color Flow plaque that tops this cake creates an interesting play of light and shadow. Other trim is simple and tailored to set off the flowery design.

MAKE COLOR FLOW PLAQUE and eight side pieces using patterns in The Wilton Way Pattern Book and recipe on page 76. Outline all pieces with tube 2 and beige icing. Thin icing as directed and flow in colors, leaving spaces between flowers and leaves open. Dry thoroughly, then loosen from wax paper by carefully slipping a piece of parchment or wax paper under pieces. Handle with extreme care as they are very fragile.

BAKE 10″ x 4″ SQUARE CAKE. Ice sides yellow and top blue. Place on a foil-covered board. Pipe tube 16 stars on sides and extending ¾″ in on top of cake all around.

ATTACH COLOR FLOW PIECES. Pipe small dots of icing on backs of side pieces to secure them to cake. Place in position on corners and gently push into the stars on the sides of the cake.

Mark on cake top where larger flowers will be positioned, using pattern as a guide. Pipe small mounds of icing on marks to support plaque. Place plaque on cake top, pressing very gently into icing. Serves 20 guests.

CINDERELLA *(shown on page 313)*

Re-create a fairy tale in Color Flow! This spectacular cake will thrill young and old alike. Gum paste is used as a base to strengthen the upright pieces.

MAKE COLOR FLOW PIECES. Make gum paste following recipe on page 142. Roll 1/16″ thick and cut pieces using patterns in The Wilton Way Pattern Book. (Fire, candlesticks and plates do not have gum paste backs.) Make mantel and supports separately from fireplace. Let pieces dry. Transfer markings from patterns to gum paste pieces.

Make Color Flow icing using the recipe on page 76. Outline all pieces with tube 1. Flow in colors. Dry all pieces thoroughly.

ADD DETAILS. On Cinderella, pipe tube 55 lines on skirt and other lines on dress with tube 1. Add tube 101s ruffles. Make tube 1s piping gel buttons and

tiara. Mix half icing and half piping gel and pipe design on dress with tube 1.

On fairy godmother, pipe tube 1 dots on dress and tube 13 stars. Add lacing on bodice with tube 1s. Pipe trim on bucket and broom with tube 1. Add tube 4 hearts on bench. Attach mantel and wood supports to fireplace with dots of icing. Secure plates and candlesticks above mantel. Attach back fireplace wall in position and secure fire to it small dots of icing.

On horses, pipe trim with tube 1, making dots with piping gel. Outline heart-shaped windows on coach with tube 55 and pipe trim on door with tube 2. Let all pieces dry thoroughly, then attach popsicle sticks to backs of all pieces (except broom) with royal icing and dry again.

MAKE DROP FLOWERS with tube 225 and mount about half of them on wires as described in Chapter Twenty. Pipe tube 65 leaves on wires. Dry.

BAKE AND DECORATE CAKE. Ice a piece of styrofoam 12″ x 16″ x 1″ and pat with damp sponge to create stucco effect. Secure to foil-covered board. Bake a 9″ x 13″ x 4″ cake. Ice and place near back of styrofoam so at least 2″ is exposed in front of cake. Pipe tube 7 bottom bulb border and tube 5 bulbs around top and down corners.

Push sticks on Color Flow pieces into top of cake and secure with a bit of icing. Lean broom on bench and secure with icing. Make small holes in styrofoam and carefully insert sticks on coach and horses, securing with a bit of icing. Prop with cotton until dried. Attach flowers and leaves at front corners of cake, pushing wires into styrofoam and attaching others with dots of icing. Serves 24.

MAJESTIC EAGLE *(shown at right)*

This spectacular Color Flow eagle plaque is made in four layers then assembled with icing to give a 3-dimensional look. It's a striking cake for any patriotic occasion.

MAKE COLOR FLOW PIECES using recipe on page 76 and patterns in The Wilton Way Pattern Book. Cut pieces of cloth-covered wire the length of the flag staffs. Insert into a decorating bag fitted with tube 2 to cover them with icing. Place in position on wax paper-covered patterns. Proceed with Color Flow method. Outline flags, shield and side banner with tube 1. Flow in thinned icing and dry thoroughly. Pipe tube 13 stars and add tube 1 ropes and tassels, then dry again.

Outline eagle with tube 2. Flow in thinned icing. Dry thoroughly. Pipe arrows with tube 2 and dry again. Loosen pieces from wax paper by slipping a

piece of parchment or wax paper under the edges and working it gently back and forth until entire design is loosened.

ASSEMBLE PLAQUE. Handle Color Flow pieces very gently as they are quite fragile. Begin with layer one as the base. Attach flags and eagle wings from layer two in position with small mounds of icing. Pipe leaves with tube 2, connecting eagle wings and flags of layer two. Dry. Attach flags and eagle body from layer three in position on mounds of icing. Dry. Finish plaque by attaching shield and eagle head from layer four on small mounds of icing. Dry thoroughly.

BAKE AND DECORATE CAKE. Bake a 9″ x 13″ two-layer

cake. Ice and place on a foil-covered board. Pipe tube 7 balls for bottom border, placing two tube 13 stars between them. Transfer pattern for side shields to corners of cake. Outline with tube 2 and fill in with tube 13 stars, leaving every other stripe plain. Attach Color Flow banner to side of cake with dots of icing. Pipe tube 7 balls for top border, placing two tube 13 stars between them just as for the bottom border.

SECURE PLAQUE IN POSITION. Cut a wedge of styrofoam about 2½″ high and cut at about a 45° angle. Ice with royal icing over entire surface of wedge and dry. Secure wedge to cake with dots of icing, then attach plaque to wedge with icing. Serves 24.

GOLDEN ROSE *(opposite page)*

This lacy shower or petite wedding cake is trimmed with hand-modeled marzipan roses.

MAKE MARZIPAN ROSES, using recipe on page 76. To begin, form a cone shape about 1″ high. Roll marzipan for petals very thin between sheets of wax paper, then cut with medium rose cutter. Cup slightly with fingers. Attach two petals around cone for bud with egg white. Complete flower by adding more petals opening out. Make nine roses and 20 buds. Cut leaves with large rose leaf cutter.

PIPE EIGHT LACE PIECES using The Wilton Way pattern and tube 2. Dry, turn over and pipe again.

DECORATE CAKE. Bake a 12″ x 4″ petal cake. Ice and place on foil-covered 17″ diameter cake board. Pipe tube 7 bottom ball border. Pipe a tube 2 line of beading 1″ in on top. Edge with scallops. Pipe tube 8 zigzag garland at base of each "petal". Using tube 3, pipe scallops above and drop two strings on each garland. Then drop two strings from top of each "petal" and pipe scallops beneath them. Pipe tube 6 top ball border. Attach roses, buds and leaves on cake top and board with icing. Secure a lace piece between each "petal" with icing. Serves 26 party-style or 44 wedding guests.

DOUBLE CAMEO *(below)*

Here's a sample of the exciting art of painting on marzipan with thinned food color.

MAKE CAMEOS. Cut two 2¾″ x 2″ oval plaques from marzipan (recipe on page 76). Dry on 5″ x 4″ egg molds. To paint flowers, thin paste food color with kirschwasser to achieve the desired shades. Using a small artist's brush, paint freehand flowers and leaves on plaques. Add shading and other details. Pipe centers of flowers with tube 1s. It is a good idea to practice your design on an extra plaque first

so you can master the technique. Let plaques dry, then pipe tube 2 beading around the edge.

MAKE CAKE. Bake a 10″ x 4″ square cake. Ice and place on foil-covered cardboard cake board. Pipe tube 8 bottom ball border. Pipe a bow on each side of cake with tube 104. Also pipe four tube 104 bows on top of cake, with streamers curving around corners. Pipe tube 6 top ball border. Attach cameos with small mounds of icing. Serves 20 guests.

GOLDEN ROSE
Directions on opposite page.

LEAPING PORPOISES
Directions on page 320

HAPPY POLAR BEARS
Directions on page 320

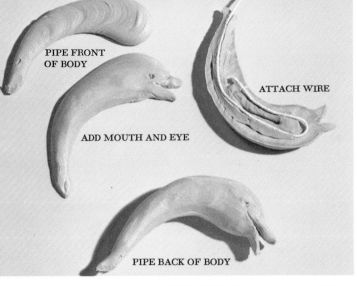

PIPE FRONT OF BODY

ADD MOUTH AND EYE

ATTACH WIRE

PIPE BACK OF BODY

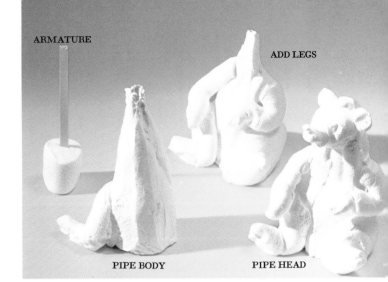

ARMATURE

ADD LEGS

PIPE BODY

PIPE HEAD

LEAPING PORPOISES (*shown on page 318*)

Three-dimensional figure piped porpoises leap and splash on this easily-made cake.

MAKE TWO PORPOISES. Using tube 12 and royal icing, pipe from head to tail on wax paper. Make the curve about 5″ long and ⅞″ wide at the head. Smooth with a wet finger. Pipe mouth with tube 4 and smooth again. Make an indentation in the icing with a toothpick to designate the eye. Dry thoroughly (about 24 hours) before proceeding.

Turn porpoise body over and attach a 10″ long piece of heavy florists' wire to the back with icing, curving as shown. Pipe the back right on the front, covering wire. Smooth with a wet finger and conceal the seam. Dry. Pipe fins and tail with a parchment cone, the tip cut in a "V" shape. Dry.

MAKE LEIS. Pipe tube 33 drop flowers and pipe centers with tube 2. Dry. Form two pieces of fine wire (not cloth-covered) into 1″ x 2″ ovals. Attach flowers to them with royal icing and dry.

BAKE AND DECORATE CAKE. Bake 6″ x 3″ square and 6″ x 3″ round cakes. Cut round cake in half and place halves at opposite ends of the square to create a tank-shaped cake, 12″ long and 6″ wide. Place on a foil-covered board and ice.

Pipe tube 7 bottom ball border. Heap more icing on top and create "waves" with a spatula. Push two flower spikes into the top of the cake. Insert the wires on the porpoises into the flower spikes and secure with icing. Pull up "waves" of icing with a spatula around them to conceal the wires. Attach the leis around the necks of the porpoises with tiny dots of icing. Serves 14.

HAPPY POLAR BEARS (*shown on page 319*)

PIPE MAMA BEAR. To begin, push a popsicle stick into a marshmallow to create the armature to pipe on and place it on a piece of wax paper. With tube 2A and figure piping icing (recipe below), start at base of marshmallow and pipe upwards. Continue around until entire armature is covered. Smooth icing with a spatula. Pipe back legs with tube 2A and smooth pads of feet with spatula. Add tube 12 front legs and head. Pipe tube 4 ears and press with damp fingers to shape.

Brush thinned gray icing onto the pads of the feet, on and around the muzzle and on the inside of the ears with a small artist's brush. Brush inside of mouth with pink icing. Pipe fur with tube 1s. Add eyes, nose and mouth with black piping gel and tube 1s. Dry thoroughly.

PIPE BABY BEAR. Make armature the same as for mama bear, but break off popsicle stick to 3″ length. Pipe the baby bear using the same method as for the larger one. Use tube 12 for the body and back legs, tube 10 for the front legs and head, and tube 4 for the ears. Finish baby bear the same as mama bear. Dry thoroughly.

DECORATE CAKE. Bake 10″ round, two-layer cake. Place on foil-covered board and ice. Spread boiled icing on the top of the cake and extending down the sides to create the impression of snow. Sprinkle with edible glitter. Set polar bears in position on top of the cake. Serves 14.

FIGURE PIPING ICING

A heavy consistency icing for piping large upright figures. For regular figure piping, reduce confectioners' sugar by one cup.

    3 cups granulated sugar
    ⅔ cup water
    ¼ teaspoon cream of tartar
    4 tablespoons meringue powder
    ⅔ cup lukewarm water
    2¼ cups sifted confectioners' sugar

Cook first three ingredients to 234°; set aside. Beat meringue with lukewarm water until peaks form. Add confectioners' sugar slowly, then beat at medium speed until blended. Pour in cooked mixture and continue beating until peaks form. (Note: You must use a heavy-duty mixer.)

CHAPTER TWENTY

A Summary of Useful Information

Within this chapter is a body of information to which the decorator will have occasion to refer frequently. Here you will find proven recipes for icings, simple ways of lining pans of various shapes with paper, ways to put flowers on wire stems, charts that explain how to cut a wedding cake and how to estimate the number servings various-sized wedding cakes will provide. There is also a simplified explanation of how cake decorators and bakers can begin to make an orderly, workable transition to the use of metric measurements.

DECORATING ICING RECIPES

Choose the icing that bests suits your purpose. We recommend Wilton Snow-white Buttercream to cover, fill and pipe the borders for most cakes in the Wilton-American style, but Classic Buttercream and Boiled Icing—Egg White are also excellent. You will also enjoy the flavor and good-handling properties of Chocolate Buttercream.

Most flowers should be piped with royal icing for clear accurate details. These can be stored an almost indefinite period of time before using as cake trims. Only royal icing piped flowers can be mounted on wire stems. For simple flowers to decorate a cake top, you may use either of the buttercream recipes in this chapter or Boiled Icing—Meringue.

Royal icing has many other uses. Filigree, lace pieces, stringwork that hangs below a tier and assembled structures such as the bi-plane on page 59 are all piped with royal icing. It is a strong "glue" to join dried gum paste or pastillage sections like the Three Bears' House on page 207.

Each of the following recipes has been tested and re-tested by the Wilton staff and has proven to be easy to handle in the decorating bag or cone and to have an excellent flavor. All of them can be made with a regular electric mixer. Do not attempt to use a hand mixer. When making a large quantity of icing, be sure to use a heavy-duty mixer.

To THIN THE ICINGS for flowers and leaves, add one teaspoon of white corn syrup per cup of icing for flowers and two teaspoons of white corn syrup per cup of icing for leaves. This gives a glossy look. Do not thin Chocolate Buttercream Icing.

QUANTITIES OF ICING needed for various cakes are not given because usage varies greatly from decorator to decorator. The best guideline we can give is that four cups of any icing is enough to ice and completely decorate a 10″ round or an 8″ square cake. You will probably use less. Only experience and practice can tell you how much icing *you* will need for a particular cake.

To COLOR ICINGS, add a few drops of liquid food color for a pastel tint. For a deeper tint, add a small amount of paste color. For deep-colored buttercream icing, mix and tint it several hours ahead. The color will deepen as the icing ages.

WILTON SNOW-WHITE BUTTERCREAM

This pure white icing is a perfect choice for wedding cakes. It handles well, tints to clear and attractive, pastel colors and performs particularly well when piping borders or simple flowers to use to decorate tops of tiers.

⅔ cup water
4 tablespoons meringue powder
1¼ cups solid white shortening, room temperature
¾ teaspoon salt
¼ teaspoon butter flavoring
½ teaspoon almond flavoring
½ teaspoon clear vanilla flavoring
11½ cups sifted confectioners' sugar

Combine water and meringue powder and whip at high speed until peaks form. Add four cups sugar, one cup at a time, beating after each addition at low speed. Alternately add shortening and remainder of sugar. Add salt and flavorings and beat at low speed until smooth. Thin with two teaspoons of white corn syrup for borders and strings. May be stored, well-covered, in the refrigerator for several weeks, then brought to room temperature and rebeaten. Yield: 8 cups. Recipe may be cut in half or doubled.

WILTON CLASSIC BUTTERCREAM

This is an excellent icing that covers thoroughly and handles well. It can also be used to pipe simple, edible flowers for a cake top. Flowers can be piped in advance and air-dried if the weather is not too humid. Or they can be piped and frozen to be placed on the cake top just before serving.

⅓ cup butter
⅓ cup solid, white vegetable shortening
1 teaspoon clear vanilla
⅛ teaspoon salt
1 pound confectioners' sugar, sifted
5 tablespoons cool milk or cream

Cream butter and shortening together with an electric mixer. Beat in sugar, 1 cup at a time, blending well after each addition and scraping sides and bottom of bowl with a spatula frequently. Add milk and beat at high speed until it becomes light and fluffy. Keep icing covered with lid or damp cloth and store in refrigerator. Bring to room temperature and rebeat to use again. Thin with corn syrup for flowers and leaves. Yield: 3 cups.

WILTON CHOCOLATE BUTTERCREAM

This is exceptionally good-tasting and easy to use. Follow the recipe for Wilton Buttercream. First cream butter and shortening. Then add mixture of:

½ cup cocoa
½ cup milk

Proceed with the remainder of the recipe for Wilton Buttercream above. Store in the refrigerator until ready to use, bring to room temperature and rebeat. Stiffen with a little confectioners' sugar for piping flowers to be used on cake top. Do not thin for making leaves. For a very dark color, add one or two drops of brown food coloring. Yield: 3¾ cups.

WILTON ROYAL ICING—MERINGUE

This is a very durable hard-drying icing. Do not use to cover cakes, since it dries much too hard. It makes sharp borders and trims and precisely-formed, long-lasting flowers. A home mixer can be used, but a heavy-duty mixer makes a better royal icing. Do not double recipe unless using a heavy-duty mixer. Useful for "gluing" sections of trim and for dummy or "show" cakes.

3 level tablespoons Wilton Meringue Powder
1 pound confectioners' sugar
3½ ounces warm water
½ teaspoon cream of tartar

Combine ingredients, mixing slowly, then beat at high speed for seven to ten minutes. Keep covered at all times with damp cloth, as icing dries very quickly. To restore texture after storing, simply rebeat. Yield: 3½ cups.

WILTON ROYAL ICING—EGG WHITE

This icing dries even harder than meringue royal icing and is used for piping precisely-formed borders and flowers. It is particularly useful for piping lace, fine stringwork and delicately-formed structures. Like meringue royal icing, it is also excellent for "gluing" dried pieces.

3 egg whites (room temperature)
1 pound confectioners' sugar
½ teaspoon cream of tartar

Combine ingredients, beat at high speed for 7 to 10 minutes. Dries quickly—keep covered with damp cloth. Rebeating will not restore. Yields 3 cups.

WILTON BOILED ICING—MERINGUE

This pure white icing is good for piping borders and flowers. It gives a fine appearance and is easy to use, but dries too crisp for covering the cake.

4 level tablespoons Wilton Meringue Powder
1 cup warm water
2 cups granulated sugar
¼ teaspoon cream of tartar
3½ cups sifted confectioners' sugar

Boil granulated sugar, ½ cup water and cream of tartar to 240°. Brush side of pan with warm water to keep crystals from forming. Meanwhile, mix meringue powder with ½ cup water, beat 7 minutes at high speed. Turn to low speed, add confectioners' sugar, beat 4 minutes at high speed. Slowly add boiled sugar mixture, beat 5 minutes at high speed.

Keeps a week in refrigerator, covered with damp cloth. Rebeat before using again. Yield: 6 cups. Use a heavy-duty mixer if doubling recipe.

WILTON BOILED ICING—EGG WHITE

A snow white icing noted for its excellent flavor. It covers the cake excellently, but is too light and fine-textured to use for piping borders or flowers.

2 cups granulated sugar
½ cup water
¼ teaspoon cream of tartar
4 egg whites (room temperature)
1½ cups confectioners' sugar, measured then sifted

Boil granulated sugar, water, cream of tartar to 240°. Brush sides of pan with warm water to prevent crystals. Brush again halfway through, but do not stir. Meanwhile, whip egg whites seven minutes at high speed. Add boiled sugar mixture slowly, beat three minutes at high speed. Turn to second speed, gradually add confectioners' sugar, beat seven minutes more at high speed. Rebeating won't restore texture. Yield: 3½ cups. Unless using a heavy-duty mixer, do not double recipe.

BEST-EVER APPLESAUCE FRUITCAKE

This recipe makes a good-tasting, firm fruitcake suitable for use in the English, Australian and South African methods of decorating.

3 cups all-purpose flour
2 teaspoons baking soda
1 teaspoon baking powder
½ teaspoon cloves
½ teaspoon nutmeg
½ teaspoon cinnamon
½ teaspoon salt
1 pound candied cherries
½ pound mixed candied fruit
1 jar (8 ounces) candied pineapple
¾ cup dates
1 cup raisins
1½ cups pecans
1½ cups walnuts
½ cup butter
1 cup sugar
2 eggs
½ cup grape juice
1½ cups applesauce

Cut up fruit and coarsely chop nuts. Mix the fruit and nuts together. Set aside.

Sift together flour, baking soda, baking powder, spices and salt. Set aside.

Cream butter and sugar. Add eggs and beat well. Beating until blended after each addition, alternately add dry ingredients and grape juice to the creamed mixture. Mix in fruit, nuts and applesauce.

This recipe will fill a 10″ tube pan for a cake 4″ deep—an 8″ round pan for a cake 3½″ deep—or an 11″ ring pan for a cake 3″ deep. Bake at 275°F about 2½ hours or until toothpick inserted in center comes out clean. Line pans before filling.

Run a knife around sides of pan and cool 10 minutes. Remove cake and cool thoroughly.

This magnificent cake, originally introduced to Wilton by *Celebrate!* reader Helen Wooldridge, keeps well for 2 months or more when tightly wrapped. It freezes well, too. Yield: 6 pounds.

HOW TO LINE PANS WITH PAPER

Before baking a fruitcake, the pan should be well-lined with two thicknesses of brown wrapping paper and three of parchment paper. This helps to insulate the cake and to keep the edges from over-browning while baking.

When filling the pan, make sure that the mixture is worked well into each corner. To level the surface evenly, lift the pan a short distance above the table and drop flat. This breaks any air pockets in the mixture, settles the fruit evenly and assures a level surface after baking.

SQUARE CAKE PAN. Place pan in center of paper. With a pencil, trace around the pan. Measure out from the outline 3″ and cut off the excess paper. Make a cut at each corner from the edge of the paper to the outline of the pan as shown. Fold the paper along the pencil lines to make a box with the overlapping flaps to the outside, so they will be against the inside surface of the pan. Insert the paper liners into pan and fill.

HEXAGON CAKE PAN. Make paper liners for a hexagon pan the same as for a square pan.

ROUND CAKE PAN. Place the pan on the paper and trace around it, then cut out. Cut a strip of paper about 4″ wide and long enough to line the side of the pan with a 4″ overlap. Fold up one long edge about 1¼″ and fringe the paper from the edge to the fold. Place the strip into the pan with the fold against the bottom, the circular pieces over it. The pan can now be filled.

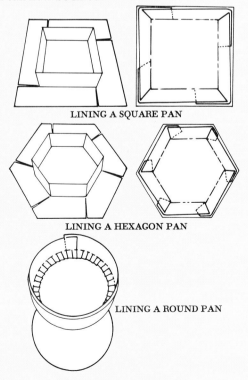

LINING A SQUARE PAN

LINING A HEXAGON PAN

LINING A ROUND PAN

WEDDING CAKE CUTTING GUIDE

This serving chart for wedding cakes is based on 1″ x 2″ servings, two layers high. If you wish to serve larger pieces, adjust the number of servings accordingly. To cut any tiered cake, start by removing the top tier. Then begin cutting the second tier, third, and fourth. The count of servings includes the top tier, although many people remove this and freeze it for the first anniversary.

To CUT A ROUND TIER, move in two inches from outer edge, cut a circle and cut 1″ wide slices within it. Move in another two inches, cut another circle, and slice into 1″ pieces. Continue until each tier is cut.

To CUT SQUARE TIERS, move in 2″ from outer edge and cut straight across. Slice into 1″ pieces. Move in another 2″ and slice this section into 1″ pieces. Continue until entire tier is cut.

CUT HEXAGON TIERS like round tiers.

CUT PETAL-SHAPED TIERS like round tiers.

DIVIDE HEART-SHAPED TIERS vertically. Slice 1″ pieces within rows.

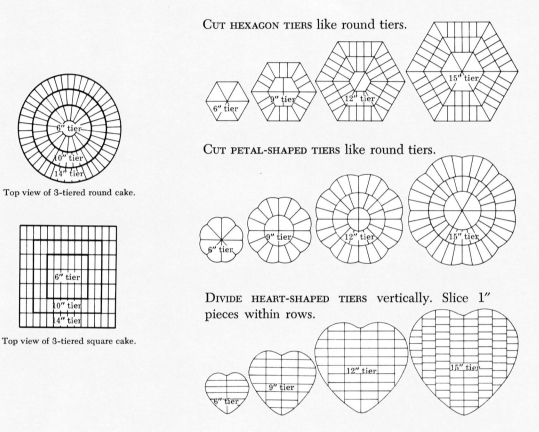

Top view of 3-tiered round cake.

Top view of 3-tiered square cake.

WEDDING CAKE SERVING CHART

Following the cutting procedures above, here's an approximation of the number of servings you can expect from each cake tier.

Shape	Size	Servings
Round	6″	16
	8″	30
	10″	48
	12″	68
	14″	92
	16″	118
	18″	148
Square	6″	18
	8″	32
	10″	50
	12″	72
	14″	98
	16″	128
	18″	162

Shape	Size	Servings
Hexagon	6″	6
	9″	22
	12″	50
	15″	66
Petal	6″	8
	9″	20
	12″	44
	15″	62
Heart	6″	12
	9″	28
	12″	48
	15″	90

PARTY CAKE SERVING CHART

Here is an approximation of the number of dessert-size servings to expect from various-sized party cakes. One-mix cakes, of any shape, serve twelve.

Shape	Size	Servings
Round	6″	6
	8″	10
	10″	14
	12″	22
	14″	36
Square	6″	8
	8″	12
	10″	20
	12″	36
	14″	42
Rectangle	9″x13″	24
	11″x15″	35
	12″x18″	54

Shape	Size	Servings
Heart	6″	6
	9″	12
	12″	24
	15″	35
Hexagon	6″	6
	9″	12
	12″	20
	15″	48
Petal	6″	6
	8″	8
	12″	26
	15″	48

CONVERTING TO THE METRIC SYSTEM

The measurements in this book continue to be based on the U.S. Customary system of weights and measures, because it is felt that the United States is still some years away from complete transition to metric. It is, however, important to begin to *think metric* to be ready for the change.

LEARN FOUR ESSENTIAL MEASURES FIRST. Cake and food decorators need really only become acquainted with four metric measures:

LITER OR LITRE (symbol "l")—volume;
GRAM (symbol "g")—weight;
METER OR METRE (symbol "m")—length; and
CELSIUS (symbol "C")—temperature

Teachers qualified to give advice on how best to adapt to the metric system stress two points:

LEARN THE SYSTEM as a *new language*, rather than trying to relate at all times to the U.S. Customary system, and,

GET THROUGH THE TRANSITION PERIOD quickly.

In the metric system, simple prefixes are added to the designations "liter", "gram" and "meter" to make larger or smaller units, as needed. The prefixes derived from Latin indicate *division* (such as 1/10) and prefixes derived from Greek indicate *multiplication* (such as 10 times). The following are the most frequently used prefixes:

DIVISION	MULTIPLICATION
Deci—1/10 or 0.1	Deka—10 times
Centi—1/100 or 0.01	Hecto—100 times
Milli—1/1000 or 0.001	Kilo—1000 times

Accordingly, a millimeter is 1/1000 part of a meter, and a kilometer is 1000 meters.

Decorators and cooks need have no concern about having favorite recipes or books made obsolete by the transitions from U.S. Customary measures to metric measures. But, if there is any worry about this situation, the solution is a simple one: keep U.S. Customary measures for use with U.S. Customary recipes and use new metric-marked measuring utensils for *new metric recipes.*

CONTINUE TO USE PRE-METRIC RECIPES. Except for the most delicately-balanced recipes, either U.S. Customary or metric measuring utensils can be used, if this one important rule is followed: *be certain the same measuring system* (U.S. Customary or metric) *is used for the entire recipe.* Since a metric cup (¼ of a liter) is less than 5% more than a U.S. Customary cup (¼ of a quart), a customary recipe can *usually* be made with metric measurements with no other effect than that the metric rec-

ipe will provide a slightly higher yield—5% higher on the average.

New recipe measurements will be largely by volume, as in the past. Accordingly, the only conversion needed will be in oven temperatures. These will be given in degrees Celsius in new recipes.

METRIC EQUIVALENTS

THE LITER

U.S. MEASURE		METRIC EQUIVALENT
¼ teaspoon	=	1.25 milliliters
1 teaspoon	=	5 milliliters
3 teaspoons	=	15 milliliters
1 tablespoon	=	15 milliliters
2 tablespoons	=	30 milliliters
1 fluid ounce	=	30 milliliters
2 fluid ounces	=	59 milliliters
4 fluid ounces	=	118 milliliters
8 fluid ounces	=	236 milliliters
16 fluid ounces	=	472 milliliters
1 cup	=	.24 liter
2 cups	=	.47 liter

THE GRAM

U.S. MEASURE		METRIC EQUIVALENT
1 ounce	=	28 grams
2 ounces	=	56 grams
4 ounces	=	113 grams
8 ounces	=	226 grams
16 ounces	=	452 grams
¼ pound	=	.11 kilogram
½ pound	=	.23 kilogram
¾ pound	=	.34 kilogram
1 pound	=	.45 kilogram
2 pounds	=	.90 kilogram

THE METER

1 inch = 2.54 centimeters
1 foot = 30.40 centimeters
1 yard = 91.44 centimeters

COOKING TEMPERATURES*

HEAT	FAHRENHEIT (F)	CELSIUS (C)
Very Slow	250-275	121-135
Slow	300-325	149-163
Moderate	350-375	177-191
Hot	400-425	204-218
Very Hot	450-475	232-246

OVEN TEMPERATURES*

°F	°C	°F	°C	°F	°C
200	93	350	177	475	246
250	121	400	204	500	260
300	149	450	232	525	274

*For each additional 25°F, add 14°C

FLOWERS AND ADMISSION DATES OF THE 50 UNITED STATES

STATE	ADMISSION	STATE FLOWER
Alabama	1819	Camellia
Alaska	1959	Forget-me-not
Arizona	1912	Saguaro, Cactus Flower
Arkansas	1836	Apple Blossom
California	1850	California Poppy
Colorado	1876	Columbine
Connecticut	1788	Mountain Laurel
Delaware	1787	Peach Blossom
Florida	1845	Orange Blossom
Georgia	1788	Cherokee Rose
Hawaii	1959	Hibiscus
Idaho	1890	Syringa
Illinois	1818	Violet
Indiana	1816	Peony
Iowa	1846	Wild Rose
Kansas	1861	Sunflower
Kentucky	1792	Goldenrod
Louisiana	1812	Magnolia
Maine	1820	Pine Cone
Maryland	1788	Black-eyed Susan
Massachusetts	1788	Mayflower
Michigan	1837	Apple Blossom
Minnesota	1858	Lady's Slipper
Mississippi	1817	Magnolia
Missouri	1821	Hawthorn
Montana	1889	Bitterroot
Nebraska	1867	Goldenrod
Nevada	1864	Sagebrush
New Hampshire	1788	Lilac
New Jersey	1787	Violet
New Mexico	1912	Yucca
New York	1788	Rose
North Carolina	1789	Dogwood
North Dakota	1889	Wild Prairie Rose
Ohio	1803	Carnation
Oklahoma	1907	Mistletoe
Oregon	1859	Oregon Grape
Pennsylvania	1787	Mountain Laurel
Rhode Island	1790	Violet
South Carolina	1788	Yellow Jessamine
South Dakota	1889	Pasqueflower
Tennessee	1796	Iris
Texas	1845	Bluebonnet
Utah	1896	Sego Lily
Vermont	1791	Red Clover
Virginia	1788	Dogwood
Washington	1889	Rhododendron
West Virginia	1863	Rhododendron
Wisconsin	1848	Violet
Wyoming	1890	Indian Paint Brush
District of Columbia		American Beauty Rose

MOUNTING FLOWERS ON WIRE STEMS

Putting flowers on wire stems gives a new dimension to your decorating. Stems allow you to raise flower clusters from the surface of the cake, to arrange flowers in baskets, vases or bouquets.

To attach a blossom to a wire, first make an icing calyx. Using green icing and tube 6, pipe a small mound of icing on a wax paper square. Insert a 6″ length of florists' wire into the mound and brush it up onto the wire in a tapered shape. Dry. Remove the wax paper and attach a flower to the calyx with royal icing. Insert the stem into a block of styrofoam to dry.

Wired leaves add a natural look to groups of stemmed flowers. To make them, pipe a small anchoring base on wax paper with tube 67 and green icing. Lay a 6″ length of florists' wire on the base. Pipe the leaf over this so the wire becomes a visible center vein. Dry. The leaves can then be taped into clusters with floral tape or used individually.

To make ferns, insert a length of florists' wire into a bag fitted with tube 3 and filled with green icing. Squeeze the bag with steady pressure and slowly pull out the wire, curving as you pull. Dry. Pipe tube 67 ruffled leaves on the wire, alternating from side to side.

INDEX

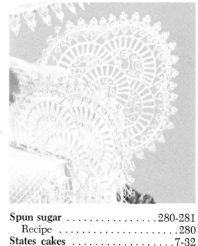